PREFACE

With constant developments and changes taking place in the field of Social Research, it has become necessary to revise this book.

The contents of the book have been designed in a way, to suit the scientific procedures of the contemporary research and fulfill the needs of the teachers and scholars engaged in various fields of academic and programmatic research across the country.

We feel obliged to acknowledge the help from Dr. B.K. Swain, Head of the Department of Sociology, Rashtrasant Tukdoji Maharaj, Nagpur University, Vijayalaxmi Nandapurkar, V.B. Indurkar and Pratibha Khadse for their invaluable help.

AUTHORS

PREFACE TO THE FIRST EDITION

Thre is no alternative to truth and therefore to research. To research is to get nearer to truth, to understand reality. Research in some form or the other, has been a passion with mankind at all times; for some, an obligation they owe to themselves.

With the growing complexity of social life and the attendant challenges which modern societies typically characterize, survey-researches in disciplines dealing with different aspects of the social reality have become imperative. That *serious students of theses social sciences* should be fa*miliar with the process* of designing and conducting research needs no emphasis, and understandably this is already a formal requirement for post-graduate studies in quite a few universities.

Our attemt in this book has been to present a concise, cogent comprehensive and critical exposition of the varied techniques employed in social research and the methodological bases underlying them. The book is, Sociology in particular, who are engaged in post-graduate or predoctoral studies. Consequently especial efforts have been made to make the contents of the book relevant to the syllabi of the various universities in the country.

We have tried to piece together the important ideas scattered in different works and have presented these in a cogent, concise and lucid manner for the average student. It is with this end in view that suitable illustration, diagrams, tables, etc., have been provided.

We are thankful to our colleagues in the department, particularly to Late Dr. N.S. Vaidya and Dr. M.C.B.J. Raju, whose suggestions have often proved valuable.

Wilkinson

Bhandarkar

CONTENTS

Chapter I

Scientific Social Research

The nature and content of research can barely be grasped without an appreciation of the method, we designate as Scientific. Research, simply stated, is an endeavour to arrive at answers to intellectual and practial problems through the application of scientific methods to the knowable universe. The scientific methods and procedures have been evolved and developed to increase vastly the likelyhood that a class of questions, viz., What? How? and to a limited extent, Why? concerning the experiential phenomena are successfully answered. *Einstein and Infeld* state the essence of science in the following words, "Science is the attempt of the human mind to find a connection between the world of ideas and world of phenomena. All the essential ideas in Science were born in a dramatic conflict between reality and our attempt at understanding the same."[1] This implies that science cannot always come up with an answer, let alone a definitive and correct answer to our problems. We need not look very far to realize for ourselves that science has failed to unravel some of the persistent mysteries of human existence. *Thompson* observes, "The vulgar belief that science has explained everything is a hopeless misunderstanding."[2]

It should be noted that science has become relatively humble with the twentieth century revolutions, especially in physics. Today nobody is sure of being able to forecast a train of worldly events on the basis of observations, here and now. It may perhaps no longer be said the science is the only process of knowing reality. There may well be other paths leading to this goal, but scientific procedures are more likely to lead us there than any other method devised by man. Concentrating on science to the exclusion of other ways of approaching the world may not always be justified.

The following statement of *Karl Pearson* represents, by and large, one deep faith of the modern age. Says Pearson, in his *Grammar of Science,* "There is no shortcut to the truth ... no way to gain knowledge of the universe except through the gateway of scientific method."

Pearson further observes, " The Scientific method is one and same in all branches (of Science) and that method is the method of all logically trained minds ... the unity of all sciences consists alone in its method, not in its material. The man who classifies facts in any kind whatsoever, who sees their mutual relations and describes their sequence is applying the Scientific method and is a man of science." [3] These facts may belong to the history of mankind, to the social statistics of our great cities, to the atmosphere of the most distant stars, to the digestive system of a worm or to the life of a microscopic bacillus. It is not facts themselves which make science,"[4] but the method by which they are dealt with.

Science is independent of any particular subject matter or order of facts. "It takes the knowable universe for its subject. It deals with physical as well as psychical processes; with man as much as with nature. It has to do with everything to which its methods can be applied. What makes a science is not of course, the nature of things with which it is concerned but the method by which it deals with these things. Study of a skylark is a not necessarily zoological."[5]

There is indeed some ambiguity about the concept of unity of science. This concept may be conceived formally as referring to logical or methodological elements common to various sciences. It must be admitted that there are different observational bases the contents of which are explained by different sets of propositions and that these cannot be conventionally amalgamated. Where theory is dealt with in the abstract without regard to particular empirical contents, the logical similarity between the sciences is implicitly assumed. Methodological considerations might seem to lead to diversity rather than unity, since the operations which are actually carried out and the calculations which are actually made by workers in the various sciences seem to be insurmountably different. It is easy to exaggerate differences between the experimental situations of the physicist and that of the social scientist. Of course, in obvious and gross ways the meter-reading of the physicist are nothing like the interview schedules of the social scientists but the obvious and gross elements here are irrelevant to the situation. In fact the physicist's experiment is very much like an interview with his apparatus; he asks questions of it and writes down the answers just as the psychologist does; only; the questions are not verbal. The differences between the various sciences, then are not essential differences, there is a genuine logical and methodological unity underlying their apparent diversity.

Against this backdrop, it may be helpful to distinguish between (1) the structure of science defined in terms of the rules of procedure, and (2) the *corpus of science* at a given time, i.e., the set propositions accepted at a given time in accordance with the rules of procedure. Says *Bernal*, "Science at any time is the total result of all that science has been up-to-date."[6]

It should now be clear that science has a reference to a method; not so much to a field of specific matter. *Lastrucci* aptly observes, "Science is an objective, logical and systematic method of analysis of phenomena devised to permit the accumulation of reliable knowledge. It is a systematized form of analysis ... not any particular body of knowledge."[7]

Little doubt, *Aristotle* was referring to this very method of dealing with facts when he said of science that it " begins when, from a great number of experiences, one general conception is formed which will embrace all similar cases."[8] To put it somewhat differently, science attempts to account for particular events by reference to general laws together with the actual conditions under which these laws act or to account for laws by reference to principles still more general.

As we shall see a little while later, the greater part of the summing up which science accomplishes is not so much in forming some new general conception or proposition as in bringing new sets of facts within the grasp of an old one. Science is an intellectual construction, a working thought model of the world and its aim is to describe and conceptualize the impersonal facts of experience in verifiable terms as exactly as possible, as simply as possible, as completely and meaningfully as possible. In the words of *Will Durant* "Science is the captured territory (in the siege of truth). As soon as a field of enquiry yields knowledge susceptible of exact formulation, it is called science."[9]

Science is a human activity among others and an intelligent person is quite capable of mastering its principles. There is indeed some distinctiveness in the scientist's ways of thinking. It is however, hard to specify what this distinctiveness is. One would say that science is more precise but nothing could be more precise than classical philology. Some would say that science is more concerned with truth, but nobody could be more concerned with truth than a biographer. Quite a few would point out that science looks more carefully at nature, but nobody looks more carefully at nature, than the artist. Understandably, different activities induce different habits and the longer and harder the course of study needed to acquire one set of habit, the more alienated they are likely to get vis-à-vis somebody who has been at pains to acquire a different set. It is impossible and unnecessary to learn many such sets. The physicist neither needs the skills involved in collecting old archaeological pieces, nor does a literary critic need the manual dexterity involved in manipulating experimental subject; but there is no reason why each should not know in a general way the part played by different people and the *modus operandi* involved. We may define the three aspects of the human activity known as science, leading in effect to three objects as follows:

Classification which leads to description, explanation which leads to understanding and prediction which leads to control.

In a sense all these three aspects are subsumed by one, namely, *explanation.* It can be easily appreciated how classification functions quite so often as explanation. Let us take the question: why does that animal have spots? And the answer could be, 'it is a leopard and leopards always have spots.' Take any classification; it involves such an attribution to a singular event of some universal characteristic — precisely, those that mark off the members of that class from those of other classes. One may not of course, be always satisfied with an answer of this kind and explaining why leopards have spots might warrant reference to the genetic basis of pigmentation or the evolutionary environment in which the particular animal developed. Admittedly then, the principles ultimately invoked are themselves glorified classification statements. When an event has been categorized as a case of some universal law, explanation can hardly go farther. Events are explained. And prediction can be conceived of as the application of an explanatory scheme to future events, on the assumption that if the principles held and the conditions fulfilled which are called upon to explain some events, the event will follow. Four rules may be identified as forming a compendious summary of almost everything which is of central importance for modern science.[10]

Rule I

We are to admit no more causes of natural things than such as are both true and sufficient to explain their appearances.

Rule II

Therefore, to the same natural effects we must as far as possible assign the same causes.

Rule III

To the qualities of bodies, which admit neither the intention nor remission of degree and which are found to belong to all bodies within the reach of our experiments, are to be extended the universal qualities of all bodies whatsoever.

Rule IV

We are to look upon propositions collected by general induction from phenomena as accurately or very nearly true, notwithstanding any contrary hypotheses that may be imagined, till such time as other phenomena occur by which they may either be made more accurate or liable to exceptions.

The above rules do not so much specify scientific method as they suggest certain restrictions which must be observed if mistakes are to be avoided. Rule I is obviously rule of economy or *parsimony*. Which restricts the number of explanatory categories. Rule II is the principle of *induction* and restricts variety in these categories. Rule III is the principle of explanation which together with Rule IV restricts scientific fantasy, while Rule IV is the recognized fundamental principle, namely, *empiricism*.

Scientific method referring as it does to a procedure or a mode of investigation by which scientific and systematic knowledge is acquired, is based in certain faith "articles of faith." Among these are: (1) reliance on *empirical evidence*, (2) use of *relevant concepts*, (3) commitment to objectivity, (4) *ethical neutrality,* (5) *generality,* (6) *predictions* based on probability, and (7) *public methodology* affording testing of conclusions through replication. It would be helpful to discuss each one of these in some detail. We shall discuss them in the above-mentioned order.

1. Reliance on Empirical Evidence

The man of science is firmly committed to the belief that "truth"[11] can always be established on the basis of evidence that our sense organs can get at. Of course, science never expects us to reach the ultimate truths.

"At their best her theories are not and never pretend to be more than diagrams to fit, not even the possible facts, but simply the known fats."[12]

The scientist believes that the sole source of our knowledge is experience (i.e., data of senses) and that there are no universal and necessary truths from which valid existential inferences can be drawn. He further believes that since knowledge existing outside oneself is reached through experience, it must always be uncertain and tentative. All this is not to say that the scientific attitude is one of uncritical empiricism. It may be sensible to describe this attitude as critical empiricism, that is, the scientist does not accept uncritically whatever the sense datum presents before him. To this sense datum, he applies the screws of *reason* so as to comprehend its true character. In other words, the man of science regards rational ideas as the guiding principles for making predictions or formulating explanations to be tested subsequently by observation, i.e., empirical evidence, now or at some point in future. But as stated already, science does not accept a proposition derived from a given set of rational ideas as constituting a reliable proof of its validity or truth. The scientist may be likened to a creative artist who fashions a block of marble into a statue. While the insights of reason would suggest the shape and form of the statue, the artist in this process of fashioning cannot afford to remain unconcerned with the grains on and the dimensions of the marble block (empirical data) except at his own peril.

It may be instructive to regard the development of science as a continuing dialectical process.[13] This implies no commitment any special version of dialecticism, it simply takes account of the fact that what is required for the advancement of science is a continuing interplay between its logical frontiers *rationalism* and its experimental frontiers *empiricism*. The logical aspect is embodied in the doctrine which has generally been known as rationalism. *Rationalism* proceeds from the rational investigation of connections between concepts without special regard to the adequacy of the concepts of experience, developing formal structures in a free and creative way. *Empiricism* in doctrine, proceeds from an empirical investigation of connections between events, without special regard to the significance of those events in any total scheme of things, accumulating factual information in a disciplined and receptive manner. Both these aspects are absolutely essential and scientific progress may be regarded as dialectical process of reciprocal feedback between them.

If empirical findings outrun logical constructions (theories, laws) science is at a loss; logical construction would have to catch up before the new empirical findings can be put in their place. Conversely, if logical constructions go ahead of empirical investigation, that may not be regarded as so serious because there will always be a scope for something to come up in the empirical realm to fill the new breach in logical development and provide an interpretation for part of the structure that was not interpreted before. But till such a time as it does so the logical construction is bound to remain a mere exercise of intellectual ingenuity.

The rationalists of old, interpreted science as a *deductive system* of propositions. For them, there stood at the head of the system, a set of self-evident propositions and from these, other propositions (theorems) could be derived by the process of reasoning. At the other end are the avowed inductionists (empiricists) who believe that science must construct its axioms from the sense data relating to particulars by ascending continually till it finally arrives at the most general *axioms*.

As we have suggested, science operates on the twin wheels of deduction and induction, both equally germane to the goals of science. Deduction involves inferring from the premises or general statements some bits of information about the world. Deduction is a device for the discovery of the truth that lies concealed within a set of statements. In fact, there is nothing new in deduction; all information contained in the conclusion is already contained in the premises. Nevertheless, it helps us to know and understand the world around us since it opens our eyes to the information that viewed otherwise, we would not get at. But the method of deduction is definitely limited by the facts ascertained empirically. The empirical method of extending one's palm out of the window to see if it is raining, has the advantage of rendering us safe from false premises. But the advantage of the deductive method in the instant case is that one does not have to go out and get wet to arrive at the answer. It is to be noted that the deductive method is a method of getting information just as the empirical method of getting information.

In a sense, in established facts have more claims on being called 'knowledge' than inferences arrived at deductively. When an empirically established fact collides with a deduced proposition, deduction must yield to the power of empirical fact. As someone has said, "Many a beautiful theory has been slain by an ugly fact...."

The case in point may be variously illustrated. If a plane that theoretically would not fly at all, does fly despite the deduction to the contrary; the theory; the basis for deduction, in consequence, would have to be revised for, it is in error. The conflict between deduction and empirical knowledge cannot, however, be settled so easily. Often the empirical facts are not so clear because measurements are uncertain. In such situation a strong deductive argument can be more persuasive.

If one of the major aims of science is explanation, the most usual pattern of explanation in science is evidently deductive, i.e., from a universal statement or statements (laws or principles) together with some particular statement conditions (which together comprise the explanations) is deduced a statement describing the event to be explained. The criteria for sound explanation of this sort are that deduction should genuinely involve the universal statement and that those statements and the statement conditions should be true as nearly as this can be ascertained.

Induction contrarily, moves from particulars to arrive at general propositions. It operates on faith that in the course of things for a long period is a basic regularity to warrant the inference that it will continue in the future too. Induction is thus a leap of faith. Many a philosopher has indicated the paradox of induction, pointing out that past experience can hardly be a secure guide to learning about nature of bodies. Their secret nature and consequently all their effect and influences may change without any change in their sensible qualities. If this happens sometimes and with regard to some object, it will happen always with regard to all objects, they point out. And then there is no logical or process argument that would secure us against this supposition. It is not inconceivable that new evidence might be forthcoming sometime and this would be the only way in which the theory of induction could escape the paradox. It may nevertheless be difficult to imagine what might constitute this new evidence.

If the *premise* and conclusion, in the logical case, are both known, some probability relations may be established between them and this may serve as a paradigm of an inductive inference. But where the inductively arrived at prediction has not yet been observed, where the conclusion is not known, the situation is akin to trying to guess where rest of the triangle lies, if one is given one side. Without further information the task is impossible and the only way to get such information is to wait. In absence of any other principle, we use, of course, the relation defined by previous sequence of observation but that the new case will conform to the pattern cannot be known until it has already done so. If we must not act except on certainty (not probabilities) we ought not act on religion, for it is not certain; but there are many things we do on uncertainty, sea voyages, battles, life insurance etc. So often when we are working for tomorrow we are doing so on uncertainty, but we do not act unreasonably; for we work for an uncertainty according to the doctrine of chance or probability, i.e., that certain events are more likely to take place under certain circumstances.

Induction has an importance to us and hence we are more sympathetic to proposals for providing it with some logical foundation. But the truth or falsity of the principle of induction is not altered by such efforts, any more than the truth or falsity of the existence of God is. Electing one side or the other, as a result of logical calculation, is futile any way.

In any case, the best attitude to induction is to make induction the subject of a resolve that in the absence of any better guide to future behaviour, we would use the lessons of past experience. It would be absurd to pretend that we need reassurances about the course of events in the distant future, just as to pretend that we know anything about the course of events in the distant past.

Scientific observations have been made with some accuracy for perhaps 5,000 years; they have been made in quantity and variety only for about past 500 years. An extrapolation on inductive grounds into the past suggests that these periods represent an almost infinitesimal fraction of the whole life of the universe. Further, all those observations have been made within a very thin spherical shell surrounding one planet of a small star (Sun). It could be that an animal species thus restricted in time and space has, in fact, succeeded in discovering the principles according to which the universe operates, but were it not for the fact that human beings as ourselves are members of this species, we should find *a priori* probability of this rather small. What success we can claim lies in our constructing a theoretical account of a hypothetical universe which, supposing it existed, would be like our universe in those places and at those times where the latter has been observed. We expect that in limited predictions, the fit of the theoretical universe to the real one shall still be fairly close. Saying something beyond this would be presumptuous.[14]

The extreme empiricist view of the matter is that laws are arrived at by induction, often understood as, by simple enumeration. But here the problem of induction is bound to arise because there is no satisfactory way of explaining empirically how we can come to a position —"in all cases of acts or events" and not, all observed cases of acts or events. But the failure of philosophers to solve the problem of induction has not prevented scientists from discovering laws. The fact is that the process of reasoning by which these laws are arrived at are not of induction at all. In fact, they start with universal propositions as hypotheses and when they have tested them, regard them as laws.

The hypothetic reasoning runs as follows:

(1) C is observed

(2) But C would follow only if A were true.

(3) Therefore, there is reason that A is true.

This is the sort of reasoning by which scientists often arrive at propositions of universal kind.

It is quite often asked what the method of science is: whether induction or deduction? The only answer to this is: both. *Larrabee* beautifully scores the point when he remarks, " If extreme rationalist (deductionist) is like a spider spinning out theories from within, the extreme empiricist (inductionist) is to be compared ... to an ant which piles useless heaps of facts. Better than either the spider or the ant is the bee, which selectively gathers pollen and transforms it into honey...."[15] We must remember that in actual scientific practice, induction and deduction are mingled in intricate ways. None could have put it better than *Auguste Comte* who said, "Induction for deduction with a view to construction...."

2. Use of Relevant Concepts

Concepts are logical constructions or abstractions created from sense impressions, percepts and experiences. Concepts are the symbols that science works with; they constitute the linguistic apparatus of science. The language of science evolves in order to deal with problems of nature for which ordinary language has proved inadequate and wanting.

The world in which we live, and in which science is discovered at work, is apparent nature. The world which science describes is a creation of the human intellect which, while it may bear some resemblance to causal nature, is not identical with it. Neither of these taken by itself is adequate to be considered in the role of the nature which is referred to in the definition of science. Science while it is the explanation of nature in its own terms, is not the explanation of apparent nature simply. What is explained is of course, discovered within apparent nature. Were it not for this, we could have no access to it. But in order to be explained, it is rendered, even at the descriptive level, in characteristically scientific terms, and to that extent given entry into a new realm. Explanation, being logical relationship, lies entirely within the fields of thought and language. The nature which is explained is given in perception, but rendered in conceptual and linguistic terms. The nature in whose terms the explanation is provided, on the other hand, is not given at all, but conjectured. There are, of course, events and processes to which, for one reason or another, we cannot gain access. These constitute causal nature, having a directly productive relationship with apparent nature.

As we shall see, the scientific procedure consists in evolving, defining and manipulating concepts or symbols with a view to contributing variously to the established corpus of systematic knowledge and/or to establish some new bit of knowledge. In his passage from concrete sense data to the higher and higher levels of abstraction (hypotheses, theories and laws,) the man of science is constantly shaping, formulating, relying on and using relevant concepts.

3. Commitment to Objectivity

The subjective-objective dichotomy is very old, going back in the history of thought beyond the foundation of most social and behavioural sciences. In basic outline, this dichotomy suggests that there are two fundamentally opposite ways of theoretically treating man and his social organization. One is the objective way, which views man and human society as basically similar to other aspects of the physical world. But social sciences typically prove too hazardous a ground in reference to which the object frame of reference as the right one for scientific knowledge is not totally acceptable. The objective frame of reference has proved immensely useful for the physical sciences and it is not surprising, given the success of the physical science that many have attempted to use this frame of reference to order and explain human behaviour. Unfortunately, human behaviour often does not lend itself to the explanation used in the physical sciences. Human behaviour entails elements which may be called ideational, i.e., intentional, meanings, values and beliefs that cannot be described in terms of sensory dimensions. The scientific method with its emphasis of objectivity bristles with problems in social sciences because of their direct or indirect concern with the study of man and his social organization. Human behaviour can be studied by other human observers alone and they are always likely to distort the facts being observed. These facts, in turn, can be appreciated only on the intentional frame of reference which implies a lot of subjectivity thrown in. The problem of objectivity in social sciences has been discussed at length in a separate chapter. Here we only address ourselves to the ideal of objectivity for a practitioner of science.

The nature of scientific method is such that a practitioner of science must set aside the subjective considerations; he must be prepared to suppress his hopes and his intuitions. The adoption of scientific approach may sometimes be painful but must be accorded due recognition.

The man of science is firmly committed to the belief that to go nearer to the goal of truth, he must "above all things ... strive at self-elimination in his judgements and provide an argument which is as true for each individual mind as his own.[16]

Objectivity according to *Galtung* [17] is a composite of

(a) *intra-subjectivity;*

(b) *inter-subjectivity.*

The test of intra-subjectivity (or reliability) is that repeated observations of a constant phenomenon by the same observer will yield constant data while the test of inter-subjectivity consists in finding that repeated observations of a constant phenomenon by different observers will yield constant data. Inter-subjectivity is only a more adequate formulation of what is generally meant by the "objectivity" in science. What is here involved is not only the freedom from personal or cultural bias or partiality, but even more fundamentally the requirement that the knowledge-claims of science be in principle capable of test (confirmation or disconfirmation, at least indirectly and to some degree) on the part of any person properly equipped with intelligence and the technical device of observation or experimentation. The term inter-subjective stresses the social nature of the scientific enterprise. If there be any "truths" that are accessible only to privileged individuals, such as mystics or visionaries, that is, knowledge-claims which by their very nature cannot be independently checked by anyone else, then such "truths" are not of the kind we seek in the sciences. The criterion of inter-subjective testability thus delimits the scientific from the non-scientific activities of man.

The scientist is thus expected to avoid at all costs what *Francis Bacon* termed the "false idols."[18] Social sciences present typical difficulties when it comes to translating into action, the pious wish to commit one-self to objectivy.

The critics have made much of this, some even going to the extent of insisting that the social sciences in view of their dubious objectivity would not qualify as sciences in the true sense of the term. The whole range of criticisms and defense thereof is presented in the next chapter.

4. Ethical Neutrality

What *Faraday* said of the philosopher, applies with equal force to the scientist, "(He) should be a man willing to listen to every suggestion but determined to judge by himself. He should not be biased by appearances; have no favourite hypotheses: be of no school, and in doctrine have no master. He should not be a respecter of persons, but of things. Truth should be his primary object.[19] A man of science is wedded to the faith that affectivity or commitment to an ideology is likely to distort his perspective and his judgement of things may thus become partisan or value-laden. He certainly cannot afford the luxury of prejudices, i.e., believing what is comforting to believe. As *Schroedniger* says, "Science never imposes anything, science states. Science aims at nothing but making true and adequate statements about its objects.[20]

However, since social sciences are called upon to explain aspects of human life, it is natural that these would be sensitive to any discussion about values and moral questions. The argument for value-neutrality in social sciences makes out a case in support of it as follows:

"In order to discover what is and to properly conceptualize what is, it is necessary for social scientist to bring no personal prejudice or bias to his study."[21] This does not mean that they should cease to be moral men, but for the purpose of description, for one's desire to know what is, one must observe, describe and theorise dispassionately. If disinterestedness is not maintained, what one believes may get in the way of what is. Dogma would interfere with thought.

The position on ethical neutrality arose curiously among those who adopted a subjective approach to social problems. It was felt that proper understanding of social structure, processes and behaviour demanded inference from data and an interpretative appreciation of abstract human relations. Value freedom was essential. For the data to be obtained only in this way, the observer would have to hold his feelings in check for the duration of his observation and conceptualization. Since all data collection was subjective in nature, if there were no attempts at ensuring ethical neutrality, the social scientific ventures would surely raise controversies of opinion. In sum, it was thought that the social scientist should describe things as they are, to the best of his ability, keeping moral values out. He needed techniques that would actually measure things he wants to measure and not fool himself by measuring something else.

But this kind of argument eventually led to a new attack on the proper goal of social theorising, one which blurs the distinction between explaining something and altering it.

The attack tends to point out that explaining things as they are amounts to putting an emphasis on the forces leading to stability and status quo and to distract people away from what might be possible by way of improvement. People who argue in this vein often impugned the motives of social science theorists, arguing in effect, that ethical neutrality or value free interpretations of the social states of being were given by them in a calculated effort to justify them and keep them that way. Thus, the attack on value-neutrality usually ends up by advocating some biased viewpoint in social analysis.

If the objective of social theory is simply to explain what people do and to deduce these explanations from descriptive data organised into concepts then the problem of value-neutrality does not really arise because regardless of what one's values are in regard to the subject-matter, the same results will continue to surface. If on the other hand, explaining also means understanding or having insight into situations, perhaps in some unique human terms, then, the value problems will arise. When this happens, the distinction between social theory and bias gets blurred. One becomes deliberately biased, then, at the risk of damage to the accuracy of his results but this risk is sometimes worth its price in terms of the quality of insights rendered possible. This is a more palatable stance for a numerically dominant section of the social scientists today. Much more will be said about this in a separate chapter in this book.

5. Generality

The conclusions of any import in science are generalizations, i.e., statements of general applicability. Typically, a series of observations of some class of objects, say X, are made by the scientist with a view to determining whether or not the members/items of this class have some property, say, Y. The result of these observations may be a series of protocol sentences. 'This X is Y' and so on. To avoid confusion, the scientist tries to identify the Xs in some to keep them distinct from one another so that the sentences read: 'X_2 is Y,' 'Xn is Y.' If among a large number of such observations no X is found which is not Y and also that no X-like objects are known which exhibit great variety in Y-like properties, the scientists tend in such situation to jump from the collection of singular statements about X_1 X_2–Xn to a universal statement about the class of Xs, viz., all Xs are Y. Such a leap is a generalization and the statement resulting from it, an empirical generalization. Generalizations emerge naturally after a large enough number of particular observations.

There can be no science without a belief in the inner harmony of the world and in the fact that reality may be grasped with the abstract theoretic or general construction. Say *Einstein and Infeld,* "This belief is and will always remain the fundamental motive for all scientific creation. Throughout our efforts, in every dramatic struggle between old and new views, we recognise the eternal longing for understanding, the over firm belief in the harmony of our world continually strengthened by the increasing obstacles to comprehension."[22]

The scientist is constantly aware of his obligation to discover "under the surface level of diversity, the thread of uniformity. Around a discovered uniformity, a logical class is constructed; about the class and its observed pattern a descriptive generalisation is formulated. Scientists are alert to opportunities for combining comparable classes into a broader class and for formulating a wider and more abstract generalization to comprehend the discrete generalizations thereby embraced.[23] Thus are the scientific theories and propositions generated. *Francis Bacon* suggested, precisely this when he presented his new method *NovumOrganum. Bacon* advocated the method of constructing axioms from senses and particulars by ascending continually and gradually till the most general axioms are finally arrived at.

It is obvious that sciences differ in respect of the levels of generalization attained. More mature a science, the greater its generalizing potential. This has been conveyed with amazing felicity by *Medawar*. He observes, "... the factual burden of a science varies inversely with its degree of maturity. As a science advances, particular facts are comprehended within, therefore in a sense annihilated by general statements of steadily increasing explanatory power and compass. In all sciences we are being progressively relieved of the burden of singular instances — the, tyranny of the particular. We need no longer record the fall of every apple."[24]

6. Predictions Based on Probability

The principal aspects of the scientific activity are classification which leads to description, explanation which leads to understanding and prediction which leads to control. The human attempt to anticipate and therefore control events relies on the ability of science to predict, i.e., to obtain knowledge of future events.

Prediction is just a special type of generalization; one from the past to the future. Prediction is always a leap of faith for there is no guarantee that tomorrow will be like today. It is one's judgement and depth of knowledge about the subject matter which lends support to the supposition based on what happened in the past, that same thing will take place in the future; prediction is reasonable to make if our assumption is sensible that the past and future belong to the same continuum, i.e., the conditions which held in the past will obtain in the future, too. "The prediction that the sun will come up tomorrow morning is implicitly a statement that tomorrow morning comes from the same universe as have all mornings in the past."[25]

Reliable predictions can well be made even when changes in conditions are bound to occur if one knows the important conditions that created the trend are changing in a certain way. Since the past is never a guarantee of the future and prediction is not just a mechanical extrapolation, the safer basis of projections of an observed trend onto the future is an understanding of the various forces that underlie the process. Prediction shares this aspect with all generalizations: from the known to the unknown. The usefulness of some generalizations in prediction naturally depends on the scientist's ability to trace out the sequence of propositions embodied in the general principle faster than nature traces out the sequence of causes, so that the scientist gets there first.

The man of science believes that predictions about phenomena are possible and must rest on a solid basis of the trend repeatedly observed and the probability that very same trend would manifest itself in terms of some concrete results in the future too. The attempt to anticipate events and hence, to control them relies on the ability of science to predict. Predictions cannot be derived by deduction from any "self-evident" or "ultimate" truths. The tincture of science liberates man from the load of prejudices. Without it, the world tends to appear definite, obvious, common objects, would arouse no questions and familiar possibilities get contemptuously rejected. It is thus clear that the scientific expectations or predictions are grounded in the established knowledge about the order among facts. It is well to bear in mind that these expectations may not always come true. If they do not, the scientist is under an obligation to research the corpus of knowledge or theory which initially afforded the basis for predictions and suitably amend it or even reject it. It is a part of the scientific attitude that pronouncements of science do not claim to be certain but most probable on present evidence. Probability reflects a state of the mind, best characterizes not negatively, as his ignorance of the future but positively as his expectation with respect to it. As *Feynman* says, "Scientific knowledge is body of statements of varying degrees of certainty, some most unsure, some nearly sure, none absolutely certain."[26]

It is typical of social sciences that they have a far lower predictability compared to the natural ones. The reasons are obviously the complexity of subject matter inadequacy at control, etc. It is often said of the social sciences that the predictions made by them are hedged with so many preconditions (such as the well-known, "other things being equal" *(Ceteris Paribus)*, that they are denuded of any practical worth. The much heard of distinction between the "exact" and "inexact" science stems from this though the usage 'exact' science is itself tautological, since all sciences are as exact as possible. It has now been generally agreed that the social sciences though relatively inexact are "sciences" nevertheless and that central criterion of conferring scientific status on any branch of study should rightly be its method of study rather than the nature of results it comes out with. In other words, a science would refer to the branch of study which has progressed to a point where its analysis reveals a logical structure, that is, its categories of classification, definitions and rules of correspondence are as free as possible from vagueness and ambiguity. Given time, social sciences might also vastly improve their predictive prowess.

7. Public Methodology Affording Testing of Conclusions through Replication

Science is a public institution practising a public methodology. A scientist has to make known to others how he arrived at the conclusion he did. This way alone can the scientist expose his own methods and conclusions of his research to critical scrutiny. Criticism, according to Karl Pearson, is "the very life-blood of science." It is through such criticism alone that science as an on-going historical institution continually improves upon the means and methods of inquiry — an obligation that every true scientist shares with the rest.

Furthermore, such criticisms signal at the right moment the drawing of unwarranted conclusions which in turn might bring about considerable harm considering the fact that we, as of now, depend so very much on the products of science. Science is a collective, co-operative endeavour geared to the discovery of facts and it is, as pointed out by *Dewey*, "a method of knowing which is self-corrective in operation, that learns from failures as from successes."[27]

Unless the method of scientific inquiry is made public, it would not be possible for the fellow scientists (and critics) to replicate the initial inquiry to verify if the same conclusions are reached by recourse to the methods in question. Subsequent replications lend added credibility and support to conclusions of inquiries if these replications arrive at the same conclusions (assuming, of course, that similar mistakes of method do not get repeated). These are the solid bedrocks on which the corpus of science rests and from which it advances into many directions. As has just been pointed out, frequentative verification of conclusions is basic requirement of science. This requirement brings to the fore one of the most central aspects of research; for, etymologically, research means repetitive search. Such repetitive searches may lend confirmation to established conclusions in the field, help propose certain modifications in them or even invalidate them. We will do well to remember that invalidation, no less than verification of propositions is an important contribution to science.

A word about replication or repeatability since the repeatability criterion cannot be smoothly applied in the realm of social sciences. The requirement of scientific research in regard to replication may be simply laid down as follows. The researcher must describe his empirical work in such a way that other people could exactly know what he did. The problem is here. The more the observer interprets what he has seen the less repeatable the study. Understandably, there is much scope in social science for the researchers to interpret their observations before recording them for subsequent presentation. Hence the subjective or impressionistic elements may be so strong that replication in the desired sense is not possible. For example, different observers may come to different assessments of the kind of people certain tribals are, owing to different impressions gained by them in the course of their living with them.

Modern science in contradiction to ancient science is characterised by a certain measure of tentativeness with which it holds its conclusions. New data may invalidate them any moment. Developed science has removed the dogmatic arrogance of those who have never travelled the region of liberating doubt. It has kept alive our sense of wonder by showing familiar things in unfamiliar contexts. Frequentative tests or verification are a necessary condition for this.

It was pointed out at the outset that for a proper appreciation of the nature and content of research a thorough understanding of the scientific method is called for. In the preceding pages the salient features of scientific method were discussed at some length. An understanding of the scientific method for a student of theory and practice of research was thought necessary in as much as research is as *Best* puts it, "is the more formal systematic, intensive process of carrying on the scientific method of analysis."[28] Formal aspects of the scientific method will become clearer as the following pages unfold the steps involved in doing research.

Meaning of Research

The Webster's International Dictionary proposes a very inclusive definition of research as "a careful, critical inquiry or examination in seeking facts or principle; diligent investigation in order to ascertain something." The above definition while helpful in indicating in a very general way what people mean when they talk about research is not specific and precise enough to afford us a thorough and clear idea of what research involves. As suggested earlier, the activities that go by the name of research involve mainly a 're-search', i.e., activities undertaken to repeat a search. Thus, perhaps improving upon the definition presented above, it may be said that research refers to "a critical and exhaustive investigation or experimentation having as its aim the revision of accepted conclusions in the light of newly discovered facts."

The researcher is constantly concerned with researching the accepted conclusions of his field, i.e., the theories with differing levels of generality and degrees of confirmation (trust worthiness) existing at a given point of time. He does his researching by probing for facts of the empirical world that confirm one or several predictions generated by accepted conclusions, his acceptance, a consequence of his assumption about the correctness of the existing theories. Thus, researching may in effect turn to the construction of new theories to take the place of those no longer able to fit the data of the empirical world. Research, stated otherwise, is a systematic attempt to push back the bounds of comprehension and seek beyond the horizons of our knowledge some "truth" or come reality, shrouded in a subtle way and consequently, to keep extending as also consolidating these horizons without end.

D. Slesinger and M. Stephenson in the Encyclopedia of Social Science propose a very comprehensive definition of research as "the manipulation of things, concepts or symbols for the purpose of generalilzing to extend, correct or verify knowledge, whether that knowledge aids in construction of theory or in the practice of an art."

(a) Manipulation of Things, Concepts or Symbols

Sciences deal with things. In a laboratory, the physicist deals with things, e.g., balls, the psychologist deals with say, white mice. In order to know how things respond to or change under specific conditions, what common denominators are discernible in their responses under various conditions are and what law they abide by etc. the scientist subjects them to purposeful control, e.g., starving the rats for a specific period or letting the balls roll on different degrees of incline, etc. Such purposeful handling we call manipulation, which is an aspect of experimentation. We cannot here afford to miss out on an important point that scientist dealing with things is not dealing with things only but also with concepts or symbols, corresponding to things or phenomena. For the things that a particular science deals with, it has and must have some terms. As pointed out earlier, the terms defining the things about which a science tries to make sense are its concepts. If the scientist were dealing with things only, he would be working and be constrained to remain at the level of the concrete and his results would at best be limited to the particular things in a specific situation investigated by him and none else, i.e., this ball, this rat (which again does not make much sense, considering the fact that verily, our thought process depends on concepts). Thus, the scientist dealing with things is also at the same time dealing with concepts which sympmbolize them and their various properties. The physicist, in our example is thus dealing with the abstract notions of spheres, circles, velocity, acceleration, angles, pluses and minuses. The psychologist dealing with rats is dealing with abstract notions organism, hunger, deprivation and problem-solving potential, etc. All these abstract notions relate to things that are being dealt with but in themselves, are not things; these are simply the mental shorthands for things. The scientist can carry them in his head, or on a piece of paper; not so the things. Since concepts or symbols are abstract forms denuded of content, it is as though the scientist working with them was working with certain classes of things at a higher level of abstraction. Concepts have thus the relevance of things but not their bothersome content and load. The astronomer cannot get the planets and stars into his laboratory nor can he get at them and yet he can deal with them, i.e., conduct controlled inquiries into their movements. Because he knows the value of the variables relevant to the concepts.

It should now be clear how the concepts or symbols are subjected to manipulation just as things can be, only with greater facility and effect. Research involves thus, manipulation of things and/or concepts or symbols.

(b) For the Purpose of Generalizing

The manipulation or purposeful control of things, concepts or symbols illustrated above is undertaken with definite purpose, the purpose being to arrive at statements of generality. That is, the net result of a controlled inquiry should be a proposition or a conclusion which tells us about conditions influencing them. Of course, generality is a matter of degree, i.e., the conclusions arrived at on the basis of observations under exercise of manipulation will vary in their degrees of generality. The level of generality may be high or low; the significance or worth of a research may perhaps be judged in such terms, but absence of generality cannot characterize science. " This thing worked with Mr. X today" is no wise a conclusion of research since the concern with generalization is definitionally central to research. Slesinger and Stephenson would consider an automobile mechanic and a physician as espousing the role of a researcher to the extent each attempts to generalize about all automobiles and patients of a given class respectively.

(c) To Extend, Correct or Verify Knowledge

Generalizations thus drawn have, obviously, certain effects for the established corpus of knowledge. A general proposition having been established as an outcome of research may extend the bounds of knowledge existing at a point in time. It may, if it does not fit a certain body of existing knowledge in the sense of not auguring well with the expectations that can be legitimately drawn from it, exert pressure on the scientist to bring about certain amendments or modifications in this body of knowledge in view of the discordant note struck by this new general proposition. Contrarily, if the generalization fits the established corpus knowledge, it lends added credibility to it.

It will be in order to elaborate at some length the points made above. The role of general propositions in enlarging or extending systematic knowledge may take various forms. The generalization can be instructively used to understand a certain region of phenomena or aspects of them that were not examined in these terms before. That is, a new observation inhered by the generalization may afford a basis for a better and deeper understanding of a phenomenon. Reviewed in terms of the new observation, the phenomena under inquiry may reveal itself as one governed by a law applicable to a class of phenomena which, in turn, may be a constituent unit of a still larger class of phenomenon. In this manner, a new general conception helps us to appreciate the deeper linkages obtaining amongst several concrete phenomena or classes of phenomena. It is thus that a new set of facts is brought within the grasp of the established corpus of knowledge in a meaningful way. In consequence, the bounds of knowledge get enlarged not just quantitatively (i.e., more units covered under a conceptual scheme) but also qualitatively). For example, general conception of "relative deprivation" may serve as a useful means for examining the relation between rise in wages and productive efficiency of a worker. The problematic and paradoxical observation that wage-rise does not always accompany productive efficiency (it may at times even hamper it) can be more aptly understood by means of this abstraction.

This behaviour of workers, i.e., low productivity despite wage-rise, then appears to be a corollary of reference group behaviour. What we have gained is a deeper understanding of a specific phenomenon. This, of course, is only one possibility. The matter will become more clear when the relation between research and theory is discussed.

Another way in which a general conception may enlarge systematic knowledge is by bringing to light the seeming inconsistencies in the existing corpus of knowledge and attempting to reconcile these. For example, the findings of studies on the effects of "authoritarianism" and democratic classroom atmospheres on learning are not seen to be consistent. A new general conception in the nature of a research finding, helps us to reconcile these findings by pointing that whatever the classroom atmosphere, the important thing is the extent to which the teacher behaves according to the expectations of the students.[30]

Yet another way in which a new general conception extends knowledge is by pointing out or identifying certain gaps in the existing corpus of knowledge and attempting to bridge these up. These gaps have a reference to the failure or inability of a conceptual scheme or theory to explain and account for certain aspects of a phenomenon to which it should expectedly or principally apply. The theory that "uniformities of social behaviour represent conformity to norms" betrays such a gap since it cannot explain existence of certain social regularities which are not culturally mandated. This inadequacy of the theory represents a gap in knowledge. [31] The role of a new general conception may be to bridge this gap and to the extent this is successfully done, knowledge gets extended.

The general conception or finding emanating from research may have another impact on the established body of knowledge, i.e., correcting the errors in it. If the new general proposition derived through manipulation of things, concepts or symbols is discordant with what one would expect logically on the basis of the existing body of knowledge or theory, the only alternative, since the empirical observations and corpus of knowledge cannot for long stay divorced from and immune to each other in mutual indifference is to effect corrections or modifications in the original theory in the light of the new evidence. In case the existing scheme of propositions has no place whatsoever for the new observations, i.e., the situation is such that either the observations are incorrect or the theory, then scientific obligation demands that the prevailing system of propositions, should be revisited and revised. Proving that something considered to be true thus far is in fact wrong, is also an important contribution to knowledge. We shall have an occasion to illustrate this point later.

That the new statements of generality emanating from research serve as scales for verification of the existing system of knowledge is only repeating the obvious. As has been noted, research involves testing to find out whether the empirical observations presented as general statements are in accord with the predictions that may be made on the basis of the existing body of knowledge. If the observations are in accord with these predictions, the corpus of knowledge which afforded these, gains greater strength and confirmation. If such is not the case, the system needs to be revised or even rejected. An important aspect of scientific activity is verification of conclusions which have found a place in the established system of knowledge. This involves frequentative scrutiny. To use an analogy, the inspector is duty-bound to examine before each performance, the ropes on which the trapeze artistes in a circus perform their perilous tricks. The ropes should have indubitable reliability. Everything depends on it. So too, in science, the established facts must be really established, for they are the rallying points and the bases for the abstract super-structure. Should verification prove them to be unreliable or false, like the ropes in our circus example, they should be cut down.

(d) (This) Knowledge may be used for Construction of a Theory or Practice of an Art

The extended, corrected and verified knowledge may be put to two possible uses:

(a) Theoretical, (b) Practical.

Knowledge thus acquired may be used for constructing theoretic models. In other words, knowledge maybe organized into propositions and these propositions may then be meaningfully articulated to form a more abstract conceptual system affording estimations about a class of things or phenomena governed by a specified set of conditions. Such use of knowledge is often labeled as theory-oriented, and the activities of a scientist who seeks knowledge for the sake of building theories of 'non-utilitarian' import are often known as 'pure', 'basic' or 'theoretical' research. Knowledge for the sake of knowledge, i.e., only for the satisfaction of 'knowing' is the attitude that underlies scientific activity of this order.

Knowledge, on the other hand, may be used as a means to some practical or utilitarian goal and not construed just as an end in itself. For example, the knowledge about people in respect of certain things they need, like and aspire for, may be used to work towards their welfare, ameliorating their practical problems or even exploiting them for certain personal or 'ideological' ends.

Science is a double headed weapon. It can do immense good but it can be made to serve sinister ends too. It has powerful muscles but no personality. It cannot lead, it can only serve. It has a sharp eye for methods and tools but is blind to ends and values.

The researches which seek knowledge mainly for the sake of serving some practical ends are often called 'applied', 'action-oriented', or 'practice-oriented.' We shall be considering this aspect in greater details very shortly. Suffice it, here, to say that one should not consider these two orientations as comprising a perfect dichotomy. As we shall see later, there is nothing practical as a good theory and that endeavours to solve practical problems have many a time given birth to theories. That is, practice is quite often a "blessing for the development of theory."[32]

Thus far, we had concerned ourselves with research in general terms. The frame utilized was so broad as to encompass researches both in the fields of natural as well as social sciences. We shall now turn to 'social research' since this is the subject of the book in the main. 'Social Research' is again a broad term having a reference to different kinds of scientific inquiries conducted in the field of social sciences and the behavioural sciences (the distinction between social sciences and behavioural sciences is itself not very clear). Sociological research, for example, which may be an especial concern for quite a few may be considered a part and parcel of the general category or rubric that is designated as 'social research'. It may be said that, all sociological research is 'social research' but not all 'social research' would qualify as sociological research. 'Social Research' would refer to a large class of researches while sociological research may be considered a sub-class within it. In practice, i.e., during the conduct of a study, it hardly makes much difference how one labels the study. What matters is the scientific character of one's procedures and how successfully one can solve the difficulty (theoretical or practical) that originated the study. Whether one calls study 'A sociological study of old people' or just plane, 'A study of the old people', it does not make much difference as long as it is a scientific study of the old people. It is not the label that by itself determines a researcher's procedures, insights, emphases and his findings, it is rather his training and capabilities, which does it. A rigid division of researches on the basis of the traditional division of sciences is not only not practicable but also not quite desirable. It is well to take heed of Francis Bacon's reminder that 'The divisions of sciences are not like different lines that meet in one angle but rather like the branches of trees that join in one trunk." [33] Lavoisior, in 1773, stated in a Memorandum to the French Convention: All forms of knowledge are threads in one great tapestry and we are assured of one ultimate pattern and design because there in a unity behind all knowledge.

In modern times, research is often a corporate affair in as much as the complex techniques of collecting and processing data require interdisciplinary cooperation. The scholars belonging to different fields of specialised studies applying different forms and techniques work together and pool their knowledge and insights at one point to solve some common problem which initiated research.

In so far as the social or behavioural sciences differ from the natural or physical sciences in quite significant ways and also, in as much as they share among themselves certain common problems of control, measurement, quantitative analysis etc. with more or less equal intensity (so much so that at one time 'scientific study' of social phenomena was thought of as impossible), it would not be improper to use the term 'social research' to embrace all scientific inquiries within the large field of social behavioural sciences. Convenience also advises this.

It will do the subject to harm if we adopt the broad definition of research discussed in the preceding pages to what is generally known as 'social research.' By this token, social research may be defined as "a method of studying, analyzing and conceptualizing social life in order to extend, modify, correct or verify knowledge, whether that knowledge aids in construction of a theory or in practice of an art."[34] It will be seen that social research is nothing more than the application of scientific procedures of manipulation (purposeful control), of analysis and of synthesis at a higher level of generality, to the social-human phenomena with a view to test, modify and enlarge systematic knowledge about social facts and social life, generally. Thus, social research has a reference to an investigation focused on social phenomena processes and organization which aims to discover new facts about social reality or verify old ones, to analyse their sequence, interrelationships, causal connections and laws governing them by means of logical and systematized methods. It is clear that social research does not aim at finding the ultimate truths. Rather, it aims to understand and clarify the behaviour of man, the social world he lives in, the relationships he maintains, the influences which are exerted on him and the effects these have upon him and subsequently, upon the social institutions of which he is a part and through which his behaviour is mediated.

A recent tendency to equate research with a particular method of investigation calls for comment. Such tendency stems from a misconception of scientific method, resulting in the setting up of a criterion which ignores its many important contributions to knowledge. It hardly needs to be over-emphasized that a "A study is scientific when its data are subjected to a logical analysis resulting in the development of a theory whether those data are secured by experiment, by statistics or common sense.[35]

The fact that experiment cannot be performed in a particular case does not negate the possibility of scientific study. The term ' experiment' is sometimes used in a more restricted sense, to apply only to situations in which objects or events involved can be deliberately manipulated by the investigator. This amounts to assuming that manipulation is just about the only method of control. As we said earlier, an astronomer cannot manipulate the stars and the planets and yet he can conduct controlled enquiries into their relationship because he knows the values of the variables. So also can the social-scientist study the miniature social systems in a controlled manner if he is able to determine the significant properties of these systems (i.e., groups). The historic reason why manipulation is sometimes confused with control is that at one time manipulation was necessary to reduce the number of variables to just two, thus making them amenable to mathematical treatment. The development of methods of 'multivariate analysis' has removed the necessity of manipulation and laboratory. Though control is not synonymous with manipulation, some scientists, Ackoff tells us, consider it useful to make a distinction between the general class of controlled manipulation. This special class they call 'experimentation' while the general class is designated as 'research'.[36]

This practice has had the unfortunate consequence of according to the non-manipulative inquiries a status lower than the manipulative ones. In fact, the emphasis ought not to be on manipulation but on control, where it belongs. For our purposes, research would also involve experimentation.

Research : Pure and Applied

Research may be motivated by a desire to understand for the sake of knowing (often called 'pure' or 'basic' research). This subject was initiated earlier but was postponed for a fuller discussion. Here we take it up. While the division between the two, i.e., 'applied research and 'pure' research is a matter of degree, it may be said that the 'pure' researcher derives greatest satisfaction from increasing his knowledge in a field of inquiry where many questions remain unanswered. To him the challenge of not knowing is paramount. If he can solve the problem, he is satisfied; the results may or may not have any practical use. The 'pure' scientist would probably argue that knowledge itself is, in the last analysis, always of some practical use. To him, scientific enquiry is noble in itself, it is its own reward. To keep digging away at the layers of intellectual questions is a challenge enough for a 'pure' scientist. To him "knowledge is the highest good, truth is the supreme value; all the rest is secondary and subordinate."[37] The 'applied' scientist, however is apt to see his research in a practical context. He would define a problem as one with reference to which some action should be taken to improve matters.

The applied scientist thus is much more likely to be working within a certain set of values and norms to which he feels committed. Sociologists for instance, study a host of problems, viz., the problem of juvenile delinquency, of old people, of ganges, etc. The 'pure' sociologist would study them just to find out the 'what' and 'how' of these, whereas the 'applied' sociologist would study these mainly with a view to finding out how best to go about arresting delinquency or helping old people. The applied scientist, of course, is working on the same data as the pure scientist but while the latter would perhaps stop short of advocating changes, the applied scientist is prepared to step in and propose the measures to ameliorate the situation. But once he starts to indicate what ought to be done, the applied scientist is stepping outside the structure of scientific investigation and is becoming a moral human being devoid of (scientific) neutrality.

As was suggested earlier, the controversy between 'pure' and 'applied' science need not be made much of, because the two are not mutually exclusive and there is a continual interplay between them. History shows how often in fact the development of science, has taken place in response to technical or even economic needs, and how in the economy of social effort, science even the most abstract and recondite kind pays for itself again and again and in providing the basis for radically new technical developments.[38]

Much has been said in favour of both sides, viz., the 'pure' science and the 'applied' science. *Huxley* disliked heartily the term 'applied' science and went a long way singing praises to the 'pure' science. He pointed out the risk in over-emphasizing the utilitarian criteria for judging the worth of sciences. *Francis Bacon*, a staunch advocate of 'pure' uncontaminated science said, "Just as the vision/of light itself/is something more/excellent and/beautiful than its manifold use, so without doubt the contemplation of things without superstition or imposture... is in itself a nobler thing than the whole harvest of inventions."[39] It is an intolerant narrow-minded view which supposes that a science is to be judged only by its practical fruits and not by illumination it affords."

Morris Cohen's perceptive statement epitomizes the importance of pure research, i.e., the purely theoretical contribution of research. He observes, "purely theoretical contributions to astronomy and mathematics, by increasing the precision of navigation have saved more lives at sea than its many possible (technological) improvements in carpentry of lifeboats."[40]

Parsons also argues in the same vein thus: "It is not a question of whether we try to live up to our social responsibility but of how. If we should put the overwhelming bulk of our resources ... into immediately practical problems, it would do some good but ... it would have to be at the expense of our greater usefulness to the society in future. For it is only by systematic work on problems where the probable scientific significance has priority over any immediate possibility of application that the greatest and most rapid scientific advance can be made."[41] *Parsons* points to the importance of 'pure' research directed at solving abstract theoretical problems. To him the application is only a technological by-product of abstract relationship among concepts, which is potentially a generator of many more applications.

The history of science testifies to the fact that the practical value of science has been in direct proportion to the precision of scientific methods and that most 'theoretical' or 'pure' investigations have practical implications of extraordinary magnitude. No great law of science has ever been discovered for its practical applications but instances abound of investigations apparently quite useless practically, which have led to most valuable results.

To quote *Dixey*, "knowledge pursued for its own sake without any direct view to future utility will often lead to results of most unexpected kind and of highest practical importance."[42] Thus, undue insistence on the practical utility of science is not historically justified and a hasty criticism of a certain scientific work being purely 'theoretical' is likely to be very unjust.

The contrary view holds that "Science is for life; not life for science." Robert S. Lynd's book, *Knowledge for what?* gave vehement expression to the feeling, "what good was knowledge if it did not have practical utility in terms of affording solutions to day-to-day problems?" *Samuel Stouffer,* the research-director of the well-known 'American Soldier Studies,' saw considerable merit in the insistence on the practical and its value for 'pure' research. Stouffer pointed out that practical application of a science enhances public recognition of the importance accorded to it and influences public co-operation and financial support for its prosecution. Secondly, applied research stimulates the improvement in the known tools and leads to the discovery of better ones. 'Pure science benefits from techniques developed by practitioners in applied field, Stouffer further points out that 'applied' research can speed up the process of building basic theories. The pressures to 'explain' or interpret surprising or unexpected practical findings, may lead to a reflection which organizes many such findings. The concept of 'relative' 'deprivation' for instance came to surface owing to the pressure to explain an anamolous or surprising observation in a practical situation, viz., the Negro soldiers who wanted to be stationed in the Northern American camps were less well adjusted there to army life as compared to the Negro soldiers who were stationed in Southern camp against their wish.

We have had a glimpse of the interplay between 'pure' research and 'applied' research. There are contributions to the other from each side. As *Dewey* aptly observes: "the method and conclusion of science do not remain penned within the science. Even those who convey of science as if it were a self-enclosed, self-actuated, independent and isolated entity cannot deny that it does not remain such in practical fact."[43] Ultimately, the great power of science appears to lie in the development of general principles which are applicable to many practical problems. *Comte* said, "knowledge is Foresight and Foresight is power."[44]

As we have already seen, 'pure' and 'applied' researches do not constitute an 'either-or' dichotomy. Historically, knowledge for its own sake and knowledge for practical application have both characterized the scientific enterprise. "... it has always been a tradition in science guiding the activities of many generations that science should be applied to practical purposes and the practical application should be a check on the validity of results and a justification for the efforts."[45] The dual emphasis is meant to provide for the development of a body of general principles about human (nature) behaviour and relationships. Secondly, because of its social orientation, it is expected to provide practical guidance in solution of social problems and issues.

Qualities of a Researcher

A question quite often asked is "What are the qualities of a researcher." To this question, a simple answer could be that being a scientist, the researcher should be firmly committed to the 'articles of faith' which underlie scientific method. This only amounts to saying that a researcher should be a man of science in the true sense of the term.

Sir Michael Foster's statement identifying the distinctive qualities of a scientist cannot perhaps be bettered. *Sir Foster* specified, in the main three qualities that characterize a true scientist.[46]

(1) Above all other things, his nature must be one that vibrates in unison with that of which he is in search, the seeker after truth must himself be truthful, truthful with truthfulness of nature; which is far more imperious, far more exacting than that which men sometimes call truthfulness.

Truthfulness corresponds to the desire for accuracy of observation and precision of statement. First, to make sure of facts is a fundamental precept in science. But this is not an easy matter. The difficulty here may be due to the untrained eye, which sees only that which it has the power of seeing, sometimes little indeed. It may be due to preconceptions which often make men see what is not to be seen. It also may be due to lack of discipline in the method of science. The unscientific man is often content with 'approximately', 'nearly' and so forth but nature never is. It is not her way to call the same two things which differ, however minutely. She resents the conduct of men who treat such differences in any other way than she treats them herself.

(2) The man of science must be of alert mind. Nature is ever making signs to us, she is ever whispering to us the beginnings of her secrets. The scientific man must be ever on the watch, ready at once to lay hold on nature's hint, however small, to listen to her whisper, however low. Receptivity to the hints and gestures of nature to the ignorant and the common place to see the unusual behind the routine demands a systematic immersion into the subject of concern to be able to catch the slightest hint that might give birth to significant research problems.

As *Cohen and Negel* so rightly point out, "The ability to perceive on some brute experience, the occasion for a (research) problem is not a common talent among men. It is mark of scientific genius to be sensitive to difficulties where less gifted people pass by untroubled by doubt,"[47]

(3) Scientific enquiry, though preeminently an intellectual effort, needs a moral quality of courage; not so much the courage which helps a man to face a sudden difficulty as the courage of steadfast endurance. The prosecution of science is a thorny affair. There are times when the scientist feels defeated and lost in wilderness. This is when he needs a supreme courage of conviction. He must learn to endure hardship intellectually. *Darwin* said, "It's dogged that does it."

The sacrifice demanded of a scientist at the altar of truth requires no less a courage than that exemplified by Von Siebold and associates who swallowed bladder worms to certify the truth of their 'theory.' It takes qualities of courage to be able to stand by one's conclusions or scientific conviction at the risk of social disapproval.

To the above three qualities of a researcher, we would like to add a fourth. This is a quality of cautiousness of statement. As Huxley puts it, "The assertion that outstrips the evidence is not only a blunder but a crime."[48] The researcher should habituate himself to withholding any judgement when data are obviously incomplete. According to W.K. Brooks, " The hardest intellectual virtue is philosophic doubt; the mental vice to which we are most prone is our tendency to believe that lack of evidence for an opinion is a reason for believing something else ... suspended judgement is the triumph of intellectual discipline."[49]

Cautiousness then, is the essence of science. One form of cautiousness most difficult of attainment and yet indispensable, is distrust of our personal bias in forming judgements. *Karl Pearson* aptly remarks, "The scientific man has above all things to strive at self-elimination in his judgements, to provide an argument which is as true for each individual mind as for his own."[50]

Nature of Social Research

The distinctive nature and character of social research derives in a significant measure from the real and supposed nature of the social phenomena which poses certain difficulties when it comes to application of the sophisticated scientific procedures characterizing the natural science to social phenomena.

It does not mean, of course, that social sciences are not science in any real sense. We may like to see what the typical limitations of social science research are:

In case of the softer social sciences so little spontaneous guidance is afforded by the subject matter than in some of the natural sciences which have a logic of their own unobtrusively pointing the way that substantive research often yields place to repetition discussion on methodology. A natural scientist need not worry about his laboratory experiment getting vitiated by his mood or by declaration of a foreign policy and other social events, however, his breath may affect the chemical elements in the course of a chemical experiment while all these and many more such factors need to be carefully controlled lest a social scientist should foul up his work. Also, certain properties of the subject-matter that social scientists deal with give rise to special problems. The results of social science inquiry are statistical, that is, presented in probability terms. They are never strictly categorical and clear cut. A certain new technique of advertising may work better than the conventional method with a certain proportion of the manufacturing while, the conventional method would appear to suit the rest. In other words, the differences between two or more categories within a social system may be so small that nothing can be said conclusively on the basis of comparison.

Besides, more than one important variable is generally involved in social science problem. Quite often it is nearly impossible to segregate or disentangle the different variables to ascertain their effects individually. This difficulty is nearly insurmountable when these different variables operate jointly and also are not amenable to experimentation. For example, when people are less educated they usually have lower income too. Hence, it is difficult to determine whether less educated people are less mobile than other people because of their education or because of their income operative together or because of both.

Furthermore, the researcher himself, being a human being a member of groups a buyer etc., frequently affects the subject matter and in effect changes the whole situation.

Again, as contrasted with the natural sciences the social sciences can barely construct a complete system. A physicist can discuss and set up equations for the entire system in which electrons flow in a circuit. But interactions among human beings cannot be so described for the human 'systems' get punctured so often and so easily that predicting a long-term sequences of events becomes well nigh impossible since a number of new influences enter with each interchange among human being; the system is never really closed.

Quite too often, the social scientists are criticized for labouring hard to contribute snake bites of knowledge. In all fairness to the critics it may be said that they are not far wrong when they make lead a criticism of this order. Conceivable, two factors can explain the poor output of social scientists. There is no denying the fact that many a serious problem of the world has barely been scratched. What causes war? What will ensure peace? Why so much of dehumanization? Social science may, of course, be said to have made some gains in certain fields, especially in the economic discipline, but many a huge human problem still remains untouched.

However, we are used to learning much about our social world in a very simple way. Most social questions can be answered seemingly very easily. Why people in slums suffer from ailments? Because they are poor. Why don't many women seek legal redressal of their genuine grievances? Because they feel it is unbecoming of women as a class to do so; on and on. Such and many other questions can be answered quite well (we feel) by consulting our own experience, by relying on our habits of thinking or by asking other people. These questions are not trivial but most of these have no single clear answer. In each case, some third factor is held responsible for what happens. But in the social sciences, it is a major task to unravel even such problems.

The behaviour of human beings is affected by diverse influences such as environmental, temporal, biological, psychological and socioculural, all of them affecting it contemporaneously. The complexity of human or social data may be largely attributed to this. It is difficult for an observer to see the underlying uniformities in the profuse diversity of human behaviour which is in a sense unique for each person. Hence, it is a formidable task for a scientist to discover another order principle which would apply to all men or the bewilderingly complex human data.

In social sciences, the laboratory is the society and the objects in the main are conscious and active human beings. "The observer and observed both being similar become so confused that an objective approach is really difficult to make. Moreover, except in totalitarian society, a controlled experiment in the laboratory of society with free men as objects ... *sine qua non* of an empirical science, is well nigh impossible in social science, generally."[51]

At this stage, it may be well to answer the emphasis on the distinctive features of Social Sciences. For instance, the complexity of social data is not so well founded. In the midst of the apparent chaos, there is indeed some pattern. If social life were so utterly complex, it would be unlivable. All social interactions are based upon expectations of behaviour, it may be an interaction between thousands of people in highly complex groups or an interaction in small cohesive groups. This means that a reasonable prediction about people's behaviour is possible — nay, it is an important aspect of social life. Talking of complexity, we should realize that complexity is a relative term. Social phenomena are complex to us, because our knowledge of them is inadequate and our tools of study have developed a little beyond infancy.

It has been pointed out above that as contrasted with the physical sciences, the social sciences lack the power of exact prediction. This is attributed to the 'erratic, idiosyncratic and irregular' nature of human behaviour.

It must be said that the case of unpredictability of social behaviour is a gain, not so well-founded. While individual behaviour may be unpredictable, one can predict with quite a high degree of accuracy the behaviour of a whole group (on the basis of knowledge of the pattern). *Lundberg* has rightly pointed out that the low predictive potential of social sciences is due mainly to our limited knowledge of relevant variables operative in the groups.

"As our knowledge of the variables increases and we will be able to judge the effort of various variatites involved, it will be possible for us to predict social events with much greater accuracy."[52]

Whereas the physical phenomena may be known directly through senses, the social phenomena are known only symbolically through words or terms referring to such phenomena, e.g., tradition, custom, values and the whole range of the subjective world, which makes verification of conclusions very difficult.

It may be pointed out in this connection that there has come about a standardization of concepts connoting social facts, and also that techniques have been developed to measure many of the so-called subjective items in objective terms, e.g., anthropometrics or sociometric measures.

Lundberg feels that most of the subject-matter of social science so qualitative and does not admit of quantitative measurement. This contention leaves some ground for criticism for, qualitative and quantitative measurements are only different stages in the growth of a science and it is not as though some data are by nature quantitative and others qualitative As science develops, what were previously thought of as a qualitative data may be transformed as quantitative ones. Secondly, we should not forget that qualitative expressions and analyses have their own place of importance in a social inquiry.

It has been argued that social phenomena compared to the physical ones are categorized by greater heterogeneity. Even if we accept this, it is possible by adequate stratification or classification effected in terms of certain traits or poverties, to ensure a fairly high degree of internal homogeneity within each stratum or class. Thus, social research may reach conclusions of broad applicability.

It has to be conceded that most physical sciences also known as exact sciences, allow for controlled laboratory experiments, hence their exactness. The social sciences suffer from this handicap, although to a limited extent laboratory experiments are possible here too. As social sciences develop, a number of human problems may hopefully be brought within the reach of laboratory experiments.

One of the characteristics of the social phenomena is that cause and effect (better still the producer and product) are hard to be segregated or disentagled clearly. In social sciences, it does not many a time, make sense to ask which is the cause and which is the effect (e.g., poverty and lack of skill). It is obvious that unless we realize this fact, we could be asking wrong questions and finding wrong answers.

The readers would have realized in the light of the above exposition that social data typically pose certain problems when it comes to these being treated by the highly developed quantitative methods of the physical sciences. It should be now clear also that quite a few critiques of the stature of social science research do not hold much water. At least the difficulties are not insurmountable. The difficulties which appear to preclude the possibility of a 'science of society' derive from our underdeveloped techniques and methodology of study and our consequent unfamiliarity with data rather than from the inherent differences between the data related to these two types of sciences.

It is an acknowledged fact that social sciences in their present state of development are far behind the physical science. Says *R. K. Merton,* "We, social scientist, happen to live at a time when some of the physical sciences have achieved comparatively great precision of theory and an abundance of technical by-product ... many social scientists take as a standard of self-appraisal ... they want to compare biceps with their bigger brothers. But this is to ignore the distinctive forehistory of each : between 20th century physics and 20th century sociology stand billions of man-hours of sustained, disciplined and cumulative research."[53]

Merton advises social scientist not to despair and harbour doubt whether a science of society is really possible, but, with the present limitations in view, "develop special theories applicable to limited ranges of data"[54] and slowly build their way up toward more general theories of broader applicability.

Utility of Social Research

To the question "what use is social research?" one may reply "of what use is a new-born child?" in the manner of *Benjamin Franklin* who replied thus, when asked the utility of his findings about the relationship between thunderclouds and electricity. This means that new knowledge like the new-born baby, holds great potential of worth and maturity. Also like the new-born child, it gives us pleasure. It gives us satisfaction of knowing the unknown. This points to a value that the scientist is committed to, i.e., the self-justifying goodness of 'new knowledge' about anything big or small. "Social research is persistently opening our eyes to the social reality, simplifying the mysterious within the seemingly common place in social life and shattering its garments of make-believe by which pious hands have hidden their uglier features. The obvious function of research is to add new knowledge to its existing store, but its power of cleansing our minds of clichés and removing the rubbish of inapplicable theory are equally notable. Scientific research is a cumulative process. It is also a rejective process, especially in social sciences ... understanding can be (advanced) not only by gains in knowledge but also by discarding outworn assumptions."[55]

A social researcher is interested in the discovery and interpretation of social processes, patterns of behaviour, similarities and dissimilarities that apply to typical social phenomena and social systems, generally. That is the social researcher is concerned with types and classes of social situation, persons or groups of which the unit he is studying at the time, is a specimen or an instance. His facts are selected and related according to their intrinsic nature and the susceptibility to organization into a logical system. This search for knowledge has a definite relation to people's basic needs and welfare. The social scientist assumes that all knowledge is potentially useful in the end. It must be remembered, however that science and society have a two way relationship. There is a give and take between science and social conditions. Science helps to create social conditions; social conditions recharge the accumulators of science.

In a general way, some of the direct practical benefits and theoretic implications of social research may be listed as follows :

(1) Social research has a crucial role to play in guiding social planning. Adequate social planning depends for its success on a systematic knowledge above the social resources and liabilities, of the people and their culture; of their similarities and differences, of organizations and operative controls, of their needs, hopes, aspirations and problems. Any effort at social planning is bound to fail of it is based on fictitious assumptions of planners in relation to what the consumers of planning need, what their problems are, what they want remedied, and what kind of system they want as an emergent product of planning.

Social planning, or for that matter any planning, requires a store of reliable, factual knowledge on the basis of which a blue-print may be designed and the difficulties in its implementation anticipated and guarded against. Nor is it all; such a foundation of scientifically gathered knowledge affords a basis for evaluation the net gains of planning for the social system in question. Social research is of immense help in securing such knowledge. It happens so often, that the overly zealous practical men with a programmatic orientation consider social research an unnecessary expense only to realize subsequently that the factual data would have helped them avoid the vast wasteful expenditure of money; time and energy occasioned by the failure of their designs on the place of practice. Social research is generally worth much more than the costs incurred over it.

(2) Since knowledge is a particular kind of power, social research, by affording first-hand knowledge about the organization and working of society and its institutions, gives us a greater power of control over the social phenomena and action. Thus, social research may be visualized as having practical implications for formal and informal types of leadership, patterns on influence and reform in different spheres of society.

(3) It is a very apt saying that knowledge is enlightenment. It dispels the thrust of outworn assumptions, superstitions and stereotypes. Social research thus, may be expected atleast to afford a more solid basis for people to hold whatever opinions they do. Some authors have claimed that social researches may have the effect of promoting better understanding and social cohesion, since it brings to light the underlying oneness in the midst of a bewildering variety or diversity of human societies. But this is claiming too much for one side and ignoring the other possibility; social research may also unravel diversity in the midst of apparent unity.

(4) It is obvious that social research has direct implications for social welfare. By virtue of the deeper understanding of the casual nexus underlying various social 'maladies', social research provides a secure basis for effective remedial measure. Social researchers analyse the problem basis for effective remedial measure. Social researchers analyse the problem in the 'total context' (this is desirable) and as such are in a better position to identify social structural anomalies and ambivalences that get reflected in the form of these problems and hence, structural changes would be necessitated. The 'remedies' suggested by research are thus deep going. They hit where they must. Many of the laymen reformer's 'remedies' create other new problem or 'side effect.' Scientific social research provides sound guidelines for appropriate measures of welfare of reform. It is no accident that a large portion of legislation and reformative measures own its origin to reports of social surveys.

(5) A researcher is charged with the responsibilities of asserting some order among facts. Thus research affords a considerably sound basis for prediction. Despite the admittedly low predictive potential of social research, reasonably reliable predictions, perhaps 'culture-bound' or 'context-bound', can be made. These have the effect of setting our efforts at social planning and control on a sounder footing. The success of planning for social development depends to a great extent on our intimate knowledge of our own society as also of other societies. Thus, social research has the effect of initiating and guiding social growth on proper lines and towards the cherished goals.

(6) Every scientist is obliged to effect constant improvements in the tools and techniques of his trade, i.e., research. The social researcher, in so far as he has to work in reference to different spatial-temporal contexts, each challenging his attack, is constantly faced with the need to improve upon his tools or if need be, to fashion new tools to match his skills with the task prompted by the exigencies of the situation. Samuel Stouffer and his associates working on the adjustment problem in the context of racial prejudice — to cite only one instance out of the many — had to effect modifications

in the prevailing techniques of research and when occasion demanded, to invent new ones to take the best out of the situation.

In concrete developmental parlance the major possibilities of utilizing social science research may be identified as under :

(a) Social research may afford valuable background data to be capitalized by social planners for assessing the existing state of affairs; particularly the magnitude, complexity and ramifications of the problem they are expected to grapple with; the critical may be illuminated by analytical studies. The observed and hidden dimensions of the problem thrown up by such studying may be expected to proffer certain measure of foresight to planners to deal with the problem effectively.

(b) Such social science exercise may provide a basis for testing the validity of certain assumptions that our planners are prone to make in laying down their short-term and long-term goals. These researches conceivably, may help the planner to anticipate the consequences and cost of alternative strategies which may be pressed into operation for achieving the settled goals.

(c) Social science researches may bring into sharp focus the varied influences and factors that contribute to the failure of certain projects. Hence the policy planners may stand forewarned about these.

(d) If social science research finding becomes a part of public knowledge, a general awareness about the situation and challenges, as also, the desired policy to meet them squarely may result. This would prepare people for accepting a particular policy and for exerting popular pressure for reformulation of amending current policies, or rejecting of modifying them.

Let us now turn to consider the utility of social research, especially, for a developing country like ours.

Value of Social Research in India

The field of social research is as broad as the range of human behaviour and its systematic manifestations. A realization of what this means should make it clear to us that the store of potential problems for social research is almost inexhaustible. The state of social sciences with the exception perhaps of economics, is characterized by researches being conducted with a view to propounding special theories of limited applicability. These sciences are not yet prepared to ascend to the level of higher building up of what *Merton* terms, the middle range theories, applicable to not too broad and not too specific aspects of human phenomena and secondly, their synthesis in more general conceptual schemes. The social sciences, as of now, are not far up from the bottom of the ladder.

In this continuing process of social research, quite a few specialized throries have emerged. The emphases of concentration on areas of study and avenues of theorizing has kept shifting from time to time. Unfortunately, very few areas (if at all) have been subjected to an intensive attack in terms of sustained attempts at replication or verification of theories, with the result that many of the prevailing theories might perhaps be on the level of plausibility. It is also possible that some of them might be 'context bound' or 'culture-bound' (i.e., valid only in a particular spatio-temporal context or a particular culture). What is needed, therefore, is the testing of such 'theories' on the anvil of different concrete socio-cultural contexts. Needless to say, the theories to be representative must fit different social situations of a given class. Hence researches are needed to probe whether the theories hold good, irrespective of contexts.

It is well-known that some anthropological studies, e.g., *M. Mead's* study of Samoa, conducted in simple 'primitive' societies sounded the death-knell for some earlier sociological and psychological theories. Just as the 'primitive' societies serve as testing points for certain theories of human behaviour, so also many developing countries like India serve as test bases for the existing theories of (just to mention, two) social organization and change. It is not difficult to appreciate the replication of existing ideas in a new context, besides testing the theory developed elsewhere, enriches our understanding of what the theory principally applies to. The developing countries are eminently suited as an anvil for the testing of theories or hypotheses of social change; for instance, of modernization of development, because it is here that one can vividly see change as a live process. A study of 'modernization' in the Indian context which may be considered a unique magnetic field of social forces pulling on opposite directions, is rightly expected to be quite revealing and enlightening besides its significant feedback value for theory.

Questions such as : What are the tangible indices or referents of modernization? How can revival of certain traditional patterns in India be reconciled with the process of modernization? What would be the phases of the continuum of modernization? How can these be rendered in operational terms? Just to mention, a few are questions that social research may be expected to answer. To expect the last, these answers can help clarification of the concept which is no small a contribution to theory building. It should be clear now that research designed to test hypotheses deduced from social theories developed in different socio-cultural contexts, besides testing and clarifying the theories by unfolding the ramifications of their operation, also help to define them by pointing out their limitations and thus add to their representativeness. Social researches conducted in different socio-cultural context thus go a long way on providing rich insights whereby different concrete phenomena may be grouped under a concept, and by enlarging the limits of the concepts, i.e., the building blocks of theories help to enlarge the scope of the theories. Thus, the process of 'Sanskritization' may be seen as an instance or reference group behaviour and as such may become amenable to scrutiny in terms of the orientation afforded by the theory of reference group behaviour. Needless to say that any specific phenomenon in a particular socio-cultural context which may legitimately be considered a concrete referent of a concept in a part, introduces a problem. The solution of this problem by research has definite consequences for the theory in terms of its possible revision or clarification or even rejection. But this has to be the function of research conducted anywhere as we shall see more clearly when we examine the place of empirical research via-a-vis theory. Why then, do we have to essay highlighting the importance of researches conducted in diverse socio-cultural setting, especially those preferred by the developing societies?

The thing is that the outcomes of researches conducted in particular socio-cultural settings, i.e., the generalizations of theories, cannot be expected to apply automatically to other socio-cultural contexts since typically, these contexts differ from one another in important respects. The natural sciences, in this respect are in a more fortunate position attributable in turn to the homogeneity could in part be a result of scientific insight and depth of understanding on the part of those who deal with the subject matter.

To the heterogeneity of the subject matter of social sciences may be attributed the reason why the social scientist is skeptical of (and, it is a desirable quality of the scientific mind) conclusions and theories based on researches in particular societies. A virtual transplant of research products, i.e., theories, on to any other socio-cultural context uncritically is rightly improper because the native soils are different. Spatio-temporal contexts and cultural operative in too subtle and imperceptible ways in influencing human behaviour. This warrants acceptance of these products of research only after he screws of scientific test have been properly applied to them. It is here that researches in diverse socio-cultural setting have their own importance. The developing countries have a very special status of import in this respect, precisely because these typify the conflicting social forces; some of which work for continuity of certain patterns and others against it — a conflict between tradition and modernity or industrialism, for instance. Such societies are characterized, on the one hand by 'norms' that are pressing and striving for social acceptance or institutionalization, and 'norms' which are on their way out but not quite gone, on the other. Such societies are not at rest with themselves; no society ever is; but unrest here is undeniably critical. In them, the social processes can be seen in their highly accentuated form; their problems are serious. So not only as testing points for theories but also in view of sheer riches, profuseness, challenge-ladenness of their social realities, such societies have a pride of place as areas for fruitful conduct of research.

The practical value of social researches for such societies in terms of social policy formulation and planning, etc., shall be briefly illustrated with reference to India. For the sake of convenience, we shall confine our discussion on the utility of social research of India to the period 1947, for the attainment of independence heralded a new era of consciousness and development of progressive policy formulation and legislation, and of multitudinous changes and attendant problems. This was when the new born democratisation started to take its first faltering steps towards its distant cherished goal of welfare through socialism.

Social planning had to be the first need. This was planning for development — material, social and cultural, in such a manner that the weaker and more vulnerable sections of the population, in particular, would benefit from its fruit and smoothly enter the mainstream of national consciousness.

With this end in view, the Planning Commission, constituted of outstanding persons representing major fields of expertise, formulated development plans which were enthusiastically implemented.

The results, however, were not always what the planners would have liked them to be; wide divergence was often evidenced between the overt aims of policy and its consequences in practice; there was considerable waste of national funds, energy and talents. The evaluation reports brought into sharp focus the need for systematic social survey/researches in areas where plans were proposed to be implemented. This need was recognized by planners themselves but the evaluation reports afforded a vivid demonstration of how social surveys or researches could have avoided much of waste. It was not long, before the planners realized that if planning was to be meaningful to people for whom it was intend, if it was to be realistic in a particular context of needs and aspirations, if the programme of its implementation was to be a people's programme and not one foisted upon them, then it should be based on complete and reliable data on the people who are to be the benefactors of planning, their need structure (priorities), their values, attitudes, their strengths and weaknesses. That 'social' surveys/researches are as important as the 'physical' surveys of the area in that the success of programmes depended, in the ultimate analysis, on people's acceptance and participation, was a realization which gave impetus to the initial setting up Research Programmes Committee in 1953 under the aegis of the Planning Commission of India and its eventual culmination in the establishment of the Indian Council of Social Sciences Research (ICSSR) in 1969.

The community development programme, an integral part of the Five Year Plans, was perhaps the most important single constructive activity "so big in content and so revolutionary in design"[56] undertaken by the national government to bring about a rounded development of rural India in planned democratic manner. Persistent difficulties in the implementation of these programmes in different parts of the country have brought about a clear realization that planning for human material presupposes a thorough knowledge of this complex material. Failure to appreciate this was bound to decrease the fruits of planning for a community. Each community is in a sense unique, hence no standard designs of a programme can be rewardingly applied to a community, neglecting its peculiarities in terms of human needs, cultural values and the unique intermeshing of forces operating therein. Thus, the systematic studies of communities came to be reckoned as a prerequisite to any successful developmental programme.

The unimaginative application of the C.D. formula to the tribal communities has time and again illustrated how important it is that a community should be developed in terms of its own values and goals. It has been pointed out by many an official that our ideas of development do not augur well with those of the tribal. What we deem necessary for a 'civilized existence' (so-called) has no place in their scheme of thinking and mosaic of values. Hence, any scheme for their 'development' unrelated to the viewpoint and the philosophy of the tribals will not be an unwarranted interference their affairs but may bring them more harm than good. Hence the need for scientific studies conducted to ascertain the whole kaleidoscope of the life pattern of tribals and of communities in general. It is gratifying to note that an important part of the role of tribal research institutes and anthropological surveys fulfills this need to some extent.

India is a welfare state. In addition to the general social services like education, health, etc. and the specialized social services intended for the benefit of the weaker and vulnerable sections of the population, e.g., women, children and the physically, mentally and socially handicapped, the state is in the process of passing progressive and protective legislation. The social welfare services need professionally competent personnel serving the cause of the handicapped of various kinds. Such services in order to be beneficial and fruitful have to be based on reliable information about people whose welfare is being contemplated. Welfare in the true sense implies giving just the right kind and degree of support to the purported beneficiaries in view of their problems so that the afflicted will acquire enough strength, capability and motivation to help themselves grow. Such help or support that will not corrupt a person or a class of persons but will ennoble them, can only be administered on the basis of reliable data afforded by scientific social studies. It hardly needs to be emphasized that legislation which is a means to a amelioration, must be based on a reliable assessment of the needs and feelings of the people and not on mere assumptions.

As an up and coming industrial nation, India is faced with certain characteristic challenges, which need an urgent coming to grips with. The First and the most obvious social alteration of the country under industrialization has been in the productive organization itself. Compromises with traditional norms of conduct, their effect or workers' efficiency and the extent to which such compromises impede full social transformation are important questions concerning work relations in India. Industrial technology has imposed some minimum requirements on the organization of productive units. The bureaucratization of labour force — an accompaniment of industrialization, presents various transitional problems not only for factory recruits but also for the elite groups. The need for subjective attitudes and objective incentives favourable to novel jobs and conditions of employment is implicit in the requirement of new work-relations and the new forms of productive organizations. Various obstacles in the way of fuller commitment of persons to the norms of industrial work are evident. Industrialization involves gross changes in the occupational structures mooted by the economic sector and finer changes necessitated by demand for specialized skills. A vital economic problem of India is the shortage of capital; the budgetary behaviour of people also needs to be taken into active account.

The population explosion and the rapid rate of urbanization are evidently connected with industrialization in India. Infant mortality has gone down; there is in evidence a high cityward migration; age composition has changed and with it has emerged the problem of dependency. All this has serious implications for the varied spheres of social life. In India, cities seem to have grown at a rate surpassing both expansion of employment opportunities and of public services or amenities.

Technological modernization in India seems to be linked with profound changes in the family and kinship organization. A common symptomatic feature of industrialism appears to be the disintegration of the family. Industrialization has given rise to many a problem of community organization, e.g., problems of residence, transportation, and congestion. Slums have appeared, constituting one major environmental source of a number of problems of social control. Crucial questions of social strategy are not involved in formulating an educational policy in view of industrial demands. The correlation between education supply and man-power demand is hardly perfect. The mass media of communication supply the technical basis for promotion of a national public participation in political events and policy-making. Political participation seems to have been organized around unions or other occupational groups for a variety of interests and loyalties. Industrialization seems to have influenced, in important ways, the religious organization and beliefs.

Realism appears to be the disintegration of the family. Industrialization has given rise to many a problem of community organization, e.g., problems of residence, transportation, and congestion. Slums have appeared, constituting one major environmental source of a number of problems of social control. Crucial questions of social strategy are now involved in formulating an educational policy in view of industrial demands. The correlation between education supply and man-power demand is hardly perfect. The mass media of communication supply the technical basis for promotion of a national public participation of political events and policy-making. Political participation seems to have been organized around unions or other occupational groups for a variety of interests and loyalties. Industrialization seems to have influenced, in important ways, the religious organization and beliefs.

Industrialization has provided a new set of social positions and new criteria of placement and valuation. It has, therefore, resulted in the complication of the system of social stratification. This has been responsible in some measure for status ambiguities.

The above is a very brief outline of the major social implications of technological modernization or industrialization in India. The manifold and multi-faceted implications of industrialization for India seriously spell out the need for scientific social research on a fairly large scale, to provide for a systematic understanding of nature of problems, a sound diagnosis and an effective treatment plan. In fact, the complexity of the situation (of which little is known) calls for some kind of an inter-disciplinary collaboration among researchers from specialized disciplines — economists, political scientists, sociologists, psychologists and anthropologists etc., making for an effective multi-pronged attack on these social maladies, and for devising long-term social policies of real consequence.

STATE OF SOCIAL SCIENCE RESEARCH IN INDIA

The Role of State of Social Research in India

The role of social science in the social and economic development of the country is being increasingly recognized in India. Besides the government, public and private organizations are providing impetus to researches in the social sciences. The notion that social science research can contribute variously to the social, cultural and economic development of the country has been gaining ground ever since the Planning Commission after its creation realized the need for social science research in the relevant spheres of national development. The universities and other research institutions have been activated to work out and administer various schemes of research into social; economic and administer various schemes of research into social; economic and administrative problem germane to national development. The first five-year plan provided for a sum of rupees fifty lakhs to further these objectives.

Among the activities of the ICSSR, promotion of social science research has a central place. These promotional activities consist in financial support for research to social scientists and institutes award of fellowships. As many as 708 research projects were sanctioned by the ICSSR during the period commencing from 1969-70 to 1976-77. The development of the institutional base was mainly the responsibility of the university system. But subsequently, the needs for social science research outside university system was also recognized.

The University Grants Commission has stepped in a big way to promote social science research. Since the year 1975-76, the UGC has been implementing the teacher fellowship scheme. The UGC also has a scheme for award of scholarships and fellowships for the development of social science research in universities and colleges. There are certain foreign agencies like USEFI and Rockefeller Foundation which provide financial support. Big industrial organizations and business families have also provided assistance for social science research. Social science, however, have had a low priority in the matter of research funding. The allocation of funds for research as compared to the natural sciences is meagre.

Social science research says *S.C. Dube,* "is not a substitute for national development; in many instances it would not even indicate a clear policy line. Social scientists are nowhere close to being social engineers .... The power of social science is exploratory and its practitioners are essentially analysts."[57]

We may critically evaluate the present status of social science research in India. Admittedly, most of it lacks a national focus and it is not relevant to the major issues of the day, very few right questions are being asked by social researchers and even when asked they are not pursued seriously. Outworn methodology is being used and there is little evidence of methodological innovation which will prove equal to the unique problems of the Indian context. There is in evidence a heavy reliance on concepts formulated in foreign soils and uncritical use of borrowed methodology. Dube laments, that "social scientists in India tend to work upon the trivial and count barren theoretical and methodological exercise as triumphs. Alternatively, we refuse to examine empirically the social reality and try to answer the contemporary questions from the ancient texts and traditions."[58]

There, of course, are a few exceptions of good research work in the realm of social science but these have a narrow focus. The insights emanating from them are hardly subjected to systematic verification and hence the extent of their applicability to wider areas remain unknown. As a result, a macro-national perspective cannot emerge. Hence, while such studies do fill a gap, it is difficult to generalize from them.

During the last few decades, financial assistance is being given on an increasing scale to support social science research. A considerable volume of data has been gathered through such funded projects. But, how far these data were utilized for planning? Knowledgeable persons feel that planning was by and large done in total indifference of these data. Very few if any, significant conceptual or methodological gains have registered through these projects. "Some of them were poorly organized and indifferently executed ...." The government sponsorship of social science research projects did provide an impetus to it. But on the negative side, this resulted in a great deal of mechanical and some shoddy work. The research tradition has definitely not been enriched by such studies.

Quite a few government agencies are also involved in social science research, "where one gets picture of a great deal of mechanical work and of a general sterility in respect of significant ideas (perhaps) these organizations have some built in devices to distract them from the path of creativity." The record of some government organizations is certainly one of high productivity, but the scale of its operations is such that quite so often, quality has to be sacrificed for quantity. Nevertheless, these organizations are a rich source of social data. A few research organizations outside the university system are also producing insightful studies, especially in regard to the development hazards. There is a good case for looking into and correcting the organizational incompatibilities and contradictions in the government run research institutions. Bureaucratic strangleholds and the typical frustrations of the social science intellectuals need to be examined and remedied; comparative and long-term research needs to be looked into, management guidance in this sphere can be of great help.

The function of social research may be said to be mainly exploratory. It cannot be expected to project a definite course of social action; it can best offer policy alternatives. That social scientist makes it possible for the policy planner to move from the known towards the desirable but the unknown is a help of major consequence. Towards this end, he has to sharpen his tools and define his focus. Needless to stress that in the final analysis the social scientists will be judged by the quality of their study-products and by their success in communicating to the community in general and to the policy planning in particular.

Scientific Social Survey and Research

We now turn to discuss what is known as 'social survey.' Until quite recently, it was customary to distinguish between social survey and social research, indeed without much justification. The contemporary trend consists, however, in viewing survey as an aspect of research and such confluent terms as 'survey-research' has gained currency in methodological writings.

A social survey in its broadest sense, has a reference to a first-hand investigation, analysis and co-ordination of economic, sociological and other related aspects of a selected community or group. A survey may be undertaken with the primary purpose of formulating a programme for amelioration of the conditions of life and work of a community or a group, implying some 'frame' in the mind of the surveyor as to what the conditions ideally ought to be. The purpose of a social survey may also be to provide scientifically gathered facts or materials affording some empirical basis for the social theorists to set up their conclusions.

If the term 'social survey' is mainly thought of as referring to an operation having as its central concern 'social action', i.e., social engineering, social reform, social planning and social survey, it is to the distinctive history of social survey movement that one would have to turn for explanation.

As the history of the development of survey movement unfolds itself, we come across such trail-blazers as *John Howard,* a philanthropist and reformer, *Fredrick Leplay,* a reformer and economist; *Charles Booth,* a reformer and statistician. The life and works of all these men were governed by a deep-seated conviction that constructive reforms must be founded only on the secure ground provided by scientifically gathered facts. Thus, the survey-operation might be regarded as a pre-requisite to social reform and often the former implied the latter. Thus, the terms, 'social surveyor' and 'social practitioner' came to be used almost interchangeably. It is in this particularized sense that quite a few books treat of social survey; for them it means "scientific study of social problems acute enough to arouse public opinion and to take a "hand in their solution"[59] or a "scientific study for the purpose of presenting a constructive programme of social advance."[60]

It is worthy of note, however, that the notion of social survey as an operation undertaken basically to afford scientifically gathered material as a basis for theory construction, found its way into the sociological thought as a result of *Leplay's* work.

Threaded though the survey work of *Leplay* was an insistent concern, for theoretical generalization which has ever since exerted a powerful influence on the French and German sociology. Social survey with social action as its central concern while gaining substantially from the impetus provided by *Leplay's* work had its actual inception with the pioneering work of Charles Booth and associates and attained its full bloom in USA. The influence of the Booth survey in the field of social planning was as significant as that of the survey method for the study and analysis of social phenomena as well as one affording a substantive base for a programme of social planning is of comparatively recent origin.

At the present time, the development of varied types of survey, both the voluntary, semi-public and governmental agencies, marks the disappearance of social survey as a clearly defined form of social investigation having direct relevance for social planning or reform. Today, the influence of social surveys is not restricted to the field planning, programmes of amelioration and change. Quite a number of surveys seem to include only incidentally the programmatic.

Because of complexity of objectives and diversity of the uses of social surveys there is in evidence a lack of uniformity in defining and employing crucial variables and the qualitative and quantitative indices devised for their measurement. This has created problems, since surveys cannot be used, comparatively speaking, on a broader field of social generalization although they may be undertaken with reference to some specific problem in a specific group. It is precisely this that explains why the social survey method is no longer restricted to any particular school of thought.

The foregoing discussion should make it abundantly clear that from a broader perspective, social survey and social research do not constitute an 'either-or' dichotomy. While a social survey may provide basis for theory-construction or generalization, in addition to its implications for social planning and reform, social research may provide just the clues which may be utilized for solving certain practical problems or which may help setting up of programmes on right lines, e.g., the theory of group morale may guide planning to step up the output in a factory.

Those who are given to differentiating sharply between social survey and social research, as though they constituted a clear-cut dichotomy, seem to be governed by a considerably narrowed down conception of each.

Looking at the matter from this angle, differentiation, even if arbitrary, is indeed easy to effect. The social surveys are concerned with specific persons, specific places, specific problems, and situations, whereas the social researchers are inclined to make the more general and abstract problems as their principal concern. Whereas "the social surveyor is interested in fact-finding in order to improve the current social conditions of a specific locality, the social researcher seeks to build a body of tested general knowledge of mankind, a body of knowledge — timeless, spaceless — which may lead to formulation of theories and general laws." [61]

To use *R.S., Lynd's* striking differentiation, "The former (social researcher) works in a leisurely world in which the hands of the clock crawl slowly over a vast dial; to him the precise penetration of the unknown cannot be hurried. In this time universe of the research scholar, certain supporting assumptions have grown up, such as ... objectivity ... the self-justifying goodness of 'new knowledge' about anything big or little, the practical man (surveyor-planner) ... works by a small time dial over which the second-hand of immediacy and urgency hurries incessantly."[62]

REFERENCES

(1) Einstein, A. and Infield : *The Evolution of Physics,* N.Y. 1938, p. 280.

(2) Thompson, Sir J.A.: *Introduction of Science,* Geoffrey Cumberlege, Oxford University Press, reprinted in India, p. 27.

(3) Pearson, Karl: *The Grammar of Science* (Third edition), Part A, A & C Black, London, 1911, pp.10-12.

(4) *Ibid.*

(5) Thompson, *op. cit.,* p. 25.

(6) Bernal, J.D.: *Science in History,* Pelican, p. 18.

(7) Lastrucci: *Scientific Approach,* Cambridge, 1967, p. 6.

(8) Thompson, *op. cit.,* p. 24.

(9) Durant, W.: *Story of Philosophy,* N.Y., 1971, p. XXVI.

(10) See Caws, P.: *The Philosophy of Science,* D. Van Nostrand Co., London, 1965, p. 903.

(11) Bertrand Russell has pointed out that there are four theories of truth: (a) Warranted assertability for truth (Dewey) (b) Probability for truth (Reichenbach); (c) Truth as coherence (Hegelians) (d) Correspondence Theory (Russell); See Kaufmann, Felix: *Methodology of Social Sciences,* Oxford University Press, 1944, p. 95.

(12) Wells, H.G.: *Science and Utimate Truth,* Great Essays in Science, p. 324.

(13) For a fuller discussion, see Caws, *op. cit.,* pp. 267-70.

(14) *Ibid.*

(15) Larrabee, H.A. : *Reliable Knowledge,* Houghton Mifflin Company, 1945, p. 5.

(16) Pearson, *op. cit.,* p. 6.

(17) See Galtung, Johan: *Theory and Methods of Social Research,* London, 1967.

(18) Francis Bacon mentions four types of false idols : (1) Idols of the tribe (2) Idols of the cave (3) Idols of the market-place (4) Idols of the theatre.

(19) Thompson: *op. cit.,* p. 6.

(20) Schroedniger Mind and Matter, Cambridge, 1958, p. 37.

(21) For fuller discussion, see Smith, C.W.S., A. Critique of Sociological Reasoning, Oxford, 1979.

(22) Einstein and Infield: *op. cit.,* p. 313.

(23) Greenwood, Ernest: cf., Young P.V.: *Scientific Surveys and Research,* Prentice Hall, p. 113.

(24) Cf., Gupta S.P.: *Science, Technology and Society,* Ajanta, Delhi, 1977, p. 52.

(25) Caws, *op. cit.,* pp. 256-65.

(26) *Ibid.,* p. 53.

(27) Dewey. J.: *Reconstruction in Philosophy,* N.Y., 1952, p. 22.

(28) Best, J.W. : Research in Education, Prentice Hall of India, 1963, p. 4.

(29) The Encyclopedia of Social Sciences, Vol. IX, MacMillan, 1930.

(30) For a detailed discussion, see "The Sociology of Education" (art.) by Neal Gross in *Sociology Today,* Merton R.K. *et al.* (Ed.), Vol. 1, Harper and Row, New York, 1965, pp. 128-52.

(31) *Ibid.,* Vol. 1, Chapter I, for a detailed discussion.

(32) Slesinger, D. and M. Stephenson. "Social Research" (art), *Encyclopedia of the Social Sciences,* Vo. IX, 330, The MacMillan Company, 1930.

(33) Cf. Thompson, *op. cit.,* p. 59.

(34) Cf. Young, *op. cit.,* p. 44.

(35) Slesinger and Stephenson : *Encyclopedia of the Social Sciences.*

(36) Ackoff, R.L.: *The Design of Research University of Chicago Press,* Chicago and London, 1953, pp. 1-11.

(37) Huxley, A.: *Brave New World,* Penguin, London, 1970, p. 174(17).

(38) Oppenheimer: *Great Essays in Sciences* (ed.) Gardener, p. 194.

(39) Cf. Thompson: *op. cit.,* p. 176.

(40) Cohen, M.: *Reason & Nature,* Essay on the Meaning of Scientific Method, MacMillan, N.Y., 1931.

(41) Cf. Abraham, Francis M.: *Modern Sociological Theory,* Oxford University Press, 1982.

(42) Thompson, *op. cit.,* p. 181.

(43) Dewey, *op. cit.,* p. 121.

(44) Thompson: *op. cit.,* p. 185.

(45) Heisemberg: *Tradition in Science, Science and Public Affairs,* Vol. 29, No.10.

(46) Thompson: *op. cit.,* pp. 53-8.

(47) Seltiz, Jahoda *et al., Research Methods in Social Relations,* Methuen and Co., Ltd., 1969, p. 31.

(48) Cf. Thompson: *op. cit.,* p. 13.

(49) *Ibid.,* p. 14.

(50) *Ibid.*

(51) Gupta svp.: *op. cit.,* p. 13.

(52) See Lundberg, G.A.: *Social Research,* Longmans Green and Co., New York, 1926.

(53) Merton, R.K.: *Social Theory and Social Structure,* Free Press of Glencoe, 1968, p. 9.

(54) *Ibid.*

(55) Young : *op. cit.,* p. 36.

(56) Nehru, Jawaharlal: Cf. *Social Welfare in India,* Ministry of Information, GOI, p. 106.

(57) See foreword to Sharma, B.A.V., (edited) *et al., Research Methods in Social Science,* Hyderabad, 1985.

(58) Sharma, B.A.V.: *Research Methods in Social Science,* Hyderabad, 85, p. IV.

(59) Kelogg P.S. Harrison, G. Palmer, cf. Young, *op. cit.,* p. 17.

(60) *Ibid.*

(61) Young, *op. cit.,* p. 2.

(62) *Ibid.,* p. 78.

Chapter II

The Problem of Objectivity in Social Research

We may now say that science studies everything which can be publicly inspected — its subject matter is the class of public events. All public events are, however, seen from the private point of view of an individual scientist; atleast one may assume that each scientist has such a private point of view, the only one of whose existence I can be sure is again my own. These private points of view cannot be studied scientifically and they are the only things which cannot be studied. An analogous situation which may throw some light on the question would be a group of cameras constantly taking pictures of the world. Apart from limitations of focus and so on, the only place of which the pictures could not be taken would be the inside of a camera even if some cameras were opened there would still have to be atleast one closed camera to take pictures of their insides and that closed camera corresponds to the individual from whose point of view the whole thing is considered. The pictures stand of course, for scientific knowledge.

The social-behavioural sciences, in so far as they attempt to approximate the ideal of 'science', a term which according to the more conservative thinkers can be more appropriately used for man's investigation of his natural surroundings, are committed to several articles of faith. Among these are predictions based on probability, avoidance of value judgments, a search for all evidence relevant to the problem and a public methodology which affords testing of conclusions through replication etc. Some feel, however, that the above features are characteristic of the physical sciences and that a procedure in social inquiries which inheres one or another of these features is either ineffective or impossible. Quite a few social scientists too opine that application of the methods of natural sciences, beyond their domain, to the realm of social phenomena is indeed illegitimate and even harmful.[1] The consequence of such an application they argue, implies a simplistic and reductive treatment of man as if he were an animal or a mechanism without free will or spontaneity. They also argue that the idea extensively prevailing among social scientists that they know how to proceed impartially and objectively and that they know how to counteract or get rid of personal bias in their works is an illusion.[2] We shall evaluate critically the major arguments offered in support of these contrary points of view.

The problem of impartiality or biaslessness is in part, a problem of objectivity. The problem of objectivity is one of knowing reality. In addition to questions related to being, objectivity involves two other considerations, viz., the correct method of dealing with any question and of how we know anything (Epistemology).

It has been argued that the social scientists are of necessity and by advertence less objective than the natural scientists since social scientists, are themselves human beings, living in societies, do have certain social interests. They are participants in social movements and accept certain values and ways of life. The problem in the nature of a relative lack of objectivity, i.e., of emotional detachment, arises from the fact that the social scientists have a large stake in the outcome of their studies, that is, their own interests may be affected by the findings of their inquiries and their wishes may seriously influence the results of their studies. The folkways, mores and social usages usually come to be accepted as naturally valid and thus appear to provide complete and adequate schemes of living and thinking for members. For a social scientist to detach himself from them is often an extremely difficult task, and he runs the risk of unconsciously using them to prejudge the social situations he studies. It is, the argument runs, a major psychological feat to achieve objectivity required for scientific inquiry especially on those frequent occasions when the inquiry is likely to challenge the existing frames of social reference. The critics assert that the general circumstances of the social inquiry are such as to prevent the social scientists from using the evidence at their disposal dispassionately. The social observers so to speak, are placed in the hands of their own observation. It is these arguments that we shall now deal with.

We must consider precisely the influences which may prevent the social scientists from taking full account of the evidence at their disposal. These influences may be summed up as adverse influences of (1) Personal motives, (2) Custom and (3) Social situation of which the social scientists himself is a part. An inquirer should not let his beliefs be influenced by the above factors. Objectivity by itself will not, however, ensure that an inquirer will come to hold rational beliefs but failure in objectivity will certainly prevent him from holding such beliefs.

We cannot help admitting that one's motives do sometimes affect beliefs adversely; at times leading him to adopt beliefs without considering evidence at all or to make a defective estimate of the evidence. "Prejudice and biases are like fantasies — to believe what is comforting to believe." [3] When our motives predispose us in this way to believe something that is comforting without good evidence, we are, of course, rarely aware that this is so. At any time, there are many habits of thought which simply because they are generally accepted, are not easy to detect.

While effects adverse to objectivity may be produced, when a person's social situation gives rise to certain interests, leading in turn to prejudice and bias, it cannot be denied that in some cases the effect of social situation may in no way be inconsistent with objectivity, since all it may do is to impose limits on the availability of evidence. There are cases, however, where an effect adverse to objectivity arises in the form of an intellectual error consisting in placing undue weightage on evidence which is near at hand. This evidence in turn varies with the person's social situation, i.e., his place in the social structure.

Having considered the influences adversely affecting objectivity, we may now ask whether these influences are so potent as to render an objective social inquiry impossible. Doubtless, these influences have some effect on the beliefs of the social inquirers. Denying objectivity (to social enquirers) must be understood as influences being so powerful as to prevent normally the accomplishing of worthwhile results. One reasonable way to refute this charge would be to point out that these influences have been overestimated. The onus is on the critics to establish their case and it would suffice if it was shown that they fail to put it up.

We may approach the estimation of objectivity in two ways:

(a) We may ask in general terms what effects the general circumstances of social inquiry are likely to have on the objectivity of the scientist pursuing it.

(b) We may also do well to start with particular social theories and ask what influences might have contributed to their acceptance and generalize from this.

Some of the typical considerations which have prompted critics to doubt the realization of objectivity in social enquiry may, after a careful appraisal, be dismissed as irrelevant, as would be clear from the following discussion.

Thus, failure of objectivity in social inquiries is often attributed to the simple fact that the social scientist as a social being is also actively participating is social affairs. In answering this objection, we may point out that the biologist is himself an organism and a physicist also a body of given mass, interacting with other organisms and bodies. We would not assume simply for this reason that the theories of the biologist and the physicist would be unduly subject to the influence of biological and physical environments, at the expense of evidence. We would no more, by the same token, assume that the interaction of the social scientist with his social environment will interfere with his objectivity and rationality. Indeed, no one is casually detached from the subject-matter he is investigating.

Those who accuse social scientists of lacking in detachment from their social environment generally point to the special potency of interests and emotions which are centered around their interrelationships with other people. In this regard, we should not forget that potent interests and emotions do not inevitably give rise to prejudice or bias. They only do so that where satisfaction is gained by our escaping from or evading the difficulties rather than by overcoming them. Our interests do incline us towards prejudice and bias when we are dealing with social questions. Individuals do not find it easy to alter the course of events to their own liking and/or where there is a practical programme to be carried out, a realistic or objective appraisal of means and assets becomes inevitable. Where there is nothing effective that is desired be done, we may possibly relish the luxury of prejudice.

We now turn to the effect of 'vested interests' on people's beliefs. It is obvious that those who enjoy a position of distinct advantage in terms of wealth, power and prestige etc. under the existing system and dispensation do not wish to disturb the *status quo* and often resist changes even in the superficial overtones of the integral structure. But ordinarily, this in itself would not distort their views about the factual working of the system and its effect on other members who are a part of it. Distortion of views about the actual state of affairs implies the presence of certain incompatible motives such as a vital concern for fellowmen who can be helped only by a modification of the existing social order. A practical way to avoid this conflict is and has been to presume that the existing order contains benefits for one and all and each one is free to share them as a matter of course.

We cannot afford to overlook the fact that social prejudices and custom-based beliefs, irrespective of the truth-value of their content, do have their own peculiar form of survival value. Considering carefully their manifest and latent functions for society, it may be said that social prejudices do sometimes pay, and deliver social goods of significant import. An irrational faith in the justness and virtue of a cause may serve as an energizer, providing the necessary impetus to persons to carry it on to a point of fruition, whereas an unbiased and critical appraisal of evidence may provide just that discouragement which so often results in failure. To the extent this occurs, comforting beliefs cannot be easily written off from the popular mind. The custom-based beliefs generally contribute to social cohesion and stability. It is precisely this that makes them less susceptible to challenge and erosion.

Social beliefs are especially vulnerable to the influence of differing points of view. Since social situations are more varied compared to physical ones, it follows that the readiness to generalize from the evidence near at hand will have more drastic consequences. That people belonging to different social positions or living at different periods of time will most likely have their social theories tainted by distorting effects unparalleled in the physical sciences is, therefore, not difficult to visualize.

The above considerations have a general and extensive applicability. There are hardly any special circumstances which can claim immunity from such distorting factors. *Karl Mannheim* has suggested that a detached intellectual with no social class affiliations will probably be able to achieve a measure of objectivity which may well be beyond the reach of others. But the mere fact of detachment of this kind does not necessarily ensure that the desired results would follow. For, howsoever one may wish, the fact remains that the intellectual has also a special position which is likely to distort his view of evidence. Again, he is not above the special interests in practical terms, such as the need to maintain his standard of living or even, his desire to preserve his scholarly seclusion and detachment.

It has been shown that especial dangers confront the social scientist. But it is also seen that these are not sufficient to establish the ubiquitous inability of the social enquirers to base their conclusions on nothing but evidence. With reference to the special dangers to which the social scientist as a representative of a class has been made out to be especially subject it may be asked whether the social enquirers do typically succumb to these. The answer to this question must wait till we have considered at some length, the working of the influences referred to above as these relate to the origin of social theories.

In this connection we may have to examine whether the theory a person holds is one which he would hold if he were to notice only those facts that were near at hand (because of his situation) or lastly, whether the theory is similar to those currently held. If we notice that the differences between theories held by persons reflect the differences in interests, customs and social situations, this would more or less support the view that these factors have had some subtle part in shaping the theories.

It must be remembered, however, that the mere fact of a person's views and reactions happening to coincide with his interests, motives etc. cannot be a really firm basis for inferring that the theories are not based on a proper consideration of evidence. It would be erroneous to suppose that a person's theories must always clash with his interests before he can claim any measure of objectivity. The argument is more cogent admittedly, where there is objectivity. The argument is more cogent admittedly, where there are different views on the same question. The absence of an agreed conclusion is a sign that certain persons have not taken full account of the evidence.

In the absence of any reliable direct measure of objectivity, the usual practice is to fall back upon a simple and well-thumbed measure, i.e., to ask whether the theory is or is not a reasonable one to hold. If someone puts forward a theory for which evidence is insufficient and we know that he is unlikely to make a mistake through failure of intelligence, it will follow that his objectivity is at fault. The use of this kind of a test, however, presupposes that we are capable of considering the evidence for ourselves and that our own conclusions would be free from bias. It is, therefore, useless to ascertain whether or not the social enquirers at large lack objectivity since we must ourselves be included in this group.

It would thus seem that we ought to dismiss as inconclusive the attempts to establish that there is a general failure of objectivity among social scientists, to the extent that their enquiries are rendered futile and worthless. This being so, we may not feel it necessary to pursue the matter any further. But then those who make the attempt, run the risk of succumbing to their own charge. For, an enquiry into the origin of social theories principally belongs to the general rubric of social inquiries and hence any theory about the origin of social theory must equally apply to itself. The critic of objectivity is thus involved in a deep-rooted circularity. This point, of course, hardly helps to establish the lack of objectivity of social scientists.

The only conceivable way to avoid this difficulty would be to claim that statements about the origin of theories form a special class by themselves and therefore are exempt from the general charge. It is, of course, true that 'theories' about the origin of theories differ from theories about other kinds of social facts. But these are not good enough grounds to suppose that this difference is relevant when it comes to estimating the degree of objectivity of those who put them forward. It may be added that it is very comforting to explain away the theories of the opponents, for in so doing, we avoid facing their arguments. This is why this sort of polemic often indulged in. In any case, it can hardly be claimed, that those who investigate the origins of social theories must exhibit an objectivity which others lack.

In the light of the foregoing discussion, we may conclude that a tight case has not been made against the feasibility of effective objectivity in social inquiry. The dangers, however, are present and if we wish to proceed scientifically, we must find the best means of avoiding these. From what has been said so far, it should be plain that it is not sufficient merely to try to avoid the dangers by seeking a special position of detachment. Those who try to keep themselves above the battle cannot but have their own social interests and points of view.[4] No one lives in a social vacuum. Loyalty to scientific procedure demands that no one should ignore the possible sources of adverse influences on his beliefs.

Ultimately then, the true remedy seems to lie in making oneself conscious of these influences. To admit that one's theories may have been socially conditioned does not, in itself, stop these theories from being thus conditioned. But, it may help alter them for the simple reason that neither prejudice nor influence of custom survive detection for long. The efficacy of this remedy should not, however, be overestimated, for it does not help to overcome distortions which are simply due to the limitations of one's social situation. Even in the case of other influences, it is well worth remembering that they are often extremely difficult to identify and detect.

In view of those limitations, it may be necessary to resort to another remedy in the form of controversy. If all with the same evidence at their disposal took a perfect account of it, all would arrive at the same conclusions, hence the possibility of disputes between them may not be ruled out. But this does not unfortunately happen for reasons discussed earlier. An effective way to eliminate these influences would be to bring the different theorists together and ensure that they are able to engage in an open criticism of one another without the fear of consequences. Criticism, in the ultimate analysis, is one of the most important forms of co-operation. To label the activity of a critic as destructive is misleading. By pointing to a person that he has departed from the right path, we help him and his followers. This is thus a positive contribution for the larger institution of science. For "invalidation, no less than verification of proposition is a progress in inquiry.[5] As *Karl Pearson* aptly remarks, "criticism is the very life-blood of science."[6]

Left to ourselves, we may fall an easy prey to influences detrimental to objectivity. We do not easily become aware of our own biases, unreflective presuppositions or limitations of our own points of view; we need, most of the time, to have them pointed out to us by others. A heavy stress on the intellectual and mutual understanding among scientists particularly the social scientists, is now warranted. The power of argument rests on this understanding and when the foundation is too weak, it is the argument of power that triumphs.

Ensuring that social enquiry is, in a real sense, a "competitive, collective enterprise" would guarantee such measure of objectivity as we can lay claim on. We must admit our present imperfections; the failure to do so would amount to a divorcement from truth, the cause we are wedded to. We need to realize that we have a long way to go and that in social sciences what is needed more than ever is perfecting of tools which will register, record and classify finer qualitative distinctions and finally, that we lack the adequate testing and verification procedures for the intangible though very real aspects of social reality and human nature. Such an honest admission unto ourselves, would act as a spur to our persistent efforts aimed at unearthing of "that knowledge which will arm man for his greatest victory; the conquest of himself."[7]

REFERENCES

(1) For a fuller discussion, see Schoeck H. and J.W. Wiggins (ed.): *Scientism and Values*, Von Nostrand, New York, 1960.

(2) *Ibid.*, pp. 22-47.

(3) Gibson, Quentin: *The Logics of Social Enquiry*, Routedge and Kegan Paul, London, 1963, p. 78.

(4) Gibson, *op. cit.*, p. 87.

(5) Kaufmann, F., *op. cit.*, p. 244.

(6) Pearson, *op. cit.*, p. 11.

(7) Cf. Young, *op. cit.*, p. 115.

Chapter III

The Research Process

The usual rigmarole of steps presented in most research reports, monographs and texts on research methodology is likely to give out an over-simplified and mechanistic version of what all is involved in doing research. A research report as it generally appears in technical journals or dissertations approximates the following format:

(a) A statement of the purpose of research is made in the form of a problem so formulated as to be tackled.

(b) A description of the design of study is presented, involving discussion on the techniques (and the methodological rationale underlying them) of data collection and sampling employed in the study.

(c) The data are analyzed and the results of the study presented.

(d) The results are interpreted and conclusions put forth.

Thus, published researches may lead one to arrive at the notion that research comprises a definite sequence of procedures — each step in the sequence taking its pre-designated place no sooner than the term of its predecessor expires. The 'model' presented above may seem justified in the interests of convenience and economy of scientific reporting, it hardly ever helps one to appreciate in depth the fluid aspects of the research process. It is well worth remembering that the research process involves a number of interrelated activities or operations that overlap continuously rather than follow a neatly prescribed and synchronized sequence.

With these introductory remarks, we may turn to describe the research process.

To begin with, the research is expected to decide the general area or aspect of a subject-matter the researcher would like to inquire into. This decision at best, points to a general area of the scholar's interest and concern. It would be like saying that one desires to visit the northern part of the country during the vacations. Such a decision affords only a crude indication. It does not help much in planning and organization, because the specific details are lacking.

The range of potential areas of general interest in any particular discipline is very extensive indeed. Speaking of sociology, such area may be, planned social change, race relations, family disorganization, organizational structures and so on. Such topics may be suggested to the researcher by some scientific or intellectual interest or some practical problem which the researcher feels is in need of solution. The operations involved in a research process are so interdependent that the earlier steps or operations determine to an appreciable extent the nature of the later ones.

Serious difficulties may arise, often preventing a successful completion of the study, if the researcher has not taken into active account the subsequent procedures during the initial stages of the inquiry. Thus, the researcher has to be constantly anticipating at each step in the research process, the requirements of the subsequent steps.

As a research progresses from the formulation of the problem through collection of data to presenting the conclusions, the focus of researcher's attention necessarily shifts from one kind of activity to the other. Such shifts, it should be remembered, reflect differing emphases at different points on specific operations involved in research process, rather than a singular concentration at any time on any particular step.

Major Steps in Social Research

We now turn to describe what may be called the major phases attendant upon the process of social research. The organization of the subjectmatter requires that these steps be discussed separately and consecutively. Hence, we shall be adopting the sequence of steps proposed above, not forgetting of course, that the research process never corresponds to any neat sequential pattern of procedures as may be apparent from the published research reports.

It should also be borne in mind that designating certain steps as 'major' only implies that each of such steps subsumes under it a set of interrelated operations, each of which is important in its own way in affecting the value of the research results and their worth. Thus, 'major' steps should advisedly be considered as groupings or classes of operations or activities — hundreds of which are involved in research, each corresponding to some requirement of research. For example, 'data collection' phase subsumes decisions about the kinds of data needed, the most efficient way of collecting them, the activities to be carried out in the development and pre-testing of the data collection instruments etc. In addition, such decisions as constitute responses to the practical requirements of research are also covered, i.e., planning of budget, procurement and administration of funds, selection of personnel, training of personnel (e.g., interviewers), strategies of eliciting co-operation from people who are to be respondents and so on. It is obvious that each one of these operations will have some effect on the quality of research. A small omission anywhere will affect as adversely the quality of the study, just as a small lapse, even in the manner it is catered will affect the satisfaction people get from a recipe as it is served.

Topics prompted by intellectual concerns differ from those mooted by practical ones in that the former are less likely to involve the study of specific situations primarily as objects of interest in themselves. The specific situations have only an illustrative relevance, i.e., they are studied as specimens of some larger class of structure or processes in which the researcher evinces theoretic interest.

The researcher's decision as to what his general area of interest is going to be, i.e., problem formulation, i.e., the topic, hardly puts him in a position to start considering the procedures for data collection and analysis of data in right earnest, since at this stage, he does not know precisely what specific questions within his general area of interest he would want to be answered. Hence, the researcher needs to formulate a specific problem from within his general area of interest before he can take any decision relating to collection and analysis of data. Many a time, investigators may be tempted to jump immediately from the selection of a general topic to the collection of data. But this only means that they would have to face the task of formulating a problem at some later stage when only the lucky ones may be able to produce a worthwhile scientific inquiry. Obviously, without a problem the heaps of data would hardly mean anything. The meaningfulness of data collected can be assessed only after their scrutiny and organization with a view to finding out how these data would answer a specific problem. The problem is, indeed, the organizing principle for the processing and organization data of.

At first glace, it would seem fairly easy to see and pose a problem for study. But the experience of scientists is summed up in the adage: "It is often more difficult to find and to formulate a problem than to solve it."[1] In most scientific work the difficulty lies in framing problem or questions rather than in finding their solution. The researcher has to put a great deal of thought into the formulation of problems if he expects to get anything worthwhile from his efforts to solve them. *Cohen and Nagel* aptly remark: "No enquiry can get under way until and unless some difficulty is faced in a practical or theoretic situation. It is the difficulty or problem which guides the search for some order among facts in terms of which the difficulty is to be removed."[2] In point of fact, research really begins when the researcher experiences a difficulty or a challenge which is the basic component of a research problem.

How researchers experience difficulties in theoretic and practical contexts is discussed in the next chapter. The formulation of a specific research problem is the first material step in a scientific inquiry must be influenced basically by the requirements of scientific procedure. There is no surefooted and infallible principle which can guide an investigator in posing some conditions which have over the years proved very helpful in formulating significant problems for research. A careful study of literature having some bearing on the general area of the researcher's interest, systematic immersion into the subject-matter, analysis of 'insight stimulating' cases, etc., are some of these conditions. Formulation of problem for research, sensibly, involves on the plane of practice, researcher's concern for reducing the research task to a manageable size.

The problem, thus delimited to make it more specific and manageable, the researcher proceeds to take several interrelated steps, e.g., formulation of hypotheses (where feasible), explication of concepts that enter into the hypotheses and consideration of methods for relating the study to other studies using similar or kindred concepts. These steps are so closely intertwined that they cannot be worked on, one at a time. But for the sake of clarity we can only discuss them individually.

The suggested explanations or solutions to the problem formulated as propositions are called hypotheses. Such tentative explanations, i.e., hypotheses, may be the solutions to the problem. The inquiry is directed at finding out whether they really are the solutions to the problem.

Whether or not explicit hypotheses are proposed at this stage, the researcher needs to define the concepts which would be used in organizing the data. Such definitions include formal definitions that are designed to convey the general nature of the process or phenomenon. But no matter how simple or elaborate a researcher's formal definition of concept, he cannot usually proceed without devising some way of translating them into observable events or referents. In other words, the researcher has to devise some operations that yield data which will serve as satisfactory tangible indicators or referents of the given concepts.

Threaded through all these processes is the concern for generality of finding of the study and their relation to other knowledge, which means that the researcher is required to study critically the work already done in the field and formulate his problem in terms so general and abstract as to make clear its relation to other knowledge and permit replication of study in other concrete situations.

Once the research problem is formulated in clear-cut terms such that the types of information needed to answer it is clearly indicated, the researcher turns to the task working out a design for the study. A study/research design is a plan comprising the researcher's decisions about the procedures of sampling, data collection and analysis of data in respect of a given study, which aims to fulfill the objects or purpose of the study without wasteful expenditure of time, energy and money. If one can anticipate problems or difficulties that he may have to face subsequently, that is, before he actually conducts a given inquiry, to that extent he is in a position to face them as and when they arise, to decide beforehand what can be done to overcome them. This way, a researcher can increase his chance of deliberate anticipation directed towards bringing some expected situation under control. The researcher in the process of making decisions is also required to evaluate the methodological basis for making such decisions.

Designing a research ensures researcher against its failure. It is economical in the long run, because it forestalls the possibility of fruitless inquiry and its intractable failures. The researcher engaged in formulating a research design prepares, advisedly, an idealized research design, which is concerned with laying down the optimal research procedure that would be followed if there were no practical restrictions.[3] However, every researcher has to work in a practical situation characterized by varied constraints. Hence, he is required to take up the task of translating the idealized design into a reliable working procedure, i.e., the practical research design. The practical requirements of a study are designed in such a manner that compromises between the ideal and the practical aspects are accomplished without much damage to its scientific merit.

The research designs differ according to the research purpose.

Research purposes may be grouped into four broad categories, viz., (1) Exploration, (2) Description, (3) Diagnosis, and (4) Experimentation.

Design requirements would understandably vary for different kinds of studies. For example, the studies whose purpose is exploration, require a flexible research design, whereas those aiming at description and diagnosis would warrant a more rigid design.

The process of working out a research design involves, as has been pointed out, making decisions (with reference to the research problem or purpose) about the techniques to be employed for collection of relevant data, the safeguards to be employed in the interest of validity, reliability and precision of the instrument of data collection, the mode of drawing the sample from the 'universe' and the size of the sample that would best serve as a basis for drawing fairly acceptable inferences about the population of which the sample is a part, organizing or analyzing the data, interpreting the results of analysis and effecting 'compromises' prompted by practical exigencies, without adversely affecting the quality of work beyond a tolerable limit, etc. The researcher engaged thus, has to anticipate the field situation which goes a long way toward helping himself to get prepared and armed against future hazards. 'To be forewarned is to be forearmed' is indeed an old and wise dictum. Through designing the research, the investigator ensures that he will most probably achieve his research objective without having to spend prohibitive amounts of time, money and energy.

With the completion of the designing phase, researcher turns to the implementation aspect of it. Thus, he addresses himself to the task of formulating the instruments or tools of data collection, such as the questionnaire, interview schedule and observation guide, etc.

The task of formulating these measuring instruments is not an easy one by any reckoning. Usually, considerable preparation in terms of a deep understanding of the research problem, discussions with experienced and knowledgeable persons, systematic study of pertinent literature, reflection and imaginative 'role-taking' etc. has to go underway before the researcher is in a position to formulate meaningful and effective measuring instruments. These tentatively formulated instruments have to be 'pretested' with a view to detecting their shortcomings before their final deployment in the field.

The choice of techniques to be utilized for collection of data and the form in which these are to be pressed into service, depend on such considerations as: who are to be the respondents, what is sought to be known from them, when, where and how. Some techniques have a distinct advantage over others in certain kinds of situations. Certain techniques are especially suited to certain kinds of respondents and information whereas other techniques are virtually inapplicable in such situations. Certain situations and problems require that not one but two or more techniques be used for obtaining the information. Different forms of the same technique may be used with differing degrees of efficiency and advantage in different situations and settings.

Alongside with the formulation of measuring instrument, the researcher defines the 'population' or 'universe' of his study, i.e., the total number of items/objects/people of a specified class which is directly related to or covered by the research problem. It is rarely necessary and feasible (also, sometimes even undesirable) to study all the items which constitute the 'universe' or 'population' in order to provide an accurate and reliable estimate of its characteristics. More often, a sample of the 'population' under study is enough to afford a reliable base and it will closely match those that would have been obtained had the 'universe' in toto been studied. The researcher thus selects sample, in such a way that there is a probability that the selected sample, for the purpose at hand, is sufficiently representative of the 'universe', i.e., the conclusions based or the sample would by and large be the same as one would be arrived at, by studying each and every item, person, family, groups comprising the population or universe. There are times, however, when the time incurred in drawing a sample would be higher than what it would be if the entire 'population' was studied. In such a situation the researcher investigates the 'universe' in its totality.

The basic distinction in the sampling theory is between the probability sampling design and the non-probability sampling design. It is only by recourse to the probability sampling plan that the researcher can specify for each element of the 'population' the probability or chance of its being included in the sample and on this basis, estimate the extent to which the inference based on the sample may be accepted as one virtually based on the study of the 'universe.' While the non-probability sampling design does not afford a basis for making such estimates. It is utilized for reasons of convenience and economy. The researcher may in certain cases adopt a mode of sampling that combines certain ingredients of the probability and non-probability sampling procedures.

Having drawn a suitable and numerically adequate sample from the 'universe' the researcher proceeds to administer the measuring instruments or tools of data collection on the items comprising the selected sample. In order to ensure that the data are reliable and free from bias, the researcher needs to consider what mode of administering the instruments or tools of data collection would be most desirable in view of the kinds of responses sought and the nature of the objects or persons covered by the study. The administration of the data generating instruments brings to the fore the need for recording responses or Measurement presents difficulties all its own. Faulty recording of responses, understandably, has serious implications for the ultimate worth of the study. In fact, the recorded responses comprise the data. The researcher proceeds to examine them for completeness, comprehensibility, consistency and reliability.

The data collecting phase over, the researcher turns to the task of analysing them. The process of data-analysis subsumes a number of closely related operations. The overall purpose of data-analysis is to summarize the completed observations in such a manner that they yield answer to the research questions. Heaps of collected data would not mean anything unless these were organized in manner that conclusions or answers having a bearing on the problem of research can be arrived at. It goes without saying that the concern of analysis of data enters each of the earlier phases of study in a variety of ways. In fact, the analysis-plan of a study is shaped to a considerable extent even before the data are collected.

The broad task of analysing data may be viewed as comprising various specific sub-tasks such as the establishment of analytical categories, the application of these categories to raw data through coding, tabulation and drawing of statistical inferences, etc.

A partial obligation relating to the task of analyzing the data requires that the researcher classify the raw data into certain purposeful and usable categories. Classification or categorization facilitates the tabulation operations to be undertaken subsequently.

Coding operation has a reference to the technical procedure by which the data are categorized. Through coding the categories of data are transformed into symbols that may be tabulated and counted. Editing is a procedure involved in data analysis which is employed to improve the quality of the data for coding. Although in certain cases it is the respondent himself who assigns his response to a particular category (e.g., in poll-type questions), the categorization and coding of complex data are usually taken up after the entire data are in. The researcher has to install safeguards against factors which might operate to make the judgment of the coders unreliable.

With coding, the data are ready for tabulation. Tabulation is a part of the technical procedure involved in the statistical analysis of data. The essential operation involved in tabulation is counting to determine the frequencies or numerical strength of different categories of data. As was just indicated tabulation is just one part of the statistical analysis of data. Further statistical computations are needed in a study of any complexity. The researcher may need to work out central tendencies, deviations, correlations etc., to describe and summarize the data obtained on the sample based conclusions. He may also be required to utilize methods of sampling statistics to safeguard against drawing unjustified inferences.

With this, the stage is now set for restating the initially-stated hypotheses (if any were stated explicitly) against the generalizations or conclusions drawn on the basis of data with a view to testing their accord with these. Here retention or discarding of the hypotheses in if any, are formulated is bound to take place. In case an hypothesis fits the findings, the theory or perspective which suggested the hypothesis would be proved. If the hypothesis is disproved, the blow of disproof will pass on to theory which originated the hypothesis. In some cases, sometimes the blow may not be so severe and the theory may still survive with modification prompted by the research findings. If the researcher had no hypothesis to start with, the generalizations established on the basis of data may be stated as hypotheses to be tested by subsequent researches.

If the researcher had not proposed any hypothesis to start with, he might seek to explain his findings on the basis of some theory. This whole operation is geared to the search for broader meanings of given research findings through seeing linkages between the findings and some existing theory or established knowledge. This is termed as interpretation. The process of interpretation quite often triggers off new questions, prompting in turn further researches.

Although research is a continuous process, as limited to specific problem or issue the researcher has by now nearly reached the end of his journey. But he has an important scientific obligation to fulfill, i.e., reporting the research. The research exercise is not really complete till such time as the researcher has faithfully reported it. Science is public institution and in the interest of its growth on the right lines, every scientist is duty-bound (except in certain situations) to make his findings as also the method by which he arrived at these, known to the public. Reporting the research, to be sure, requires an order of skills somewhat different from those needed in the earlier phases of research. The chief purpose of a report is communication with an audience. It is expected that the research report will enlighten the readers on the following aspects:

(a) The problem of research.

(b) The research procedures consisting of the study design, method of manipulation (in experiment), sample, techniques of data collection and analysis.

(c) The results or outcome of the research.

(d) The theoretical and practical implications of the findings.

As was said in the previous chapter, social research often necessitates the services of any persons or categories of person; each person or category of persons is specially trained and skilled in a particular aspect of the research process. For example, a large-scale research programme involves various categories of persons such as investigators, samplers, coders, etc., with the researcher or scientist as the person directing or supervising their operations. He is, so to say, the brain behind the project and articulates the specialized operations to get to the solution of the problem. We have, in describing the major steps, opted for a model of inquiry in which the researcher scientist alone has to perform all those operations but the research process detailed above is equally applicable to inquiries in which many specialized categories of persons are involved as collaborators.

Quite a few fruitful analyses of the process of inquiry have been made and as a result, our understanding of inquiry is now expanded. Those analysing an inquiry from the point of view of science have generally conceived as problem solving process. Social scientists looking at the process of inquiry as a complex of interactions between individuals and environment have come to view it as a communicative process.

R. L. Ackoff has offered a model representing the process of inquiry which illustrates both its problem solving and communicative phases.[4] The communication model of inquiry involves four communicants:

(1) the consumer, who has a problem;

(2) the scientist/researcher who purports to solve it;

(3) the observer; and

(4) the observed.

We will do well to remember that these four communicants need not be four distinct individuals, rather they refer to four communicative roles. All four roles may be performed by a single person. Regardless of the number of people involved, one or hundreds, these roles are present in every inquiry. The communicative operations involving these four roles may be depicted in a diagrammatic form as under:

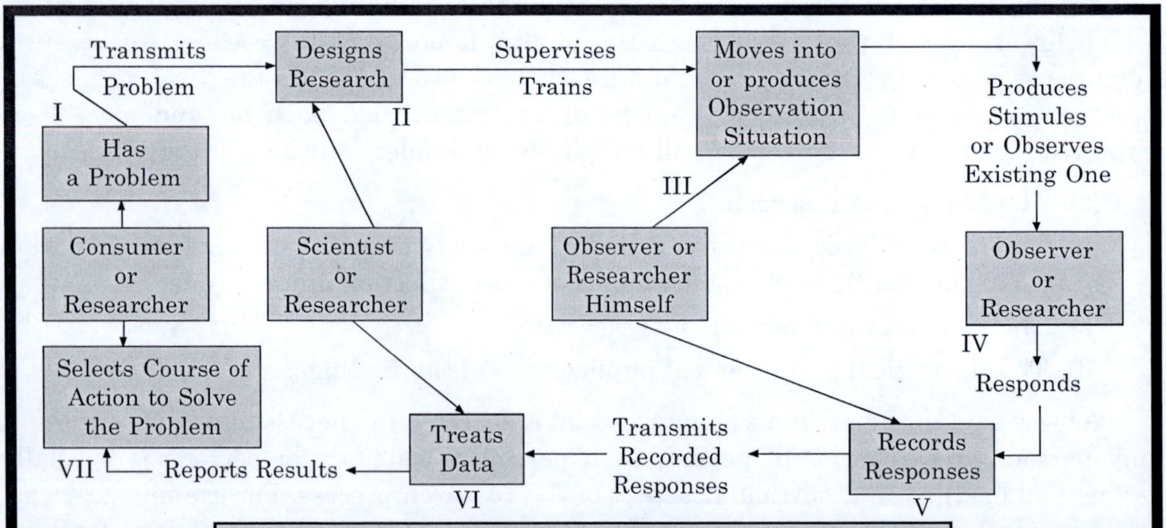

Diagram showing Communication Aspects of an Inquiry

This formulation of the communication aspects of inquiry also serves a very useful purpose in pointing out the potential sources of research error. It is clear that each of these roles may be a possible source of error.

The diagrammatic representation makes it quite clear that the problem solving phases of inquiry are: (1) Existence of a problem; (2) Formulation of the problem and designing a methodological strategy for solving it; (3) Movement into or creation of the environment in which observations are to be made (i.e., data-collection); (4) Recording of data; (5) Treatment of data (analysis and interpretation); (6) Action based on the reported results to solve the problem.

It is not difficult to see that the communication and the problem solving aspects of research exhibit the very same pattern that was presented in the preceding pages. The chapters that follow deal with different phases of the research process at some length.

REFERENCES

(1) Merton *et al.* (ed.), *op. cit.*, Harper and Row, N.Y., p. XI.

(2) Selltiz *et al., op. cit.*, p. 159.

(3) See Ackoff, *op. cit.*, p. 10.

(4) *Ibid.*, pp. 8-11.

Chapter IV

Formulation of Problem in Social Research

As was suggested in the last chapter, research really begins when the researcher experiences some difficulty, i.e., a problem demanding a solution within the subject-area of his discipline. This general area of interest, however, defines only the range of subject-matter within which the researcher would see and pose a specific problem for research. In other words, the subject-area only indicates where to look for a problem without specifying what the problem is like. In its diffuse form, the subject-area simply represents broad zone of issues within which the researcher expects to find his specific problem.

The general area or topic of a study may be either suggested or known. The researcher may also be interested in the phenomena that have already been studied to a certain extent, in which case, the researcher may be interested in identifying more exactly the conditions that affect the given phenomena in a particular way. If the researcher is working in a field in which there has developed a well articulated theoretical system, he may want to test specific predictions or expectations based on that theory.

A wide variety of practical concerns may also suggest a topic for research. Need for a factual evaluation of a programme, information pertinent to policy-making or social planning or need for finding out a practical solution to a certain problem facing a community etc., may suggest certain topics as well worth selecting for research.

Personal values play an important role in the selection of a topic for research. Social scientists with different values tend to choose different topics for investigation. Of course, personal values are not the only determinants in selecting a topic for inquiry; social conditions do often shape the preference of investigators in a subtle and imperceptible way. There are also number of powerful inducements to selection of one topic rather than another. Societies differ in respect of the premium they place on the work in different fields. These differential premia affect the choice of research topics. In a given society, it may bring, greater prestige — to do research on a deadly disease rather than, say, the patterns of child socialization.

More research funds are available for research in a particular area, e.g., on the less controversial topics rather than on controversial ones relating to politics and religion. Better paid positions may be available to researchers working in certain areas than in certain others. Needless to say, few social scientists would not be indifferent to such considerations as income, personal prestige, research funds and public or state co-operation.

It should be noted that selection of a topic for research is only half a step forward. This general topic does not help researcher to see what data are relevant to his purpose, what methods he would employ in securing them and how he would organize these. Before he can onsider these aspects he needs to formulate a specific problem. The problem defines the goal of the researcher in clear terms. It is obvious that in absence of a problem the inquiry would only become a meaningless exercise. A research like any other human activity is goal-directed. If the goal itself is unknown or ill-defined, the whole rigmarole of research operation will lead us nowhere. Thus, without a problem research cannot proceed because there is nothing to proceed from and proceed toward. There is nothing but wisdom in the saying: "If you start from nowhere you will generally reach there."

This is not to deny that sometimes a researcher's problem or difficulty consists in not perceiving a problem at all; he faces the problem of problemlessness. In social sciences especially, quite a number of researcher may be faced with this problem, i.e., the problem of not being able to see a problem. But being a particular kind of problem in itself, it guides the researcher in exploration — a process that involves a progressive narrowing of the scope and sharpening the focus of questions till the specific challenging questions are finally posed (resembling a pyramid with the general topic as the base and the specific challenging questions as the pinpoint or apex of top.)

The formulation of the topic into a research problems is, really speaking the first step in a scientific enquiry. A problem in simple words is some difficulty experienced by the researcher in a theoretic or practical situation. Solving this difficulty is the task of research.

Let us now appreciate what is meant by experiencing a difficulty in a theoretical situation. Observations not fitting the theoretical expectation, e.g., a theory may predict that particular type of societies will have a low rate of suicide but observations do not substantiate this prediction. This gives rise to a problem faced in theoretic situation. A difficulty in a practical situation may be felt, for instance, when there is a decline in production in spite of improvement in wages of workers. We shall be discussing these points in detail very shortly.

R. L. Ackoff's analysis affords considerable guidance in identifying a problem for research. Aackoff visualizes five components of a problem.[1]

(1) Research-consumer : There must be an individual or a group which experiences some difficulty. The individual may be the researcher himself and the group could be a group of researchers or scientists. For most problems, there are also other participants. The researcher, if he is different from the research-consumer, is participant in the problem. So are all individuals or groups who may be affected by a decision taken by the research-consumer.

(2) Research-consumer's Objectives : The research-consumer must have something he wants to get at or some ends he seeks to achieve. Obviously a person who wants nothing cannot have a problem.

(3) Alternative Means to Meet the Objectives : The research-consumer must have available, alternative means for achieving the objectives he desires. Means are courses of action open to the research-consumer. A course of action may involve use of various objects. Objects used thus are the instruments. A scale may be an instrument, but the use of a scale may be conceived of as a means. An instrument refers to any object, concept or idea which can be effectively incorporated in the pursuit of the objective.

It needs to be remembered that there must be at least two means available to the research-consumer. If he has no choice of means, he can have no problem. His problem, however, may consist of how to make the alternative means available for himself.

(4) Doubt in Regard to Selection of Alternatives : The existence of alternative courses of action is not enough; in order to experience a problem, the research consumer must have some doubt as to which alternative to select. Without such a doubt there can be no problem. The research-consumer must have a question concerning the relative efficiency of the alternative means and he must want to answer it.

All problems understandably get reduced ultimately to the evaluation of efficiency of the alternative means for a given set of objectives. It may be a bit difficult to appreciate this, particularly in reference to a pure research directed toward knowledge for the sake of knowledge. Since information is an instrument and its use a means, the inquiry directed toward obtaining correct information is directed toward identifying and securing efficient instruments. Since instruments cannot be separated from their use, such inquiry also reduces to determination of relative efficiency of alterative means.

(5) There must be one or More Environments to which the Difficulty or problem pertains : A change in environment may produce or remove a problem. A research-

consumer may have doubts as to which will be the most efficient means in one environment but would have no such doubt in another. For example, a person may have a problem involving a decision as to what kind of coat to wear on a clear day. But should it rain, he would have no doubt about the propriety of wearing his raincoat.

The range of environments over which a problem may be said to exist varies from one to many. Some problems are specific to only one environment while others are quite general.

The formulation of the problem consists in making various components of the problem explicit.

Says John Dewey : "It is a familiar and significant saying that a problem well put is half solved. To find out what the problem or problems are which a problematic situation presents, is to be well along in inquiry. To mistake the problem involved is to cause subsequent inquiry to be irrelevant. Without a problem there is blind groping in the dark."[2]

If we go merely by appearances, it would seem fairly easy to pose a problem for research. But this is not so in reality. Even so great as scientist as *Darwin* has testified to the difficulty in posing a problem. In his *Origin of Species,* he wrote, "Looking back, I think it was more difficult to see what the problems were than to solve them...."[3] This is so, explains *Merton*, because "in science, the questions that matter are of a particular kind. They are questions so formulated that the answers to them will confirm, amplify, or variously revise some part of what is currently taken as knowledge in the field. In short, although every problem in science involves a question or a series of questions, not every question qualifies as a scientific problem."[4]

Merton presents a powerful case for investigating the process of problem-finding. Although the process of problem solving has been subjected to intensive investigation, inquiries into the process of problem-finding, *Merton* points out, have suffered a relative neglect. *Merton* distinguishes three principal components in the progressive formulation of problem for social research :

(1) The originating questions (what one wants to know?)

(2) The rationale (theoretical or practical) (why one wants to have the particular questions answered?)

(3) The specifying questions (possible answer to the originating questions in terms that satisfy the rationale).

(1) Originating Questions

The originating questions represent the beginnings of certain difficulties or challenges which, formulated in much specific terms would indicate where exactly the answer to them can be searched for, attain the status of a research problem. Thus, the originating questions constitute the initial phase in the process of problem formulation.

Originating questions are of various types. One class of originating questions calls for discovering a particular body of social facts. Such questions may express a doubt as to whether the alleged social fact are really facts. Needless to say that before social facts can be explained, it is advisable to ensure that they are actually facts. It is not unusual for scientists to provide explanations for things that never were. It is to be noted that, "if the facts used as a basis for reasoning are ill-established or erroneous. Everything will crumble or be falsified .... Errors in scientific theories most often originate in errors of fact."[5]

A recognition that social facts are not always what they appear to be, leads the researcher to raise questions aimed at discovering a particular body of facts. These questions, as has already been suggested, do not yet constitute the problem, although they do constitute an essential step in that direction. Such questions are typically prompted by efforts to 'explain' social patterns which the researchers feel have not yet been established as genuine patterns. Such questions, sometimes called 'fact-finding' questions, hold a particular significance for social science. This is because men are apt to assume that they know the facts about the working of society or polity without hardy investigation, because society and polity are after all their native habitat. Contrary to this assumption, not all plausible beliefs about our native habitat are essentially true.

Another type of originating questions directs attention to the search for uniformities of relations between classes of social variables. An example of such a question is 'what is there about the structure of societies that determines the kinds of deviant acts that occur within their confines?'

Such questions, it would seem, are formulated in terms of broadly delimited categories of social variables but they do not indicate specifically which particular variables in each class may be germane to the issue. Such questions usually derive from a general theoretical orientation rather than from a well-articulated theory.

It is quite evident that the originating questions differ in their scope as well as their degree of specificity. For example, in the discipline of sociology, a large number of originating questions are addressed to sociological variables within one or another institutional sphere of society. 'Does the degree to which management takes the teacher's views into account in their decision-making process affect the degree to which the teacher takes the students' views into account, in the class room?" Would be a question of this type. But such relatively specific questions concerned with a particular institutional sphere (e.g., the school system) may have a potential bearing on comparable organizations in which role incumbents may reproduce in their behaviour *vis-à-vis* a subordinate his experience in relation to his/her superior.

Originating questions of another kind are put in such a form that they can be addressed to a variety of institutional spheres, e.g., the questions, 'Do the diverse social roles that members of different social classes are called upon to play have consequences more important for their personalities than have their class positions'? is one of this kind. It should be borne in mind that neither the more general nor the more specific versions of the originating questions claim an exclusive value; each has its own value in augmenting knowledge of a particular kind.

In sum, the originating questions are of different kinds and emanate from different sources. Some are questions of descriptive fact, about observed empirical generalizations, some enquire into the sources of the observed patterns of social organization and others are concerned with their consequences, and so on.

(2) Rationale of Questions

The originating question is just one component of the problem. Another is the rationale of the questions. Rationale is the statement of reasons why a particular question is worth putting across. The rationale states what will happen to other parts of knowledge or practice if the question is answered, i.e., how the answer to the question will contribute to theory and/or practice. In this way, the rationale helps to effect a distinction between the scientifically consequential and trivial questions. In short, "the rationale states the case for the question in the court of scientific opinion."[6] The requirement of a rationale arrests the flux of scientifically trivial questions and enlarges the volume of important ones.

As a rationale for science as a whole, it refers simply to knowledge as a self-contained end. It ignores rather than denies, the possibility that a new bit of knowledge will contribute to practical concerns, viz., power, comfort, safety, prestige, etc. The scientist may regard his deep interest in a question as a strong enough reason for pursuing it. But sooner or later, if the question and its answers are to become a part of the corpus of science, they must be shown to be relevant to other ideas and facts in the discipline.

The practical rationale makes out a case for the question by pointing out that its answers will help people achieve practical values, i.e., health, comfort, productivity, etc. This is not to deny that a question raised mainly with an eye on the practical value of its answer may have important consequences for the theoretic system. It is evident that a particular question may have import both for systematic knowledge and for practical uses largely, because the inquiry undertaken with an eye on any one has unintended consequences for the other.

(a) Theoretical rationale of a question may be considered as one worth asking because its answer would enlarge the scope of an existing theory or conceptual scheme. Such a question would ask whether the existing ideas or concepts could be instructively used to understand aspects of phenomena that have not yet been subjected to examination in terms of these concepts or ideas, e.g., an examination of a particular rebellious 'cult' or movement within the theoretical frame of 'Anomie.' If the observations fit the conceptual scheme, it in effect gets enlarged or extended. This is precisely what is meant by bringing new set of facts within the grasp of an old one.

(b) Theoretical rationale of a question may direct the scientist's attention to observed inconsistencies in currently-accepted ideas or findings and may prompt him to ask whether these inconsistencies are spurious for apparent rather than real. Such questions invite re-examination of these ideas that initially led to the expectation. Are the ideas faulty, or the inferences drawn from them faulty? These questions about inconsistencies lead to posing of new problems for research. We had an occasion to illustrate such inconsistent results in the first chapter. In so far as much inconsistencies set the stage for instituting new problems, researchers are expected to be on the look out for 'deviant cases', i.e., cases that depart from the prevailing pattern. The deviant cases are then examined with a view to arriving at a single unified interpretation of the prevailing regularity and of departures from it. Properly investigated, the exception can improve the rule.

(c) A question may be considered well worth asking, because its answer is expected to bridge the gaps in the existing ideas or theory that do not account for aspects of phenomena to which they should in principle apply. In some cases, the gap may be bridged by ideas that are consistent with the existing theory, which is then seen as incomplete but not wrong. In other cases, the new theoretical proposal might require some revision of the earlier theory. *Merton* cites as an illustration, the question of accounting for regularities of social behaviour that are not prescribed by cultural norms or that may even be at odds with these. The question expresses doubt for on the familiar assumption that uniformities of social behaviour necessarily represent conformity to norms. That is, it identifies a gap in the narrowly cultural theory of behaviour which considers social regularities as culturally mandated. Yet as anyone would agree, many social regularities need not be culturally prescribed, e.g., men tend to have higher suicide rates than women, though cultural norms do not invite males to put an end to themselves. *Durkheim's* work on suicide partly bridged this gap. It was his contention that the designated properties of groups (e.g., the degree of their social cohesion) determine the rates of behaviour which are either not prescribed by culture or tabooed.

Once the theoretic gap is identified, it may spark off further questions, each with its distinctive rationale. There is no doubt, for instance, that much of patterned social behaviour is culturally prescribed. This is, after all, what we mean by institutionalized behaviour. When this fact is made to confront the theory that social regularities are the indirect properties of social structure, we are at once in a position to pose a series of new questions such as, "How does a social structure produce new cultural norms prescribing behaviour that was previously unperceived resultant of it"? With this, the inquiry gets focused on the formation of norms in groups similarly situated in the social structure.

Questions having a rationale consequent upon a gap in theory being identified, have a particular forces and significance when the gap is such as can be bridged simply by recasting the earlier assumptions. For example, a question may be raised about the assumptions that "Group equilibrium is a function of the extent to which group members conform to each other's expectations."[7] This assumption in turn is based on the idea that each act in a sequence of identical conforming acts will yield the same or increasing degree of appreciation or satisfaction to the actor and to other participants in the interaction system. These assumptions are put to question. It can be argued in this reference that the same act will have different consequences according to the phase of the system of interaction in which it occurs. That is, longer the sequence in which one person conforms to another's expectation, the more will his conformity be taken for granted and the less will be the other's reward for his conformity. On this view, the successive acts of conformity will yield smaller increments of reward.

It is observed that in the course of its evolution, any particular discipline and its specialized fields have given vent to distinctive problems at each of its stages of development. When for example, early modern sociologists were zealously engaged in trying to establish a distinct intellectual identity, they placed a heavy premium upon the autonomy of the field and largely ignored the methods, ideas and data from related disciplines. *Durkheim*, for instance, objected to and bred a school of objectors to the systematic use of psychological explanations of social phenomena. Similar has been the case with special branches of the discipline of sociology, e.g., sociology of law, sociology of science or sociology of medicine, etc. in each branch of sociology for example, sustained emphasis on one range of problems has evoked after a time, corrective, emphases upon problems that had so far come to be neglected. On occasions, this calls for the revision of analytical models or schemes that have led sociologists to concentrate on a restricted range of problems at the expense of other problems that the model tends to neglect.

As corrective emphases of theory develop, attention is redirected toward problems under temporary neglect. For example, the relation of population growth to human welfare, one of the oldest problems of population theory, has been periodically reformulated to accord with new concepts and to make it amenable to new methods of investigation.

Investigation of a range at problems has gone as far as it can with the use of existing concepts. The concepts useful for a time in the past, may now prove to be inadequately differentiated, typically introducing the problem of devising appropriate classifications. The concept of role, for example, proves inadequate to deal with many problems so long as it has to depend on the vernacular for depicting social positions, e.g., father, leader, physician, etc. Such inadequacies give rise to the problem of devising a standard set of concepts or categories which can be used to describe any role or set of roles in a way that does adequate justice to its complexity and permits systematic comparison with other roles. The solution of an inadequacy is a pre-condition to getting on with a broader programme of research.

(3) Specifying Questions

This is the stage of culmination in the process of formulating a research problem. The originating questions, as we have seen, differ in their degree of specificity. Some may be quite diffuse; some relatively more specific. In their most diffuse form, they simply register a dimly felt sense of ignorance, a general concern with 'something' that seems to be in need of solution but this 'something' is not clearly or sharply identified. In somewhat more focused form the originating questions point to a class of variables that may be involved in bringing about an observed state, without specifying the pertinent variable in that class. At this stage, the problem has yet to be fully instituted. The originating question must still be recast to indicate clearly the observations that will provide an answer to it.

This objective of transforming the originating questions into specifying question with an eye on a series of observations in particular concrete situations warrants a search for empirical materials in reference to which the problem can be investigated fruitfully. Although, sometimes, the investigator stumbles upon these materials by some lucky coincidence quite often, he selects them by deliberate design realizing their strategic character in arriving at the answer or the solution to the problem. In sociology, we may cite cases where answer to certain antiquated problems were attempted by investigating them in concrete situations that strategically exhibited the nature of the problem. Inquiry into the modes of interdependence among various social institutions was greatly advanced by Max Weber's decision to study this general problem in the specific instance of the connections between ascetic protestantism and modern capitalism. Weber realized that the concrete phenomena, i.e., protestant ethic and modern capitalism, had a strategic character in as much as it afforded in a miniature but representative form an essential understanding of the general nature of inter-institutional dependence.

No concrete situation or observation, however, is strategic in itself. It is a certain insight the researcher brings to the situation that makes it strategic.[8] The signal importance of this phase in the definition of a problem has been widely recognized. But it presents difficulties all its own. We can only illustrate here how as final phase in the formulation of a problem, a general originating question can be transformed into specific one so as to indicate the types of situations that will afford the strategic observations to answer them. It is well-known that social organizations have latent functions. The originating question may ask "What are latent functions or the unintended consequences — positive and negative — of the present 'rational' organizational structures for the clients?" The hospital system being such an organization, would afford a strategic site for investigating this question. The question in its more specific form may be phrased thus: "What are the unintended consequences of the rationally organized hospital system for the care of the patients?"

It should be clear that not even a beginning of the solution can be found so long as the questions remain in such an undifferentiated or different fused form. The question must, therefore, be broken down into several specifying questions related to particular aspects or organization of hospitals and their consequences for the care of patients. (e.g., hierarchy of statuses, formal rules etc.). These simple, pointed, focused and empirically verifiable questions are the final resultant of the phased process we call the formulation of a research problem. It is only such specific questions that provide answers which in their synthesized form afford the solution to the problem. This solution, as we have stated earlier, has implications for theory, systematic knowledge and/or for practice.

We may here consider the social determinants of sociological problems. Many problems in social sciences are brought into focus by influences external to specific discipline itself. A brief prelude to this was provided when we considered the practical rationale of questions.

Changes in the patterns of social life may give a new or renewed significance to a broad subject of sociological inquiry.

A renewed interest in the study of face to face groups, for instance, is attributed mainly to the preponderance of formal organizations in contemporary society and a growing need for such societies for face to face 'primary' groups in modern society characterized by instrumental orientations.

It can hardly be assumed, however, that all social and cultural changes will automatically induce or reinforce interest in a particular sphere of inquiry. When changes in a society come to be defined as a social problem and are occasions for acute social conflict, then only do such spheres begin to attract interest. For example, sociologists paid scant attention to the institution of science although it was recognized as a major dynamic force. A limited renaissance of interest in this field occurred only when a spate of limited historical events subjected the institution of science to stress, e.g., in Nazi Germany. Also, the state imposition of secrecy upon scientific work in many societies had the result of violating the values and moral conviction of men of science and of curbing the flow of scientific information.

Historical events can affect the value-commitments of sociologists and lead them to work on a restricted range of problems. *Merton* suggests that the Great Depression and the social strains it created in its wake, led any American sociologists to study problems of social disorganization.

The social organization of the inquiry itself may affect the selection of problems. The choice of subject-matter as also the ways in which problems are construed has been demonstrated to be related to the recruitment pattern and working conditions of researchers.

Thus far, we were engaged in considering the steps involved in the formulation of a problem for research within the general area of a discipline, drawing the illustrative materials from the discipline of sociology. We have also seen how difficult it is to be able to pose a significant problem for research. This is really speaking the first and perhaps the most crucial step in the research process. Many a researcher is stuck at this point and look for guidance in the matter of posing the problem. This perhaps is the stage where others can help him the least.

A question so often asked is, "where to look for a problem?" The answer can only be, "Your own mind, where else?" It is a sensitive mind that alone experiences a problem or a difficulty, in a particular situation. This difficulty or curiosity as we have seen, arises because some new observations do not fit into the person's (researcher's) scheme of ideas about the true nature of being and becoming or because the diverse bits of knowledge acquired by him do not fit together meaningfully or something cannot be explained on the basis of what he knows or finally, because there is some element of challenge in a practical situation. It is quite understandable, therefore, that the problem is something that the researcher has to experience from within. It arises, in a way, from what one already knows, and what, on this basis, one would like to know if he were to satisfy his creative impulse. One who does not know much will hardly have problems. It is in this sense that 'ignorance is bliss.' A person may have acquired wrong ideas, but on this very basis, he may experience problems which will ultimately change his initial ideas.

Systematic knowledge acquired by the individual, his training and personal talents, all contribute toward sensitizing him to see the difficulties and pose pertinent questions of real import. *Cohen and Nagel* rightly point out that "the ability to perceive in some brute experience, the occasion for a problem and especially a problem whose solution has a bearing on the solution of other problems, is not a common talent among men. It is mark of scientific genius to be sensitive to difficulties where less gifted people pass untroubled by doubt."[9] Raising new questions, new possibilities or regarding old problems from new angles requires a creative imagination and reflects a real advance in science. The mythical tale about Newton testifies to this. Apples have been falling and must also have fallen on the heads of people before Newton's time but it was the sensitive Newton alone who raised that strategic question which sounded the beginnings of the law of gravitation.

We may now list some of the conditions that experience has proved to be conducive to formulation of significant research problems.

(1) Systematic Immersion in the Subject through First-hand Observation : The researcher must immerse himself thoroughly in the subject-area within which he wishes to pose a specific problem. For example, if the researcher was interested in the broad problem of juvenile delinquency, if would serve him well if he visited remand homes, juvenile centers, juvenile courts, the families of the delinquents and the localities where

the incidence is high. He should try to know at first-hand the various aspects of the life of delinquents by interviewing them, their family members and supervisors, etc., by observation; no experience is more rewarding in terms to getting a deep feel of the situation. This exercise helps a great deal in suggesting to the researcher the specific questions that may be posed for the study to answer. This process is known by various names, e.g., pilot survey, preliminary survey or exploration.

(2) Study of Relevant Literature on the Subject : We have already seen that to be able to pose a problem, the researcher must be well-equipped to experience some difficulty or challenge. This in turn would depend upon how well the researcher is conversant with the relevant theories in the field, reports and records, etc.; this would help the researcher to know if there are certain gaps in the theories (his problem then will bridge these) or whether the prevailing theories applicable to the problem are inconsistent with each other or whether the findings of different studies do not follow a pattern consistent with theoretical expectations and so on. All these will afford occasions for institution of research problems. This is also an aspect of exploration.

(3) Discussion with persons having Practical Experience in the Field of Study : This is often known as an experience survey, which again is an exercise at exploration. Administrators, social workers, community leaders, etc., are persons who have a store of rich practical experience in different fields of social life. These persons, therefore, are in an effective position to enlighten the researcher on different aspects on the fields of his propose study. Such persons represent in a nutshell, years of experience, hence their advice, comments, information and judgements are usually invaluable to the researcher. They can help and guide him to sharpen his focus of attention on specific aspects within the broader field.

Important as these conditions are in formulating a research problem, they hide a danger. In social science as elsewhere, habits of thought may interfere with the discovery of the new or the unexpected, unless the preliminary observations, reading sad discussions are conducted in a constantly critical, curious and imaginative frame of mind.

We now know that research begins with a problem or a difficulty.[10] The purpose of the inquiry is to find a solution of this difficulty. It is advantageous and desirable that researcher should propose a set of suggested solution or explanations of the difficulty which research purports to solve. Such tentative solutions or explanation, formulated as proposition are called hypotheses. The suggested solutions (formulated as hypotheses) may or may not be correct solutions to the problem; whether or not they are in the task of inquiry to test and establish. The next chapter is devoted to a fuller exposition of the concept of hypotheses and their role in science.

REFERENCES

(1) See Ackoff, *op. cit.*, pp. 28-30.

(2) See Dewey, John: *Logic — The Theory of Inquiry*, Henry Holt & Co. N.Y., 1938.

(3) Merton, *et al.* : *op. cit.*, p. ix.

(4) *Ibid.*, p. x.

(5) Cf. Merton, *et al.* : *op. cit.*, p. xiii.

(6) Theobald, D.W. : *Philosophy of Science,* Methuen, London, 1968.

(7) Merton, *et al., op. cit.*, p. xix.

(8) *Ibid.*, p. xxv.

(9) See Merton, *op. cit.*, p. 151.

(10) Selltiz, *et al., op. cit.*, p. 31.

* **Note :** The inquiries termed "exploratory" or "formulative" do not start with a problem; their problem is to find a problem. Hence, such studies do not begin with a hypothesis, rather they end up by formulating hypotheses.

Chapter V

Hypotheses: Their Nature and Role in Social Research

Once the problem to be answered in the course of research is finally instituted, the researcher may, if feasible proceed to formulate tentative solutions or answers to it. These proposed solutions or explanations are called *hypotheses* which the researcher is obliged to test on the basis of fact already known or which can be made known. If such answers are not formulated, even implicitly, the researcher cannot effectively go ahead with the investigation of his problem because, in the absence of direction which hypotheses typically provide, the researcher would not know what facts to look for and what relation or order to search for amongst them. The hypotheses guide the researcher through a bewildering Jungle of facts to see and select only those that are relevant to the problem or difficulty he proposes to solve. Collection of facts merely for the sake of collecting them will yield no fruits. To be fruitful, one should collect such facts as are for or against some point of view or proposition. Such a point of view or proposition is the hypothesis. The task of the inquiry or research is to test its accord with facts.

Lundberg aptly observes, "The only difference between gathering data without a hypothesis and gathering them with one, is that in the latter case, we deliberately recognize the limitations of our senses and attempt to reduce their fallibility by limiting our field of investigation so as to prevent greater concentration for attention on particular aspects which past experience leads us to believe are irrelevant as insignificant for our purpose."[1]

Simply stated, an hypothesis helps us see and appreciate (1) the kind of data that need be collected in order to answer the research question and (2) the way in which they should be organized most efficiently and meaningfully.

Webster's New International Dictionary of English Language, 1956, defines the term *"hypothesis"* as "proposition, condition or principle which is assumed, perhaps without belief, in order to draw out its logical consequences and by this method to test its accord with facts which are known or may be determined."

Cohen and Nagel bring out the value of hypothesis thus: "We cannot take a single step forward in any inquiry unless we begin with a suggested explanation or solution of the difficulty which originated it. Such tentative explanations are suggested to us by something in the subject-matter and by our previous knowledge. When they are formulated as propositions, they are called hypotheses."[2]

Once the scientist knows what his question (problem) is, he can make a guess, or a number of guesses as to its possible answers. According to *Werkmeister,* "The guesses he makes are the hypotheses which either solve the problems or guide him in further investigation."[3]

It is clear now that a hypothesis is a provisional formulation; a tentative solution of the problem posed by the scientist. 'The scientist starts by assuming that the solution is true without, of course, personally believing in its truthfulness. Based on this assumption, the scientist anticipates that certain logical consequences will be observed on the plane of observable events or objects. Whether these anticipations or expectations really materialize is the test of the hypothesis, its proof or disproof. If the hypothesis is proved, the problem of which it was a tentative solution is answered. If it is not proved, i.e., falsified owing to non-support of proof, alternative hypothses may be formulated by the researcher. An hypothesis thus stands somewhere at the midpoint of research; from here, one can look back to the problem as also look forward to data. The hypothesis may be stated in the form of a principle, that is, the tentative explanation or solution to the questions how? Or why? May be presented in the form of a principle that X varies with Y. If the from the book inquiry established that an empirical referent of X varies with the empirical referent of Y in a concrete observable situation (i.e., the hypothesis is proved) then the question is answered. Hypotheses, however, may take other forms, such as intelligent guesses, conditions, propositions deduced from theories, observations and findings of other scholars etc.

Proceeding on the basis of hypotheses has been the slow and hard way of science. While some scientific conclusions and premises seem to have arisen in the mind of the investigator as if by flashes of insight, in a majority of cases the process of discovery has been a slower one. "The scientific imagination devises a possible solution, a hypothesis—and the investigator proceeds to test it. He makes intellectual keys and then tries to see whether they fit the lock. If the hypothesis does not fit, it is rejected and another is made. The scientific workshop is full of discarded keys."[4]

Cohen and Nagel's statement that one cannot take a single step forward in any inquiry without a hypothesis may well be a correct statement of the value of hypothesis in scientific investigation generally, but it hardly does justice to an important function of scientific research, i.e., the "formulation hypotheses." Hypotheses are not given to us readymade. Of course in fields with a highly developed theoretic structure it is reasonable to expect that most empirical studies will have at least some sharp hypotheses to be tested. This is so especially in social sciences where there has not yet evolved a highly developed theoretic system in many areas of its subject-matter which can afford fruitful bases for hypothesis-formulation. As such, attempts to force research into this mould are either deceitful or stultifying and hypotheses are likely to be no more than hunches as to where to look for sharper hypotheses in which case the study may be described as an intelligent fishing trip. As a result, in the social sciences at least, a considerable quantum of research endeavour is directed understandably toward 'making' hypotheses rather than at testing them. As we shall see later, a very important type of research has as its goal, the formulation of significant hypotheses relating to a particular problem. Hence, we will do well to bear in mind that research can begin with well formulated hypotheses or it may come out with hypotheses as its end product.

Let us recapitulate the role of hypotheses for research in the words of *Chaddock* who summarizes it thus: "(A hypothesis) in the scientific sense is ... an explanation held after careful canvass of known facts, in full knowledge of other explanations that have been offered and with a mind open to change of view, if the facts disclosed by the inquiry warrant a different explanation. Another hypothesis as an explanation is proposed including investigation all available and pertinent data either to prove or disprove the hypothesis.... (A hypothesis) gives point to the inquiry and if founded on sufficient previous knowledge, guides the line of investigation. Without it much useless data maybe collected in the hope that nothing essential will be omitted or important data may be omitted which could have been easily included if the purpose of inquiry had been more clearly defined"[5] and thus hypotheses are likely to be no more than hunches as to where to look for pertinent data.

An hypothesis is therefore held with the definite purpose of including in the investigating all available and pertinent data either to prove or disprove the hypothesis.

Types of Hypotheses

There are many kinds of hypotheses the social researcher has to be working with. One type of hypotheses asserts that something is the case in a given instance; that a particular object, person or situation has a particular characteristic. Another type of hypotheses deals with the frequency of occurrences or of association among variables;

this type of hypotheses may state that X is associated with y a certain (Y) proportion of times, e.g., that urbanism tends to be acompanied by mental disease or that something is greater or lesser than some thing else in a specific setting. Yet another type of hypotheses assert that a particular characteristic is one of the factors which determine another characteristic, i.e., S is the producer of Y (product). Hypotheses of this type are known as causal hypotheses.

Hypotheses can be classified in a variety of ways. But classification of hypotheses on the basis of their levels of abstraction is regarded as especially fruitful. *Goode and Hatt* have identified three differential levels of abstraction reached by hypotheses."[6] We shall here be starting from the lowest level of abstraction and go over to the higher ones.

(a) At the lowest level of abstraction are the hypotheses which state existence of certain empirical uniformities. Many types of such empirical uniformities are common in social research, for instance, it may be hypothesized with reference to India that in the cities men will get married between the age of 22 and 24 years. Or, the hypotheses of this type may state that certain behaviour pattern may be expected in a specified community. Thus, hypotheses of this type frequently seem to invite scientific verification of what are called "common sense propositions," indeed without much justification.

It has often been said by way of a criticism of such hypotheses that these are not useful in as much as they merely state what everyone seems to know already. Such an objection may however be overruled by pointing out that what everyone knows is not often put in precise terms nor is it adequately integrated into the framework of science. Secondly, what everyone knows may well be mistaken. To put common sense ideas into precisely defined concepts and subject the proposition to test is an important task of science. This is particularly applicable to social sciences which are at present in their earlier stage of development. Not only social science but all sciences have found such commonsense knowledge a fruitful item of study. It was commonsense knowledge in the olden days that sun revolved round the earth. But this and many other beliefs based on commonsense have been exploded by patient, plodding, empirical checking of facts. The monumental work, *The American Soldier* by *Stouffer* and associates was criticized in certain quarters, for it was according to them mere elaboration of the obvious. But to this study goes the credit of exploding some of the commonsense propositions and shocking many people who had never thought that what was so obvious a commonsense could be totally wrong or unfounded in fact.

(b) At a relatively higher level of abstraction are hypotheses concerned with complex 'ideal types.' These hypotheses aim at testing whether logically derived relationship between empirical uniformities obtain. This level of hypothesizing moves beyond the level of anticipating a simple empirical uniformity by visualizing a complex referent in society.

Such hypotheses are indeed purposeful distortions of empirical exactness and owing to their remoteness from empirical reality, these constructs are termed 'ideal types.' The function of such hypotheses is to create tools and formulate problems for further research in complex areas of investigation.

An example of one such hypothesis may be cited. Analyses of minority groups brought to light empirical uniformities in the behaviour of members of a wide variety of minorities. It was subsequently hypothesized that these uniformities pointed to an 'ideal type'. First called by *H. A. Miller* the 'oppression psychosis,' this ideal-typical construction was subsequently modified as the 'Marginal man' by *E. Stonequist* and associates. Empirical evidence marshalled later substantiated the hypothesis, and so the concept of marginality (marginal man) has very much come to stay as a theoretic construct in social sciences, and as part of sociological theory.

(c) We now come to the class of hypotheses at the highest level of abstraction. This category of hypotheses is concerned with the relation obtaining amongst analytic variables. Such hypotheses are statements about, how one property affects other, e.g., a statement of relationship between education and social mobility or between wealth and fertility. It is easy to see that this level of hypothesizing is not only more abstract compared to others; it is also the most sophisticated and vastly flexible mode of formulation.

This does not mean, however, that this type of hypotheses is 'superior' or 'better' than the other types. Each type of hypotheses has its own importance depending in turn upon the nature of investigation and the level of development the subject has achieved. The sophisticated hypotheses of analytical variables owe much of their existence to the building-blocks contributed by the hypotheses existed at the lower orders of abstraction.

Sources of Hypotheses

Hypotheses may be developed from a variety of sources. We examine here, some of the major ones.

(1) The history of sciences provides an eloquent testimony to the fact that personal and idiosyncratic experiences of the scientist contribute a great deal to type and form of questions he may ask, as also to the kinds of tentative answers to these questions (hypotheses) that he might provide. Some scientists may perceive an interesting pattern in what may merely, seem a jumble of facts to the common man. The history of science is full of instances of discoveries made just because the 'right' person happened to make the 'right' observation owing to his characteristic life-history and exposure to a unique mosaic of events. Personal life-histories are a factor in determining the kinds of a person's perception and conception and this factor may in turn direct him to certain hypotheses quite readily. An illustration of such individual perspectives in social sciences may be seen in the work of *Thorstein Veblen* whom *Merton* describes as a sociologist with a keen eye for the unusual and paradoxical. A product of an isolated Norwegian community, *Veblen* lived at a time when the capitalistic system was barely

subjected to any criticism. His own community background was replete with deprivational experiences attributable to the capitalist system. *Veblen* being an outsider, was able to look at the capitalist economic system more objectively and with dispassionate detachment. *Veblen* was thus strategically positioned to attack the fundamental concepts and postulates of classical economics. He was an alien who could bring a different experience to bear upon the economic world. Consequently, he made penetrating analyses of society and economy which have ever since profoundly influenced social science.

(2) Analogies are often a fountainhead of valuable hypotheses. Students of sociology and political science in the course of their studies would have come across analogies wherein society and state are compared to a biological organism, the natural law to the social law, thermodynamics to social dynamics, etc. such analogies, notwithstanding the fact that analogies as a class suffer from serious limitations, do provide certain fruitful insight which formulated as hypotheses stimulate and guide inquiries. One of the recent orientations to hypotheses formulation is provided by cybernetics, the communication models now so well entrenched in the social science testify to the importance of analogies as a source of fruitful hypotheses. The hypothesis that similar human types or activities may be found occupying the same territory was derived from plant ecology. When the hypothesis was borne out by observations in society, the concept of *segregation* as it is called in plant ecology was admitted into sociology. It has now become an important idea in sociological theory. Such examples may be multiplied. In sum, analogy may be very suggestive but care needs to be taken not to accept models from other disciplines without a careful scrutiny of the concepts in terms of their applicability to the new frame of reference in which they are proposed to be deployed.

(3) Hypotheses may rest also on the findings of other studies. The researcher on the basis of the findings of other studies may hypothesize that similar relationship between specified variables will hold good in the present study too. This is a common way of researchers who design their study with a view of replicating another study conducted in a different concrete context or setting. It was said earlier that many a study in social science is exploratory in character, i.e., they start without explicit hypotheses, the findings of such studies may be formulated as hypotheses for more structured investigations directed at testing certain hypotheses.

(4) An hypothesis may stem from a body of theory which may afford by way of logical deduction, the prediction that if certain conditions are present, certain results will follow. Theory represents what is known; logical deductions from this constitute the hypotheses which must be true if the theory was true. *Dubin* aptly remarks, "Hypothesis is the feature of the theoretical model closest to the 'things observable' that the theory is trying to model."[7] *Merton* illustrates this function of theory with his customary felicity. Basing his deductions on *Durham's* theoretic orientation, Merton shows how hypotheses may be derived as deductions from theoretic system.

(1) Social cohesion provides psychic support to group members subjected to acute stresses and anxieties.

(2) Suicide rates are functions of unrelieved anxieties to which persons are subjected.

(3) Catholics have greater social cohesion than protestants.

(4) Therefore, lower suicide rates should be expected among Catholics than among protestants.

If theories purport to model the empirical world, then there must be a linkage between the two. This linkage is to be found in the hypotheses that mirror the propositions of the theoretical model. It may thus appear that the points of departure *vis-à-vis* hypotheses-construction are in two opposite directions : (a) conclusions based on concrete or empirical observations lead through the process of induction to more abstract hypotheses and (b) the theoretical model through the process of logical deduction affords more concrete hypotheses. It may be well to bear in mind, however, that although these two approaches to hypotheses formulation seem diametrically opposed to each other, the two points of departure, i.e., empirical observations and the theoretical structure, represent the poles of a continuum and hypotheses lie somewhere in the middle of this continuum. Both these approaches to hypotheses-construction have proved their worth. The Chicago School in American sociology represents a strong empirical orientation whereas the *Mertonian* and *Parsonian* approach is typified by a stress on theoretic models as initial bases for hypotheses-construction. Hence hypotheses can be deductively derived from theoretic models.

(5) It is worthy of note that value-orientation of the culture in which a science develops may furnish many of its basic hypotheses. That certain hypotheses and not others capture the attention of scientists or occur to them in particular societies or culture may well be attributed to the cultural emphases. *Goode and Hatt* contend that the American emphasis upon personal happiness had had considerable effect upon social science in that country. The phenomenon of personal happiness has been studied in great detail. In every branch of social science, the problem of personal happiness came to occupy a position meriting central focus. Happiness has been correlated with income, education, occupation, social class, and so on. It is evident that the culture emphasis on happiness has been productive of a very wide range of hypotheses for the American social science.

Folk-wisdom prevalent in a culture may also serve as source of hypotheses.

The sum and substance of the discussion is aptly reflected in *Larrabee's* remark that the ideal source of fruitful and relevant hypotheses is a fusion of two elements: past experience and imagination in the disciplined mind of the scientist.[9]

Characteristics of a Usable Hypothesis

We now turn to address ourselves to the question 'what are the characteristics of a 'good' hypothesis?' Let us try to answer it. All hypotheses of science are seized by some kind of insight and intuition, a leap of imagination. But the important methodological point is that a hypothesis so reached must be tested against data to be convinced of its adequacy. The power of a statement to explain its data determines its truth. But no amount of converging evidence can transform a factual statement into an analytical one and so free it from the principle of permanent control.

The criteria for judging the usability of the hypotheses are none else than those that help the hypotheses perform their designated functions vis-à-vis research and the existing edifice of knowledge, generally. Hence a 'good' usable hypothesis would be the one which satisfies many of the following criteria:

(a) A hypothesis should be empirically testable. It should be so stated that it is possible to deduce logically certain inferences close to the level of concrete observation so that they can be tested by observation in the field. That is, the hypotheses should have empirical referents. The concepts embodied in the hypothesis must have clear empirical correspondence and should be explicitly defined. For example, 'Bad parents beget bad children' is hardly a statement that can qualify as a usable hypothesis, since 'bad' cannot be explicitly defined.

(b) Hypotheses should be closest to things observable. Failing this, it would not be possible to test their accord with empirical facts. *Cohen and Nagel* rightly remark"... hypothesis must be formulated in such a manner that deductions can be made from it and consequently, a decision can be reached as to whether it does not explain the facts considered."[10]

(c) The hypotheses must be conceptually clear. This point is implicit in the proceeding criterion. The concepts utilized in the hypothesis should be clearly defined — not only formally but also, if possible, operationally. Formal definition or *explication* of the concepts will clarify what a particular concept stands for, while the *operation definition* will leave no ambiguity about what would constitute the empirical evidence or indicator of the concept on the plane of reality. An ambiguous hypothesis characterized by undefined or ill-defined concepts cannot be tested since, understandably, there is no standard basis for knowing what observable facts would constitute its test. It is advisable that the concepts embodied in the hypotheses be defined in a manner commonly accepted and communicable. This would ensure continuity in researches and go a long way in bringing about a cumulative growth of scientific knowledge.

(d) The hypotheses must be specific. One may hypothesize that something will happen in next five minutes, with absolute confidence but just because it is refuted it is empty of concrete information. We need to know what will happen and as soon as we commit ourselves to one view or another we become vulnerable; our prediction will be refuted if what was said would happen does not happen. A scientific statement is useful to the extent it allows itself to be exposed to a possible refutation. Often the researchers are tempted to express their hypotheses in terms so general and so grandiose in scope that they are simply not amenable to test.

This temptation can be suicidal. The researchers would do well to avoid employing concepts in their hypotheses for which suitable tangible indices have not developed. An hypothesis should include a clear statement of indexes which are to be used. For example, the concept of social class needs to be explicated in terms of such indicators as income, occupation, education, etc. Such specific formulations have the obvious advantage of assuring that research will be practicable and significant. It also helps to increase the validity of the results because more specific the statement or prediction, smaller the probability that it will actually be borne out as a result of mere accident or chance.

(e) Advisedly, the hypotheses should be related to a body of theory or some theoretical orientation. This requirement concerns the theoretic rationale of a hypothesis, i.e., what will be the theoretical gains of testing the hypothesis? If the hypothesis is related to some theory, research will help to qualify, support, correct or refute the theory. A science can become cumulative only through interchange between the existing body of fact and theory.

Will not deriving hypotheses as a rule from some theoretical base throttle ventures into new fields in which no articulate theoretical system has developed? Will not such hypotheses lead to unnecessary repetitions? Doubts of this order may be raised by some. Theses objections do not have much substance since such hypotheses formulate imaginatively, besides serving the function of elaborating, extending and improving the theory, they may also suggest important links between it and certain other theories. Thus, the exercise of deriving hypotheses from a body of theory may also be an occasion of a scientific leap into newer areas of knowledge. As *Parsons* put it, "Theory not only formulates what we know but also tells us what we want to know."[11]

If hypotheses were derived from a body of theory, to that extent it would be possible to formulate them as statements about what will happen, that is, the roots of hypotheses in theory would invest these hypotheses with the power of prediction. One of the valuable attributes of a good hypothesis is its power of prediction. The potency of hypotheses in regard to predictive purposes constitutes a great advancement in scientific knowledge. To quote *Cohen and Nagel,* "... the hypothesis to be preferred is one which can predict what will happen, and from which we can infer what has already happened, even if we did not know (it had happened) when the hypothesis was formulated."[12]

In the example cited earlier, the hypothesis that lower suicide rates should be expected among the Catholics than among the Protestants besides having a predictive potential would also afford by virtue of its theoretical moorings, the basis for saying that married persons or a minority community or a tribal community by virtue of high social cohesion would have lower suicide rates. It is in this sense that a 'good' hypothesis helps us make statements about what is already there or what has already happened although we were not aware of it.

(f) Hypotheses should be related to available techniques. This is, of course, a sensible methodological requirement applicable to any problem when one is judging its research ability. The researcher who does not know what techniques are available to test his hypotheses is in a poor way to formulate usable questions. In other words, the hypotheses should be formulated only after due thought has been given to the methods and techniques that can be used to measure the concepts or variables incorporated in the hypotheses.

This should not mean as implying, however, that formulation of hypotheses which are at a given time too complex to be handled by contemporary technique is a taboo.

We must not forget that if the problem is significant enough as a possible frame of reference, it may be useful regardless of whether or not it is amenable to verification or test by the techniques available at the time. The works of *Marx* and *Durkheim* have been of paramount importance to sociology even though at that time their larger ideas were incapable of being handled by available techniques. Lastly, it would be well to remember that posing of 'impossible' questions may stimulate the growth and innovations in technique. There is no doubt that some amount of impetus to modern developments in technique has come from criticisms against significant studies which were at that time considered inadequate because of limitations of available techniques.

Let us turn to the questions, "How should the researcher ideally formulate hypothesis for research?" *R.L. Ackoff* has attempted to answer this question in a systematic way. As was stated in the previous chapter, all research problems ultimately reduce to the question, which of a set of alternative means is the most efficient one. Once those alternative means are formulated, the researcher is in a position to pose a question of each of the means, as to what may constitute the evidence that this particular means is the most efficient one among the alternatives. The answer to this questions would usually be in the form: "The particular means can be accepted as the most efficient among the alternatives under specific conditions." Such specific conditions should be formulated for each of the alternative means. The statements of these acceptance conditions are the hypotheses. The researcher does not, of course, know which of these alternative hypotheses is true; this is precisely what the research is designed to determine.

Ideally, a researcher should start with trying to determine all the alternative means (solutions of explanations) of coming to grips with his problem. This means that the researcher needs to undertake a 'resource survey' which includes survey of related theories or orientations, which may bring to light what alternative means, solutions or explanations may be applied to the problem. As has already been said, the researcher will attempt to determine which of the alternative course of action or solution or explanation is most efficient in terms of certain criteria, e.g., economy predictability etc. Let us now suppose that a researcher has a problem whose solution depends on certain predictions and the researcher knows that there are three alternative theories (means) which are germane to the problem. Now, if one of the three theories is more likely to predict events more accurately than the other two, it may be taken as the most efficient one as a solution to the problem. If the problem happens to be one dealing with practical or programmatic concerns, the criterion of efficiency of alternative course of action may be economy in the realms, of time, money and energy. The alternative hypotheses which the researcher sets out to formulate are nothing but statement of conditions for each of the alternative means under which conditions, it (each alternative means) may be seen to be the most efficient. Simply stated, the alternative hypotheses are the statements of acceptance conditions for each of the alternative courses of action or alternative solutions to the problem. Suppose the researcher's problem is to decide which of the two types of teaching methods should be recommended for a particular educational institution. The research decides to use, let us say, the student's examination scores as a measure of efficiency (of the means). Then, for each of the alternative teaching methods, his statement of acceptance conditions, i.e., alternative hypotheses, will be as under:

H1: The average examination score produced by teaching method No. 1 is greater than the average test score produced by teaching method No. 2.

H2: The average examination score produced by teaching method No. 2 is greater than that of teaching method No. 1. Therefore recommend Method No. 2 if H2 proves to be correct.

We note here that one possible outcome has not been considered, i.e., the test scores are equal for both teaching methods (No. 1 and No. 2). Now, if the test scores were really equal, i.e., if both methods were equally efficient, the researcher will have no course of action to select for recommendation, consequently, he may have to add another course of action.

It is clear now that formulation of alternative hypotheses involves the following steps:

(1) A measure of efficiency applicable to all the alternative courses of action is selected (Examination Score: sales, productivity etc.)
(2) On the basis of this selected measure of efficiency a set of acceptance conditions for each alternative course of action is assigned.
(3) The acceptance conditions are reformulated as hypotheses which are mutually exclusive and jointly exhaustive.

In all research (theoretical or action oriented) alternative courses of action (solutions, explanations) acceptance conditions (economy, predictions etc.) or hypotheses should be made explicit. In fact, if the acceptance of one set of alternative hypotheses rather than another would make no difference whatsoever to subsequent behaviour (scientific or practical) then the problem or its formulation is scientifically meaningless.

It is obvious that there is no scientific way of selecting one of the alternative hypotheses as valid save when there is some index of efficiency which can be applied to each of the alternative courses of action. The applicability of the measure of efficiency to alternative course of action depends on certain conditions holding. For example, in our illustration of the alternative methods of teaching, the use of examination score as a measure of efficiency may be suitable only if each student is allowed an equal period to complete the common test. Such conditions constitute the points of agreement among the hypotheses. These points of agreement among the hypotheses are either known or assumed to be valid. Should such an assumption be made, the researcher must make it explicit.

If the researcher sets up two hypotheses, there must be at least one point of agreement among them and one point of variance or disagreement. These alternative hypotheses may be represented symbolically as under:

H1 – MN1

H2 – MN2

H3 – MN3

H4 – MN4

The alternative hypotheses should encompass all possible outcomes of research, that is they should be exhaustive with respect to the points of disagreement which will be tested. Secondly, of course, the hypotheses should be mutually exclusive. Failing these two requirements, research will not indicate which one course of action or solution should be selected from among the entire range of possibilities represented by the alternative hypotheses.

A very effective way of assuring ourselves that the hypotheses are mutually exclusive and jointly exhaustive of the universe of possibilities is to use the logical technique known as the "*Boolean expansion.*" Suppose we have one common point of agreement (M) among the later native hypotheses and three points of disagreement (e.g., N, O and P), then the alternative hypotheses according to the requirements of exhaustiveness and mutual exclusion could be presented as under. The common point of agreement among these hypotheses may be the examination score under specific conditions. Thus, M = Examination score. The points of difference may be N = more than x; N' = less than x; similarly O = more than y, O' = less than y and P = more than z, p' = less than z.

(Read H4 as Examination score is more than x and y but less than z.)

H1	–	MNOP	H5	–	Mn'OP'
H2	–	MN'Op	H6	–	MN'OP'
H3	–	MNO'P	H7	–	MNO'P'
H4	–	MNOP'	H8	–	MNO'P'

In general, if there are in points of disagreement, there will be 2 n (2 x 2 x 2 x 2.n times) alternative hypotheses in an exclusive classification. Only one of them can be true and must be true.

In a research involving more than two hypotheses, it is advisable to formulate the points of disagreement symbolically in a manner indicated to facilitate the construction of hypotheses. Intuition is often not a satisfactory guide.

It was suggested earlier that ideally there should be one hypothesis for each alternative course of action. Such a problem is one which involves estimation, e.g., estimating an optimum number of workers for a production unit — 100, 250, 300 etc. The selection of the most efficient course of action depends on an estimate of the value of a critical variable (i.e., the exact number of workers) in such cases, it is not economical to formulate explicitly each alterative course of action and to associate a hypothesis with respect to each. We can use only a shorthand formulation. The alternate hypothesis can simply be stated as: "K workers are needed" and the problem of research is to estimate this K. Now, since the estimate of the value of any variable is subject to error, it is advisable to express the estimate as a range of values rather than a single value, e.g., 300 = 50 workers (250 to 350) are needed.

We may now introduce the readers to the concept of *null hypothesis.* The alternative hypotheses and the null hypotheses together constitute the framework for the statistical testing of hypotheses. Fuller significance of null hypothesis can be grasped by the students at later stage.* Suffice it here to say that the null hypothesis in its simplest form asserts that there is no difference between two populations in respect of some property and that the difference found between the sample drawn from these populations is only accidental and unimportant. H. E. *Garrett* remarks: "The null hypothesis is akin to the legal principle that a man is innocent until he is proved guilty. It constitutes a challenge and the function of a (research) is to give facts a chance to refute this challenge."[14] A null hypothesis in its other form may assert that the results found in research do not differ significantly from the results to be expected on a probability basis or as stipulated in terms of a certain theory. An alternative hypothesis may state, for instance, that:

H1: The females commit suicide more often than the males.

The null hypothesis (Ho) may be stated as:

Ho: The females and males do not differ in respect of the rate of suicide.

A null hypothesis is decidedly more useful than other hypotheses because it is exact. It is easier to disprove the contrary of an hypothesis than to prove it with complete certainty. In other words, while a hypothesis cannot be shown to be true without factual consequences, it may be falsified conclusively if the expected consequences fail to occur. This enables the researcher to eliminate some of the alternative hypotheses and while this does not finally establish the one he thinks to be true, he can never be sure that he has identified and eliminated all the alternatives; still his confidence in it will grow if it continues unrefuted. It might also be the case that it cannot possibly be refuted, but in this case it would not be of much practical use. According to *Karl Popper,* the real basis of science is the possibility of empirical disproof. No amount of positive confirmation of the hypothesis, in Popper's view, entails its truth. One can only say tat certain statement are definitely incorrect. Besides, the statistical techniques available to us are better adapted to test a *null hypothesis*.

REFERENCES

(1) Lundberg: *op. cit.,* p. 119.

(2) cf. Selltiz, *et al.: op. cit.,* p. 38.

(3) Werkmeister, W. H.: *Basis and Structure of Knowledge,* Harper and Bros., New York, 1948, p. 300.

(4) Thompson: *op. cit.,* p. 49.

(5) Chaddock, R.E.: *Principles and Methods of Statistics,* Houghton Mifflin Co., New York, 1925, p. 372.

(6) See Goode, W.G., and Hatt, P.K: *op. cit.,* p. 73.

(7) Dubin, Robert: *Theory Building,* Free Press, N.Y., 1969, pp. 211-2.

(8) See Merton, R.K.: *op. cit.,* p. 33.

(9) Larrabee: *op. cit.,* p. 172.

(10) Cohen and Nagel: *op. cit.,* p. 207.

(11) Parsons, T : *The Structure of Social Action,* Vol. 1 Free Press, New York, 1962, p. 9.

(12) Cohen, and Nagel: *op. cit.,* p. 207.

(13) Ackoff: *op. cit.,* pp. 27-46.

*The students are advised to refer chapters on hypotheses and testing of hypotheses in Ackoff, R.L.: *Design of Social Research.*

(14) Garrett, H.E.: *Statistics in Psychology and Education,* Vakils, Feffer and Simons Ltd., Mumbai, 1967, p. 212.

Chapter VI

Concepts — their Role in Scientific Investigation and Development of Science

The aim of science is comprehension as complete as possible of the connections between sense experiences in their totality and "the accomplishment of this aim by the use of a minimum of concepts...."[1] A concept is an abstraction of observed things, events or phenomena. *McClelland* defines the term concept, as "a short-hand representation of a variety of facts. Its purpose is to simplify thinking by subsuming a number of events under one general heading."[2] Wherever any degree of abstraction is involved, whether in sophisticated scientific observation, in interpretative understanding or in the simple commonsense statements of fact, concepts are always used. *Talcott Parsons* rightly remarks: ".... There is no empirical knowledge which is not in some sense and to some degree conceptually formed."[3]

Science is based on facts, i.e., such propositions as are supported by material evidence. Science not only observes them but is charged with the responsibility of stating them. For stating such aspects as constitute the subject-matter of a particular discipline, the science must have some terms. As we have just suggested, the terms having a reference to things about which a science tries to make sense are its concepts. *Abraham Kaplan* has put the matter succinctly. He says: "The important terms of any science are significant because of their semantics (they) reach out to the world which gives the science its subject-matter. The meaning of such terms results from a process of conceptualization of the subject-matter. In this process, the things studied are classified and analyzed; several things are grouped together and particular things assigned to the several groups to which they belong. The concept 'paranoid', for example, puts into a single class certain set of persons and is itself analysed into such patterns as delusions of persecution, grouping together a set of actions, verbal or otherwise, as the case may be, and without regard to the actors performing them."[4]

The language of science evolves in order to deal with the problems of its concern for which the ordinary language has proved inadequate. Each science thus develops and utilizes certain concepts in order that it may be able to pose a range of significant problems for investigation, conduct empirical observation, organize its data to provide answers to the problems and to communicate its findings. Of course, science employs as stated at the outset, *the Occam's razor,* the principle of *parsimony,* in its language. The rule of scientific analysis is, 'as few concepts as you dare and as many as you must.' The principle decrees that science should attempt to explain all its phenomena in the most economical way, employing as few terms, concepts, symbols or formulae as possible. The process of scientific investigation comprises, what to the investigator may appear to be flashes of insight, glimpses or conditions between things or events and awareness of distinctions and differences. In order to be retained, these have to be symbolized (as concepts) if they do not initially occur in an already symbolized state. The ultimate goal of scientific investigations may be said to be the establishment of general theories which are indeed the larger conceptual schemes at a higher level of generality or abstraction.

To reach this level of theorizing or conceptualization, the investigator needs to conduct his empirical observations and to analyse these observations in a particular conceptual framework at the lower levels. In sum, scientific enquiry involves understanding the relationship among various concepts which symbolize objects, events, properties etc. that constitute the subject-matter of a given discipline. Concepts are needed to formulate the problem and to design ways of solving it.

It is our experience that some concepts are quite close to the objects or facts they represent. For example, the meaning of the concepts 'Man' may be easily clarified by pointing to specific men. The concept is an abstraction of the characteristics all men have in common; characteristics that are either directly observable or easily ascertained or measured. Other concepts cannot, however, be so easily related to the facts or phenomena which they are intended or represent; motivation, need-disposition, attitude, role, adjustment, commitment etc. widely used by social scientists are concepts of this kind. They are inferences, at a higher level of abstraction, from concrete events and their meaning cannot be easily conveyed by pointing to specific concrete objects, individuals or events. The greater the distance between the concepts used in a study and empirical facts which they are intended to refer to, greater the possibility of their being misunderstood and thus greater the care that must be exercised in defining them precisely. The social sciences have, admittedly fallen by the way at this greatest hurdle of them all, viz., the exact definition of constructs.

A precise definition or explication of concepts being utilized by the researcher is a natural and sensible methodological requirement for any study. In one's own private world, it would hardly matter what one means by what. This personal idiosyncratic vocabulary which perhaps serves him alright as long as he is conversant with it, may keep things going. But in the world of the scientists, it would be disastrous if one's concepts did not mean the same thing to other as they meant to scientist himself. It would create serious problems of communication and correspondence among scientists (as also between scientists and common citizens) and affect the cumulative and integrated growth of knowledge adversely, if the same concept was used by different scientists in different senses or different concepts were used to describe really similar and indistinguishable entities or phenomena. This would create, as one can easily visualize, confusion worst confounded. Such a confusion does unfortunately exist in the larger domain of the social sciences which have borrowed a majority of the words from current popular terminology, even though the meaning attached to them have been sharpened or adapted to serve their more exacting use.

It should now be plain why the need for a clear-cut definition of concepts utilized by the scientist at various stages in his research has been laid so much stress on. *Explication* refers to the process of making explicit what is implicit in the concepts. In the absence of explication of concepts, others would not know what one is talking about, let alone whether he is talking sense. *Ackoff* aptly states, "the function of a scientific definition of a concept is to make explicit the conditions under which and the operations by which we can answer questions about that which is conceptualized."[5] Scientific requirement calls for explication of concepts at two levels.

(1) The concepts must be defined in abstract terms, giving the general meaning they are intended to convey. This may be called the 'formal definition.' Such a definition is designed to convey the general nature of the process or phenomenon in which the scientist is interested. And as suggested above, (2) the concepts must be defined in terms of the operations by which they will be represented in particular research. Such a definition is known as the 'operational definition' (sometimes, called the 'working definition') of the concept. Such definitions are designed to make possible the collection of data which the scientist or researcher is prepared to accept as the indicators or empirical referents of his concept.

Let us discuss each of the two types of definitions at some length.

At first glance, providing unambiguous formal definition for the concepts might appear to be a very simple task. Such may be the case in respect of certain standardized concepts that are in scientific currency. But formal definition usually present a host of difficulties of the kind Durkheim experienced. As *John Madge* [6] points out, Durkheim chose the topic 'suicide' for his study as it ('suicide') could be easily defined. Although he started by asserting that defining 'suicide' was fairly easy, almost at once, he experienced formidable difficulties. For example, if a man is so unhappy that he refuses to eat and wastes away, will this amount to suicide or an illness of some kind or, when soldiers march into battle in circumstances under which they are certain to be killed, would that be suicide? In formulating a definition, it is not always possible to be certain about whether to include particular instances. *Durkheim* after many years of examination of these different considerations, started with a preliminary definition. Subsequently, he found out its inadequacy and kept on modifying it. His first definition was formulated thus: " The term suicide is applied to any death which is the direct or indirect result of a positive or negative act accomplished by the victim himself." But again Durkheim realized that his definition neglected one important feature: namely, that suicide should be an intended act. He therefore arrived at the following subsequent definition:

"Suicide is applied to all cases of death resulting directly or indirectly by a positive or negative act of the victim himself which he knows will produce this result." This definition of suicide is recognizable and augurs fairly well with the reckoning by which official suicide statistics are kept. The above example drives home the point that it is usually not so easy to define a concept formally.

Let us now turn to a very simple case. Suppose we were interested in getting an answer to a 'simple' question in a housing survey. "How many people live in your house?" A moment's consideration makes us realize that we will be concerned with a variety of such questions — should a son who is away at college most of the time during the year be included among those living in the house? Should a boarder who travels during the week and is in his room only on week-ends be included? Should the maid who sleeps in three or four nights and spends the others at her family home be included? Theses questions amply testify to the difficulties one could come across in the course of providing formal definitions to concepts.

Lack of clarity in meanings of many psychological and sociological concepts is considerable since, understandably, the nature of the language of science depends on its methods of observation. Says *Theobald,* "An investigator whose methods are limited to unaided perception will present his observation in the common descriptive language which will not have critical precision. On the other hand, the indirect method of observation will require precise abstract language to present its case."[7]

We shall here discuss the procedure required if adequate standardized formulation is not available. Comparing the definitions of a concept offered at different times in the history of science or different definitions offered at the same time, we generally find that there is a common core of meaning which runs through all the definitions. The meaning toward which various definitions of the concept point is the true meaning of the concept. Some scientists advocate looking for a definition with which most scientists would agree, but if this were to become a general rule there would be little progress in defining. We should, of course, seek to improve upon the definitions but improvement is possible only by taking the past and present definitions into account. The following procedure has proved very useful in arriving at better definitions of conepts.[8]

(a) Examine as many definitions of the concept, past and present, as possible. Keep chronology of the definitions in mind.

(b) Try to get at the core of the meaning toward which most of the definitions seem to point.

(c) Formulate a tentative definition based on the 'core.'

(d) See if the tentative definition covers all the cases you think it should, relative to your research objectives; where it does not, make necessary revisions.

(e) Submit the definition to as wide a critical appraisal as possible. Include scientists as well as non-scientists from various fields among the critics.

(f) Make final revisions on the basis of the legitimate criticisms you receive.

It was stated earlier that formal definitions of concepts entering the scientific corpus of a discipline are not enough. In addition, quite often the researcher-scientist needs to offer an *'operational definition'* to the concepts. To this point we now turn.

The operational definition of a concept purports to specify the operations which observe, measure and record the phenomena symbolized by the concept.

Thus, the scores on a particular scale for measuring I.Q. may be said to be the operational definition of the concept 'intelligence.' *Samuel Stouffer,* the director of the 'American Soldier Studies', defined the crucial concept *'personal adjustment'* operationally as under: ".... It is assumed that, on the average, men who said they were in good spirits, that they were more useful in the army than the civilians, that they liked the Army, were better adjusted to the Army than men who were negative in several of those expressions."[9]

Bradburn tried to define operationally, the elusive concept of 'Happiness.' He states "one way to find out whether people are happy is to ask them. "Respondents were accordingly asked to answer the following question: Taking all things together, how would you say things are these days — would you say, you are very happy or not too happy."[10]

Now that the nature of operational definitions has been exemplified, the reader should be able to appreciate their value in scientific research. The operational definitions afford an understanding of the 'true meaning' of the concept. "The true meaning says professor *Bridgman* the inventor of operational definitions, "is to be found by observing what a man does with it, not by what he says about it."[11] What is important for us to know is what the researcher assumes to be the empirical indicators of his concept. This is what really matters. No word has meaning if the circumstances under which it is used are not specified. A concept, on this view, is synonymous with the corresponding set of operations. What the researcher says social cohesion is, cannot be regarded as being of much consequence; how he goes about assessing the degrees of social cohesion through the use of certain instruments is what constitutes the true meaning of social cohesion for purposes of his research. Thus operational definitions insist on meaning in deed and not in words.

Dodd, in the *Dictionary of Social Science,* states: "A definition is an operational definition to the extent that the definer (a) specifies the procedure (including materials used) for identifying or generating the definiendum and (b) finds high reliability or (consistency in application of) his definition." In short, as *Bachrach* says, "the operational definition of a dish ... is its receipe."[12]

Among sociologists for instance, operational definitions have been postulated by *Chapin, Lundberg, Alpert* and *Kirkpatrick.* In Alpert's words, no definitions have any meaning apart from the methods which have been employed. Says *Lundberg,* on the basis of such premises, "space is that which is measured with a ruler, time is that which is measured by a clock, force is that which makes pointers move across the dial."[13]

Very useful as these operations often are, we must constantly remind ourselves that an undue emphasis on such definitions is likely to defeat the ultimate purpose of social science research. Sociologists do not seem to be agreed among themselves about the importance of operational definitions. The critics have justly opined that a concept does not merely mean a set of operations. The operations are simply the techniques one has to use in order to get at and measure something behind these operations and the phenomenon itself. An operational definition is best applied to uncomplex concepts such as time, temperature etc., but not to such complex ones as social cohesion, morale, love, anxiety etc. It can without doubt offer a high level of precision when applied to uncomplex concepts. But it fails us just when we are in most need of clarity.

The crux of the matter with reference to operational definitions is that we do not say we are measuring unless we know what we are doing, that is, unless we know both how to get the numbers and what the numbers stand for. A set of numbers, operationally generated, means nothing unless it is taken as indicating a relationship between aspects of the world which in their theoretic setting are concepts.

One cannot maintain that the concept is just a set of operations, because sometimes a situation arises in which one has a perfectly clear concept and is trying to discover an operation whereby to measure its values; there are as yet no operation, although there certainly is a concept.

It would, however be a wrong attitude to scale down operational definitions, for the social science also depends on empirical confirmation which is best obtained by operational definitions.

After all our best efforts to reduce qualities into quantities through operationalization, the qualities essentially remain qualities and the magic of quantification does not change their innate texture.

Blummer rightly states that "the vagueness of a concept is equivalent to a difficulty in observing clearly a thing to which the concept is presumed to refer to, indeed this difficulty of knowing what to observe, being able to observe it and knowing how to observe it, is the crucial obstacle in bringing the concept into touch with experience."[14]

At the present stage of social sciences, we find a compromise between these positions. We may deal with the problem more easily by remembering that the concept is a set of directions. It directs the communicant to a particular kind of experience, one which to some extent has been shared. If it does not do so, communication becomes hazardous. Thus whether the concept is defined in a purely formal manner or in an operational manner, the definition turns our attention to this experience.

REFERENCES

(1) Einstein: cf. Gupta: *op. cit.*

(2) Cf. Selltiz, *et al., op. cit.*, p. 41.

(3) Parsons: *op. cit.*, p. 28.

(4) Kaplan, Abraham: *The Conduct of Inquiry,* Chandler Publishing Co., San Francisco, 1964, p. 50.

(5) Ackoff: *op. cit.*, p. 55.

(6) Madge, John: *Origins of Scientific Sociology,* Free Press, Paper-back, The MacMillian Co., pp. 16-18.

(7) Theobald: *op. cit.*, p. 18.

(8) See Ackoff: *op. cit.*

(9) Stouffer, *et al.*, cf. Simon, Julian: *Basic Research Methods in Social Science,* Random House, N., 1968, p. 17.

(10) Cf. *Ibid.*, p. 17.

(11) Cf. Madge, John: *The Tools of Social Science,* Longmans, London, 1965, p. 49.

(12) *Ibid.*, p. 20.

(13) Lundberg, George: "The Thoughtways of Contemporary Sociology," *American Sociological Review,* 1963, pp. 710-11.

(14) Blummer, H.: *Social Science Research Council Bulletin,* No. 44, New York, 1939.

Chapter VII

The Design of Research

In the course of the present chapter we shall be concerned with the problems of how the various phases of research can be brought under control. The problem of control can be handled by 'designing' the research. Let us therefore approach the meaning of 'design' and understand what all is involved in 'designing.'

An architect is said to 'design' a building. In the process of 'designing' he considers each decision that is required to be made in constructing the building. Bearing well in mind the purpose for which the building is to be used, the architect takes decisions, such as, how large the building will be, how many rooms it will have, how these rooms will be approached, what building materials will be used and so on. The designer engages himself in such decision-making well before the actual construction begins. He proceeds in this manner because he wants to get a picture of the whole before starting the construction of a part. This picture helps him to visualize clearly the difficulties and inconveniences that users of the building would face when the building would come up according to the plan. On the basis of this paper-picture, he can effect corrections or modification and make improvements before the actual commencement of construction. It is obvious that the building may inhere many defects and engender many inconveniences for its users and thus the very purpose for which it is to be constructed may be defeated if careful thought was not given to the matter at the 'designing' stage. The professional architects in India often complain, indeed with justification, that people often think it an unnessary wastage of funds to hire the services of architects. They would better 'utilize' this fund for adding a few more rooms to their building. More often than not, the self-styled architects realize almost immediately that their 'economy' in terms of saving of the fees of a professional architect was misplaced or misconstrued and that it would now cost them a lot more for now they would be required to make drastic modifications to remove the inconviences that they had not paused to anticipate. Despite this unnecessary and avoidable expense of money, time and energy, they are lucky who can really 'save' the worth of the building.

Designing by forewarning us about the future difficulties ensures against wasteful expenditure of money, time and energy, so to we can be armed against them in good time. To design is to plan, that is designing is the process of making decisions before the situation actually arises in which the decision has to be carried out. Designing is thus a process of deliberate anticipation directed toward bringing an expected situation under control.

The lesson we have learnt from the foregoing discussion applies with equal force to any research. If we anticipate before we conduct a research inquiry, the various difficulties that may have to be encountered in the course of this exercise and decide what to do about these, then, we increase to that extent our chances of rationally controlling and articulating the research procedure and forestalling the possibilities of failure.

The research designer understandably cannot hold all his decisions in his head. Even if he could, he would have difficulty in understanding how these are interrelated. Therefore, he records his decisions on paper or record disc by using relevant symbols or concepts. Such a symbolic construction may be called the research design or model. The model makes possible an overall evaluation of the total plan. It is on this basis that the researcher can appreciate the whole study structure as also the operations, the place and importance of the successive steps that he will be required to take in the total scheme.

The research design results, as said earlier, from certain decisions taken and ordered in a certain sequence by the scientist. The major design decisions are in reference to the following aspects:

(a) What the study is about and what are the types of data needed?

(b) Why the study is being made?

(c) Where the data needed, can be found?

(d) Where or in what area the study will be carried out?

(e) What periods of time the study will include?

(f) How much material or how many cases will be needed?

(g) What bases will be used for selection of cases?

(h) What techniques of gathering data will be adopted?

(i) How will the data be analysed?

(j) How best can these above questions be decided upon and decisions articulated in a manner that research purpose will be achieved with minimum expenditure of money, time and energy?

As *Selltiz, Jahoda, Destsch and Cook* describe, "A research design is the arrangement of conditions for collection and analysis of data in a manner that aims to combine relevance to the research purpose with economy of procedure."[1]

The decisions in respect of the data to be collected, the sample to be selected, the manner in which the collected data are to be organized etc., which constitute the trunk of the research design, must be based on good grounds. In the interest of science, the design decisions must be based on an accepted methodology. The researcher must investigate or make investigable the method of making design - decisions. To the extent he does it, he is methodologically designing the researchre. It must be remembered, however that no inquiry is completely methodological just as none can be completely unmethodogical. Researchers vary between these two extremes. A completely methodological design is a scientific ideal which the researcher may never attain but which he is obliged to constantly try approximating.

Let us now turn to consider the need for methodologically designed research.

(1) In many a research inquiry, the researcher has no idea as to how accurate the results of his study ought to be in order to be useful. Where such is the case, the researcher has to determine how much inaccuracy may be tolerated. In quite a few cases he may be in a position to know how much inaccuracy his method of research will produce. In either case he should design his research if he wants to assure himself of useful results. A researcher gets into trouble not only when he fails to obtain results which are accurate enough but also when he gets results that are much too accurate. If the required degree of accuracy can be obtained with little trouble, and greater accuracy only with very great difficulty, then the researcher would only be wasting time, efforts and funds in working for greater accuracy.

(2) In many research projects, the time consumed in trying to ascertain what the data mean after they have been collected is much greater than the time taken to design a research which yields data whose meaning is known as they are collected. Modern research suffers a great deal from a 'lust' for fresh data. Researchers rush off to collect data without a concern for what they mean until they are collected. At this stage it is often very late to improve upon them. It is true that in some cases the delay produced by research-planning may result in obtaining stale data. But it should be remembered that failure to plan a research may produce more inaccuracy than designed research project run later. For example, suppose the researcher rushes to make observations before he has

developed adequate instruments. The errors produced by his inferior instruments may be greater than the degree of inaccuracy he would have obtained had he waited to develop better instruments even at the obvious risk of his data getting a bit stale.

(3) A scientist owes certain obligations to the institution of science. His right to the title 'scientist' rests in part on his ability to develop better and still better ways of inquiring. This is true of all sciences but particularly so, of social sciences today. The hope of any future for sciences of society may well depend on the extent to which the social scientists demonstrate how major social problems can be solved effectively in a scientific way. The scientist cannot afford to remain complacent with his methods. As a scientist he is obliged to question each and every phase of his method, opening up in effect, the possibilities of continuous improvement. He cannot wait for lucky discovery to improve his methods. He must improve upon them and take what luck has to offer as a bonus.

Once the research problem is formulated in clearcut terms, the researcher is in a position to consider how he will try to solve it. The first step toward obtaining a solution should advisedly be in the nature of designing an ideal research procedure; that is, the procedure the researcher would have liked to adopt for solving a problem if he was completely unrestricted by practical exigencies and limitations. This is the idealized research design. *Ackoff* defines the idealized research design thus: "The idealized research design is concerned with specifying the optimum research procedure that could be followed were there no practical restrictions."[2]

At first glance, such a step, i.e., of designing an idealized plan, might seem very impracticable and even an unnecessary one. The researcher may be inclined to ask why he should bother himself with procedures that cannot be carried out. Why dream idly of realizing an ideal almost impossible of attainment? The answer to this can be that concern with ideal or optimum research conditions is neither idle dreaming nor wishful thinking. It is really important, if we want to know how good the results are that we would eventually obtain. The ideal conditions and procedures act as a standard by reference to which we can evaluate the practical research conditions and determine their shortcomings. If these shortcomings are made explicit, it is possible in many a case to determine their effects on the observed results and thus to adjust the results with a view to minimizing the effects of the shortcomings.

The use of idealized research model or the research standard for adjustment of actual data is common throughout the sciences. For example, the ideal model for determining the acceleration of freely falling bodies requires a perfect vacuum in which the bodies could fall with complete freedom. But in actual practice, the physicist can never create a perfect vacuum. Still he can conduct his experiment in such a way that he can determine how a body would fall if it were in a perfect vacuum. He determines how acceleration is affected by variations in atmospheric pressure. He calculates the relation between the changes in the atmospheric pressure and changes in acceleration. On this basis, he determines what would occur in a complete vacuum and can thus infer the acceleration of freely falling bodies. The idealized research design then, comprises the specifications of the most efficient conceivable conditions and procedures for conducting the research. But the procedures and conditions specified in the idealized research model can seldom if ever be met in practice.

The next design-job for the researcher is to translate the idealized research model into a practical one. The practical research design has a reference to the translation of idealized design into a realizable working procedure. The practical research design is necessary because certain factors do keep the researcher from meeting the idealized conditions. In a concrete research situation, practicality may impose many restrictions on the researcher's activities. The number of subjects or events he may ideally want to study may be much larger than his time, money and energy would allow. In such a case, he can only observe a portion of the whole population or converse. Once this restriction is imposed, the use of statistics of sampling becomes necessary. Hence, the translation of the ideal model into a statistical model is a necessary step for the actual conduct of research.

Even where there is only one subject, event or property to be observed, the researcher is aware of the fact that his observations are always subject to error and he will thus need more than one observation for each set of variable-values. He would like to make an infinite number of observations of some single subject. This is obviously impossible. Hence, he must deal with *a sample* of the possible observations. Thus, sampling possible observations requires a translation of the idealized model into a practical statistical model.

Even if situations existed in which the researcher could make an infinite number of observations on each subject, it might be wasteful to do so. He may not even need the degree of accuracy that such a large number of observations would yield. Therefore, if he wants to do just as much work as is necessary to get the degree of accuracy he requires, he will again want to use only a sample of the possible observations, which means that he will render a statistical translation of the idealized research model.

In many social situations, manipulation of the totality of variables involved is not possible, hence research must be conducted in situations which differ from the idealized one. Thus, we must determine how we can infer from the result obtained in some real concrete situation what we might observe if we had managed to produce the ideal situation. This requires that we make explicit the kind of real situation we will look for, how we will characterize it and how we will adjust the results observed so that assertions about the idealized situation can be made. This too will require the statistical translation of the idealized research design and formulation of the research operations to be actually performed.

The practical research design may be conceived of as comprising the following four phases :

(a) *the sampling design,* which deals with the method of selecting the subjects or evetents to be observed for the given study.

(b) *the observational design,* which relates to the conditions under which the observations are to be made or the data are the secured.

(c) *the statistical design,* deals with the question of how many subjects are to be observed and how the observations are to be organized with a view to securing answers to the research problem.

(d) *the operational design,* which deals with the specific techniques by which the procedures specified in the sampling, statistical and observational designs can be carried out smoothly. In other words, the operational design deals with the administration research project.

It must be remembered that none of these sub-designs and the resultant models is autonomous *vis-à-vis* the others. A decision in respect of any phase of the design may influence or affect a decision subsumed under any other phase. Consequently, these phases generally overlap.

As should be clear now, that the practical research design represents a compromise prompted by a number of practical considerations that are related to the actual conduct of social research. As *E. A. Schuman* puts it thus, "Research design is not a highly specific plan to be followed without deviations but rather a series of guide-posts to keep one headed in the right direction."[3]

Research designs differ depending on the research purpose just as the plan of a building would depended upon the purpose for which it is intended to be used. The research purpose may be grouped broadly under the following four broad categories :

(a) To gain familiarity with the phenomenon or to achieve new insights into it, often in order to formulate more precise research problem or to develop hypotheses. Studies having this type of a purpose are known generally as *Exploratory or Formulative studies.*

(b) To portray accurately the characteristics of a particular situation or group or individual (with or without specific initial hypotheses about the nature of these characteristics). Studies characterised by such aims are known as *Descriptive studies.*

(c) To determine the frequency with which something occurs or with which it is associated with something else (usually but not necessarily, with a specific initial hypothesis). Studies having this type of purpose are known as *Diagnostic studies.*

(d) To test a hypothesis suggesting a causal relationship between variables. Studies characterised by this purpose are called, *Experimental studies.*

It must be remembered that a fixed typology of the studies suggested above is inevitably arbitrary in as much as the different types of studies are not absolutely separable from one another and therefore, for purpose of classification, the 'major intent' of each becomes the basis for assigning them to different categories. In this connection it needs to be recognized that the development of knowledge rarely progresses in a direct step-wise manner. Each step forward in the resolution of a problematic situation is, at the same time, a step in the direction of posing new questions and of reformulating older ones. As *Max Weber* has said: "Every scientific fulfillment raises new questions it asks to be surpassed and outdated."[4]

In the formulative or exploratory studies the premium is on discovery of ideas and insights. Therefore, the research design corresponding to such studies must have enough flexibility to permit consideration of different aspects of a phenomenon.

In the descriptive and diagnostic studies, the major concern is with accuracy. Hence, the research design for such studies must be such that the bias will be minimized and the reliability of the evidence collected maximized (we shall have occasion to consider 'bias' and 'reliability' in a later chapter). These two studies, namely, descriptive and diagnostic, though somewhat different in their aims, present similar requirements with respect to the research design.

Studies which aim at testing causal hypotheses, i.e., the experimental studies, require procedures that will not only minimize bias and increase reliability but also permit inference about causality. Experiments are particularly suited to this end.

In practice, however, these different types of studies or researches are not always sharply separable. Any given research may have in it elements of two or more types of the functions we have described above. In a single study, however, the primary emphasis is usually on only one of these functions and the study can be thought of as falling into the category corresponding to the major function aimed at.

Design for Exploratory or Formulative Studies

Exploratory studies have, in the main, the purpose of formulating a problem for more precise and structured investigation or of developing hypotheses. An exploratory study may, however, have other functions too, e.g., increasing the investigator's familiarity with the phenomena he wishes to study in a subsequent, more structured investigation or with the setting in which he plans to carry out such an investigation. An exploratory study may also serve as a basis for clarifying concepts, establishing priorities for further research, gathering information about practical possibilities for carrying out research, data gathering in research in specific real-life setting, etc. "Exploratory studies," says *Katz,* "represent the earlier stage of science." From its findings may emanate the knowledge that helps the research in formulating a problem for research or in developing hypotheses to be tested subsequently.

Let us try to understand to some satisfactory extent the nature of an exploratory study by an analogy. A doctor who is called upon to attend to a patient whose malady he is totally unfamiliar with, will ask him various questions concerning his complaints, will examine the various parts of the patient's body using different instrument at his disposal and peruse the patient's pathological reports or records (if any) and so on. On the basis of this exploration, the doctor may find himself in a position to pose a question like, "could it be typhoid?" One of his hypotheses relating to the above question may be, 'it is typhoid.' The doctor's subsequent treatment in the nature of antibiotics will constitute a test of the hypothesis. If the patient responds favourably to the treatment there is room for believing that the typhoid hypothesis is tenable. If the post-treatment observations suggest unfavourable response, the typhoid hypothesis is falsified. Such a test of hypothesis does not belong to the realm of exploratory studies.

The above example illustrates the nature of an exploratory study and also how it differs from the problem-solving and hypothesis testing studies. In the initial stage when the doctor was asking the patient all manner of questions and was examining him, using various instruments and scrutinizing various reports, the doctor was simply exploring, i.e., conducting some sort of an exploration study. The end-result of this exploration was the question (problem) that suggested itself to him.

After this phase of exploration, the doctor proceeded to test his proposed hypothesis by resorting to a more controlled or structured method of investigation. This second phase was the hypothesis testing phase of the inquiry. The exploratory study may thus be considered an earlier step consisting in problem finding or hypothesis formulation, to be followed by other steps aimed at problem-solving or hypothesis-testing, on a continuum of research processes. The flexible nature of the research design characteristic of exploratory studies should be clear from the above example. The doctor's questions to the patient were neither pre-determined nor was his use of certain instruments. The doctor was continually accommodating newer facts as they were becoming known to him, changing in effect, his tentative and formative idea about the nature of disease from time to time till finally he could put forth his tentative diagnosis (hypothesis).

The relative youth of social science and researches in the realm of social science make it inevitable that much of social science research, for a time to come, will be of an exploratory nature. Few well-trodden paths exist for the investigator of social life to follow. Most existing theories in social sciences are either too general or too specific to provide any clear guidance for empirical research. Under the circumstances, exploratory research is necessary to obtain experience that will be helpful, in formulating worthwhile hypothesis for more definitive investigations. For a general area of problems about which little knowledge is available and a general state of ignorance prevails, an exploratory study is most appropriate.

Quite often we see a tendency to undermine the importance of exploratory research and to regard only experimental research as more scientific. But if experimental work is to have any theoretical or practical value, it must be relevant to issues that are much more broader than those posed in the concrete confines of the experiment. Such relevance can result only from adequate explorations of the dimensions of the problem with which the research it attempting to solve.

Path-breaking explorations or formulative researches are particularly complex affairs. One starts from a scratch, without guide-posts or yard sticks. Any intellectual framework and categories within which to classify, what one sees, are absent. The researcher's only resource is whatever concepts he can borrow from other fields or from the common language. He needs to create his own guide-post and scheme of classification. He must decide what to look for, and what to ignore, what to record and what not, which clues to follow and which to abandon, what is of consequence and what is trivial. The explorer has great freedom but the same can so often be terrifying.

We have already noted that more appropriately the exploratory study should be considered an initial step in a continuous research process rather than an exercise in isolation. The most difficult phase in an inquiry as we have had an occasion to see, is its initiation. The most careful methods during the later stages of enquiry are of little worth if an incorrect or irrelevant start was made. Adequate exploration ensures against such an eventuality. *Selltiz, Jahoda, Deutsch and Cook*[5] suggest that the following methods are likely to be very fruitful in exploratory research directed toward the search for meaningful hypotheses.

(a) A review of related social science and other pertinent literature.

(b) A survey of people who have had practical experience of the broad problem area to be investigated.

Most exploratory researches utilize these methods. These methods to be used must, of course, be flexible. As the initial vaguely defined problem gets transformed gradually into one with more precise meaning and reference, frequent changes in the research procedures become necessary in order to provide for the gathering of data relevant to the evolving hypothesis.

Survey of Literature

Frequently, an exploratory study is concerned with an area of subject-matter in which explicit hypotheses have not yet been formulated. The researcher's task then is to review the available material with an eye on the possibilities of developing hypotheses from it. In some areas of the subject-matter, hypotheses may have been stated by previous research workers. The researcher has to take stock of these various hypotheses with a view to evaluating their usefulness for further research and to consider whether they suggest any new hypotheses. A researcher working in the field of sociology will find that such publications as the Sociological Journals, Economic Reviews, the Bulletin of Abstracts of Current Social Science Research, Directory of doctoral dissertations accepted by Universities, etc. afford a rich store of valuable clues. In addition to these general sources, some governmental agencies and voluntary organizations publish listings or summaries of research in their special fields of concern and service. Professional organizations, research groups and voluntary organizations are a constant source of information about unpublished works in their special fields. It could be too narrow an outlook, however, to restrict one's bibliographical survey to studies that are directly relevant to one's area of interest. The most fruitful means of developing hypotheses is the attempt to apply to the area in which one is working, concepts and theories developed in quite different research contexts. Thus. the theory of perception developed in the area of psychological problems may provide stimulating clues for researchers desiring to work on the problems of group morale or group tensions. The sensitive descriptions to be found in the works of creative writers or novelists may also provide a fertile ground for the generation of hypotheses.

The Experience Survey

Some people in the course of their day-to-day experience, by virtue of their peculiar placement as officials, social workers, professionals, etc. are in a position to observe the effects of different policy actions and to relate these to problem of human welfare. The block development officer and his village level workers, for example, are likely to develop certain rare insights into the characteristics of the rural people and the estimated effectiveness of various approaches to their welfare. The professionals too may acquire rich insights in respect of the relevant categories of clients. The administrators are typically very advantageously positioned to obtain fruitful insights into what really works in a practical situation. The specialists acquire in the routine of their work, a rich fund of experience that can be of tremendous value in helping social scientists to develop awareness about the important influences operating in a situation they may be called upon to study. It is the purpose of the experience survey to gather and synthesize such experience.

Since the aim of experience survey is to obtain insights into the nature of the problem and useful leads or clues to the possible hypotheses and since the experience surveyor is looking for provocative ideas and useful insights, the cases are chosen on the basis of the likelihood that they will be able to contribute such ideas and insights. It is indeed a waste of time in an experience survey to interview people who have little competence, relevant experience and communicability. The best method of selecting informants may be to ask strategically placed administrators working in the field one desires to study, to point out the most experienced and informative people.

Efforts are made to select informants so as to ensure a representation of different types of experience. Variations in the points of view also need to be given adequate representation in the sample of respondents selected. Thus, in an experience survey of factors likely to resist, say, planned rural development, it may prove advantageous to interview the officials charged with plan-implementation as well as the village leaders. It would be ideal to interview people at different levels in each group.

In an experience survey, the best way to determine the sample size to identify the point during the process of interviewing after which additional interviews do not provide new insights and answers seem to fall into the pattern which has already emerged from the earlier interviews.

Before any systemic attempt is made to collect the insights of experienced persons, it is, of course, necessary to have some preliminary idea of the important issues in the general area of the subject-matter. In the systematic interviewing of the informants, it is necessary to maintain a considerable degree of flexibility. The formulative or the discovery aspects of the experience survey require that the interviewer allow the respondent to raise issues and questions the investigator has not previously thought of.

Even at the cost of repetition, it must be stated that the problem before a person undertaking an exploratory study is that he has no clearly formulated problem; at the best, he may have a vaguely or dimly felt 'originating question.' His exploration is directed toward problem-finding. Naturally, the researcher does not have any clear-cut idea as to what specific, predetermined set of question he should put to the informants to be able to get the 'relevant' information or answers. Since he has no specific problem, every information is relevant, every information, irrelevant. Hence, the investigator cannot frame definite questions in advance of the actual questioning of the informants. He thus casts his net wide; asks the informant all manner of general, flexible questions, viz., "what would you say about the people of this area?" On picking up a clue in the course of conversation, for which maximum opportunity and freedom is allowed to the informant, the investigator slowly tightens the net, i.e., asks the respondent more pointed questions. If this leads to the strengthening of the hunch initiated by the earlier clue, he tightens his net further still, asking definite and pertinent questions. The culmination of this process, if all goes well, is the discovery of the problem and/or meaningful hypotheses. Thus in an experience survey, it is the 'non-structured' flexible methods of data collection that are generally used. Of course, as the clues start maturing and insights begin developing, the information-seeking devices also shift toward greater pertinence and structuredness.

An experience survey, in addition to being a source of hypotheses, can also provide information about the practical possibilities for doing different types of research, e.g., where can the possibilities for the research be obtained? Which factors can be controlled and which not, in the situation intended for study? How ready are the agencies or citizens to co-operate in study of the problem in question? In addition, the experience survey may provide information about the problems considered urgent by personnel working in a given area. This information may prove to be useful in establishing priorities in specific research programme. The report of an experience survey also provides a consolidated summary of knowledge of skilled practitioners about the effectiveness of various methods and procedures for achieving specific goals.

Analysis of 'Insight-stimulating' Cases

Scientists working in relatively unformulated or uncharted problem-areas where there is little experience to serve as guide have found intensive study of selected examples and especially fruitful method for stimulating insights and for suggesting hypotheses for more structured inquiries. The anthropological studies of certain 'primitive' cultures have contributed profound insights in the regard to the relationship between the individual and society. The famous psychoanalyst *Sigmund Freud* based many of his theoretical insights about the working of the human psyche on the finding of his intensive studies on patients.

The following characteristics of this approach which is geared to developing insights are worthy of mention :

(a) The attitude of the research must be one of alert receptivity, of seeking significant clues.
His enquiry is in a process of constant reformulation and redirection as new information keeps coming. This implies frequent changes in the focus in relation to data to be obtained and in the criteria for selection of cases proposed to be investigated.

(b) The second feature is intensity of the study of the person, group, culture or situation selected for investigation. In the study of the individual, for example, an extensive examination of his present situation and his life history may be undertaken.

(c) The third characteristic of this approach is its reliance on the integrative powers of the investigator, i. e., on his ability to thread together many diverse bits of information into a unified interpretation. Since evoking new hypothesis is the central concern of such an approach, this characteristic is very desirable, for after all, the emerging hypothesis will be tested on the anvil of empirical evidence subsequently.

The experience of the social scientists working with this approach has been that a study of certain types of cases produces a harvest of new insights. We list below some such type of cases. Since experiences indicate that for particular problems certain types of cases are more appropriate and fruiful we shall also indicate which types are particularly apt for what category of problems.

(a) The observations of strangers or newcomers to a particular community may point out the characteristics of a culture of community that might otherwise be overlooked by an investigator reared in that culture. A stranger's eye is more sensitive to social customs and practices that are generally taken for granted or explicitly rationalized by the members of the community and thus do not incite surprise or bewilderment in them as they do in the newcomer-stranger. A way of seeing is indeed, also, a way of not seeing.

(b) Marginal individuals or groups which are moving from one cultural grouping to another and hence are on the periphery of both group are typically exposed to conflicting pressure of these groups. Therefore, they can reveal dramatically the major influences operating in both groups.

(c) Study of persons or groups who are in transition from one stage of development to the next has proved fruitful in providing insights into the relations between culture and personality. The study of groups or societies in transition may be of substantial value in understanding the process of social change and disorganization.

(d) Deviants and pathological case do throw light on the more common cases. The study of deviants may highlight the normative reference from which they are deviating, as also, the types of pressures to conform and the socio-psychological case to the understanding of personality are illustrations of the insights that may be gained by a study of pathological cases which frequently serve to underscore the basic processes of the diametrically opposite type of cases, i.e., non-pathological or normal cases.

(e) The characteristics of individuals who fit well in a given situation, as also, of those who do not fit well provide valuable clues about the nature of the pressure in the situation. The contrast in the characteristics of the two types of individuals provides an insight into the distinct nature of a community or group.

(f) A rounded view of any situation can be had if the individuals intended to be covered by the study are selected in such a manner that they represent different positions in the social structure. Persons occupying different positions are likely to see a given situation from different perspectives and this very diversity is a potent producer of insights.

(g) A review of investigator's own experience and a careful examination of his own reactions as he attempts to project himself on to situation of the subjects he is studying *Freud's* valuable insights emanated from his efforts to understand himself. This, of course, involves subjective introspection on the part of the investigator. Nevertheless, it must be emphasized that in maintaining a great distance between themselves and the objects of their study, i.e., an overly objective attitude, the scientists often neglect a very powerful source of ideas. During the specific phase of research when one is, in the main, looking for ideas such objectivity may not be appropriate.

There are many more cases which could have been included in this list; the above list of insight-stimulating cases this list is not exhaustive. Which type of case will be of most value will depend largely on the problem under investigation. Nevertheless, by way of general statement, it may be said that cases that provide sharp contrasts or engender striking features are the ones that are likely to prove most useful.

In closing, it is important to remind ourselves that the exploratory studies merely lead to insights or hypotheses; they do not test them. An exploratory study may rightly be regarded as a first step; more carefully controlled studies are needed to test whether the hypotheses that emerge (from the exploratory study) have a broader applicability and generic significance.

Design for Descriptive and Diagnostic Studies

We have already stated that the descriptive studies are the ones that aim at describing accurately the characteristics of a group, community or a group of people. A researcher may be interested in studying the people of a community, their age composition, sex composition, caste-wise distribution, occupational distribution and so on.

A researcher may be concerned with estimating the proportion of people in a particular population who hold certain views or attitudes. How many favour lowering the age of voting? How many students favour student representation on university bodies?

Quite a few other researchers, may be concerned with specific predictions. What percentage of people will vote for a particular party candidates? What will be the volume of unemployment within a decade?

It is understandable that when one does not know anything at all about a problem, he must attempt to understand it in a general way before beginning to make specific the various aspects of the subject. Explorers and missionaries write such descriptions of many exotic lands. They chose to describe what they thought to be important and interesting unconcerned with any rigid rules of scientific proof. Even such reports had their importance, for anthropologists subsequently rushed to study these 'natives' who were only hinted at in the explorer's reports.

Descriptive studies often provide a jumping pad for the study of new areas in social sciences. It is worthy of mention that *Freud's* compilation of case histories of patients laid the foundation for clinical psychology. *Freud* remarked "the true beginning of scientific activity consists in describing phenomena and (only) then, in proceeding to group, clarify and correlate them...."

Most anthropological research may be characterized as descriptive in as much as the thrust is on portraying a rounded picture of a total culture or some aspect of it. In more mature social sciences, sophisticated theories and statistical techniques of description may also be used. A general picture helps one grasp the essence of the problem.

It may not be very useful to conceive of descriptive research only as a phase on the evolutionary continuum of researches. This is so, firstly, because a piece of descriptive research may be of important scientific value in itself, although it cannot be generalized to apply to other situations. It can provide information which is of value in policy formulation and secondly, because the notion of stage assumes that we have knowledge about the various stages in the supposed continuum. There is hardly any firm evidence to substantiate such an evolutionary view of scientific research.

Another class of researches called diagnostic, may be concerned with discovering and testing whether certain variables are associated, e. g., do more villagers than city dwellers vote for a particular party? Are people who have co-educational background better adjusted to married life than those who did not have this background? As was indicated earlier, both descriptive as well as diagnostic studies share common requirements in regard to the study design. So we may group those two kinds of research interests as descriptive and diagnostic, together, since from the point of view of research procedure both these studies share certain important characteristics. It should be noted that in contrast to the problem (of problem finding) which froms the basis for exploratory studies, the research questions characteristic of the descriptive and diagnostic studies demand much prior knowledge of the problem to be investigated. Here the researcher must be able to define clearly what he wants to measure and must identify adequate methods for measurement. In addition, the researcher must be able to specify who are to be included in the definition of the given population with reference to which conclusions are to be drawn. In collecting evidence for studies of this type, what is needed is not so much the flexibility (as for exploratory studies) as a clear formulation of what is to be measured and the techniques to be adopted for precise, valid and reliable measurements.

The procedures to be used in descriptive/diagnostic study must be carefully planned since here the aim is to obtain complete and accurate information. The research design for these studies must make a much greater provision for protection against bias. Because of the amount of work involved in descriptive/diagnostic studies, concerned with economy (of time, money and labour) in the course of research is extremely important. Considerations of economy and protection against bias permeate every stage of the research process.

Let us now turn to consider some of the ways in which economy and protection against bias are taken into account in the design of a descriptive/diagnostic study.

The first step in a descriptive/diagnostic study, is to define the question, that is to be answered. Unless the questions are formulated with sufficient precision to ensure relevance of the data collected to the questions raised, the study will be fruitless. It is necessary to formally define the concepts entering into the question and also to indicate how the concept is to be measured. Considerations of economy would need to be entertained at the stage of specifying the research questions. This restricts the area of the study to bounds of manageability.

After the problem has been formulated specifically enough to indicate what data would be required, the methods by which data can be obtained must be selected. Tools for collecting the information must be devised if no suitable ones already exist. Each of the various methods of data collection — observation, interview, questionnaire etc. — has its peculiar advantages and limitations. The researcher would have to consider the nature of the problem, the scope of the study, the nature of respondents, type of information needed, the degree of accuracy needed, etc., and in view of these, balancing the gains and losses, should select one or more methods of data collection.

The stage of developing the data-collection procedures is one of the major points at which safeguards against bias and unreliability would need to be introduced. Questions to be asked to the respondents must be carefully examined for the possibility that their wording may suggest one answer rather than another. Interviewers must be instructed not to ask leading questions, observers need to be trained so that all the observers involved in the study record their observations uniformly. Once the data collection instruments are constructed, they must be pre-tested. Pre-testing the data-collection instruments before they are used in the study proper, greatly minimizes difficulties of comprehension, ambiguousness and sterility of questions.

In many descriptive/diagnostic studies, the researcher wants to make statements about some specific class of people or objects. However, it is rarely necessary to study all the people comprising the group in order to provide an accurate and reliable description of certain characteristics of its members. Quite often a sample or a fragment of the population about which inferences are to be drawn, affords an adequate basis for making such statements.

Much work has been done on the problem of designing the sample in a manner that it would yield accurate information with a minimum amount of expenses and research effort. It is important that the study findings based on the sample (a part of the population under study) should be reasonable accurate indicators of the state of affairs in the total group (population). This means that the sample should be selected in such a way that findings based on it are likely to correspond closely to those that would be obtained if the 'population' were studied. The researcher must select his sample in full consideration of the relative advantages and limitations of different methods of sampling and adopt the one (or a combination of two or more) that will provide the most accurate estimate of the population it represents, with maximum economy.

With a view to obtaining consistent data free from the errors introduced by different interviewers, observers and others working with the project, it is necessary to supervise the staff of field workers closely as they collect and record information. Effective checks must be set up to ensure that the interviewers continue to be honest and that the data they collect are unbiased. As the data are being collected, they should be examined for completeness, comprehensibility, consistency and reliability.

The process of analyzing the data after these are in, involves coding the responses, i.e., placing each item in the appropriate category, tabulating the data and performing statistical computations. These steps will be discussed elaborately in a later chapter. Here, we may simply note that both the considerations, i.e., of economy and need for safeguards against error, enter into each of these stepss. The considerations of economy indicate that analysis be planned in detail to the extent possible, before work on it is started. Of course, complete and intricate planning of analysis is neither always possible nor desirable. But excepting exploratory studies, it is generally feasible and advisable to work out in advance the basic outlines of analysis.

Safeguards against errors in coding ordinarily take the form of checking the reliability of coders through continual supervision. Decision needs to be taken on whether the tabulation is to be done by hand or by machine. But machine tabulation while more efficient, may prove prohibitive in cost if the responses to be tabulated are not large in number.

Accuracy of tabulation must be checked. Statistical computations, e.g., averages, dispersions, correlations etc. would need to be computed (as and when needed). Statistical operations of another sort are needed to be introduced for the purpose of safeguarding against drawing unjustified conclusions from the findings. These involve such procedures as estimating from the sample-findings the probable occurrence of some characteristic in the population which the sample purports to represent and estimating the probability that difference found between the sample sub-groups represent the true differences between the two sub-groups in the total population, etc. We will have more to say about this later.

The following table attempts to show the salient points of difference between the exploratory and the descriptive/diagnostic study designs. A note of caution, however, is warranted. The table-represents only an 'ideal-typical' formulation, i.e., exploratory studies have been considered as an ideal type; so also the descriptive studies. The points of difference highlighted in the table must, therefore, be understood as those between the two 'ideal models' of studies. In practical situations, these differences may not be found in such a clear-cut form.

Study type	*Basic design*	*Observational design*	*Sampling design*	*Statistical design*	*Operational design*
Exploratory	Flexible	Flexible (ustructured instruments)	Flexible (Non-probability; judgement)	Flexible No Pre-planned design for analysis	Flexible No fixed decisions about operationalizing
Descriptive; Diagnostic	Rigid	Rigid (structured Instruments)	Rigid (probability design) Random Samples	Rigid preplanned design for analysis	Rigid Advance decisions about operationalizing the study

We now turn to consider the study designs necessitated by the class of studies we call the experimental studies.

Experimental Study Design

The experimental studies form a sub-class of the studies which attempt to deal with problems in reference to which we ask how events are related to one another. Experimental studies deal with cause and effect problems, i.e., experimental studies are the ones concerned with testing the causal hypotheses. An hypothesis of causal relationship asserts that a particular characteristic or occurrence (X) is one of the factors that determine another characteristic or occurrence (Y). Before setting out to consider the kinds of research design that can best test the hypotheses of this type, it is necessary to discuss at some length the concept of causality.

The concept of causality is an extremely complex one and it is not possible to present a thorough analysis of this concept here. Indeed, we may not do better than bring out the basic points necessary for a workable conversance with the concept.

What is a' cause'? The first point that we must be clear about is that in science the causes which are discovered are, secondary' or 'caused causes.' They are only 'efficient' causes not the 'final' causes. They do not provide an answer to the question, 'ultimately why?' Purpose does exist in human affairs, there may be cosmic purposes also; but in science a final cause does not exist. *Francis Bacon* decreed that concern for final causes be better left to philosophy. Scientists hold that purpose is not a necessary concept in the research for scientific laws. In sciences, the word cause is used in the sense indicated by J.S. Mill, "a cause which is itself a phenomenon without reference to the ultimate cause of anything. "As Mill puts it, "causation is simply uniform antecedece."[6]

But even after gaining a clear understanding that science does not concern itself with, a first cause or a final cause, great ambiguities still remain. Professor *Bergeson* has pointed out that even in scientific discourse, three different meanings of the term 'cause' are frequently confused. A cause may act by impelling, by releasing or by unwinding. The billiard ball that strikes another determines its movement by impelling, the spark that explodes the gunpowder acts by releasing and the gradual relaxing of the spring makes the gramophone turn or unwind the disc, acts by unwinding. Only in the first cause, would the cause seem to explain the effect. In the other two causes the effect is more or less given in advance and the antecedent invoked is its occasion rather than its cause. In the first case, where the cause acts by impulsion, what is in effect is already in the cause. In the second cause where cause acts by releasing, it is an indispensable condition; it pulls the trigger, apart from which the effect would not occur. But it does not explain more than the rate or duration of the effect.

Causality

In regard to this immensely complex concept of causality we cannot afford to miss out on the *Humean* view of causality.[7]A central point of the Humean view is that when someone states that X causes Y he only expresses some reflection in his mind of the material objective world and not the material world directly. It is as though he is talking of a moving picture of a landscape rather than of the landscape itself. The moving picture may be very public and most of us might agree on what the picture is of. But this moving picture is man-made just as the association or prediction is a product of human mind for it requires an observer to notice the association or to interpret the association.

David Humean did not, of course, insist that there was no real world in which things happen but what *Humean* is saying is simply that when a scientist observes an association and abstracts from the real world to make some scientific statement, the statement is not the same thing as what he has been observing. It is a product of his mind or a picture of the world filtered through his perception. This is true of a statement of causality as of every association.

Hume says, "All reasoning concerning matter of fact seem to be founded on relationship of cause and effect, "We judge that the appearance of a table indicates the factual presence of the table on the grounds that presence 'causes' appearances and we judge that the table is there (if in fact, it is) as a result of the earlier causal chain such as growth of a tree and subsequent actions of a carpenter. To know the matter of fact involves for *Hume* the necessity of knowing the causal relation which links them to our perceptions or which links one event to another. But when we turn to look for this causal relation among the events which we perceive, we find no trace of it. These are mere events; the pattern of events has a certain regularity but we are never able to dictate a relation between events — certainly not a causal one. We may observe that one event is linked with another through a series of intermediate events or that one event never seems to occur except just before or just after another. Nevertheless they are all events. The most *Hume* would concede to, was by characterizing causal relation as possessing three elements, viz., contiguity, succession and constant conjunction — these relations themselves being defined by means of pairs of events both of which must be observed if the relation is to be taken to obtain. But this kind of relation is clearly useless in establishing truths about the matters of fact, since one would have to have the matter of fact as well as the perceptions of them in order to appreciate that the former caused the latter. Unfortunately, we can never get directly at the matters of fact but only at the perceptions of them and hence all falliable empirical knowledge is falliable resting as it does on totally unprovable surmises about the cause of what appears.

The same argument would apply in a slightly different way to the attempts at making predictions about the future on the basis of past observations.

The analysis of causality into contiguity, succession and constant conjunction (Hume) has been a centerpiece of controversy.

Many philosophers have felt that the internal necessity which compels one state of affairs to give way to another is clearly open to rational if not to empirical scrutiny. They have thus dismissed Hume's skeptical conclusion as an unworthy loss of faith in philosophy. But the alternative analyses have brought out that *Hume's* intentions were not properly understood. *Hume* did not deny that our idea of causality is derived from regularity in experience nor did he doubt that men have a tendency to expect such regularity in future experiences; he only denied that we can have any knowledge other than the experience of regularity itself to base these expectations which are philosophically groundless. Some other philosophers seem to have felt that logical connections in the realms of thought and of language were so clear that they indicate real connections in the world of precaution and the natural world. Hume admitted the plausibility to this argument to the extent of defining causality as the tendency of our mind to produce the idea of what is called the 'effect' when the idea of what is called the 'cause' is presented to it. But the fundamental epistemological problem is exactly to discover the grounds on which we may presume the connections and tendencies in the world. Indeed, no theory of causality has succeeded in doing this.

From *Aristole's* four causes: material, efficient, formal and final to Mill's inductive method of determining which element of some antecedent situation is to be matched with which element of consequent situation has cause the effect, this parallel between the real and ideal relation has been assumed. Some theorists like Hegel have tried to identify them but even this is of no help since it leaves us with the question whether our understanding of amalgem of what is actual with what is thought, affords us an accurate representation of it. Mill's methods are no doubt an elegant recipe for detecting constant conjunction that Hume speaks of. Mill's methods of residues and the method of concomitant variation. The first three deal with sets of antecedents and consequents.

If we are looking for the cause of some consequence C and suppose a number of sets of antecedent (A) after each of which C is observed, the method of agreement directs us to look for the cause of C among those antecedents which are members of all the sets. Alternatively, suppose the consequence C follows after only one of these sets of antecedents, the method of differences directs us to look for the causes among those members of that set which it does not share with any of the other sets which failed to produce C. The method of residues prompts us to discard from the set of antecedents any elements whose effects are known to be different from the consequence in question and to look for its cause among those which are left out after the operation is competed. Lastly, the method of concomitant variation directs our search towards the cause of any event or process whose intensity varies with time among other phenomena whose contemporaneous or little prior intensity varies in some simple way with respect to the intensity of the first. But all these methods in the light of the rule of constant conjunction (Hume) are obvious; they barely prove helpful in solving the *Humean* problem.

Hume's answer to his critics was that as an agent he would be quite willing to concede their points but as a philosopher with some share of curiosity he would want to know the foundation of this inference. There may or may not be any internal necessity of linking events in the world and we cannot know whether there is such a linkage or not, but it is only reasonable to behave as if there was.

But then what would an answer to the question of causality come to? The law of the uniformity of nature phrased in causal language says that similar causes are always followed by similar effects and enables us to use the relation past-present as an analogy for present-future. But suppose it was suddenly revealed to us that this law was about break down and that from tomorrow similar cause may not lead to similar effects. Now, unless we are told in advance what the differences were going to be, we will have to wait for the change in order to be able to base new kinds of predictions or new kinds of observation. But this activity itself would presuppose the same regularity of causal connection to which the change was offered as a counter-example. A failure of the principle genuinely would involve complete chaos but one would have no way of knowing about it by the fact that this chaos would extend to our perception and thought. If all that is argued for is the occasional falliability of the causal principle then this argument does not hold and we are once again driven to a sceptical impasse. Hence, the solution would seem to lie not in trying to establish the truth of the principle but rather in asserting it.

It is to be noted that in any particular test, the cause and effect to be abstracted from a complex setting or background. Thus, a better formulation of the principle would be that 'similar causes lead to similar effects if the backgrounds are similar.' In other words, if other things are equal *(ceteris paribus),* we may resolve to proceed on the assumption that the causal principle holds but at the same time we may treat with courteous skepticism any claim to have decisively established it.

We may envisage the present state of universe as the effect of its previous state and the cause of what will follow. By causal relationship is meant an effectively productive relationship between antecedent conditions and subsequent results. Hume could discover no such relationship, one merely saw the antecedent conditions and then the subsequent results.

The conclusion of the pristine Humean view is that there is no difference between statement of cause and effect and all other statements of association. But this view is not very satisfactory because social scientists talk and behave as if some associations belong to a different class from other associations. Many an attempt has been made to propose an inclusive and realistic definition of causality. *M. Bunge* and Blalock have defined causality mostly by offering synonyms for it. Causality, say Blalock, is conceived as involving the notion of production, that is, causes produce effects. Production is obviously used as a synonym for causation. But giving synonyms can be useful when one is clarifying what a particular word means in a particular language. Obviously, synonymization does not help solve basic scientific problems of causal labelling.

Definition may be offered by naming some properties of the concept. This type of definition would aim to state, for instance, what causality is. This is an ontological definition in terms of certain material properties of our world. Such a definition can help us to convey to others a general feeling of what one has in mind. For example, a horse is an animal with four feet used for riding, or culture is a grand pattern comprising habits, customs, thought and adaptive skills acquired by members of a society. Such a definition of causality has been tried by philosophers for centuries now, without any success. *Bridgeman* criticizing the sub-definitions argued that defining words in terms of properties creates walls to understanding. Instead, he advocated that definitions should be formulated in terms of operations.

Hume demonstrated typical flaws in ontological definition of causality without offering a substitute definition of causality in terms of operations. Instead, he suggested that the term 'causality' was useless and should be dispensed with. This view was one of the most influential ones prevaling among the twentieth century philosophers including Bertrand Russell.

Terms can be defined denotatively, that is, with examples. But one needs more than denotations to clarify the scientific concept of causality.

When there is disagreement among scientists about the application of a term and when they are keen to increase the likelihood that the same terms will be applied to same empirical phenomena, they must turn to operational definitions, i.e., by making sense of a concept by reference to the operations involved.

An operational definition of causality may reasonably be proposed in terms of the following procedure:

(1) The stimulus is varied and variations (if any) in the response observed.

(2) A number of other stimuli are used to observe if same response occurs.

(3) If the above two steps yield appropriate results the relationship between stimulus and response may be called 'causal.'

Defining causality in situations where structured experiments are not feasible is obviously fraught with hazards. However, a worthwhile operational definition of causality in non-experimental setting would mean that the definition results in many scientists reaching the same judgement. Secondly, the proposed operational definition fits closely the hypothetical concept of causality held by most scientists.

It makes sense to say that causal relationships are a sub-class of associations. In other words, all causal relationships are associations but all associations may not be causal relationships. A causal and effect statement may be understood as a type of scientific explanation but not all explanations are causal statements. The question now is how to effect a distinction between those associations that are within the sub-class of statement and those that are not. Quite a few attempts have been made to find a method for deciding whether or not a particular association may be included in causal or non-causal associations.

Many writers have opined that association which can be verified experimentally deserves the title causal, no others. Although this has been a useful rule in much of science it cannot be said to be perfect rule. In any experiment some hidden third factor rather than changes in the hypothesized independent variable might be responsible for the changes in the dependent variable. Besides, many situations do not allow for experimentation. Since a hidden third factor may turn out to be the real cause, a single experiment understandably fails to provide a comprehensive operational definition of causality. It is necessary under the circumstances, to run related experiments varying different parameters of the situation. It is only after the important possibilities are exhausted in the course of the experiment-series that we can conclude or rightfully say that the experimental stimulus causes the response.

Where experimentation is possible, the operational definition of causality may be proposed as follows:

If the response follows the experimentation stimulus and if this experimental relationship persists even if other elements of the situation are subjected to variation, the observed relationship may be called causal.

Situations in which no experiment is possible and hence the test of experimental confirmation cannot operate as a criterion for defining casual statements which throw up a number of questions about causal statements. Such situations characterizes most social sciences.

Wold (1966) attempted to bring non-experimental situations within the reach of the experimental verification principle by asking whether or not a non-experimental situation is fictitious or the hypothetical experiment. That is whether the natural situation has in it many of the elements of an actual experiment. But this conceptualization is not without shortcomings. Firstly, the essence of the experiments as an operational definition of causality is that it is the actual observed result of a real experiment that serves to determine whether or not the relationship is to be called causal. Secondly, the very act of choosing to label relationship as causal is an operation that defines causality. But such an operational definition lacks validity because it hardly goes far toward in resolving disagreements among people.

Logicians and philosophers have tried various combinations of conditional statements of the 'if-then' variety. They have attempted to find out some logical formulation that successfully distinguishes between causal and non-causal associations. This quest has, however, failed to reach the goal. Yet another type of attempt has recently been made by H. Simon, Blalock and others abstracting from original work of P. Lazarsfeld. This group has investigated how the correlation between and among three or more variables can help the analysis to sort out which of these variables can be said to cause which. This is an implication and formalization of the analysis seeking to investigate whether a hidden third factor is responsible for correlation between two other variables. This kind of a study of causal ordering is quite useful and important but does not achieve the purported results. For instance, if the investigator starts with three variables none of which should really be said to be cause of another, the analysis can tell us nothing about whether or not the relationship between two given variables should be called causal. Schemes of this kind aimed at labelling relationship as causal or non-causal depend heavily upon the use of extraneous knowledge to help us sort out the relationship. For instance, the knowledge that a certain event precedes all the others in time and hence cannot be the effect of these events. Thus, the whole thing boils down to the assertion that a relationship is causal unless proved otherwise by tests for spuriousness. Such a scheme obviously does not afford an operational definition indicating whether a given relationship should be called causal. At best it can only suggest that within a set of variables one relationship is more causal than another.

An overview of these various attempts leads one to the conclusion, that no definition has been created that fits customary scientific usage, though this is the stated aim of all of them. It is not surprising also that no perfect or near perfect definition has yet been generated. Even the best operational definition does not lead every one to classify all examples of such concepts in exactly the same way. There always are exceptions at the border line. It is, therefore, quite understandable that such terms as cause and effect which are so very complex and abstract would be much harder to define satisfactorily and would have many more border line cases on which people disagree when classifying situations as causal and non-causal.

Whether or not a situation is closely analogous to a controlled experiment does not provide a complete definition of causality. Furthermore, even in controlled experiment there is often no help for specification error except subject-matter knowledge.

In the light of the above discussion a working definition of causal relationship may be offered as under:

A causal relationship is expressed in a statement that has the following important characteristics : Firstly, it is an association that is strong enough for the observer to believe that it has a predictive (explanatory) power that is great enough to be scientifically useful or interesting. For example, if the observed correlation is 0.6 even if the sample is large enough to justify the correlation as statistically significant, i.e., unimportant relationships are not likely to be labelled causal. Secondly, the more tightly a relationship is bound, that is, compatible with a general theoretical framework, the stronger its claim to be designated as causal. Connections with a theoretical framework afford a support to the belief that the side conditions necessary for the statement to hold true are not restricted and that the changes of spurious correction are not substantial; because a statement tends to stand or fall as the rest of the system stands or falls.

It may be noted that the term causal is more likely to have different meaning, to the decision-maker and to the scientist. The decision-maker will call a relationship causal if he expects to be able to manipulate it successfully. For example, smoking may be considered causal by a decision-maker wanting to reduce deaths from diseases statistically related to smoking. But to the scientists the word cause is likely to mean that the situation does not require further exploration. In the case of cigrettes perhaps only one ingredient in the cigarette does the damage and the scientists searching for this ingredient may choose to withhold the word cause from smoking itself.

The difference in meaning and use of causal concept between decision-making and pure investigation situation is one example of the general proposition that attribution of causality depends upon one's purpose. The causal concept is perhaps most necessary for a policy-maker especially when he is considering changing one variable in the hope of achieving change in another variable of, e.g., fertility, in reproduction parlance. The classification causal and non-causal is an attempt to discriminate between situations that he believes allow such control and those that do not. On the other hand, the causal concept is not at all necessary for a person who is expected to forecast for he has no interest in trying to manipulate the independent variables. The causal concept may or may not be necessary for the pure investigator.

Berttrand Russell and most contemporary physicists seem to believe that it was neither necessary nor useful in the physical/natural sciences. Many non-policy scholars in the social science, however seem to find the concept of causality useful in classifying situations for future research.

The difference among disciplines in respect of the variable to be called causal also illustrates how causal labelling depends upon purpose. In those cases in which variables are complementary, like achievement motivation and investment, it is perhaps unnecessary for the psychologist or economist to deny the causal label to one variable in order to apply it to another variable. But when the variables are hierarchical then they may be causally incompatible and particular investigators, depending upon their disciplines, must choose which label to give to study and call it causal on the basis of the label they consider most fruitful.

In regard to the meaning of causality as evidenced in social scientific usage of the term, there appears to be considerable consensus among scientists on which relationships are causal and which are not. *J.L.Simon* proposes an operational definition of causality. "A statement", he says, "shall be called causal if the relationship is close enough to be useful or interesting, if it does not require so many statements of side conditions as to get its generality and importance; if enough ... third factor variables have been tried to provide some assurance that the relationship is not spurious; and if the relationship can be deductively connected to a larger body of theory or...be supported by a set of auxiliary propositions that explains the mechanism by which the relationship works."[8]

The above definition is more in the nature of a check list of criteria. Whether or not a given relationship meets the criteria sufficiently to be called causal is neither automatic nor objective. The determination requires judgement and substantive knowledge of the entire context.

It should be clear, therefore, that science goes about its ordained business of events by disclosing their 'efficient causes.' This simply means that the event in question is shown to be determined by the preceding events. The remarks of the philosopher of science, *A.E. Taylor,* can barely be excelled. He says, "The notion of causation as a transaction between two things is replaced in the experimental science by the conception of it as merely the determination of an event by antecedent events. As it becomes more apparent that the antecedent events which condition an occurrence are a complex plurality, and include states of what is popularly called the things acted upon as well as the processes in the so-called agent, sciences substitutes for the distinction between 'agent' and 'patient', the concept of a system of reciprocally dependent interacting factors ... the current scientific conception of cause (is thus) the 'totality of conditions' in the presence of which an event occurs and in the absence of any member of which it does not occur. More briefly, causation in the current scientific sense means sequence under definitely known conditions."[9]

In modern science the emphasis is on a multiplicity of 'determining conditions' which together make the occurrence of a given event or effect probable. Scientific thinking is concerned with discovering 'necessary' and 'sufficient' condition for an effect. While 'common sense' leads one to expect that one factor may provide a complete explanation, the scientist rarely expects to find a single factor or condition that is both necessary and sufficient to bring about an effect. Rather, he is interested in 'contributory conditions,' 'alternative conditions', all of which he will expect to find operating to make the occurrence of a given event or effect probable (but not certain). We shall now briefly explain and illustrate the above 'conditions.'

(a) A necessary condition is said to be one that must occur if the phenomenon of which it is a 'cause' is to occur, e.g., if X is a necessary condition of Y, then Y will never occur unless X occurs. Such a relationship between X and Y may be designated as 'producer-product' relationship.[10] Such 'producer-product' relationships are the especial concerns of social and behavioural sciences.

    By way of illustration, we may say that differentiation is a necessary condition of social stratification, that is, social stratification would never occur if persons in the course of interaction did not get differentiated.

(b) A sufficient condition is one that is always followed by the phenomenon of which it is a 'cause.' If X is a sufficient condition of Y, then wherever X occurs Y will always occur. It must be borne in mind that in this strict sense of 'cause-effect', no object or event can by itself be said to be the cause of another object or event. The effect that an object or event has on another, always depends on its environment, e.g., mere striking the bell will not cause the subsequent sound if the bell is struck in a vacuum. Such a relationship between X and Y is studied primarily in 'mechanistic system.'

(c) A contributory condition is one that enhances the likelihood that a given phenomenon will occur but does not make its occurrence certain since it is only one of a number of factors that together determine the occurrence of the given phenomenon. Some sociological studies have suggested that the absence of a father-figure from the home during childhood is a contributory condition in the generation of drug-addiction among adolescents in the family.

(d) A contingent condition is one under which a given factor is a contributory factor in producing a given phenomenon (effect). In the above example, the contributory condition, i.e., absence of the father figure, may contribute to the incidence of drug-addiction among adolescents only in neighbourhoods were the use of drugs is quite pervasive. In this case, such a neighbourhood is a contingent under which the contributory condition, viz., absence of father-figure, contributes to the probability of occurrence of the 'effect.'

(e) Alternative conditions are conditions which may all contribute toward the occurrence of a given phenomenon or effect. In the example cited above, it may be seen that the absence of the father-figure (contributory condition No.1) or the father-figure expressing variously antipathy toward children (contributory condition No.1) both contribute toward producing the effect, i.e., drug-addiction. These conditions are known as the alternative conditions.

It is impossible, as already mentioned, to demonstrate directly that a given characteristic or event X determines another characteristics or event Y, either by itself or in conjunction with other characteristics or events. We are rather in a position of inferring from the observed data that the hypothesis that X is a condition for the occurrence of Y is (or is not) tenable with some particular measure of confidence. Let us now consider what evidence is necessary to justify any inference of causal relationship.

(a) One type of relevant evidence concerns concomitant variation, i.e., the extent to which X and Y occur together or vary together. Suppose we wish to test the hypothesis that X is contributory condition of Y, we shall have to find out whether the proportion of cause having the characteristic Y is significantly greater among cases having characteristic X than among the cases not having the characteristic X. Unless we can get at such an evidence, we will ordinarily conclude that the hypothesis is not tenable. Further, if the hypothesis also specifies that the amount of Y is determined by the amount of X, we will have also to find evidence to the effect that, on the whole, those cases that show a higher amount of X also exhibit a higher amount of Y. Other type of causal hypotheses, e.g., that X is necessary or sufficient 'cause' of Y or that X as a contingent cause in association with M and an alternate cause with N, would require identifying particular patterns of association between X and Y.

Let us try to understand this with the help of an example. Suppose in a small town a doctor on the basis of his observations, advances the hypothesis that eating of a particular seasonal fruit (X) may lead to severe cold (Y). An inquiry is then conducted with a view to testing the hypothesis. If consequent upon the inquiry it is found that among those who have it the proportion of those who ate the seasonal fruit (X) was almost equal, we would reject the hypothesis that X leads to Y. Of course, before rejecting the hypothesis, a careful investigation would need to be carried out with a view to finding out whether eating the seasonal fruit (X) is a contributory condition of cold (Y) under some contingent condition, e.g., say, general debility. Suppose, the inquiry revealed that the persons who had eaten the fruit and suffered from general weakness were in an overwhelming proportion in the ones suffering from cold, then we can say the seasonal fruit (X) is a contributory condition of severe cold (Y) under the contingent condition of general debility (M).

If, on the other hand, the inquiry indicated that 92% of people suffering from cold had eaten the seasonal fruit and only 25% of the people not suffering from cold had eaten the fruit, we would conclude that the hypothesis that X is the contributory ' cause' of Y is tenable. It must be remembered that the hypothesis would be simply tenable, not proved, since other possible explanations of the observed relation between X and Y may be invoked and this would be equally tenable, viz. :

(1) Affliction of cold in some way created a craving for the fruit, which means that eating fruits did not lead to cold; it is rather the other way round, i.e., cold (Y) created an urge for eating the fruit (X).

(2) Some other condition (Z) led to both eating the seasonal fruit and having cold.

(3) Yet another condition (W) like impurity which merely happened to be associated with eating the seasonal fruit was responsible for cold, i.e., tap water.

(b) Second type of evidence relevant to inference about causality is the time order of two events X and Y. One event reasonably be considered the cause of the other if it occurs after the other events. By definition, an effect cannot be produced by an event which occurs only after the effect has taken place. In our example, X cannot be considered the 'cause' of Y, if as proposed in the alternative hypothesis No. 1, the condition of severe cold (Y) led to a craving for the seasonal fruit (X).

It would be well to remember that time order may not be accepted by some as an automatic test of causality. This argument may be replied by pointing out that just because there is no logical connection, it would not follow that the time lags are no help in establishing causality. We must recognize after all that to use time lag or time order to infer the direction of causality in a particular relationship is to make use of one of the most general inferences based on all the experimentation that has been undertaken, namely, that actions of the present do not appear to modify the past. But this is a statistical empirical hypothesis, not without known exceptions. Therefore, to put this inference to sensible use, one needs to adduce other additional reasons to justify that the hypotheses may be believed to apply in a particular case.

It should, also be noted that the occurrence of a causal event may precede or may be contemporaneous with the occurrence of an effect. It is also possible for each factor in the relationship to be both a 'cause' and an 'effect' of the other factor. This is an instance of the symmetrical causal relationship. George Homan's hypothesis: "The higher the rank of a person within a group, the more nearly his activities conform to the norms of the group"[11] typifies the symmetrical causal relationship in as much as the reverse of the hypothesis is also true, i.e., the closer the activities of a person come to the norm, the higher his rank will tend to be.

Although symmetrical causal relationships are frequently found in the realm of social phenomena, it is useful to focus upon the influence of any one factor on the other. In distinguishing between 'cause' and 'effect' it is useful to establish which of the two events came first, assuming they did not occur simultaneously. Knowing that an increase in rank in a specific instance, preceded an increase in conformity to group norms, we understand that the increase in conformity was not the causal factor. However, knowledge of temporal priority is not in itself sufficient for inferring causality. In our example, even if we had established for certain that X preceded Y, this was not enough to say that the eating of seasonal fruit (X) caused severe cold (Y). Two other alternative hypotheses (No. 2 and No. 3) need to be considered, i.e., that some other condition led to both (X) and (Y) or some other condition associated with X was responsible for Y.

(c) We must, therefore, get at the evidence which would establish that no other factor save the hypothesized one (X) was the 'cause' of the hypothesized effect (Y). Till such time as the evidence ruling out other factor as possible determining condition of the hypothesized effect is secured, we shall not be able to say that X is the 'cause' of Y. In our example, it may be that some third factor, e.g., glandular secretions, led both to desire eating the seasonal fruit as also to severe cold. If we can disprove this, the other alternative possibility still remains to be reckoned, i.e., some other factor which merely happened to be associated with eating of seasonal fruit led to cold. Suppose it was found that people who had bought the fruit from a particular shop where the fruit was kept in the open for a long time were the ones who mostly suffered from cold, whereas the few who had bought from other shop where the fruits were kept in a cold storage mostly did not suffer from cold; then the hypothesis that the seasonal fruit (X) itself was the cause of severe cold (Y) would have to be discarded and attention would be turned on to the effects of the storing system which might have brought about a chemical reaction on fruits in one shop but not in the other. Under these circumstances, the effect Y would properly be attributed to the chemical factor.

It must be stressed that the three kinds of evidence discussed above, i.e., concomitant variation, time sequence of variables and evidence ruling out other factor as 'cause' is or in not cause of the effect. It does not, however, provide any absolute certainty. That is, we may, on the basis of our evidence, conclude that it is reasonable to believe that X is the 'cause' of Y but we can never be certain that the relationship has been conclusively demonstrated.

In our above example, the procedures suggested for testing the hypothesis that X is a cause of Y, called for a number of different studies. None of these separate studies could provide a very secure ground for testing the hypothesis because it left the alternative hypotheses unscathed and untested.

An experimental design provides for the gathering of various kinds of evidence simultaneously so that all the alternative hypotheses can be tested. In an experimental test of the hypothesis in our example, the researcher would arrange for a number of subjects to eat the seasonal fruit ('x) and for a number of comparable subjects not to eat the fruit. The groups are to be chosen such that they do not differ from each other except by chance, before eating the seasonal fruit. Now comparison of the incidence of cold (Y) in two groups after one group which has not eaten it, would provide evidence of whether eating of the fruit (X) and cold (Y) vary together. By keeping a careful record of the time of eating the fruit (X) and the time of the ons2 et of cold (Y) the researcher would get the proof as to which of the variables came first. By introducing 'controls' to protect against the possibility that different exposures or experiences during the experiment (other than eating of seasonal fruit or not eating it) which might affect the occurrence of cold, he would ensure that the two groups differ from each other only with respect to (X). The researcher, in addition, could build into his experiment, the provision for testing hypotheses about particular alternative causal factors. For example, the researcher would test the hypotheses about the effects of storing system by having some of the subjects eat seasonal fruit that had been stored in cold-storage and some eat other fruit (not the seasonal fruit in question) stored in the open. This would help him to ascertain whether the 'open' storing system alone was productive of (Y) or whether the 'open storage' interacted with the seasonal fruit (X) and the product of interaction (V) produced (Y), i.e., cold.

Thus, we see that experimental design wherever it is feasible is the most effective device for testing a causal hypothesis. But then, experiments are not possible to be set up in certain situations. Suppose a researcher is interested in studying the effects of different methods of child-rearing on the personality structure of a person. He cannot conceivably assign certain children to be brought up in one way, others in another. In such a case he would have no other alternative but to proceed by locating children who have been brought up in different ways and then assessing their personalities. Hypotheses about the effect of attributes of the individuals are not often amenable to experimental investigation since the manipulation of the 'independent' variable (experimental variable or the factor which has been hypothesized as the 'cause') is either extremely difficult or impossible. Let us say, we want to see the effect of feeblemindedness (X) on perception (Y). It would not be possible in this case to manipulate (increase or decrease) feeble-mindedness. The only alternative open to us will be to achieve this variation by selecting individuals in whom this variable is present or absent; more or less. Occasionally, natural situations may provide the desired contrasting conditions (e.g., very high I.Q.) and thus the opportunity for sufficiently rigorous procedures to mke possible a reasonably sound basis for inference. Ordinarily, however, the natural situations are complicated and do not admit of an assumption on the part of the researcher that two or more groups that he has chosen for the purpose of experimentation variable. It is understandable that without a sound basis for such an assumption which a created artificial situation affords. The results of the experiment can have only a doubtful reliability.

Of course, there is no absolute certainty about the validity of inference. No matter how carefully controlled the experiment, there always lurks a possibility that the influence of some factor was not taken into account. Especially, in social sciences, where there is little knowledge about what factors to control and where many of the relevant factors (e.g., attributes of the individual) are not quite amenable to control, this possibility has to be contended with.

Basic Outline of Experiment

For a start, two groups are chosen such that they do not differ from each other in significant respects (which might affect the hypothesized relationship among variables) except by chance. Any one of these groups may be chosen as the 'experimental' group and the other chosen as the 'control group.' The 'experimental' group is exposed to the assumed causal (or independent) variable while the 'control' group is not. The two groups are then compared in terms of the assumed effect (dependent variable). This structure makes possible the securing of three types of evidence required for testing causal hypotheses.

Evidence of the first type, i.e., of concomitant variation, is provided very simply in an experiment since the investigator can easily see or determine whether the assumed effect occurs more frequently among subjects who have been exposed to the assumed cause than among those who have not been exposed to it.

Evidence of the second type, i.e., (Y) did not occur before (X), is also easily obtained because the experimental group and control group are chosen in such a way that there is reason to believe that the two groups do not differ from each other, in terms of a referent of (Y) before exposure to (X). Alternatively, the actual before measurements of these two groups afford the basis for saying that the groups did not differ in respect of (Y) before exposure to (X). This being the case, the difference in these two groups after exposure of one of them to (X) can be said to have decisively followed the experimental variable, i.e., (X).

Evidence of the third type, which rules out other factor as the possible determining conditions of (Y) may be secured in several ways in an experiment. Such possible causal conditions may be :

(a) factors that have occurred in the past or are more or less enduring characteristics of the subjects ;

(b) contemporaneous events other that the exposure to the experimental variable;

(c) maturational or developmental changes (or changes due to inertia as in physics) in subject of the experiment during the period of the experiment; and

(d) the influence of the measurement process itself.

Different procedures have been evolved to eliminate each of the above type of factors as the possible determining conditions of the effect (Y). These shall be discussed at length when we consider the basic types of experimental design and its ramifications.

The entire design of an experiment has the function of providing for collection of evidence in such a way that influences causal relationship between the independent and the dependent variables can be legitimately drawn. However, certain aspects are especially important in this regard, viz., the method of selecting experimental and control groups, the points in time when the dependent variable is measured, the pattern of control groups used and number of possible causal variables systematically included in the study.

Let us turn to consider the issue relating to the selection of experimental and control groups when designing an experiment.

In any research design that involves comparison of two or more groups of subjects who have been exposed to different experimental treatments, there is an underlying assumption that the groups being compared were equivalent before the introduction of the experimental treatment.

Clearly, the goal of creating groups that are equivalent in all respects is impossible of attainment. Before considering how this problem can be tackled in a practical and satisfactory way, we should be able to appreciate the rationale behind having such equivalent groups. The first reason is to provide a basis for inferring that the differences which may be found on the dependent variable (assumed effect) do not result from or reflect initial differences between the two groups. This second reason is that of increasing the sensitivity of the experiment by making it possible that small effects of the experimental variable are registered which might possibly be dimmed by the effect of other factors.

The goal of protecting the validity of the experiment by ensuring that the experimental and control groups differ initially only by chance, is achieved by a procedure termed *randomization*. The other goal, i.e., increasing the sensitivity of the experiment so that the effects of the assumed causal variable will be clearly discernible even if they are relatively small and when there are relatively few subjects, is achieved by the 'matching' procedures.

Randomization

It involves random assignment of members of a group of subjects to experiment and control groups. The assignment procedures must give each subject the same chance of being assigned to any of the alternative groups. This can be achieved by flicking a coin for each subject, e.g., if it falls 'heads' the subject may be assigned to the control groups. Thus, the procedure is such that in any selection of the subject, researcher's personal judgment is inconsequential. This does not, of course, mean that the experimental and control groups will be exactly alike but that whatever differences exist between them prior to exposure to the experimental variable are solely due to chance or the operation of the probability principle. If after one of the groups is exposed to the experimental treatment the two groups are found to differ by more than what could be expected by chance, the researcher may infer that the experimental variable has led to this difference. It must be remembered, however, that this inference can be made only tentatively, subject to the possibility that some other factor may have led to it.

Matching

Matching simply stated, involves pairing the subjects for assignment to the experimental or control group in a manner that a particular type of subject assigned to, say the experimental group, is balanced by assigning its exact counterpart to the control group. For example, a male, 25 years old, living in city may be matched by a male of the same age and intelligence in the control group. Matching is typically effective in increasing the sensitivity of the experiment. Matching ensures that the experiment will reveal true difference brought about by the experimental variable, although these (differences) may be small as compared to those produced by other variables.

The matching of individuals is understandably a very difficult task for the following reasons:

(1) If matching is to be precise and subjects are to be matched on several criteria, like, age, sex, nativity, educational status, there must be a larger number of cases to select from, in order to achieve an adequate pairing. All of these cases will have to be measured in relevant respects, but only a few can be used. The more precise the matching, greater the number of cases for which no match may be available.

(2) It is often quite difficult to know exactly which factors are the most important ones for purpose of matching. Matching with some degree of precision on more than two or three factors is hardly possible.

(3) It is often difficult to obtain adequate measure of the covert and intangible factors on which matching is necessary, e.g., attitudes, intelligence, aspirations, morale, anxiety etc. It is obvious that matching is likely to be inaccurate.

It is worthy of note that matching is not a substitute for randomization; it is rather a supplement to it. Matching can take account of only a few variables; therefore, those that are unaccounted for but, nevertheless make up the complexion of group, should be randomly distributed between the experimental and control group.

Should the research interest be in a function collectivity (family, clique class room etc.), it is appropriate to match group with group rather than individual with individual.

One method of matching, technically called the frequency distribution control, is an attempt to match an experimental with a control group in terms of the overall distribution of a given factor or factors within the two groups. For example, if age was relevant to the effects being studied, frequency distribution control would ensure that the averages in these two groups (i.e., experimental and control) are alike and the distribution of ages in the two groups is similar. This method is thus an attempt to get some of the advantages of matching case by case without having to incur the costs of losing many cases (unmatched) as we do in the precision control matching.

The frequency distribution control method, however, is not without its disadvantages. Although distributions on single factors are equated, the groups may actually be badly mismatched on a constellation of these factors. It would be wrong to assume that distributions in two groups are similar simply because their averages are similar. Secondly, even though a statistical test indicates that the distributions in two groups do not differ significantly, the researcher is not justified in concluding that they are equivalent.

We now turn to consider the different types of experiment design.

If the researcher wishes to test the hypothesis that X is the cause of Y, by comparing a group that has been exposed to X with one that has not been so exposed, it is obviously essential to measure the two groups with respect to Y, either during or after their exposure to X. Sometimes, it is desirable or even necessary to have in addition, measures of their position with respect to Y before they have been exposed to X. The point of time at which the dependent variable, i.e., assumed effect, is measured provides a basis for classifying experiments into two main groupings.

The control groups instituted provide a basis for further sub-classification.

Experiments

THE AFTER ONLY TYPE

(Measurement only of the dependent variable after exposure to experimental variable)

THE BEFORE-AFTER TYPE

(Measurement of the dependent variable before and after the group is exposed to the experimental/independent variable)

- Before-After (single group)
- Before-After (with one control group)
- Before-After (with two control groups)
- Before-After (with three control groups)

The 'After-Only' Experimental Design

The After-only experiment is its basic outlines may be represented by the following procedure :

Condition	*Experimental Group*	*Control Group*
Before Measurement	No	No
Exposure to Experimental Variables	Yes	No
Exposure to Uncontrolled Factors	Yes	Yes
After Measurement	Yes (Y_2)	Yes (Y'_2)

Change = $Y_2 - Y'_2$

The procedure characteristic of the After-only experiments may be described as follows:

(1) Two equivalent groups are selected. Any one may be used as the experimental group and the other as the control group. As said earlier, the two groups are selected by randomization procedure with or without supplementary 'matching.'

(2) None of these two groups is measured in respect of the characteristic which is likely to register change, consequent to the effect of the experimental variable. The two groups are assumed to be equal in respect of this characteristic.

(3) The experimental group is exposed to the experimental variable (X) for a specified period of time.

(4) There are certain events or factors whose effects on the dependent variables are beyond the control of the experimenter. Try as hard as he might, he cannot control them. So these factors may be called uncontrolled events. Needless to say, both the experimental as well control groups are equally subject to their influence.

(5) The experimental and control groups are observed or measured with respect to the dependent variable (Y) after (sometimes, during) the exposure of the experimental group to the assumed causal variable (X).

(6) The conclusion whether the hypothesis, 'X produces Y' is tenable is arrived at simply by comparing the occurrences of Y (or its extent or nature) in the experimental group after exposure to variable X with the occurrence of Y in the control group which has not been exposed to X.

In the tabular representation above, Y_2 and Y'_2 (after measures) are compared to ascertain whether X and Y vary concomitantly. The evidence that X preceded Y in time, is acquired from the very method of setting up the two groups. The two groups are selected in such a manner that there is reason to assume that they do not differ from each other except by chance in respect of the dependent variable Y.

The final problem of eliminating the effect of other factors, such as contemporaneous events or maturational process is dealt with on the basis of the assumption that both groups are exposed to the same extent and hence undergo similar maturational or natural developmental changes between the time of selection and the time at which Y is measured. If this assumption is justified, the position of the control group on the dependent variable Y'_2 at the close of the experiment includes the influence of external uncontrolled events and natural development processes that have affected both groups. Thus, the difference between Y_2 and Y'_2 may be taken as an indication of the effect of the experimental variable. It must be borne in mind, however, that the external events and the developmental processes may interact with the experimental variable to change what would otherwise have been its effect operating singly. For example, the effect of a medicine M may be different when the atmospheric conditions or climate interacts with the medicine. Thus, babies may register a greater increase of weight when medicine and climate interact with each other as compared to the increase that may be attributed to medicine (M) and climatic conditions (A) operating on the babies independently.

The major weakness of the After-only experimental design is obvious, viz., 'before' measurements are not taken. Both groups are assumed to be similar in respect of the before measure on the dependent variable. Unless the selection of the experimental and control groups is done in such a meticulous manner that it warrants such assumptions, it is quite likely that the effect the researcher attributes to the experimental variable may really be due to the initial difference between the two groups. Again, as we shall shortly see, 'before-measurements' are desirable or advisable for a variety of reasons. This facility is lacking in the After-only design.

We cannot afford to overlook the possibility that in certain experimental situations, 'before measurements' are not feasible owing to certain practical difficulties. Again in certain situations, as we shall have an occasion to appreciate, 'before measurements' may not be advisable and the safeguards quite prohibitive in cost. Under such circumstances the After-only design may be a reasonably good choice provided, of course, that meticulous care is exercised in selecting the groups as equivalents.

The Before-After Experiments

As their very name would indicate, the 'before-after' experiments share common characteristic, namely, the groups are observed or measured before the exposure to the experimental variable. A 'before' measurement of the dependent variable that characterizes the Before-After experiments may be desirable for various reasons such as the following:

(a) A 'before' measurement of the dependent variable is necessary for matching the cases in the experimental and the control groups. This measure greatly enhances the sensitivity of the experiment.

(b) A 'before' measurement makes it possible to determine the incidences of change in the dependent variable and to take these into consideration in evaluating the effects of the experimental or independent variable.

(c) If the hypothesis of the study specifies the initial position on the dependent variable as one of determining conditions, then obviously, the before measurement is required to test the hypothesis. For example, the hypothesis may state that an educational programme will have greater effect on persons who have a set of specific characteristics than those who do not have these particular characteristics. In such a case, an initial measure of such characteristics as well as the 'after' measure is required by the hypothesis.

(d) If the experimenter is interested in finding out whether the experimental treatment has different effect on cases who were initially at different positions on the dependent variable, he must, understandably have a 'before' measure of position on the dependent variable.

(e) In the real life setting, the ideal requirement of selecting the experimental and control groups on a purely random basis is often hard to fulfil and certain compromises are called for. In such cases, the evidence from a 'before' measure that the experimental and control groups were initially equal in respect of the dependent variable helps to increase the confidence that a difference found on the 'after' measure is due to the effect of the experimental variable only.

The 'Before-After experiments may characterize various arrangements and permutations with reference to control groups :

(1) Only one group may be used in the study, with the 'before' measure serving as a control, i.e., representing the position of the dependent variable in the absence of the experimental treatment.

(2) The 'before' measurement may be on the one group and 'after' measure on a different one which is assumed to be an equivalent group.

(3) The 'before' and 'after' measures may be taken both on experimental groups as well as on one control group.

Whatever the pattern of control groups, the 'Before-After' experiment provides evidence of concomitant variations among X and Y, by comparing the occurrence of Y in the group exposed to X with the occurrence of Y in the group not exposed to X. The second evidence of causality, i.e., that X came before Y in time, is inferred from the assurance provided by randomization that the groups are likely to be equivalent with respect of the referents of Y. This initial equivalence with respect to the referents of Y can be checked by comparison of 'before' measures of the two groups.

The 'before-after' experiments may involve two or more control groups. The variations in control group arrangements relate to the attempts to take account of and segregate effects of contemporaneous events, maturational or natural development processes and/ or 'before' measurement on the experiment.

The possibility of the effects of the 'before' measurements on the dependent variable must be reckoned with. The 'before' measurement may crystallize the attitudes or views of the subjects or it may exhaust the good will of the subjects. The subjects may mentally connect the 'before' measurement with the experimental treatment as also with the 'after' measurement. The 'before' measure may thus distort the true effect of the experimental variable. The second (i.e., the 'after') measurement may introduce other problems. The subject may be bored or he may try to give responses which are consistent with his previous responses (elicited during the 'before' measurement), may also try to vary the responses just to make them more interesting or just to appear 'co-operative vis-à-vis the experimenter in his 'intended' purpose of being able to show a certain change. The process of repeated measurement, i.e., 'before' and 'after' may also affect the measuring instrument, e.g., the observer himself may get fatigued, prejudiced or grow more or less sensitive to the phenomena he is recording.

With this general outline of the 'before-after' experiments as a backdrop, let us now discuss the specific types of experiments of this class.

The 'Before-After' Experiment with a Single Group

The tabular representation of this type of experiment is given below:

Conditions	*Experimental Groups*
Before Measurement	Yes (Y_1)
Exposure to experimental factor	Yes
Exposure to uncontrolled events	Yes
After Measurement	Yes (Y_2)

Change = Y_2-Y_1

It is clear that in this design, the difference between the subject's positions on the dependent variable before and after the exposure to the independent variable (experimental factor) is taken as a measure of the effect of experimental variable. The subject is made to serve as his own control.

But it is understandable that external factors unrelated to the experimental treatment may have been in operation, leading in turn to a change in the subject's position on the dependent variable. Thus, the major weakness of this rudimentary experimental design is that it does not make possible the segregation of such effects (i.e., external, contemporaneous, developmental processes and the effects of 'before' measurements) from those of the experimental treatment.

The design may, therefore, be used only when the researcher can assume on just grounds that the 'before' measurement does not in any way affect (a) the subjects' exposure to the experimental variable and (b) the 'after' measure. In addition, the use of this design is justified if the researcher has a sound basis for believing that there are not likely to be any other influences, beside the experimental variable, during the period of experimentation which might have affected the subjects' response at the time of second measurement.

The 'Before-After' Experiment with One Control Group

The inclusion of one control group in this design is aimed at taking account of the effects both of the initial measurement and of contemporaneous, external factors. In such a design, experimental and the control group are both measured at the beginning and also at the end of the experimental period.

Conditions	*Experimental Groups*	*Control Group*
Before Measurement	Yes (Y_1)	Yes (Y'_1)
Exposure to experimental variable	Yes	No
Exposure to uncontrolled events	Yes	Yes
After Measurement	Yes (Y_2)	Yes (Y'_2)

Change = $Y_2 - Y_1$ (Experimental Group) $Y'_2 - Y'_1$ (Control Group)

(minus) (minus)

The experimental variable is introduced in the experimental group only. Since both the experimental and control group are subject to the 'before' measurement and the uncontrolled factors, the difference between the two groups is taken as the effect of the experimental variable alone.

In view of its typical limitations, this design should be used only in cases where the 'before' measure and the uncontrolled events affect the experimental and control groups in the same way. But it is quite possible that the 'before' measure or uncontrolled factors may interact with the experimental variable in such a way that its effects is changed. When such a possibility is present, the 'Before-After' study with one control group does not afford a basis for inferring the effects of the experimental variable since it cannot segregate or draw apart the singular effect of experimental variable. R.L. Solomon has devised more elaborate designs to take account of such interactions. These involve use of additional control groups.

The 'Before-After' Experiment with Two Control Groups

The design makes it possible to segregate the influence of the experimental variable from that of the 'before' measurement even if there is a likely interaction between them (i.e., experimental factor and 'before' measurement). This design may be represented as under:

Conditions	*Experimental Groups*	*Control Group I*	*Control Group II*
Before Measurement	Yes (Y_1)	Yes (Y'_1)	No (Y'_1) = (Y_1+Y'_1)/2
Exposure to experimental factor	Yes	No	Yes
Exposure to uncontrolled events	Yes	Yes	Yes
After Measurement	Yes (Y_2)	Yes (Y'_2)	Yes (Y''_2)
Change	$d_1=(Y'_2-Y_1)$	$d_2=(Y'_2-Y'_1)$	$d_3=(Y''_2-Y''_1)$

Interaction = $d_1 - (d_2+d_3)$

This design involves an addition of one more control group to the previous design, i.e., 'Before-After' study with one control group. This second control group is not pre-measured but is exposed to the experimental variable and subjected, of course, to after measurement. The 'before' measure of the second control group is assumed to be similar to the 'before' measures of the experimental and the first control group, i.e., equal to the average of the 'before' measure of the experimental group and control group I. Thus, in control group II, there is exposure to experimental variable but no possibility of interaction between the 'before' measure and the experimental variable.

If we assume, for a moment, that contemporaneous events or maturational processes are not likely to have significant effect on the dependent variable in this design, then change in control group II, i.e., d_3 may be taken as the effect of experimental variable alone. Again, the change in control group I may be taken as the effect of 'before' measurement alone. Further more, the difference between the change in scores of experimental group, i.e., d_1 and the sum changes in stores of two control groups, i.e., (d_2 + d_3) may be taken as the effect of interaction between the 'before' measurement and the experimental variable. This interaction may have the effect of enhancing or reducing (in varying degrees) the effects of the experimental variable.

Let us try to understand this by an example. Suppose the researcher wants to test the hypothesis that a new system of instruction (X) has the effect of improving the performance of students at the examination. Should he decide to use the 'Before-After' design with two control groups, he would need to follow the procedure shown in the above representation. He administers a test to two out of the three equivalent groups, i.e., the experimental group and the control group I, to know the 'before' measure on the performance of the students. The 'before' measure of the control groups II is assumed to be the average of the 'before' measure of the two groups, subjected to 'before' measurement. Suppose this measure was 50 marks in both the groups and therefore, control group II is also assumed to measure 50 marks. Next, the experimental group and the control group II are exposed to the experimental variable, i.e., those groups are exposed to the new method of instruction whereas control group I is taught in the usual way. Of course, during the time that the groups are subjected to the experimental variable, say for a fortnight, all the groups are equally subject to the effect of factors external to the experiment and beyond the control of the experimenter. Lastly, the 'After' measures are taken for all the groups and the changes, i.e., difference between the 'After' measures and 'Before' measures, are recorded.

It is clear that the change in the control group II (d_3) is due to experimental variable, i.e., the new method of instruction, and the uncontrolled events. Now assuming that the uncontrolled contemporaneous events did not have any significant effect on the dependent variable (i.e., performance in terms of marks), this change, let us say (60 – 50 = 10) of 10 marks, may be attributed to the new methsod of instruction alone. The change in control group I may be attributed to the effects of 'before' measurement, i.e., the awareness in the subjects about the experiment and thus a resultant keenness or extra efforts on their part to do better at the second examination. Let us say, the change amounts to (54 – 50 = 4) four marks. Thus, the individual effects of the 'before' measurement and the experimental variable, assuming the effect of the uncontrolled events as zero, total to fourteen (10 + 4).

Now, the experimental group registers, let us say, a change of (65 – 50 = 15) fifteen marks. This change is the integrated effect of the 'before' measurement, plus the effect of experimental variable, plus the effects of uncontrolled factors, plus the effects of the interactions between (a) the 'before' measurement and experimental variable, (b) that between the experimental variable and the uncontrolled factors and (c) that between the 'before' measurement and the uncontrolled factors. But since there is reason to believe (in our example) that the uncontrolled factors have no or very negligible effect, the interaction of this experiment would really occur only between the 'before' measurement and experimental variable differently than they would have, if they were not pre-measured. Thus, the change, i.e., 15 marks, is the cumulative effect of (1) the 'before' measurement, (2) the experimental variable and the interaction between (I) and (II). From our control groups (I) and (II) it is found that the individual effects of (1), the 'before' measurement and (11) the experimental variable, adds up to 14 marks ($d_2 + d_3$). But for the interaction the change in the experimental group, i.e., d_1 would be equal to (d_2+d_3), i.e., 14 marks. We find however, that (d_1=15) exceeds ($d_2 - d_3$) by 1 mark.

This means that the interactional effect of (I) and (II) is equal to + 1. (The interactional effect might be negative also). It is clear now that this experimental design is useful and efficient only in situations where there is a sound reason to believe that the uncontrolled contemporaneous events or maturational processes are not likely to have significant effects. 'How would we proceed in a situation where such uncontrolled factors are quite likely to have important influences on the dependent variable?' is the question that we now turn to answer.

R.L. Solomon has provided an answer to this question by proposing a further elaboration of the earlier two control groups with a view to installing safeguards when contemporaneous events or developmental changes may be expected to influence experimental results. This involves the addition of a third control group.

Before-After Study with Three Control Groups

Condition	*Experimental Group*	*Control Group I*	*Control Group II*	*Control Group III*
Before Measurement	Yes (Y1)	Yes (Y'1)	No (Y"1) $\left[\frac{Y1+Y'1}{2}\right]$	No (Y'"1) $=\left[\frac{Y1+Y'1}{2}\right]$
Exposure to Experimental factor	Yes	No	Yes	No
Exposure to uncontrolled event	Yes	Yes	Yes	Yes
After Measurement	Yes (Y2)	(Y'2)	(Y'2)	(Y"3)
Change	d1 = Y2 – Y1	d2 = Y2 – Y1	d3 = Y"2 – Y"1	d4 = Y"2 – Y"1

Interaction = d_1 $(d_2 + d_3 - d_4)$ $(y'_2 - y'_1)$

As should be clear from the above representation, the experimental group and control group I are subjected to 'before' measurement. As with the previous design (with two control groups), the control groups II and III are not pre-measured and are assumed to have the pre-measure score equal to the average of such scores in the experimental and control group I. The experimental variable is introduced to the experimental group and control group II. All the four groups are assumed to be equally subject to the effects of external contemporaneous events, let us say. Some national event or some campaign, etc., during the period of experiment. All the four groups are measured after the experiment.

In such a design, the change in control group III, i.e., d_4, represents the effect of contemporaneous events beyond the experimenter since this happens to be the only factor operative on this group. The change in control group II, i.e., d_3, represents the effect of the experimental variable and of the contemporaneous events. Change in the control group I, i.e., d_2, represents the effects of 'before' measurement and of the contemporaneous factors. The effect of the experimental variable alone, i.e., of the new method of instruction, can be assessed by subtracting the change in control group III from the change in control group II, i.e., $d_3 - d_4$. The change in the experimental group, i.e., d_1, reflects the cumulative effects of 'before' measurement, of the experimental variable, of uncontrolled events and of interaction between these factors. Now this design affords us the individual measures of the effects of uncontrolled factor, i.e., d_4 (the effect of say, some national campaign which keeps subjects more informed about certain events or things, thus, improving their performance in the examination) and of the effects of experimental variables alone (d_3–d_4) and finally the effect of 'before' measurement (d_2– d_4). Hence, we can easily calculate the interactional effect of the three factors, i.e., (a) 'before' measurement, (b) experimental variable and (c) the uncontrolled factors, on the dependent variable, i.e., the examination score by subtracting the total of the individual effects of the three factors (a), (b) and (c) from the total change registered in the experimental group. Thus, interactional effect would be equal to $d_1 - (d_2 + d_3 - d_4)$.

It may be observed that this experimental design with three control groups is tantamount to doing the experiment twice, i.e., once with a 'before-after' design with one control group (experimental group and control group I) and the second time, with an 'after only' design (control group II and III).

In the context of the discussion on the various types of experimental designs, it must be remembered that these experiments suffer from a general limitation of a practical nature, i.e., the researcher is not always in a position to test a causal hypothesis by assigning subjects to different conditions in which he directly controls the causal (experimental) variable. For example, if the hypothesis was concerned with the relation between smoking and cancer, the researcher would hardly be in a position to control the extent of smoking as per the ideal requirement of the experimental procedure by assigning different persons to smoke different number of cigarettes. All that the researcher can get at is a record of how much an individual has smoked and of whether he has cancer. The correlation between smoking and cancer may be computed.

But the existence of a correlation between smoking and cancer does not mean necessarily that one is the cause of the other. The researcher must contend with the possibility expressed by the correlation that people who smoke heavily are for some as yet unknown reason, also the kind of people who develop cancer, if, therefore, a non-experimental study (since 'experimental' control as in this example, is not possible) would provide a test of 'causal' hypothesis, it must provide ground for making inferences about causality and safeguards against unwarranted inferences. But the non-experimental studies cannot provide such safeguards as adequately as the experimental studies do. Certain substitute safeguards are available. These safeguards involve comparison of people subjected to contrasting experiences in the real life-setting, determination of the time-order of variable (supposed 'cause' and 'effect') and examination of the relationship between the variables in terms of pattern of relationship that might be anticipated if one or the other were to be the causal condition.

(a) Comparison of groups exposed to contrasting experiences: If an investigator is not in a position to assign subjects to different groups, one which will be exposed to a given treatment and one of which will not be so exposed, then the only alternate solution is to locate groups of people in the natural setting who are about to be or have been exposed to experiences that differ with respect to the assumed causal variable in which the researcher is interested. For example, if the researcher was interested in the effect of community development programme, i.e., one of these would be the one exposed to the C.D. programme and the other equivalent community would have to be the one that did get exposed to the C.D. programme. Such a study approximates an experiment in the sense that the community in which the C.D. programmes have been in operation represents the 'experimental' group and other community represents the 'control' group. The difference between the two communities in terms of certain pertinent characteristic may be attributed to the causal variable, i.e., the C.D. programme. Of course, we must be aware of the obvious difficulty involved in selecting those groups (communities) that are equivalent in all respects and differ only in respect of the exposure to the assumed causal variable. In the real life-setting, it would be a stroke of good luck to come across such comparable groups differing only in respect of the causal variable.

The type of design we have just discussed may be called the 'ex-post facto' design. Studies using the 'ex-post facto' pattern suffer from a serious limitation, namely, that the subjects cannot be randomly assigned to different conditions and there is no possibility of prior measurements to check whether the two groups were initially similar in their position on the assumed dependent variable due to absence of before measurement or in respect of other characteristics believed to be relevant to it.

As suggested earlier, the researcher may sometimes be in a position to locate two groups of comparable people one of which is about to be exposed to certain experiences (assumed causal variable) and the other, not likely to be so exposed. Such a study approximates a 'before-after' experiment with one control group. The group of subjects about to undergo a particular experience, e.g., those selected to undergo a particular orientation course, represents the 'experimental' group; those not selected represents the 'control' group.

Let us now discuss how one can get at the second kind of evidence necessary to establish causality, i.e., evidence of the time-order or variables in a non-experimental study design. In some cases, the evidence that X preceded Y and not *vice versa,* is so clear that no supplementary evidence is needed. Often, however, the time-relationship between two variables is not so clear. Even though one appears to be prior to the other, this may not really be the case. For example, in a study of the effect of early experiences on the typical response pattern during adulthood, a researcher may have to rely on his adult subjects' accounts of their childhood. What he would get out of the adults is actually likely to be statement (about childhood) that have been heavily coloured by the subjects' personal interpretations based on their personal 'theories' and their prospective reflections as adults.

Panel Studies

The researcher may utilize various procedures to secure evidence of the time-relationship between the variables. We shall discuss two of them.

(1) The investigator may ask the subjects how they felt about something before a certain event took place or whether there have been any changes in their feelings. For example, a question such as this may be asked: "Can you remember what you thought about life in an industrial complex before you moved into it?" B ut one cannot afford to overlook the danger in this case, that replies to such questions may be inaccurate. The researcher may sometimes devise indirect checks on the incidence of distortion.

(2) Gathering evidence through studies extended over time ***Panel Studies.*** *The panel study* is a special type of long view technique that measures certain attributes of a given sample of persons at different points in time. The panel study, however, differs from other long view studies in at least two significant ways. Firstly, the panel study is more likely to have a real historical interest as compared to other long view studies in that it is generally concerned with what happened at particular times. It is understandable why a study at a single point in time can hardly be used to find out how people of a certain programme of development or a certain campaign. Thus, there is no substitute for data on different points of time.

It is well worth noting that a panel study is not the only way to obtain this type of historical information. Alternatively it may be possible to take separate samples at various points of time and on this basis to attempt a historical documentation. Suppose we wanted to know in absolute terms what proportion of votes a particular political party has obtained at different times before a particular election, then it hardly matters, in conceptual parlance, whether the poll is taken on a sample of people just about a fortnight before the election or whether a poll is taken on the same sample of the above size (panel) twice. Major cost differences between these two strategies are not quite substantial.

Secondly, the panel study may be distinguished from other long view techniques in that the panel is much more efficient when charges are sought to be measured from period to period rather than on the absolute levels. For example, a manufacturer may want to know whether or not more people are shifting towards his brand of produce than moving away from it. The panel study typically grapples with such comparative problem with great statistical efficiency.

It is obvious that the panel method in comparison to non-panel long view method reveals much back and forth shifting behaviour that otherwise fails to meet the eye.

Studies which are limited to a single observation or single interview or other measurement of each respondent, and in which the researcher does not have supplementary information about individual's experiences, there is little possibility of securing evidence about time sequences except by asking the respondents to recall when events took place. But in studies that focus on the same people over a period of time, the investigator may secure direct evidence of time relationships among variable. Such longitudinal studies may take the form of repeated observations or interviews with the same subjects; the common group of informants subjected to repeated observations or measurements over a period of time constitute the 'panel' for the researcher. The 'panel' is subjected to a 'multiphased study.' The 'American Soldier Studies' conducted by *Stouffer* and associates provide an example of utilizing different kinds of data about the same subjects at different times.

Samuel Stouffer and associates were interested in the relation between the acceptance of the official value system of the Army and promotion. They interviewed a group of newly-inducted soldiers and ascertained their position on the scale of acceptance of the Army value system.

Four months later, they examined the Army records of these very men and found that a higher proportion of those who had a higher position on the scale of value acceptance, had got promotion. This led them to the conclusion that positive commitment to the Army value system was conducive to promotion.

We may point out the typical advantages of the panel technique as under:

1(a) If mini-samples of a given population are studied by single contacts and differences in the results noted from one period to another, one cannot know whether these differences are due to differences in the samples surveyed during each period includes the same persons or groups, as in the panel techniques, the variations or shifts in the results may be attributed with certitude to a real change in the phenomena studied. For example, full effect of a campaign cannot be ascertained through sequence of polls taken on different people. They show only majority changes. They conceal minor changes which tend to cancel out one another and sometimes even major changes if these are nullified by opposing trends. Most importantly, they neither indicate who is changing nor do they follow the vagaries of the individual voter along the path of his vote, to discover the relative effects of various other influencial factors on his final voting verdict.

(b) Data secured from the same persons over a period of time, affording a detailed picture of the factors involved in bringing about shifts in opinions or attitudes, can be secured for everyone in the panel. An analysis of the chartered profile of individuals in a panel may afford the researcher an insight into the causal relationships.

(c) The information collected about each person from time to time tends to be deeper and more voluminous than that obtained in single contacts. It is possible, despite certain limitations to build up an inclusive case history of each panel member.

(d) Provided, of course, that the group constituting the panel is cooperative, it may well be possible to set up experimental situations which expose all members of the panel to a certain influence and thus enable the effectiveness of this influence to be measured.

(e) It has been the experience of researchers that the members of a panel learn to open out and unload their feeling in the course of frequentative interviews and so valuable comments and elaboration of points made by them can be secured. Whereas the first interview may elicit only 'yes' or 'no' responses from the respondents, the repeated interviews or measurements spread over a continuum of time may elicit from them elaborate responses in so far as they might have thought deeply about the problem after the first administration. On first contact, the informants may be suspicious of the investigator and may have little familiarity with the problem.

The problems raised by the panel procedure are often sufficient to off-set the gains attendant upon it. We may briefly discuss the limitations of the panel techniques.

(a) The loss of panel members presents a formidable problem for the researcher. People change their locale, become ill, or die or are subjected to other influences which make it necessary for them to drop out of the panel. Thus, the panel that was initially intended as a representative sample of the population may subsequently become unrepresentative. The losses in the membership of the panel may be occasioned by the loss of interest among the panel members or a change in attitude toward the panel idea. Not infrequently, the enthusiasm of the panel members dies down after the first or the second interview.

(b) *Paul Lazarsfeld* has pointed out that the members of a panel develop a 'critical set' and hence cease to be representatives of the general public. The panel invariably has an educational effect. It tends to dramatize and increase one's interest in otherwise unobserved elements and to heighten one's interest in otherwise unobserved elements and to heighten one's awareness of things and events around him. Hence the mere fact of participation in the panel may change a person's attitude and opinions.

(c) Once the members of a panel have expressed an attitude or opinion they tend to try to be consistent and stick to it. Thus, panel members as compared to the general public are loss likely to change. Thus, the panel may misrepresent the population.

(d) The detailed records are available for the most stationary elements of the population. Of course, the mobile groups of a community belong to the panel for a shorter time. Panels composed of the same persons for many years will gradually become panels of old people and eventually die out.

A panel study, however, is not always feasible. One of the difficulties is that the events or thoughts may already be long past by the time the researcher begins. Occasionally, memory is not always reliable and the respondents may be inclined to 'construct' these part events not so much from their fading memories but from their personalised theory about their past.

Lastly, let us consider the problem of how to search for competing causal assumptions (whether Y to X is the cause) in a non-experimental situation. It is often reasonable to expect that if X were the cause it would show a higher degree of Y. But this would not be so if Y were the causal factor.

Klineberg had hypothesized that the comparatively low Intelligence Quotients of Negroes in the southern part of U.S.A. might be attributed to their poor environments. This led him to expect that the I.Q. of Negro children will increase with the length of residence in a city such as New York. His hypothesis was borne out by investigation of Negro children in New York.

In this reference we would do well to remember that the mere fact of scores on Y differing with different lengths of exposure to X does not provide a clear-cut basis for an inference of causality. The possibility is that X and Y may be mutually reinforcing. Again, it is also possible that other factors may be associated with differences in length of exposure to the independent variable (X) and it may be these other factors which really account for differences in the dependent variable (Y). In *Klineberg's* study the possibility that the more intelligent Negroes had moved to New York much earlier might really be a reflection of this characteristic (high I.Q.) of their parents.

A variety of checks for such possibilities have been used, viz. :

(a) Repetition of the study at another time might provide a basis for scrutinizing whether some factor other than the assumed one could have caused the changes in the dependent variable.

(b) Controlling factors that may be confounded with the length of exposure to the assumed causal variable. For example, the researcher controls the 'age' factor if it is likely to affect the dependent variable in conjunction with the independent variable, i.e., he compares individuals of the same age who differ in length of exposure to the causal variable.

REFERENCES

(1) Selltiz, *et al.*: *op. cit.*, p. 50.

(2) Ackoff: *op. cit.*, p. 11.

(3) Selltiz, *et al.*: *op. cit.*, *p.* 50.

(4) *Ibid.*, p. 40.

(5) *Ibid.*, p. 53.

(6) Thopson: *op. cit.*, p. 30.

(7) See Caws, *The Philosophy of Science,* D.Van Nostrand Co. Inc., New York 1965, pp. 248-55.

(8) Simon J.L, *op. cit.*, Chap: *Sampling and Probability.*

(9) *Op. cit.*, pp. 30-1.

(10) Homans, G.C.: *The Human Group,* Routledge Kegan Paul Ltd., London, 1968, p. 141.

Chapter VIII

The General Problems of Measurement

In as much as measurement of things, their properties, overt or covert, and their responses to certain stimuli, etc., are essential engagements of scientific research it hardly needs to be emphasized that the quality of research will depend on the fruitfulness of the measurement procedures employed. It is understandable that basic to any meaningful measurement is an adequate formulation of the research questions and explicit definition of the concepts utilized in the course of the study. In other words, the researcher must know besides why he wants to measure, what it is that he wants to measure. Measurement in the realms of human behaviour or social phenomena is typically hazardous since a substantial part of what is intended to be measured is covert or of an inferrential nature.

We have just stressed that the researcher must have a clear notion of what is to be measured. Failing this, he would not be in a position to decide how he will measure it. A measurement procedure consists of the techniques for collecting data and a set of rules for using these data. The purpose of various data collection techniques that we shall be considering in the later few chapters, is to produce trustworthy evidence that is germane to the research problem. The accompanying rules facilitate the use of these data in making specific statement about the characteristics of the phenomena to which the data purport to be relevant.

Data may be collected in many different ways, e.g., by observation, questionnaire or interviews, examination of records or available statistics and/or by projective techniques. The data collection techniques and the rules for utilizing the data must produce if they are to be useful, information that besides being relevant to the research problem is valid, reliable and precise. Let us briefly understand what type of a measuring instrument or procedure can produce information that is (a) valid, (b) reliable and (c) precise.

(a) An instrument is valid to the extent it measures what it purports to measure. If the researcher was interested in measuring a person's I.Q. (intelligence) and adopted as a measuring instrument a test that measured only general knowledge or memory, then the measuring instrument cannot be said to be valid. As Selltiz, Jahoda and associates state, "A measuring procedure is valid to the extent to which scores reflect true differences among individuals, groups or situations in the characteristics it seeks to measure...."s[1] A thermometer, for instance, cannot be a valid instrument for measuring pressure.

(b) An instrument of measurement is reliable to the extent that the independent and comparable measures of the same object give similar results (provided, of course, that the object being subjected to measurements does not undergo changes between the measurements). For instance, a measuring tape made of elastic would be an extremely unreliable instrument since the same object may yield different measures (values) depending upon how much the elastic is stretched. Similarly, an instrument, say an I.Q. test, would be considered unreliable if persons who were classified on the basis of the first measurements as 'geniuses' are classified as 'below average' on a second measurement taken after, say, a month of the first one.

(c) The measuring instruments is precise to the extent that it is capable of making distinctions in certain characteristic of persons or situations fine enough for the purpose it is expected to serve. A precise scale for attitude measurements will be able to distinguish between fine shades, e.g., strongly favourable, neutral, unfavourable and strongly unfavourable, of people's attitudes and not register just crude differences.

We now turn to consider the different factors which may contribute to variations among scores registered on a measuring instrument administered to a group of subjects. This consideration is very relevant (especially, in the context of human behaviour) because the result of measurement may reflect not only the characteristics being measured but the process of measurment itself. Following are the possible sources of variation in scores among a group of subjects subjected to a measuring instrument.

(a) Of course, the variations in scores in the ideal measuring situation would reflect the true differences in the characteristic which the researcher is attempting to measure. This is as it should be.

(b) Conceivably, true differences in other relatively stable characteristics of the subject may affect his score. Few techniques available to the social scientist can provide 'pure' measures of any given characteristic. Hence, the scores of individuals in a group may reflect not only differences in the characteristic being measured but also the differences in other characteristics intertwined with the one being measured.

(c) Variations in the situation in which measurement takes place often play a major part in contributing to the difference in scores among a group of subjects; for example, the interview results of a subordinate may be markedly affected by the presence of his superior officer. Comparatively, the presence of his co-workers would not affect them so substantially.

(d) Various personal factors such as latent motive, state of health, fatigue, mood, etc. may contribute to variations in scores of the subjects in a group.

(e) Lack of uniformity and inadequacies in the method of administering the measuring instrument, e.g., administration of an interview schedule to subjects, may contribute to variations in scores among subjects.

(f) Any measuring instrument, taps only a sample of items relevant to the characteristic being measured. If a measuring instrument comprises mostly items to which the subjects are likely to respond in one way rather than the other, that is, if the items did not represent the entire universe of possible aspects then the scores may vary owing to the sampling of items.

(g) The subjects will quite understandably respond to the items or questions on the basis of how they understand them. Therefore, if the subjects' understanding of the items in a measuring instrument is in uniform, variations in their responses may reflect the differences in interpretations or understanding rather than the true differences (in the characteristics).

(h) An instrument of measurement may not function effectively in reference to its purport owing to such circumstances as poorly-printed instructions, wrong check marks, lack of space for recording responses fully, etc. It is not improbable that these factors might contribute to variations in the scores of subjects.

(i) The phase of analysis of data involves many sub-processes such as coding, tabulation, statistical computation, etc. Errors entering at this stage may contribute to variations in scores of individuals.

We have seen some of the major factors contributing to variations in results obtained from any measurement procedure. The errors introduced into the data by such factors (from (b) to (i) may be grouped into two broad categories:

(1) *Constant or systematic errors* which are introduced into the measurement by some factor which systematically affects the characteristic being measured in the course of measurement itself (for example, stable characteristics like intelligence, education, social status etc.).

(2) *Random errors* are introduced into the measurement by factors likely to vary from one measurement to the next, although the characteristic that the researcher

wants to measure has not changed. For example, transient aspects of the person, situation of measurement or of the measurement procedure, etc. are factors that might introduce such errors. Thus, a random error reveals itself in the lack of consistency in reported or equivalent measurements of the same person, group, object or event.

The Problem Involving Validity of Measurements

The validity of a measuring instrument as suggested earlier has a reference to the extent to which differences in scores on it reflect the true differences among individuals or groups, etc. in respect of the characteristic it seeks to measure, or the true difference in the same person or group from one occasion to another. We have seen how the constant errors and the random errors may get introduced into the measure. Estimates or validity are thus affected by both types of errors.

In essence, validity concerns the extent to which an instrument is measuring what it is intended to measure. The formulation can be interpreted in various direction. 'Realism' could be a term to be used as a label for this goal. Realism is not the same as truth, a realistic description need not be literally true, but it must help us to get an adequate or realistic picture of the world either by telling us straightforward truths or by affording us points of view, concepts and the like, which are faithful in relation to this purpose.

Let us take an example of the thermometer. What does it measure, which variables it is assigning values to? The answer to this is minimal realism — a measurement is anchored in reality in the sense that it pertains to significant aspects of the world. But then we can go on to ask the further question of how it measures temperature, that is, if it measures temperature correctly and thus measures nothing but temperature. This is maximal realism.

We may distinguish among three different interpretations of the requirement that the result of a measurement should be about 'what it is intended', that is, three different meanings of 'realism.'

(1) The realism of a certain set of data consists of its correspondence to some facts, i.e., its truth.

(2) The realism of a certain set of data consists of its connection with some significant problem or with the purpose of the study, i.e., its relevance.

(3) The realism of a certain set of data consists of its correspondence with precisely those facts that are connected with some real problem or the purpose of the study, i.e., truth and relevance. The meaning of the term validity oscillates between (2) and (3). Krippendorf observes, "Generally, validity designates a quality that compels one to accept scientific results as evidence. Its closest relative is objective truth."[2]

Since we do not know an individual's true position on the variable or characteristic we seek to measure, there is no direct way of determining its validity. In the absence of such direct knowledge of the individual's true position in respect of the variable being measured, the validity of an instrument is judged by the extent to which its results are compatible with other relevant evidence. What constitutes relevant evidence depends, on of course, on the nature and purpose of the measuring instrument. The purpose of certain tests is to provide a basis for specific predictions about individuals, e.g., whether certain individuals will be successful in a particular type of career, profession or in solving a certain type of problem. Other tests, although they are designed to measure specific characteristics of individuals do not afford predictions about how individuals will respond to function in given situations. In the case of the former type of tests, evidence as to whether the individual actually conforms to the predictions, provides a basis for estimating the validity of the test. Investigation of validity in these terms may be described as pragmatic, i.e., validity judged in terms of accuracy of predictions made on the basis of the test results. The latter type of tests which are designed to measure characteristics that do not lead to specific predictions cannot naturally be evaluated so directly. Certain other evidence is necessary and is sought to provide a basis for judging whether the test or instrument measures the concept, it is charged with measuring. The approach has been designated as construct validation.

(a) *Pragmatic Validity:* In the pragmatic approach to estimation of validity the interest is in the usefulness of the measuring instrument as an indicator or a predictor of some other behaviour or characteristics of the individual. The investigator is not interested in the performance of the subject on the test *per se;* rather he is interested in the person's performance on the test only as an indication of a certain characteristic of the person.

What is essential in this approach is that there be a reasonably valid and reliable criterion with which the scores on the measuring instrument can be compared. In general, the nature of the predictions and the techniques available for checking them will determine what criteria are relevant. For example, if the purpose of a test is to predict success in school, one very relevant criterion could be the school grades.

Ideally, the criterion with which the scores on the measuring instrument are compared should itself be perfectly valid and reliable. But in practice the investigator rarely, if at all, finds a thoroughly tested criterion and usually selects the one that seems most adequate despite its limitations. The reliability and validity of the available criteria may be improved upon by careful defining of the various dimensions of the criterion and getting information relevant to these.

(b) *Construct Validity:* Many of the measures in social sciences deal with or relate to complex constructs, e.g., measures of intelligence, of attitudes, of modernization, of group morale, etc. Cronbach and Meehl point out that the definition of such constructs consists, in part, of sets of propositions about their relationship to other variable constructs or directly observable behaviour. Thus, in examining construct validity one would ask such questions as, "what predictions would one make on the basis of these sets of propositions about the relationships among variable scores based on a measure of this construct?" or "are the measurements obtained by using this instrument consistent with these predictions?"

It is evident that the predictions in respect of the construct validity are of a different order and have a somewhat different function from those involved in determining the pragmatic validity. For example, let us consider a prediction relating to how individuals will vote at the national elections. Since this prediction relates to examining the construct validity, such prediction about voting may be made with a view to evaluating the construct validity of a test of say, 'progressive attitudes.' The researcher may reason out that since this test measures persons with progressive orientation, people who get rated as less "progressive" on this test will be more likely to vote for a particular party which has a particular ideological bias or slant. But there may not always be a high degree of correlation between "progressive" orientation and voting behaviour, since many other conceivable influences such as family tradition, socio-economic status, religion etc. may also influence his vote. In construct validation, all the predictions that would be made on the basis of a set of propositions involving the construct enter into the consideration of validity (ideally). For example, the researcher in the above illustration may specify voting preferences for candidates within a particular political party. He may also make and test predictions about relations between voting and socio-economic status, religion, education, etc. If any one of these predictions is not borne out, the validity either of the measure or of the underlying hypotheses would become suspect.

It should be remembered that examination of construct validity involves validation not only of the measuring instrument but also of the theory or perspective underlying it. If the researcher's predictions are not borne out, the researcher may not get a clear clue as to whether the shortcoming is in the measuring instrument or in the theory on which the predictions were grouped. Consider, for example, a prediction or hypothesis that greater interaction between people leads to greater liking for each other amongst them.

If the findings do not suggest the predicted or hypothesized relationship, it may mean either that measure of 'liking' or of 'interaction' is not valid or that the hypothesis incorrect. The researcher may under the circumstances, be led to re-examine the constructs as 'interaction' or 'liking', and the entire network of propositions that led to this prediction. The outcome or result of this quest may be the refinement of the constructs.

Campbell and Fiske have suggested that the investigation of construct validity can be made more rigorous by increased attention being paid to the adequacy of the measure of the construct in question; before its relationships to other variables are considered. They propose that two kinds of evidence about a measure are needed before one as really justified in examining relationship with other variables:

(a) evidence that different measure of the construct yield similar results; and

(b) proof that the construct thus measured can be differentiated from other constructs.

In order to secure such evidence, the researcher must measure the characteristics from which he wishes to differentiate or segregate his construct, using the same general methods he has applied to his central construct.

In the light of the above discussion, it is clear that construct validity cannot be adequately tested by a single procedure. Evidence derived from a number of sources is relevant, i.e., correlation with other tests, internal consistency of items, stability of pattern over time, etc. How the evidence from each of these sources bears on the estimation of the validity of the test depends on the relationship predicted in the theoretic system in which the construct has been employed. To the extent more and more different relationships are tested and confirmed, the greater is the support marshalled both for the measuring instrument and for the underlying theory.

We have discussed thus far two aspects of validation. We shall do well to bear in mind that these aspects are not mutually exclusive. Estimates of pragmatic validity may enter into the evaluation of construct validity and principally, the construct validity of the measure shown to have pragmatic validity could be investigated.

In sum, construct validity does not lie in the correspondence between reality and results but in the relationship between results of a measurement or investigation and some theory supposed to shed light on the problems or questions behind the investigation.

It has been suggested that the measures shown to have pragmatic validity are usually arrived at by a trial and error method. The ideal requirement of science lays down that the constructs involved in these measures and their relation to the criterion variables be thoroughly considered. Such investigations typically lead to clarification of concepts and eventually to construct validation of these measures. The scientist should not, advisedly, remain content with a measurement procedure which has been validated only pragmatically. So long as the scientist cannot understand the reason behind its working, i.e., why a particular prediction comes out to be true, he has no assurance that the 'mysterious' conditions of its working still hold with reference to a particular application. It is quite understandable that so long as a particular predaiction ignores any concern for an underlying theoretical explanation as to its working, it does not afford any basis for generalization to other problems.

The Problem of Reliability of Measurements: The formulation of the requirement of reliability is often impaired by a certain vagueness. By the reliability of a measurement with respect to a given variable is meant the constancy of its results as that variable assumes different values. The variables usually considered are: the measuring event (e.g., the same person using the same ruler in successive measurement "forms" of an intelligence test)1; the person doing the measuring (e.g., different eye witnesses of the same event).

Holsti says: "If research is to satisfy the requirement of objectivity, measures and procedures must be reliable; i.e., repeated measures with the same instrument on a given sample of data should yield similar results."[3]

Here we find a connection between the concepts of objectivity and of reliability. This is only as it should be. It is natural to assume that an objective result is independent of the subject who conducted the investigation. Here, however, we must distinguish between the factual or ontological problem, i.e., what makes the result true and the epistemic or methodological problem — how do we come to know that a result is true?

Ontological independence is a two-place relation. A datum is ontologically independent of its producer (for example, scorer) when it is not about the producer.

The question of epistemic independence is, however, more complicated and controversial. Epistemic independence is a three place relation; it is a relation between a producer, P, a result, R, and a set of possible producer, S. If a certain result R1, produced by P1 is epistemically independent in relation to a population of scores, S1 to the extent that it is possible for the members of S1 to know R1 without first acquiring mental characteristics that P1 already has. A datum is thus maximally independent, in this sense, in a certain population of scores if every member of this sense, in a certain population of scores if every member of this population would produce it. The epistemic independence is a matter of degree, in so far as more or less of specific capabilities and knowledge of the scorer can be made use of in the process of measuring a phenomenon.

Krippendorf distinguishes between three kinds of reliability:

(1) *Stability* is the degree to which a process is invariant over time, i.e., yields the same results at different points of time.
(2) *Reproducibility* is the degree to which a process can be recreated under varying circumstances, different locations involving different materials, forms, i.e., yields the same results despite different implementations.
(3) *Accuracy* is the degree to which a process conforms in effect to a known standard, i.e., yields the desired results in a variety of circumstances.

Reliability is regarded to be one of the constituent elements of validity. A measurement procedure or an operational definition (of a construct) is reliable to the extent that independent applications of it yield consistent results. Julian L. Simon remarks, "reliability is roughly the same as consistency and repeatability."[4] He further elaborates that if one knows that a measuring instrument or an operational definition has statisfactory validity, he need not bother about its reliability. If an instrument is valid, it means in essence that it is reflecting primarily the characteristic which it is supposed to measure, thus there would be little reason to investigate its reliability, i.e., the extent to which it is influenced by extraneous factors.

Methodologists would not, however, be inclined to subscribe to the view that reliability is presupposed by validity. They would point out instances between these two concepts and that reliability is a necessary but not a sufficient condition for validity or in other words, that validity implies reliability but is not implied by it.

It is only rarely that a researcher is in a position to say in advance whether his instrument has a satisfactory validity. Hence, it is generally necessary to determine the extent of variable error in the measuring instrument. This applies with particular force to construct validity where simple determination of validity directly is impossible of realization.

Till such time as a satisfactory measure of validity and reliability of a measuring instrument has been demonstrated already, its reliability should be determined before it is used in a study. We now consider some of the methods of determining the reliability of measurements.

Evaluation of reliability of a measuring instrument requires determination of the consistency of independent but comparable measures of the same individual or situation. It would be desirable, therefore, to have many repeated observations or measurements of the same individual or situation as a basis for estimating errors of measurement. But in the area of human behaviour this is often not possible. Apart from other things, such oft repeated measurements may create annoyance, fatigue and may also affect the characteristics one wishes to study. When this is likely, reliability may be estimated on the basis of as few measures as possible (even two) for each individual in a sample of the 'universe' or even on the basis of one measure if it can be subjected to internal analysis. Enough measurements to provide a basis for evaluation of reliability may also be obtained by increasing the number of individuals measured rather than the number of measurements of the same individual.

Different methods of estimating reliability are focussed on different sources of variation in scores: (a) some are concerned with 'stability' of individual's position from one administration of the measure to another, (b) others are concerned with the 'equivalence' of the individual's position on different instruments expected to measure the same characteristic. They essentially focus on unreliability due to sampling of items or to substantive variations in administration, and (c) still other methods are concerned both with 'stability' and 'equivalence.'

Stability: The stability of results of a measuring instrument is determined on the basis of consistency of measures on repeated applications. Of course, where the characteristic being measured is likely to fluctuate between the subsequent measurements, e.g., attitudes, morale, etc., inconsistency in measurements would be evidenced.

This should not, however, be interpreted as unreliability of the measuring instrument. What should bother us is the effect of extraneous factors. The appropriate method for determining stability is to compare the result of repeated measurements with a view to identify whether the source of instability is genuine fluctuations in the characteristic being measured or a random error due to inadequacies contained in the measuring instrument. When the measuring instrument is an interview schedule, questionnaire or a projective test, involving subjects' cooperation, usually, only two administrations are used. In case the measuring device is observation in a natural setting, the number of observations may be repeated.

A restricted number of administrations (usually two) in case of identical repeat-interview, questionnaire or projective test is advisable because these measuring procedures require a great deal of participation by the individual subject and interest, curiosity, and motivation may get substantially dampened during the second application of the test. Consequently, the test though objectively identical to the earlier one, may actually represent a substantially different test-situation on second administration. Secondly, the subject may artificially try to maintain consistency in his responses at the second application as he may remember his responses to the first one. There is, of course, the possibility that the initial measurement has actually changed the characteristics being measured (as in the 'before-after' experiment.) Lastly, there is the possibility of a genuine change occurring between two administrations of the test. When there is the possibility of initial measure having affected the results of the second measurement and also of genuine change having been brought about by extraneous factors, the common practice is to strike a mean between waiting long enough for the effects of the first testing to fade off but not long enough for a significant amount of change to take place.

The method of 'alternate' measurement procedures administered at different times is a well-thumbed design to take account of the combined effect of these various sources of unreliability and thus ensure both 'stability' and 'equivalence.' A group of subjects receive one form of test at one time and after a lapse of time receive a different form of the test. Alternatively, the group of subjects may be rated by one observer in a particular situation and by a different observer after the stipulated lapse of time in another situation. Correlation between scores or rating at these two points of time provides an overall index of the reliability.

As in the repeated-observation method, there is the possibility that genuine changes in the characteristic being measured might have occurred in the interval between two test administrations. But again, provided that the results of two testing are reasonably independent, the effect of this possibility is to make the obtained coefficient an estimate of the minimal reliability of the measuring instrument.

Since the method of alternate measurement procedure administered at different times takes into account more sources of variation than the other methods described earlier, it ordinarily gives a lower but a more accurate estimate of reliability than either a coefficient of stability or a coefficient of equivalence.

Which method of testing reliability a researcher will use in a given research depends not only on the intrinsic worth of different techniques but also on the practical facilities available to him and the resources that can be procured to develop the measuring procedures. Sometimes, it may not be possible for him to reach the same group of subjects for the second or subsequent measurements or the cost of so doing may be prohibitive. In such a case, he has no choice but to base his estimate of reliability on the equivalence of scores. Sometimes, the measuring instrument does not lend itself to internal analysis that may be warranted as a test of equivalence.

The reliability of measuring instruments can often be increased by taking appropriate steps with respect to the source of error. For example, the conditions under which the measurement procedure is applied can be standardized to effect a similarity between conditions in which subsequent measurements are taken. Adequately trained, instructed and motivated personnel greatly helps to minimize the possibility of variations during the administration of procedures.

There are two methods of increasing the reliability of a measurement procedure. These involve the selection and accumulation of measurement operations themselves rather than any change in the conditions of the measurement operations. The first method of increasing reliability is to add measurement operations of the type with which the researcher started in the first place and to assign to the subject a score based on the sum of the results of all measurement operations. In the testing situation parlance, this means increasing the length of the test and in the observational situation it means increasing the number of observations or of observers or both. We can make the reliability of a measuring procedure approach the point of perfection (i.e.,1) provided we are able to add measurement operations indefinitely without changing their nature in any major way.

The second method of increasing reliability is to increase the internal consistency of the measurement operations of the test items. This method is mostly used in the field of psychological testing. The researcher begins with a large collection of test items, calculates a score based on each, and another score based on responses to the total set of items. Then the score for each item is correlated with the total score. Only those items (e.g., statements) are retained in the test which correlate most highly with the total score of the test. The items which are retained are then divided into two equivalent groups. New scores are calculated on these two groups and these scores are correlated to provide a measure of reliability of the 'purified' test.

The internal consistency of the test items may also be increased by dropping from the test items as cannot distinguish sharply between the high and low scorers, i.e., that have a low discriminatory power, those items which yield the largest differences in the direction of response, in other words, those items which have a high 'discriminatory power', are identified as the ones most consistent with the total set (test). We shall have an occasion to discuss the internal consistency of items in the chapter on scaling techniques.

It is well-worth remembering that the method of internal consistency can reduce unreliability resulting from lack of equivalence of items but it cannot do much to reduce unreliability resulting from instability of a subject's responses or variations in the condition of measurment. The method of increasing the number of measurement operations can be used to reduce these sources of unreliability if it is possible to spread the measurement operations out over a period of time or to distribute them over a number of different conditions of measurement.

Precision: We now turn to consider the problem relating to precision of the measuring instruments. In the interest of both accuracy of judgement as well as the discovery of constant relationship among characteristics that vary in amount as well as in kind, statements that merely affirm or deny differences have to be replaced by more precise statements indicating the degree of difference.

In social sciences, many of the distinctions are qualitative in nature, e.g., we distinguish different races, languages, cultures and communities. But it is often necessary and desirable to make distinctions of degree rather than of mere kind. Suppose, a researcher was interested in studying people's attitude toward the ceiling on urban property. Should he want to assert that two persons differ in their attitudes toward ceiling on urban property, he must at least be able to distinguish among different shades of attitude, that is, he must be able to identify certain persons as equivalent, or others as unequal or different. If the researcher wishes to state that the attitude of one person is more favourable than that of the other, he must be able to identify rank different attitudinal positions as more favourable or less favourable. If he wishes to make a statement that Mr. X, is much more favourable than Mr. Y as compared to Mr. Z, then he must be able to determine whether the difference between the former two attitudinal positions is equal to the difference between the latter two attitudinal positions. And going a step further, if the researcher wants to make some such assertion as "Mr. X is twice as favourable as Mr. Y," then he must be able to identify the existence of an absolute zero of favourableness for the given attitude as well as equal points above the zero point. The above four types of statements correspond respectively to four levels of measurment or as these are mediated through four types of scales, i.e., the nominal scale, ordinal scale, interval scale and ratio scale. The least powerful are the nominal scales whereas the ratio scales are the most powerful as devices for comparison.

Nominal Scales: The basic requirement for a nominal scale is that the researcher be able to distinguish two or more categories relevant to the attribute under study and specify the criteria for placing individuals or groups etc., in one or the other category. The categories are merely different from each other; they do not represent the more or less degree of the attitude or characteristic being measured. Classification of individuals according to race, for instance, constitutes a nominal scale. The use of nominal scales is characteristic of exploratory research where the emphasis is on uncovering relationship between certain characteristics rather than on specifying the mathematical form of relationship.

Ordinal Scales: An ordinal scale defines the relative position of objects or persons with respect to a characteristic with no implication of the distances between positions.

The basic requirement for an ordinal scale is that one be able to determine the order of positions of objects or persons in terms of the characteristics under study, i.e., whether an individual has more of the given characteristic than another individual or the same amount of it or less. This presupposes that one must be able to place each individual at a single point with respect to the characteristic in question. Of course, this is a requirement for the more powerful scales as well. In an ordinal scale, the scale-positions are in a clearly defined order but there is no definite indication of the distance between any two points. That is, distance between 7 and 8 may be equal to, greater than or lesser than the distance between 2 and 3 or 1 and 2. Thus, with ordinal scales, we are constrained to make statements of greater, equal or less, but we cannot articulately specify how much greater or how much less.

Interval Scales: On an interval scale, not only are the positions arranged in terms of greater, equal or less, but the units or intervals on scale are also equal. In other words, the distance between the scale positions 7 and 8 is equal to the distance between positions 2 and 3, 2 and 1. The thermometer is an example of the interval scale. The basic requirement for such a scale is a procedure for determining that the intervals are equal. It should be remembered that for many of the attributes that social sciences typically deal with, procedures affording reasonable certainty about equality of intervals are yet to be devised.

On the interval scale, the zero point is arbitrary (as in the nominal and ordinal scale); for example, in the centigrade thermometer the zero point is the mark at which water freezes but in the fahrenheit thermometer the zero point is much below the freezing point of water. Thus, in the interval scale one cannot state, for instance, that a person's attitude is twice as favourable as that of another person just as one cannot say that 20 degrees fahrenheit is twice as hot as 10 degrees fahrenheit.

Ratio Scale: A ratio scale contains in addition to the characteristic of an interval scale, an absolute zero. The operations necessary to establish a ratio scale include methods for determining not only equivalence (as in the nominal scale) or rank order (as in ordinal scale) and the equality of intervals (as in the interval scales) but also the equality of ratios. Since ratios are meaningless unless there is an absolute zero point, it is only the ratio scale that warrants assertions such as "Mr. X is twice as favourable towards the nationalization of Banks as Mr. Y is." If one's data conform to the criteria for a ratio scale, all relations between numbers in the conventional system of mathematics obtain between the correspondingly numbered positions on the scale. With such a scale, all types of statistical procedures become amenable.

It should be conceded that for most of the subject-matter dealt with by the social sciences, the researchers have not been able to develop procedures that satisfy the requirements of a ratio scale. For most part, the scale construction uses the judgements of people (judges) as the basis for the subject's positions on the scale.

We close this chapter with a few comments on the statements made and opinions often expressed that social sciences can never hope to reach the precision of measurements achieved in the physical sciences because the very nature of the materials with which the social scientists deal do not permit the establishment of an absolute zero point. No doubt, much of social science measurement will always be indirect and will depend upon the knowledge of the relationships between characteristic. The development of this knowledge, in turn, is partly dependent upon the development of fundamental measurement.

The gloomy prediction that the social sciences may never reach the precision of measurements characteristic of physical may well prove to be correct. But such an assertion seems premature at this stage. We can only express the hope that measurement of social and psychological characteristics or properties will, given time, progress from a lower scale to a higher one as it happened in the case of many physical properties. As Stevens has pointed out, "when people (in the olden times) knew temperature only by sensations as 'warmer' or 'colder', temperature belonged to the ordinal class of scales. It became an interval scale with the development of thermometry, and after thermodynamics... it became a ratio scale."[5]

Long ago a foot-racer would race only against another runner. Now he races against a clock and achieves a time record. Of course, the runner usually also races against other runner but his time scores has a meaning all by itself, which was not possible before the chronometer (clock) was invented.

REFERENCES

(1) Selltiz, *et al.: op. cit.,* p. 198.
(2) See Rosengren, K.E., (ed.): *Advances in Content Analysis,* Sage Publications, Beverly Hills, London, 1981, p. 51.
(3) *Op. cit.,* p. 46.
(4) Simon, J. L.: *op. cit.,* pp. 24-25.
(5) Cf. Selltiz, *et al.: op. cit.,* p. 171.

Chapter IX

Data Collection

An Introduction

Various methods of collecting data are employed by social scientists. Here we discuss the varied dimensions relevant to data generation and attempt to arrive at an abstract typology involving stimuli, responses and setting for data collection.

A datum is what is observed, is manifest or phenotypical.[1] Data in social sciences, as in other sciences, are based on our sense-observations. The word 'observation' as used here includes all forms of perception used in recording responses as they impinge upon our sensor. But response is not a datum. A response is some manifest kind of action, whereas a datum is the product of the process of recording the response. The continuum from response (which is observed) to the datum (which is observed and recorded) has been presented by Johan Galtung as under:

The Stimulus to Datum Sequence

1. Stimulus Presentation a	2. Object Manifestation b	3. Response Perception c
4. Impression Recording d	5. Datum	

The stimuli (questions, tests, pictures or other objects) presented to the respondent (subject) may be classified as: (a) systematic stimuli, and (b) unsystematic stimuli. By systematic we mean those that are kept constant while objects are changed, i.e., all units (subjects) are exposed to the same standardized stimuli systematically. Contrariwise, the stimuli are unsystematic when they lack standardisation, e.g., informal interviews where subjects are asked questions they are most likely to find meaningful.

The responses of the subjects to the stimuli may similarly be classified as: (a) systematic responses, and (b) unsystematic responses. Systematic responses have a reference to constant (definite, standardized) response categories. Thus, the responses of subject to a stimulus (S1) are recorded on a predetermined set of response category (R1). Contrariwise, the responses are unsystematic where the answer is recorded verbatim with due regard to all possible individual variations and characterological nuances (as in informal interviews).

Bringing these categories of stimuli and responses together in a single complex table, we get the main setting for data collection as under:

		Stimuli	
		Unsystematic	Systematic
	Unsystematic	Informal settings	Formal Unstructured settings
	Systematic	Impossible	Formal Structured settings

Thus, the possible setting for the collection of data are:

(a) Informal.

(b) Formal unstructured.

(c) Formal structured.

The responses of the subjects may be characterized as acts. Inaction or silence on the part of the subject may also constitute an important response, often more revealing than many responses which can be called 'acts.' Acts in the sense may be classified into (a) verbal, and (b) non-verbal.

The verbal acts may be sub-divided into oral and written. Verbal acts are acts where verbal symbols are used to communicate. The non-verbal acts are like bowing, clapping, shrugging shoulders, etc. The oral-verbal acts consist of the subject replying to a stimulus by the word of the mouth. The other kind of verbal acts consist in writing out the responses/replies to the stimulus.

If we intertwine the three kinds of manifest acts with the three settings of data collection, we get a table with nine boxes or cells. This break down table (given below) brings out most of the known procedures of data collection utilized in social sciences.[2]

The contents of different cells in the table may be considered to be general ideas that may also be used to generate other techniques of data collection. The subsequent chapters are devoted to detailed treatment of the major forms of data collection and significant ramifications of these.

The main forms of data collection responses

	Responses		
	Non-verbal	*Oral-verbal*	*Written-verbal*
Formal setting	Participant observation	Conversations, use of informants	Letters, articles, biographies
Formal unstructured settings	Systematic observation	Interviews unstructured	Questionnaire open-ended
Formal structured setting	Experimental techniques	Interviews structured	Questionnaire structured

The Paper Sources of Data

The two main sources of data (information) relevant to the research problem) in social research come from the inner world of library and the outside world of living people. We may broadly designate these two main sources simply, the 'paper' and 'people.'

'Paper' sources may provide the social or behavioural scientist a wealth of usable information. It is often unnecessary and uneconomical to expend time and energy mounting field-surveys to collect information readily obtainable from authentic 'paper' sources. Under the general rubric of documentary or 'paper' sources, we may subsume historical records, diaries, biographies and statistical records, etc.

When we turn to consider 'people' as the potential source of social science data, we identify various forms of observation but more particularly and primarily, the interview and questionnaire, as the techniques for collection of data from this source.

Documentary Sources of Data

Let us turn to discuss the typical and the major limitations of the documentary or 'paper' sources of data.

The social scientist as a rule has important facility in that the events and processes which concern him are human beings mostly living through them. Written evidence thus has straight-forward function of providing facts and figures and the indirect function of helping us project our understanding onto other times and places.

It is customary to distinguish between the sources of documentary data as primary and secondary. The 'primary' sources provide data gathered at firsthand and the 'secondary' ones are those from which data are got at, secondhand, that is, sets of data are culled from other people's original data. It is not always easy, however, to be able to determine whether a particular source is 'primary' or 'secondary.' This is so because in much published work, there is not just one writer who would have collected the information himself. For example, as for the census report, one can hardly say that the Commissioner of Census himself is the author. He does not collect data personally. But the census data are regarded as 'primary' data since the Commissioner is a single entity collecting and analysing the information gathered at firsthand through field workers under this charge.

The distinction between 'primary' and 'secondary' can be made even more useful if a further division of documents between what John Madge calls 'records' and 'reports' were to be effected.

'Record' is primarily concerned with a transaction taking place now, whereas the 'report' is usually written after the events has taken place (e.g., a historical account). Cross-tabulating these two contrast sets, i.e., Primary-Secondary and Contemporary — (Record) Retrospective (Report), we get a fourfold classification of documentary sources, as shown below:

		Primary		*Secondary*
Contemporary	(1)	Letters Contracts Court records Census of Population Tape recording and Films etc.	(2)	Historical study using actual documents. Statistical research based on census data. Research using other peoples' correspondence. Research report based on assistants' field-work.
Retrospective	(3)	Personal Diary Autobiography Report on Institutional visits, etc.	(4)	Research using diaries or autobiographies.

Cells (1) to (4) connote as follows:

(1) Compiled at the time by the writer.

(2) Transcribed from primary contemporary sources.

(3) Compiled after the event by the writer.

(4) Transcribed from primary retrospective sources.[3]

It should be noted that the cells in the above table, however, do not represent water-tight compartments; these should rather be regarded as displaying the general categories which may cut into one another. The fourfold categorization helps us, nevertheless, to identify common features of the different kinds of documents. John Madge proposes that documents, for the sake of convenience, may be broadly divided into two groups. The first of these groups would comprise the personal documents, the authors of which describe events in which they participated or indicate their personal beliefs and attitudes. Such documents are essentially subjective and are generally distinguishable from the second group which consists of the public or official documentation of social activity, hence relatively speaking, more objective.

Personal Documents. In its narrow sense, the personal document is a spontaneous first person description by an individual of his own actions, experiences and beliefs. The wide range of personal documentary material comprises autobiographies, diaries and letters and other artistic and projective documents which describe the subject's experiences and his beliefs or which give an insight into his cultural background. 'Life history' as a personal document relates to a compreshensive autobiography. But in common usage, a 'Life-history' may be almost any kind of biographical material. For Thomas and Znaniecki, the authors of 'The Polish Peasant', the personal document constiuted a perfect type of sociological material. Thomas and Znaniecki made vigorous use of the personal materials in their study of the Polish Peasants. Their stress on the use of such personal material subsequently proved to be something of a turning point in the development of social science.

At the time of publication of 'The Polish Peasant' more than 60 years now, the social scientists were very keen on making their discipline comparable in objectivity to natural sciences. From this viewpoint, personal documents (being essentially subjective) were regarded as of low scientific value. However, the sociological use of personal documents, thought to be out of the mainstream of development for a time, had not at any stage disappeared totally. Its persistence was partly due to the growing acceptance by social science of the whole range of psychological concepts and method. The major thrust of the revelation by Sigmund Freud that it was possible to conceptualise human beliefs and actions in terms of private and even unconscious motives and influences was that the subjective world is also accessible to and not beyond the scope of scientific investigation.

Blummer's criticism of the use of personal documents by the authors of 'The Polish Peasant' inaugurated a controversy. Subsequently, four authorities drawn from different social science fields, namely, G.W. Allport, L. Gottschalk, Clyde Kluckhohn and Robert Angell were invited to develop their views on the validity and limitations of personal documents as a tool of social science. These authorities reached the conclusion that subject to necessary safeguards, the use of personal document was not only permissible but also indispensable. They have indeed made a lasting contribution to social science in terms of systematically analysing the typical hazards attendant upon the use of personal documents. Two crucial issues they raised pertain to:

(1) The methodological question of how far disortions enter in the course of translating private records, and

(2) The questions of how to gather and analyse the number of personal documents needed for the derivation of abstract principles or hypotheses.

Allport indentifies thirteen motives that might induce individuals to record details about themselves, viz., self-justification by special pleading, exhibitionism, desire for order, literary delight, securing personal perspective, relief from tension or catharisis, monetary gain, assignment to write a brief autobiography, assisting in therapy (for a psychiatric patient), confession as means to absolution, scientific interest, public service and example (to achieve a reform or offer a model) and desire for immortality.

It is understandable that the individual's underlying motive is quite liable to influence the contents of the documents. Some authors, for example, may have a deliberate propagandist intention. Literary dishonesty may lead to suppression of unpalatable and undramatic sequences to form an aesthetically structured whole. It must be remembered that "... every contributor is a prisoner of his own culture."[4] It cannot be helped, therefore, that his thought processes are likely, by and large, to be determined by the society in which he lives.

We shall now discuss briefly the main forms of personal documents, namely, autobiographies, diaries and letters.

Autobiographies which are written sometime after the occurrence of events recorded in them and intended for publication, may be expected to suffer from propagandist intentions, from a tendency to rationalize and from conscious stylization. The prospective view, on the other hand, enables the writer to select and display such of his experiences and actions that subsequently come out to be significant features in his 'life history.'

Diaries are often the most revealing especially. when they are 'intimate journals.' This is so because they are less constricted by the fear of public showing and because they reveal with greatest clarity what experiences and actions seemed most significant at the time of their occurrence. But the diaries may exaggerate the conflicts and dramatic phase of life maintaining silence about the long calm and happy periods. Often the diarist assumes that the reader knows the persons and situations which he fails to adequately describe. A shrewd diarist may with some ulterior motive write a diary which will easily fall into the outsiders' hands and in effect mislead them.

Letters are often used by researchers, as evidenced in the study of the Polish Peasant. The authors Thomas and Znaniecki analysed 754 letters exchanged between the Poles in the U.S.A. and those in Poland. Letters often have some propagandist intention since they are designed by the writer to convey to the recipient some impressions more telling than mere facts. As with diaries, the letters often lack continuity and assume much of what any third party may be ignorant about.

We have seen how the personal documents by their very nature engender strong possibilities of distortion. It must be admitted that no internal test or screw exist for the analyst to correct such distortion. The only satisfactory correctives are the external ones, such as the degree of correspondence with other sources of information or with observed behaviour and the success of predictions based on the original material. Gottschalk lists five kinds of circumstances which may predispose the investigator to believe that the informant's statement is truthful.

(a) When the truth of the statement is a matter of indifference to the witness, he is likely to be unbiased (this might possibly have impaired his observation or memory).

(b) When the statement is prejudicial to the informant or his interests, it is likely to be unusually truthful.

(c) When the facts at issue are so much the matters of common knowledge that the informant would be unlikely to be mistaken or lie about them.

(d) When the part of the statement of primary interest to the investigator is both incidental and intrinsically probable.

(e) When the informant makes statements which are contrary to his expectations and anticipations as assessed by the investigator's knowledge of his thought-patterns and preconceptions.

It may be remembered here that many of the personal documents are recorded not by the informant but by the investigator (as when the informant is illiterate). In the course of recording, the investigator himself may be responsible for introducing distortions. The informants are likely to be 'blinkered' and 'polarized' by the investigator's own interests and line of approach. The informant is not only led to introduce topics which may barely be of any interest to him; he may even adopt attitudes and pretend to hold beliefs which he would not have expressed if only he had been free of investigator's influence.

Let us now turn to consider how far the personal document material might serve as a basis for generalization. It is generally believed that people whose personal documents become available are the ones who tend to be suffering from frustrated emotional lives. Should this be fair surmise, generalisations based on personal documents would clearly refer to such people and not to the population as a whole. One way of overcoming this limitation is to solicit the cooperation of a more representative cross-section of the population. The documents may be offered to be purchased. The offer of payment coupled with a promise of anonymity has been shown to induce the otherwise reluctant people to come out with personal documents. But such a practice may affect adversely their representativeness.

Even if the problem of typicality is solved, the problem of obtaining a sample of documents large enough to permit fine analysis still remains. In favourable circumstances, however, investigators have been able to obtain large samples (for example, Thomas and

Znaniecki used a number of fragmentary autobiographies, large number of letters and a considerable collection of records, newspaper accounts, etc.).

Thrasher in his study 'Gang' was able to supplement his main technique by persuading a number of gang members to write their life-stories.

The Public or Official Documents

Newspapers: Newspaper reports, where a reporter was present at the scene, might be thought of as valuable. But it has been shown too often how little reliance can be placed on them. We should recognize the pressures under which the newspaper correspondents work. Many of the correspondents may depend on their personal system of recording. In many cases, the correspondent may highlight only the 'eye-catching' and the 'dramatic' parts of the total occurrence. Typically, newspapers work very fast. Latest news is always most desirable. Staleness is a taboo. Reports are controlled by available space and newspaper's policy. The popular press is often more concerned with entertaining than informing.

Public Records and Statistics: These are, on the face of things, the most satisfactory and reliable sources. For example, the verbatim parliamentary record of what is said possibly is the most trusted document one can find. More valuable than a written record is tape-recording which preserves not only what was said, but also how it was said. An unedited sound film could be even better. Their reliability too is usually high. The inventory, balance sheet etc., are useful accessories to business transactions; there are penalties for false statements.

The Census Reports, the annual digests of statistics and statistical reports of various State departments and other national bodies produce a great deal of useful data for social scientists to work with. Official statistics, although the data on which they are based may not be directly relevant to the researcher's interests, are in most instances designed to inform rather than deceive the readers. These are normally prepared by experts and this is a point in their favour.

The range of matter covered in available records and the treatment a subject receives in such records varies with the administrative needs of which they were collected. Health statistics give birth and death rates, etc. Public and private economic organizations collect and publish data on wages, hours of work, productivity, absenteeism, strikes, etc. In addition, a small but steadily increasing body of data is being collected by various institutions like schools, hospitals, social service agencies, etc., on the psychological level proper.

Data collected in the course of such other activities have a number of advantages for social research in addition to that of economy. A major one is the fact that much information of this sort is collected periodically, making the establishment of trends over time possible. Another is that the gathering of information from such sources does not require the co-operation of the individuals about whom information is desired as does the use of techniques such as questionnaires, interviews, projective techniques and techniques such as questionnaire, interviews, projective techniques and techniques such as questionnaires, interviews, projective techniques and often observation. Moreover, since such data are collected in the ordinary course of events, the measurement procedure is less likely to reveal the investigator's purpose or to change the behaviour in which he is interested.

K. M. Landis based his study entitled 'Segregation in Washington' exclusively on the analysis and interpretation of available statistical data, e.g., census reports, official health statistics, employment data, police statistics, etc. Similarly, Leo Srole in his study of 'Status and Prestige' (in the 'Yankee City' series of investigations by Warner and Associates) utilized a rather unusual source of data relevant to his problem—the cemetery records.

It needs to be stressed that the statistical data require that the investigator is able to ask many different questions related to the research problem. If a research idea or hypothesis can be formulated in such manner that the available recorded material bears on the question, the use of such material becomes possible. The guiding principle for the use of such material becomes possible. The guiding principle for the use of available statistic consists in keeping oneself flexible in respect of the form in which research questions are asked. Durkheim's study on suicide provides a classic example of how the superior flexibility of a genius resulted in the testing of a social theory by available statistics. Durkheim started with the hypothesis that the causeszz of suicide are to be found in the social conditions. To test this theory, Durkheim studied critically the statistics on suicide in certain European countries.

Certain studies, such as Durkheim's, rely entirely on the analysis of data collected for purpose other than those of the particular study. In others, such data are used in conjunction with other procedures. Data regularly collected for other purpose may be used to measure the effects of an experimental treatment. Thus, in the Hawthorne electrical studies, Roethlisberger and Dickson found that changes in such conditions as illumination, rest periods and hours of work could not account for a consistently rising rate of productivity in the experimental groups over a period of time. They subsequently concluded that changes in social organization of work groups and their relationship to management were responsible for a rise in productivity.

Available statistics may be used for other purposes, in a study. They are frequently useful in selecting cases with specified characteristics for intensive study. Available records may also be used to supplement or to check information gathered specifically for the purposes of a given investigation. For example, in a study of the psychological impact of long-term unemployment in an Austrian village (Jahoda, Lazarsfeld and Zeisl) the 'shock' effect of unemployment was checked against such records as the accounts of the local grocer.

The records of specific behaviour may be used as an indicator of some more general concept. A series of studies by Tryon illustrate this use of records. Tryon was concerned with the problem of indentifying sub-cultural groups in more meaningful and reliable ways. One of his hypotheses was that the residents of common demographic social area will experience certain common socially relevant situations and common psychological states elicited by those situations and will behave in certain common ways. As an evidence to test this hypothesis, Tryon used voting records. Voting for him was an indicator of social attitudes.

The investigator must take certain precautions even when using statistics which are generally considered reliable.

(a) The definitions of categories used in available statistical material do not so often coincide with those used in social research. In criminal statistics, for instance, the concept of 'crime' is operationally defined in a number of ways. A social scientist interested in family composition may be grossly misled if he proceeded on the basis of the operational definition of a household as used in the census reports. In view of such confusion, the use of available records may be more misleading than enlightening unless the precise definition on which the statistics are based is ascertained.

(b) To know merely what the original collector of available data (records) set out to gather is not enough; it is also necessary to enquire into his methods. Many records are collected with the intention of covering an entire 'population' and not just a sample. Many obstacles stand in the way of realizing this ideal. It may also be that the informants from whom the original collector drew information were not willing to provide it. Income statistics based on individual tax declarations generally tend to be underestimates. This cannot but be the case.

(c) It is quite possible that the degree of inaccuracy in official statistics due to these reasons may be negligible from the point of view of the social scientist. But there are methodological errors that may lead to serious inaccuracies. This fact needs to be kept in mind especially when dealing with data collected over many years. Kingsley Davis in 'The population of India and Pakistan' has pointed out that the olden rural statistics were kept by the village chowkidars to whom the most obvious and intelligible cause of death was 'fever.' The increase of certain causes of death (other than fever) shown in later statistics is probably a reflection of the change in the techniques of reckoning.

Thus, to ignore how statistics are kept and for what purpose, is to misuse statistics badly. It is, of course, no criticism of the statistics themselves. Occasionally, it is possible to correct available records in the light of what is subsequently known about the methods by which they have been gathered. In any case, the proper qualifications in respect of such data when used for research purpose can be made only if the social scientist is aware of the possible errors inherent in the particular method employed.

We close this discussion with the brilliant remarks on the subject by Professor Bowley: "It is never safe to take published statistics at their face value, without knowing their meaning and limitations, and it is always necessary to criticise arguments that are based on them unless one is able to trust implicitly the knowledge and good faith of the persons bringing them forward. It is extremely easy to falsify lessons which numerical statements should teach. The actual use or appreciation of statistics are ultimately a matter of intelligence, special knowledge and common sense."

Biographies: A glance along the borrower's registers of a public library will show that the common borrower enjoys reading about other people's lives. The biographer generally works on people of some fame, whatever their spheres of activity. Thus, a biography is more likely to be about some famous person, his outstanding success or the eye-catching personality. The professional biographer depends on sensationalism for the sale of his work and as such he may try to make his book sensational, shocking and dramatic. There is a possibility that the biographer may be motivated by a concern with the defence of a dead person, such as biographies written by loving sons and daughters. In yet another instance, biographer may have been commissioned by the family of a person. This latter type of biography must be carefully scrutinized since it is hardly likely to contain much criticism of its subject; it is rather likely to be replete with justifications and accentuation.

Historical Documents: Conventionally, historical documents deal with events of the past about which the main source of information is documentary, the participants being dead. This definition is by no means satisfactory since there is plently of the present century alive in the minds of the living people. Nevertheless, the historical document belongs to special category of its own since it enables us to appreciate the importance of the links between social sciences and history.

Much of sociological investigation is perfected with historical background. For example, community studies bring out the historical development of the given settlement, the study of organizational structure of the trade union can only gain a good perspective by tracing the developmental chain. In all investigations such as these the sociologist must turn to documents to establish the sequence of events and try to understand the process that took place in the past. The sociologist who dives into historical research. without seeking advice from the historian will only waste time and effort in seeking out correct sources and is likely to use the sources badly if he knows little about the way in which the documents were complied.

Case Histories: 'Case-history' records are collected in the course of welfare work. The case-workers are firsthand observers of social behaviour. This material can be utilized by social scientist with great advantage. It should be noted, however, that the case-workers tend to record their observation in an impressionistic way, their descriptions are subjective based on general personal experience with little concern for classification within an integrated conceptual framework. Since there is likely, in case work, a bias toward the socially pathological (in the selection of cases) and as the case records have little uniformity, generalization is often difficult. On the other hand, it is in the nature of case-histories that they abound in richness and evocative quality. There is no doubt that the data of the large and increasing body of case-workers with experience of various forms of pathology, can be utilized by the social scientists very fruitfully in their researches.

Before the close of the discussion on documents, which afford a potent source of social science data, it is important to consider the question: "How far can documentary evidence, even when properly selected and checked for authenticity, be used as proof?" This is an issue of great importance, not only because a large part of social evidence is still entirely derived secondhand from documentary sources but also because there are reasons for supposing that the user of documents is often tempted to stretch his material to suit his imaginative thesis. He also has, to boot, unique opporunities for doing so.

It has been recognized generally that the documentary material by itself may never provide a deep insight into the motives and activities of other generations. It is also generally accepted that the ideal of objectivity, however possible for the natural scientist, is beyond the reach of any historian. This does not mean, of course, that the historical facts are a suspect. As Carr points out, "... (the facts) have the same relation to history as bricks or steel or concrete have to architecture.... But they are not in themselves 'facts of history.' It is only the decision of the historian that they are significant for his purpose which makes them into the 'facts of history....' His choice and arrangement of these facts and juxtapositions of them which indicate his view of cause and effect, must be dictated by presuppositions and (these) will be closely related to the conclusion which he is seeking to establish.... History therefore is an interaction between the historian and the past of which he is writing. The facts help to mould the mind of the historian. But the mind of the historian also... helps to mould facts."[6]

In the light of the above, a question that poses itself is how the social scientists can exploit the documentary material and how they can overcome their prejudices while using them. The classical well-thumbed method is for the scientist to search his mind until he has exposed his own biases. Even if he cannot overcome them, at least he is able to make some allowance for them (Socrates). But the psychologically naive belief that it is possible by introspection to unearth every secret interest and prejudice is no longer tenable. The most persistent, 'obvious' and 'commonsense' of the individual's presuppositions may just be those which could be restricting his understanding and preventing him from realizing the significance of many of the facts available to him. If his access to the problem is by way of documents alone, these limitations are especially prone to detract from the richness of his results.

Even within the bounds of admissible ideas, the user of documents has ample scope for distortion so long as his conclusions are based on impressions and he wants us to take a lot of trust. A more recent development which consists in the direct use of quantitative methods on documents themselves, greatly reduces the possibility of impressionistic distortion. The technique is known as 'Content Analysis.' We shall discuss this technique at some length.

Content Analysis

Berelson defines 'content analysis' as a "research technique for the objective, systematic and quantitative description of the manifest content of communication."

Content analysis is a methodologically sophisticated version of the commonsense technique of finding out how an author of a book has treated a particular subject. This can be found out easily enough by the commonplace practice of looking at the index of the book. Content analysis is a formalization of techniques that have long been used informally. As we well know, the number of references and the space devoted to a particular subject give a fair indication of the importance attached to it by the author. This commonsense technique was gradually improved upon and in 1930 the first full analysis along these lines was published (New York). The topic happened to be the amount of space devoted to foreign news in American morning newspapers. Early examples of formal content analysis are afforded by military intelligence agencies during wartime. Enemy newspapers and radio stations were monitored exhaustively and counts were made of various kinds of references to transportation, obituaries and so forth. Variations in the numbers of such references from week to week generally signified troop movements and other changes that suggested what the intentions of the enemy could be. The value of this technique a few years later, was enhanced and confirmed in Hornell Hart's analysis of trends in the space devoted to various subjects in American periodicals and books. The next important step was the adaptation in 1973 by Harold Lasswell of the technique of content analysis for the systematic study of recorded psychoanalytical interviews. Subjects covered in these interviews were systematically classified and as a result, much of the same scheme of categories could be used in a variety of other context. With the outbreak of war in Europe, Lasswell took over the directorship of an officially sponsored World Attention Survey based on content analysis of foreign newspapers. Apart from certain immediate functions, this technique was found to provide an intellectual weapon of substantial consequence. For example, the content analysis indicated that Germany was clearing the path for a sudden change in diplomatic orientation. This surmise came out to be true, subsequently.

Later, Leites and Pool used a similar technique to study changes in the Comintern policy and throughout the war, students of Lasswell and Leties undertook analyses of United State foreign language press on behalf of the U. S. Department of Justice. Over the years, internal propaganda, the speeches of politicians, the content of radio programmes, films, popular magazines, etc., have been subjected to content analysis. Content analysis was used during the initial interviewing programme in the 'Hawthorne Electrical Company Studies' and also included in the preparatory technique for the 'focussed interviews' undertaken by Merton and Kendall. R.K. White content analysed to public speeches of Hitler and Roosevelt with a view to identifying the propaganda techniques and describing the appeals of political leaders to their followers. White systematically ascertained the 'values' to which the two leaders appealed in their public speeches. In the main, he identified three values on which he compared the two leaders, one authoritarian and the other democratic, i.e., strength values, moral values and economic values. Content analysis has been used extensively on studies of mass media to determine changes in either the media themselves or in society and culture with the passage of time.

A survey of the field by Berelson brings to light the specific purposes for which documents or communication-contents have been analysed. These are as detailed below:

One of the more exciting uses to which content analysis has been put is exemplified by D. McClelland's study of the historical relationship between the motivation to achieve among the members of a society and the economic development of the society. McClelland and his associates measured the frequency of "achievement imagery" in the popular literature of society at various periods and related these frequencies to economic indication. For example, they found a close correspondence between the content analysis of data and coal imports into London from 1550 to 1850. Considering the multiple obstacles present in such investigations the closeness of the correspondence has been acclaimed to be starting. Pitrim A. Sorokin used content analysis to analyze the ground cultural changes over millenium. He clearly brought out how the proportion of philosophers of different outlooks has changed from century as a proxy for the way held by the various systems of truth.

The content of art has also been analysed systematically and the techniques has been acknowledged as a source of much of our understanding of the contacts among cultures, diffusions and the transmission of knowledge among them. Anthropologist A. L. Kroeber traced the travels of the flying gallop (an invention of artists) as a way of representing a running horse in art and established a sequence of transmission of knowledge amongst cultures.

Berelson specifically mentions, schematically, the major purpose for which content analysis has been employed.[7]

(a) Purpose of Ascertaining the Characteristics of Content:

- to audit communication-content against objectives;
- to construct and apply communication standards;
- to aid technical research operations;
- to expose propaganda techniques;
- to measure 'readability' of communication materials;
- to identify stylistic features.

(b) Purpose of Ascertaining the Causes of Content:

- to idntify intentions and other characteristic of the communicators;
- to detect the existence of propaganda;
- to determine the psychological state of persons and groups;
- to secure political and military intelligence;

(c) Purpose of Ascertaing Effects of Content:

- to reflect attitudes, interests, values of populations;
- to reveal focus of attention;
- to describe attitudinal and behavioural response to varied items of communication.

It should be remembered that any single study may have one or more of these three broad purpose.

The research procedures involved in the content analysis generally, of books, magazines, newspapers, radio programmes, T. V. serials and films etc. consist in utilizing a system or scheme of categorization on which basis the communication or documentary content is analysed from a quantitative angle and this in turn is geared to test hypotheses the investigator sets before himself. Hence, content analysis may be used to test hypotheses about the treatment of minority groups in magazine articles or in films etc., or to enquire into propaganda techniques. Communication through the media or radio, films, public speeches, etc., has been subjected to content analysis. The important point about content anlysis is that content of communication is analysed by means of systematic predetermined categories based on themes, value intents and style, etc., as the need may be, which often yield quantitative results. A simple instance would be to hypothesize that a certain newspaper has changed hands, say, a couple of years ago. Rather than leaving this as an impression of the readers, content analysis would test the impression systematically and see if it conforms to reality.

Due largely to the work of Lasswell and associates, the technique of content analysis has registered a tremendous improvement. The analysis of content proceeds under certain controls that render it systematic and objective in comparison to the conventional impressionistic review of communication content. Firstly, the categories of analysis used to classify the content are clearly and explicitly defined so that other individuals can apply them to the same content to verify the earlier conclusions. Secondly, the analyst is not free to select and report merely what strikes him as interesting but must methodologically classify all the relevant materials in his sample (which is of course, selected as a represntative of the 'universe'). Thirdly, a quantitative procedure is used in order to provide a measure of the dominance and emphasis in the material of certain ideas or themes found and to make a possible comparison with other samples of material. For example, if we took a systematic sample of newspaper editorials and counted the relative numbers of editorials expressing favourable, unfavourable and neutral attitudes toward a certain international issue, we would be carrying out a simple form of quantification that has proved feasible and reliable. We can on this basis come out with a more exact picture of the situation than would be possible if simply the general impressions or memory were relied upon. In the absence of some sort of mathematical aid, there is a limit to the amount of materials that can be digested and recalled in detail by the human mind.

Let us give some thought now, to a few inadequacies or limitations that the technique of content analysis with its characteristic emphasis on quantification typically suffers from.

Firstly, definitions of content analysis tend to emphasize the procedure of analysis rather than the character of data available in communication. In addition, they imply a somewhat arbitrary limitation of the field by excluding from it, all accounts of communication that are not cut out in the form of the number of item, various ideas or themes (or other elements) appear in the material being analysed. Secondly, concern with quantification in practice, seems to have become so dominant that it often over shadows concern with the unique content of communication. It is indeed difficult to be convinced as to why quantification should be regarded as an essential requirement in content analysis when it is not so in the customary analysis of data obtained by interviews or observation. Granted that quantification is a more precise procedure, yet it is not always feasible. It hardly needs to be stressed that both quantified as well as qualitative data have their legitimate place in the contemporary social science. Besides, the stress on measurement in content analysis often implies that one indulges in an exercise of measuring the unmeasurable, i.e., qualities.

The problem of drawing a sample of the material to be content analysed, poses its own brand of problems. Suppose a researcher was interested in analysing the concern of the national press with the issue of ceiling on urban property. The first task of the analyst will be to define his universe, i.e., the national press. For his purpose, it may not be satisfactory to list all the newspaper published in the country and to draw a systematic sample (every fifteenth or twentieth newspaper) even if he were to ensure that newspapers representing different geographical areas, political orientations, economic policies, etc., are included in the list of the newspapers. The fact is that the newspapers vary greatly in size and influence and, therefore, a realistic sample should not weigh some obscure journal with an influential metropolitan daily. Thus, it would be proper to divide the newspapers into a series of classes according to their circulation and then draw from each class a 'random' sample covering a given volume of readers. So far as the issue of ceiling on urban property is concerned, it may not be judicious to assume the volume of circulation. To overcome such problems, the researcher may more properly choose the procedure of a 'Popularity sample.' He may, for instance, choose a sample comprising the write-ups from ten largest newspapers in the country.

Another problem related to sampling of the mass media contents relates to the time order. The researcher may get a distorted impression of the general policy of newspapers if the editions for only a single day or even a single month were studied. On the other hand, if the researcher were to cover a period of several months, the task would plainly become unmanageable. Before he knows how many issues he can handle, the researcher/analyst will have to decide on the nature and size of the units that are to comprise his sample.

Frequently then, the sampling procedure in communication research consists of three stages:

(a) Sampling of sources (which newspapers, radio stations, etc. are to be analysed);

(b) Sampling of dates (which period is to be covered by the study);

(c) Sampling of units (which aspects of communication are to be analyzed).

Now we need to ponder over the problem of establishing categories for analysis. Suppose, our researcher has decided to choose a sample of editorials. His next task will be to establish categories in terms of which the editorials could be classified. The researcher has two major bases for establishment of relevant categories:

(a) The research purpose or hypotheses; and

(b) The material itself.

The newspaper's concern with say, ceiling on urban property can find expression in a variety of ways. The paper may emphasize it or it may ignore the issue. It may confine itself to straight non-committed or informative reporting or it may generate much editorial comments on it. It might use certain key words such as socialism, welfare, etc., frequently or rarely. It can treat the matter lightly or seriously. It may appeal to commonly accepted values or refrain from expressing moral implications of the issue. Each of these categories of analysis and many others can be used in content analysis depending on the purpose of the study.

Lastly, we turn to consider the problem of reliability of responses and classification should be so clearly analysed. Ideally, the methods of analysis and quantification should be so clearly defined that different judges would arrive at the same results when analysing the same materials. But perfect reliability suggested above, at the present time is something that can only be realized at the cost of a deeper interpretative understanding of the material. Merely counting the number of times a word turns up in a given volume of material does ensure reliability, but this cannot but be an analysis of a very superficial type, because the same word carried different meanings or messages in different contexts arising from its relationship with other words and the theme. The primary method of increasing reliability of classification to specify clearly the characteristics of statements (rather than words) that are assigned to a given category and to use many examples drawn from the materials being analyzed to illustrate what kind of statements are to be considered as representing a given category.

In concluding the discussion on the documentary sources of data, we would do well to remind ourselves that the rich human material which quite a few documents contains is very fertile source of ideas. Spontaneous personal documents, newspaper reports, business or official files, etc. typically provide an invaluable preliminary to direct observation. "They also supplement observation and participation in social processes by broadening the base of experience. But by themselves they tell an incomplete story and it is clearly unwise to stretch their adoption into contexts in which they can offer neither economy nor satisfaction."[8]

Social Research and History

We shall now discuss more directly the relevance and utility of data obtained from historical sources, for sociological research. At various place in this chapter, the value of historical data for social research was tacitly recognized. The following account is pertinent to the basic issues that might be posed. The following account is pertinent to the basic issues that might be posed in regard to the use of the historical approach for understanding social systems as dynamic and living entities.

A group of thinkers, during the relatively brief period in which social science has been recognized as a disciplined form of intellectual endeavour, has tried to effect a rigid differentiation between what are conventionally known as social sciences, like sociology and economics on the one hand and history on the other, in terms both of their logic and method. They have argued that history is basically an 'idiographic discipline', whereas the social sciences, generally, are 'nomothetic' ones. Definitionally, an idiographic such as history is concerned with the unique and particular events or happenings that are studied for their own sake, while the nomothetic disciplines like sociology are concerned with the unique and particular events or happenings that are studied for their own sake, while the nomothetic disciples like sociology are concerned with the unique and particular events or happenings that are studied for their own sake, while the nomothetic disciplines like sociology are concerned with the formulation of general principles through which the class of phenomena constituting their subject-matter is sought to be understood. It is this dichotomous view of sciences which has quite often been referred to by the group of historians, social scientists who would jealously want to maintain some clear line of demarcation between their repective fields.

The main argument has been supplemented by two further derived distinctions between these disciplines. It is held, for instance, that the sociologist in his quest for general propositions about social systems, of necessity, must develop conceptual schemes so as able to analyse and order the many diversities of human existence in society. The historian, so runs the argument, concerned as he is with the individuals and events in their particularistic detail, has little, if any, use for such conceptual schemes of generic applicability. In essence, the sociologist and the historian are conceived of as working on different levels of concern for abstraction.

To trace the example further distinction between the two disciplines as brought out by the group of thinkers espousing the dichotomous view, concerns the role played by the dimension of time in the two disciplines. The historian, on this view, is engaged in tracing a chronological sequence of the past events, showing how one event led to another, while, say the sociologist by contrast, is mainly interested in the functional relationships which exist between analytically distinct elements in social systems, time notwithstanding. The sociologist is seen as seeking general propositions not bound by temporal or spatial contexts, i.e., timeless and spaceless.

Yet another argument in the ultimate analysis to the same end, is advanced mainly by sociologists who are keen on guarding their rather 'newly acquired status' as scientists and to the effect that history and sociology are in the conduct of their inquiries. The sociologists according to this view, follow the methods of the hard core sciences while history does not, and for most part cannot aspire to this because of the very nature of its subject matter. It has to make do with methods that can afford only qualitatively inferior findings.

However, drawing strict lines of demarcation between History and Sociology (as a social science) as has been done both by a group of historians as well as sociologists, may involve considerable difficulties. Nagel has convincingly shown that the distinction between the idiographic and nomothetic disciplines is one which, in the ultimate analysis, can scarcely be maintained.[9] It is hard to appreciate how in a purely idiographic discipline one could acquire knowledge of anything at all. On the other hand, in a nomothetic discipline any consideration of the singular, particular or non-recurrent can hardly be avoided.

Any attempt to distinguish between history and sociology on methodological grounds is similarly fraught with hurdles; for this would imply that sociology would have to be virtually restricted to the study of present-day societies, here and now. This would result in the scope of the discipline being defined by reference to a particular set of research techniques.

The arguments advanced in favour of a strict demarcation between history and sociology would thus be seen to have rather alarming implications for the sociologists' appreciation of the uses of historical data in their own fields of research. If sociologists adhere to the view that history and sociology are logically or methodologically distinct, they understandably would be inclined to have a low estimation of the significance of history for their fields of study. Admittedly, for a sociologist considering the major task of sociologists as a class, the building up of a general theory of social systems based on logically ordered body of abstract categories, the historical materials in general may not seem to be of much value. They may, of course, be of a particular interest to him in just one respect, viz., in connection with the dynamic aspects of his purported general or trans-historical theory. It is not difficult to see that data secured through conventional methods of the historian having a continuity over time, are required to develop and test general propositions about the process of long-term social change. In fact, as Hans Genth says, "History consists of changes which social structure undergo."[10] Each change, each emerging as philosopher Whitehead noted, "is... containing within itself all its past and seed of its future."[11]

Smelser's study entitled 'Social Change in the Industrial Revolution,' testifies, in unmistakable terms, to how well historical data may be employed by a sociologist interested in testing the general propositions about the process of long-term social changes. Smelser uses a great deal of data from the industrial and social history of Lancashire covering a period of over seventy years commencing from 1770, with a view to providing an empirical test of general theory of change in social systems through process of structural differentation. The thory is a part of the wider thory of social action developed by Talcott Parsons. The procedure that Smelser followed was to show how his model of structural change could be successfully applied to change: (a) in the Lancashire cotton industry and then, to change, (b) in the family economy of the Lancashire working class, concretely two different institutional sub-systems. Both the sub-systems, Smelser argues, conform to the same pattern of structural differentiation and the process of change, in both cases could be explained in terms of a common dynamic model. Thus, Smelser claimed the general applicability of the model and corollariously of the general theory of action from which the model was derived. In this manner, Smelser utilized the data of history as a useful type of material to inject content into his trans-historic theoretical scaffold. He was not interested in the Lancashire cotton industry or the working class family for their own sake, nor even in the context of some broader theory of the industralization process, rather, he was interested in this simply because they provided data that could be used in testing a general theory of social systems. For Smelser, historicity of the two sub-systems was of no consequence.

For the group of sociologists which stresses the basic methodological difference between history and sociology the historical data have a still meagre significance as compared to what they may have for the sociologists dealing with theories of general scope. While this group may accord some recognition to the general orientation value of the general orientation value of the broad historical studies for sociologists (for, who can deny the strong historical base underlying the sociological thinking of Marx, Weber and Durkheim) the conventional historiography is regarded as a representation of some pre-scientific mode of thinking about man and society which is clearly outclassed in the study of contemporary socienties conducted with the aid of 'modern' research techniques. For them, the empirical basis of much historical argument is suspect. Lazarsfeld has criticized in strong terms the sweeping assertions so often made by historians without an adequate empirical basis.[12] These methodological purists would not, as far as possible, make use of the conventional type of historical materials even in connection with the study of social change; they would rather create their own kind of historical data using techniques like panel study. Only thus, would argue, can the data of a quality affording fruitful theoretical analysis be obtained.

Besides, the afore-mentioned two groups of sociologists for whom relevance of historical data is little more than marginal, exists a major group representing what may be called the 'classic' tradition. This group takes on an entirely different stand vis-a-vis the relevance of history for social research. This tradition stems from the faith that the study of history is one of the most important sources of sociological data. Sociological inquiries following this tradition are characterized by a focus on different forms of structure and culture exhibited by particular societies at specific points of their development or evolution and on the understanding of particular processes of change delimited in geographical and historical terms.[13] This group of sociologists, operates, to use Wright Mills' phrase, at the level of social-historical structures." The great masters of the classic tradition in sociology, to name only the most outstanding, are Karl Marx, Max Weber, Herbert Spencer, Mannheim, Schumpeter, Mosca, Michels, Veblen, Hobson and C. Wright Mills. The perspectives of the 'classic' sociologists are decidedly far wider as compared to the perspectives of sociologists who would let the modern methods of field research define for them the scope of their subject.

The classic tradition in sociology may thus be seen as occupying an intermediate place in the continuum of the various inquiry types that constitute modern sociology. Sociologists of this tradition neither aim at an entirely general theorizing nor would they be happy with mere empirical descriptions of social milieu at certain point in time. The central concern of those of the 'classic' tradition is with comprehending the diversity which is manifested in the structure and culture of societies, with identifying the limits and determinants of this diversity and with explaining how given societies or structure within them have developed in a particular way and function the way they do. This implies thinking in terms of societies developing structures and as such would call for the introduction of a historical dimension. Thus, the special relevance of historical data for sociologists of this schools is easily appreciated. Obviously any developmental approach cannot do without historical materials. When one speaks of a change from folk society to a modern society or from the informal to formal organization of production or business, he is using in effect, the conceptions which derive their validity from historical study.

The comparative method, fundamental to the classic tradition draws its breath from history. The approach consists in comparison being drawn between different societies with the view to explaining the variation in social structure and culture. Such comparison involves or must involve, in principle, the societies of the past as well as of the present. The exponent of the comparative method cannot afford to neglect the vast fund of information about man and society which the past has to offer, regardless of whatever materials are available about the contemporary socienties. For him, history is the broadest and probably also the richest field of study.

According to the classic tradition, sociology in effect is nothing short of a historical discipline and the problems of its concern cannot be approached or fruitfully formulated without adopting a historical perspective and an extensive utilization of historical data. Thus, the classic tradition refuses to admit of any clear demarcation of any kind between history and sociology. They are seen as inextricably interwined or as merging imperceptibly, one into the other. This tradition would regard the differences between them as differences of degree only, not of kind.

The above discussion affords a cognitive back-drop for the issue of the relevance of history for sociological studies. As we have seen there are on the one hand, sociologists who take the 'Natural science view' of sociology, whatever their focus of interest; formulation of a general theory or empirical social research by use of quantitative techniques, and there stands on the other hand, a strong group, committed to the classic tradition and operating at the level of social-historical structures. For the former, the relevance of history to sociological studies is just about negligible or marginal, whereas for the latter, sociology is inevitably rooted in the study of history. The former claims that a true science of society must be able to transcend history, both in theory and methods, while the latter argues that history will not be transcended. As Marx said, "... real history, history as temporal order, is the historical succession in which ideas, categories and principle have manifested themselves ... it is the principle which (makes) history, and not history... the principle."[14] They (the latter) question the value of both of the attempts to establish trans-historical theory and of the detailed empirical studies of social milieu that typically ignore the societal and historical contexts.

Although the merit of this controversy (which has gradually died down in recent years) is rather difficult to evaluate, it may be said with a certain measure of conviction that it will not be worthwhile either for the methodological purists to exclude them from the map of the sociological discipline and such studies as do not come up to the arbitrarily decreed methodological standards of validity and precision nor for that matter will it be desirable for the 'classic' traditionalists to deny the relevance of quantitative methods current in social researches on consequential sociological problems. The real import of the argument arises over questions of how the sociologists of the present generation may best direct their efforts and resources. No one can deny that studies on the 'classic' lines are of crucial significance to contemporary sociology and should be pursued enthusiastically, in the larger interest of the subject. Any proposed general theory must understandably take into active account the range of possible variations in human societies, especially, of the ways in which they are integrated and change. The Parsonian general theory has been criticized on the score that it is not as general as it purports to be; that is, certain variations or exceptions manifested by some societies have suffered neglect in his theoretic scheme.

It hardly needs to be overemphasized that studies of the historical and comparative kind fulfil the function of operating as frameworks into which detailed empirical studies of social millieu can be fitted in meaningful way. The most rewarding procedure would be to study with the help of modern research techniques particular social millieu which seem to have a particular significance in the context of some wider structural analysis. It is easy to appreciate also that studies focussing on patterns of variation in social structure or on what is taken as 'human-nature,' can be a great aid in understanding our own society and the times we live in. Comparions with other historically diverse settings typically help us understand our setting more intelligibly. Hence, the tradition of historically oriented study would continue to form the very core of sociology.

As suggested earlier, during the past few decades the importance of historical perspective has been largely recognized by the rival camp representing the 'natural science view of society.' In fact, this quarter of sociologists had to face a barrage of criticisms from within the discipline itself. Increasingly critical positions have been taken toward both the 'general theory' and methods of survey-research in recent years. The value of structural-functional theory operating on the premise of social system has been seriously questioned. While the recent years have shown significant advances in the equipment of quantitative analysis, the validity of the data subjected to such analyses has come under searching examination. The outcome of these developments according to Goldthorpe is that the concept of social action has assumed a new centrality, both from the methodological and theoretical standpoints.[15] The need to explain social structure in terms of action and interpret the meaning of action has once again become the major preoccupation of sociological analysis.[16] With this development, the void between the perspectives of the historians and sociologists has lessened considerably, and once again the possibility of a meaningful mutual dialogue between the two disciplines, typical of Max Weber's time, has come close to materialization.

The previous decades witnessed the development of new forms of social history (or 'urban' history) built from large bodies of quantitative data secured from such sources as official registers, trade directories and census reports, etc. There is thus no real basis now, for marking off historians from sociologists by reference to the kinds of data with which the two work and the way they utilize them. The historians in having to handle such data (social history) are being required to lean heavily on the techniques of analysis developed, in the main, by sociologists. They also have to depend on sociological concepts which they have now started appreciating. Reciprocally, the new social history has important functions for sociologists. The demonstration of historical data as of a systematic and quantitative breed as apparent in the new social history has encouraged sociologists to use such materials for testing specific hypotheses involving quantitative comparisons. The new social history is thus a welcome augury for sociologists to undertake empirical investigations of certain theories of the middlerange relating to the long-term effects of a certain process on other institutional mechanisms and processes.

The contemporary sociology is characterized by a renewed interest in the macro-sociological and evolutionary or developmental perspectives and it is precisely this development that calls for a cautious and critical stance toward historical data. Especially, sociologists seeking to work in the classic tradition need to be aware of the need to adopt historical data from the secondary sources with a pinch of salt. It is apparent that writers of this tradition who cried hoarse against 'positivistic' sociologists banking entirely on survey-based data are themselves exhibiting a measure of dogmatism in treating the 'facts' contained in historical works as self-evident truths rather than understanding them chiefly in the nature of inferences of the historian drawn from the 'relics' at his disposal. Any kind of historical sociology relying in the main on the secondary historical sources needs to apply the screws of critical scrutiny in the same manner as methodologically required for the quantitatively oriented sociology. Certain versions of present day sociology utilizing the evolutionary or developmental approach (such as, Bellah R. N. : *Religious Evolution,* A. S. R. 1964) seems to reveal a measure of uncertainty in regard to the relationship between historical and theoretical statements.[17] The objective in such studies is the well-intended exercise of demonstrating empirically, on the basis of historical evidence, certain sequential patterns in institutional or structural change. But the procedure of tracing historical patterns post-factum, cannot by itself lead to theoretical explanation.

A theoretical explanation entails a separate exercise. There are in evidence some recent attempts to produce 'theoretical' history, i.e., theories of social evolution or development which purport to represent the principles underlying sequential regularities and thus, afford estimations about the future. Such attempts are reflected clearly in the works of the 'new' Marxist writers like Perry Anderson and have been shown (Goldthorpe-1971) to be present, albeit covertly, in a bulk of current American writing on the modernization and industrialism themes. In the latest work of *Parsons (The System of Modern Societies,* Englewood Cliffs, Prentice Hall, 1971) an attempt of this order is discernible (revivification of structural functional theory by linkage with a *pro-naturalistic evolutionism).* In all such attempts there is according to Goldthorpe, a tendency to ignore the reasoned criticisms directed against the notion of theoretical history by writers like Karl Popper and Gellner. The authors of this methodological lineage, according to him, seek in "the classic historicist fashion, to use their theories to lend a spurious scientific basis and objectivity to what can be shown to ideological arguments."[18] Theories of social evolution and development according to Robert Nisbet,[19] are typically 'haunted' by the problem of how to make the historical record congruent with the proposed immanent processes of change. A keener awareness of the historical record and the way it is constructed would stand the sociologists in good stead, since such an awareness may be expected to sensitize them to the treacherous spots that may lie concealed in the evolutionary theories as a class.

Thus, while agreeing with Arthur Schlesinger that "No social scientist can wisley ignore the long arm of the past" [20] we need not agree with Daniel Webster that "the past is, at least secure."[21] The axiomatic belief about the past being secure may lead one to treacherous conclusions. A critical and cautious stance vis-a-vis the historial materials is, on all counts, most desirable.

REFERENCES

(1) Galtung, *Op. cit.,* p. 27.
(2) *Ibid.,* p. 110.
(3) Madge: *Tools of Social Science*, Longmans, London, 1965.
(4) *Ibid.,* p. 86.
(5) *Ibid.,* p. 105.
(6) *Ibid.,* p. 110.
(7) Cf. Selltiz, *et al.: op. cit.,* pp. 334-5.
(8) Madge: *op. cit.,* p. 116.
(9) See Nagel: (art) "The Logic of Historical Analyis," *Scientific Monthly,* p. 74.
(10) Cf. Young: *op. cit.,* p. 148.
(11) *Ibid.*
(12) Lazarsfeld, P.; In M. Komarovsky (ed.) *Common Frontiers of the Social Sciences,* Free Press, 1957.
(13) Goldthorpe, J.: in M. Blumer: *Sociological Research Methods,* Mac Millan., 1977, p. 183.
(14) Cf. Bottomore, T.B. and Rubel: *Karl Marx,* Penguin, p. 76.
(15) Goldthorpe: (art) Blumer., *op. cit.,* p. 188.
(16) *Ibid.*
(17) *Ibid.,* p. 190.
(18) *Ibid.*
(19) Nisbet, R.: *Social Change and History,* Oxford University Press, New York, 1969.
(20) Cf.: Young: *op. cit.,* p. 148.
(21) *Ibid.,* p. 157.

Chapter X

Observation

We are almost constantly engaged in observation of things, objects, processes and even thought-ways of people. It is our basic method of obtaining information about the world around us. All observation, however, is not scientific observation. Observation becomes a scientific tool for the researcher to the extent that it serves a formulated research purpose, is planned systematically, is related to more general theoretical proposition, is recorded systematically and is subjected to check and controls on validity and reliability. This is not to say, however, that observations of great scientific import cannot occasionally be made just by stumbling across the unexpected or chance coincidences. The history of science is replete with evidences of valuable discoveries founded on unsystematic, haphazard and casual observations that were unrelated to some pre-defined and established research purpose, e.g., the discovery of radium and penicillin.

Many types of data sought by the social scientists can be obtained through direct observation. Direct observation of behaviour, of course, is not the only method by which the scientist can obtain data. Interviews, questionnaires, records, etc., can under certain situations, replace and supplement observations by the scientist. "But indeed", as John Dollard puts it, "the primary research instrument would seem to be the observing human intelligence trying to make sense out of human experience...."[1]

Compared to the other methods of data collection, observation has some distinct advantages.

1. One great asset of the observational technique is that it is possible to record behaviour as it occurs. Many other research techniques depend entirely on people's retrospective or anticipatory reports of their own behaviour. But these reports are by and large given when the respondent is somewhat removed from stress and strains that influence his behaviour in the ordinary routine. However, at this time, the respondent is influenced by other pressures peculiar to the research situation. The observational techniques yield data that pertain directly to typical behavioural situations. A researcher would prefer observational methods, should he have reasons to believe that distortions in 'recall' or reminiscence are likely to occur.
2. Most items of our behaviour are so much a part of our habit that they escape an aware detection and resist translation into words. Anthropologists observing foreign cultures have noted that many facts worth recording are so much taken for granted by the native people that they do not think they are worthy of reporting.
3. Studies may deal with subjects who are not capable of giving verbal reports of their behaviour or feelings for the plain reason that they cannot speak, e.g., infants or animals. Such studies necessarily depend on observation.
4. Observation is independent of people's willingness to report. Many a time, a researcher meets with resistance from persons being studied. People may not have the time or they may be unwilling to be interviewed or tested. Although observation cannot always overcome such resistance, it must be conceded that relatively speaking, it is less demanding of active co-operation on the part of the subjects and hence less exacting for the subjects.

We assume that observations would yield data which are comparable on the inter-observer basis and hence can afford well grounded generalizations. But we can no longer talk about the 'observer' in abstract, because we have experience of only one observer, namely, the person we can talk about and observe my body even my thoughts, but whenever I regard myself as an object in this way, there is sense in which I am still the subject who observes.

If in any scientific activity an observer confronts what is observed, sometimes the observation is reflexive, and the same person plays both roles. The only experiences of observation to which I have direct access are my own, and I cannot tell if the experiences of others are like mine, even if they are described to me, for the experiences themselves are private and *'Sui Generis'*, whereas the description is public and makes use of the categories of language.

But this very thing may go against the observational method not so much for methodological, as for ethical reasons. For example, in the participant observation, insights are often gained at the expense of morality (e.g., where there is deception of subjects).

Observational techniques are, of course, not without their own brand of limitations. The major ones are as follows:

(1) It is often impossible to anticipate the occurrence of an event precisely enough to be able to be present to observe it. Even the observation of regular daily occurrences sometimes becomes difficult because of the possibility that unforeseen factors may interfere with the observational task.

(2) The practical possibility of applying observational techniques is limited by the duration of events. For example, life histories cannot be generated this way. Besides, some occurrences that people may not be willing and able to report are rarely accessible to direct observation (for example, private behaviour).

(3) It is often held that observational data cannot be quantified. This, however, is a gross misconception. It should be remembered that the anthropologists were pioneers in the use of observational techniques and did not feel the need for quantifying their observation. This is no reason to suppose that observational data are typically unamenable to quantification. Social researchers will do well to bear in mind that observational data like other data are not incapable of being quantified.

Observation may serve a variety of research purposes. It may be used to explore the given area of subject-matter or to gain insight into the research problem and provide a basis for development of hypotheses. It may also be used to gather supplementary material that would help interpretation of findings obtained by other techniques. Lastly, observation may also be used as the primary method of data-collection in descriptive studies as also, in the experimental studies designed for testing causal hypotheses.

Types of Observation

Observation may take place in the natural or real life setting or in a laboratory. Observational procedures tend to vary from complete flexibility to the use of pre-coded detailed formal instrument. The observer may himself participate actively in the group he is observing or he may be an observer from outside or his presence may be unknown to the people he is observing. We may thus classify scientific observation broadly, on three bases, as follows:

(1) controlled/uncontrolled observation.

(2) Structured/unstructured/partially structured observation.

(3) Participant/non-participant/disguised observation.

The type of observational technique to be chosen in a particular study depends on the purpose of the study. In an exploratory study, the observational procedure is most likely to be relatively unstructured and the observer is also more likely to participate in group activity. On the other hand, for studies of the descriptive or experimental type, the observational procedures are more likely to be relatively structured and involve a minimum of participation on the part of the observer. It should be noted, however, that the degree of structuredness and the degree of participation need not be together. For example, the researcher in an exploratory study may be a participant observer or a non-participant or a disguised observer. A particular research situation may demand the coupling of participant observation with a highly structured observational instrument.

The investigator, whatever be the purpose of his study, should advisedly answer four broad questions before setting out to observe, i.e., he must be sure about : (i) what should be observed, (ii) how the observation should be recorded, (iii) how to ensure accuracy of observation, and (iv) what relationship should obtain between the observer and observed and, how the desired relationship should be established.

The questions cannot be answered uniformly since the above decisions depend on the nature of the study and the extent to which observational procedures can be structured.

Let us now discuss the major types of observational procedures. One of the most useful bases for classification of observational procedures is the degree of structuredness. Accordingly, we get two ideal-typical observational procedures: (1) unstructured, and (2) structured. It will be helpful to bear in mind that in actual practice, there are degrees of structuredness, i.e., structuredness and unstructuredness constitute a continuum rather than a sharp cut and dried distinction between the structured and unstructured types of observation.

Unstructured Observation

The unstructured observation is diametrically opposed to the structured observation in its ideal-typical formulation. The structured observation is characterized by a careful definition of the units to be observed, information to be recorded, the selection of pertinent data for observation and standardization of conditions of observation. The unstructured observation represents ideally a contrasting situation in respect of all these. We shall discuss the unstructured type of observation in its relation to the four major issues posing the investigator as outlined above.

(a) What should be observed? In highly-structured studies, the well-formulated research-problem or hypotheses clearly point to what data will be most relevant. But in exploratory studies the observer does not know in advance which aspects of the situation will prove relevant. Since unstructured observation is mostly used as an exploratory technique the observer's understanding of the situation is likely to change as he goes along. This, in turn, may call for changes in what he observes. It should be noted that such changes called for in the foci of observation are often desirable. Such shifts in focus according to the exigencies of the situation is a characteristic of unstructured observation. That is, the unstructured observation is flexible, it allows for changes in focus from time to time if and when reasonable clues or doubts warrant such changes with a view to facilitate taking stock of the new observational items that appear to be pertinent or important at different points in time. The observer is always prepared to draw his clues from unanticipated events in an attitude of alert receptivity.

While no stringent criteria or hard and fast rules can be laid down as to how the observer will go about observing a particular situation it would be helpful, however, to indicate some of the significant aspects that the observer can overlook only at his peril.

(1) The observer should see who the participants are, how many they are and how they are related to one another.
(2) The observer should understand the 'setting.' He should know in addition to its overt appearance, the kinds of behaviour it encourages, discourages or prevents and its social characteristics.
(3) The observer should also understand the purpose which has brought the subject-participants together, the nature of the purpose and how the goals of participants are related.
(4) The observer must also understand what the participants do, how, with whom and with what they do it. For example, the observer should know what stimulus initiated the behaviour, what the goal is towards which the behaviour is directed, what are the qualities of the behaviour (duration, intensity, etc.) and what are it consequences?

It should be noted that in a practical situation, it is often not possible to obtain enough clues to allow such a comprehensive description. It may also be that the course of events is too fluid to permit consideration of all dimensions of a social situation or that a certain aspect of an occurrence may be so important as to need the entire attention of the observer.

(b) Recording an observation involves two major considerations, viz., (i) when should the notes be taken, and (ii) how the notes should be kept.

The best time for recording is on the spot and during the event. This results in minimizing selective bias and distortions of memory. There are, however, many situations in which note taking on the spot is not feasible because this is likely to affect the naturalness of the situation and create suspicions in minds of the persons being observed. Constant note taking may also affect the quality of observation, as the observer has to divide his attention between observing and writing. In consequence, during the process, the relevant aspects of the situation may be lost to the eye.

In a situation where on the spot detailed note taking is not possible, the memory of the observer may be too heavily taxed if recording is postponed to the expiry of an observational period. In such situations the observer should advisedly jot down significant key words so as to help him reconstruct the situation later. In certain situations, it may also help him reconstruct the situation later. In certain situations, it may also help if the observer retires from an on-going situation for a few minutes every hour to make more detailed notes. It is important that the observer should pen down as soon as possible, after the period of observation, a complete account of everything important in the situation. The facility of recording improves if the observer evolved some kind of indexing system.

(c) Ensuring the accuracy of observation is another important concern of the observer. In situations where for some reasons, immediate recording is not possible, he is likely to find that by the time he sits down to write his observations, his memory does not accurately feed in the relevant details. In order to check the accuracy and completeness of the record, the observer should, if feasible, compare it with a record made by a tape recording equipment. Of course, this is not always feasible; besides, tape recording captures only the auditory stimuli in the situation.

The next best solution is to have two or more people observe the same event. They can later compare their notes and check bias. This is an excellent way to discover one's blind spots. However, as we have suggested above, two observations may be qualitatively different; against this, two observers from different backgrounds may be employed to observe the same situation. This is understandably a limited remedy.

It happens quite often that the observer injects an overdose of interpretation into his records. This may adversely affect the validity and reliability of his conclusions. One way out of this is to have two observers record the same vent using the same system. A subsequent comparison, between their records may go some way in detecting the intrusion of interpretation.

As we shall see, the participant observer, by virtue of his typical position, faces formidable difficulties in maintaining biaslessness. Such an observer may get involved emotionally with some of the people he is studying. This affects his objectivity. To gain access to intimate data, the observer may allow himself to be absorbed into particular situation he is studying. But this very factor may make him to accept uncritically the behaviour that he should be trying to explain. This problem can be met mainly by the observer becoming aware of his proneness or tendency to take things for granted. An outsider serving as a check may bring home to the observer his blind spot.

It is also possible to detect blind spots by breaking up or dissecting the perceptual field so the factors that lead it to be seen in a particular way lose much of their force. In other words, by approaching the situation in an analytical way the observer may be able to lessen the distorting influence of certain factors that are likely to lead to bias.

The natural way of seeing the situation is to see the action as one centred around the principal actors. But an inconspicuous person, seemingly very insignificant in the situation, or sometimes even a dead person, may be the real center of the situation (e.g., in ceremonies dealing with the propitiation of the soul of a dead person).

An effective screw to control accuracy in observation and interpretations is for the investigator to establish a sort of relationship with the subjects which makes it possible for him to take them into his confidence about the research. A participant observer's situation is likely to create inner conflicts within the investigator. This, in turn, may interfere with objectivity. Should the group being observed be undergoing an emergency of some kind, there is indeed a strong pressure on the observer to become an active participant. He may have to abandon at least temporarily, his detached position as an observer. But if he does enter into the center of activities of the group, he risks the danger of losing his identity as a scientist. Thus, the participant observer is in a dilemma; resulting either way, in the loss of objectivity. Rosenfeld suggests that bias arising from inner conflicts may be minimized if one is aware of the conflicts and of the nature of one's defence.[2]

The final issue relates to the relationship between the observer and the observed. In field observation faulty approach vis-à-vis the subjects may have dire consequences for the inquiry. Since the method is applied in the actual life-sphere of the persons, the observer's mistakes cannot remain insulated incidents.

The observer must decide before he approaches the potential subjects, whether to reveal the facts that he is a researcher or to enter the situation under some other guise. There are advantages as also disadvantages in both these approaches. It may for certain reasons seem preferable to make known to the subjects his real role as the researcher. This approach is relatively simple compared to disguised observation. Secondly, it increases substantially one's opportunity to get information which he would get only very indirectly were he to approach them in disguise. Thirdly, the open declaration approach does not hold the possibility that his activity will harm any of the people in the situation whereas the disguised observer must consider this possibility seriously.

The obvious disadvantage of a direct approach is that this may make the subjects conscious only to the detriment of naturalness of behaviour the observer wants to observe. The researcher therefore has to weigh carefully the relative gains and losses of these two approaches before employing any one. Sometimes, there is no alternative to disguised observation. M. Sherif and C. Sherif have reported that the gang-activities of the boys in a summer camp could only be observed by the researcher in the guise of a labourer on the camp grounds. Similarly, in the study of socio-psychological effects of long-term unemployment in an Austrian Village (Jahoda, Lazarsfeld and Zeisl), disguised observation (research workers presenting themselves as members of voluntary welfare group) was used with advantage.

Entrance into a community requires a very careful staging. If there are many more than two sides to be approached simultaneously, the issue becomes all the more tricky. The observer must be prepared to provide a convincing reason for his presence in the community. It may sometimes be advisable to let influential persons in the community handle the explanation of the investigator's work. The observer then must decide upon the degree of his participation in the community, ranging from the bare minimum of answering when addressed, to engaging in some major activity concerning the community life.

Structured Observation

Structured observation consists in a careful definition of categories under which the information is to be recorded, standardization of conditions of observation, and is used mostly in studies designed to provide systematic description or to test causal hypothesis. The use of structured observational technique presupposes that the investigator knows what aspects of the situation under study are relevant to his research purposes and is in a position therefore to develop a specific plan for making and recording observations before he actually begins the collection of data. Structured observation may be employed in the natural field-setting or a laboratory-setting.

Structured observation, in so far as it is used mainly in studies starting with relatively specific formulation, normally allows for much less freedom of choice with respect to the content of observation than is allowed in unstructured observation. Since the situation and the problem are already explicit, the observer is in a position to set up in advance the categories in terms of which he will analyse the situation. The categories are clearly defined to provide reliable data on the questions to be asked. Of course, such a definition of categories is the end-product of the researcher's efforts at trying to solve specific coding problems. To start with, the researcher may be faced with a large number of categories. It is important that the researcher decides upon an appropriate frame of reference for categorization and trains observers accordingly.

R. E. Bales has developed a procedural system of categories for recording group interaction. He has proposed 12 standard behavioural categories applicable to a wide range of group situations. Behaviour of any group member is coded in terms of careful definition of each category.[3]

Now we turn to the problem of recording observations during a structured observation. The most commonly used system of recording is one that provides the observer with a number of duplicate sheets containing the list of categories to be coded. Mechanical recording instruments have been used in some studies. For example, Chapple devised an international chronograph. Helen has developed an audio-introspectometer. Bales and Gerbrands have devised an interactional recorder. All these devices are meant to facilitate recording of observational data according to a specific principle of categorization.

Sound recordings and motion pictures have been used when it is necessary to describe the overall nature of an event or to code certain action of a member in terms of a frame of reference provided by the entire event. Of course, each of these has obvious limitations. Although such devices as motion pictures, tape-recording and television may be very helpful in affording an overall view of a social event, their use does not by itself solve the problem of gathering data for systematic purposes. Relevant categories for recording behaviour must be established, time-units decided upon, methods set up for recording as to who initiated an action and who was the target. In sum, if the data are to be useful for research, they must be recorded in terms of such a formal scheme.

We shall now consider the problem of ensuring the reliability of observations. This problem is effectively tackled by ensuring some kind of a standardization in the observational instrument. There are, however, some special problems in achieving reliable and valid observations. These are as follows:

(1) One problem derives from the inadequate definition of the kinds of behaviour that are to be accepted as corresponding to a given concept. For example, if the concept of adjustment was not operationally defined, different observers may be inclined to regard different kinds of behaviour as empirical referents of the concept.

(2) Another factor that may lower the reliability of even a well-trained and skilled observer is the degree of confidence one must have in one's judgement before marking a given category. For example, observers may assign the same observational items to different categories because they may themselves manifest different tendencies to perceive evidence of a particular behaviour.

(3) The constant error introduced by the observer because of the distortion of his perceptions (for various reasons) is one of the major sources of unreliability.

(4) The load of work can also hamper reliability. The result of overloading is often that the observer cannot record all relevant data and may unwittingly record some aspects rather inadequately, thus, introducing bias.

As was suggested earlier, reliability can be increased by careful training of observers. A well-developed observational procedure can be damaged by differences among different observers or by failure to understand the rules for its use. It is necessary, therefore, that a good period of time be devoted to train the observers. Such a training entails several phases: (i) explanation of purposes and theory in the given study, (ii) explanation of categories and the rules for their use, (iii) purpose of each category for a theoretic scheme, and (iv) practice by observer-trainees, discussion on concrete difficulties and reliability-test of observers.

It should be remembered that all this may not always eliminate the constant bias shared by two or more observers. In such a case, the bias can be minimized by same events.

Lastly, we need to consider the relation of the observer with the observed. The observer must carefully prepare his entry into situation and make sure that all members of the group are willing to accept him. Since usually the observer is conspicuously engaged in recording behaviour, using timing device and other technical aids, it is barely possible to disguise the fact that he is doing research. Hence, it is all the more important that he obtains the group's full agreement to the inquiry.

The entry of an observer into the group, however unobtrusive, may introduce a new variable into the situation and this may change the behaviour being observed. For example, in a children's group, the presence of adult observer may have a great distorting influence. It is important that some thought is given to ways in which the observer's presence may influence the outcome of research and to develop the techniques that would reduce this possibility. On the whole, people seem to get used to observers if the behaviour of the observer convinces the subjects that he means no ill.

We shall now discuss the participant and the non-participant types of observation. This conceptual typology was introduced to social sciences by Prof. Edward Lindeman. Lindeman was very critical of studies based upon schedules of questions for which the investigator found answers by making inquiries of persons. Lindeman considered as absurd any attempt to avoid bias by posing questions requiring a simple 'yes' or 'no' reply in a study dealing not only with the 'what' of life but also with the 'why' and 'how' of life. Lindeman was of the opinion that if one wished to know what the subject was really doing one should watch him and not ask him.

Nels Anderson was a intimate participant in the life of 'Hobos', on the road, in lodging houses and in their various activities. The tremendous insight which Anderson developed through such an exercise is amply evidenced in his study entitled 'The Hobo.'

Participant observation has a reference to the observer sharing to a greater or lesser degree the life of the group he is observing. This sharing may be intermittent but active contacts at close proximity do afford an intimate study of persons. W.F. Whyte in the course of his study published as 'The Street Corner Society' was intimately associated with the various aspects of the activities of members in Cornerville. Paul Cressey in his study entitled 'Taxi Dance Hall' employed the technique of participant observation and his investigators became part of the social world of the Taxi Dance Hall to the extent it was possible.

The non-participant observation, in contradistinction, is characterized by a relative lack of participation by the observer in the life of the group that he is observing. In sum, to quote John Madge, "When the heart of the observer is made to beat as the heart of any other member of the group under observation, rather than as that of detached emissary from some distant laboratory, then he has earned the title of participant observer."[4] In other words, the participant observation is an attempt to put both observer and observed on the same side by making the observer a member of the group so that he can experience what they experience and work within their frame of reference. On the contrary, the non-participant observation involves the espousal by the observer of a detached role of the observer and recorder without any attempt on his part to experience through participation that which the observed experience.

Merits and Limitations

Let us discuss the significant merits and limitations of participant and non-participant types of observation.

Merits

In participant observation, the investigator becomes a member of the community being observed by him. The investigator need not carry out exactly the same activities as the subjects, suffice it, if he finds a role in the group which does not disturb the usual patterns of behaviour. Thus, one of the advantages of participant observation is that since the members of the community are unaware of the researcher's purpose their behaviour is least likely to be affected. Thus, the researcher is enabled to record the "natural" behaviour of the group.

Secondly, since the researcher actually participates in the group under observation, he normally has an access to a body of information which could not easily be obtained by merely looking on in a disinterested fashion. He thus obtains a great depth of experience, while he is able to record the actual behaviour of other participants. Since his period of participation may continue for months, the range of materials collected is likely to be much wider than those gained from a series of quite lengthy interview-schedules.

Thirdly, in participant observation, the researcher is able to record the context which gives meaning to expressions of opinion surpassing in richness and depth the usual questionnaire. He can also check the truth of statements made by members of the group.

Some occurrences are rarely, if ever, accessible to direct observation. Sexual bahaviour, family crisis and underworld activities, etc., are examples of events that are not amenable to direct observation by an outsider. It is here that the participant observation helps.

Limitations

Participant observation has certain disadvantages, one being that the investigator who actually becomes a participant happens to narrow his range of experience. He takes on a particular position within a group with a definite clique or friendship circle. He learns and follows a pattern of activity which is characteristic of its members. Hence, many avenues become closed to him. Further, the role he comes to occupy in the group may be important so that he may be instrumental in effecting changes in the group-behaviour.

The position of participant-observer is especially precarious when it comes to maintaining objectivity. The involvement in the situation may lessen the sharpness of observation not only because the investigator identifies himself with his informants but also because he becomes so used to certain kinds of behaviour. In certain situations, the physical and emotional endurance as well as the patience of the researcher may be put to an acid test. Even the observation of routine day-to-day occurrences may become difficult in view of the possibility that unforeseeable factors might interfere with the observational task.

To the extent that he participates emotionally, the observer comes to lose objectivity which in scientific parlance is his single greatest asset. He may react in anger when he ought to be recording. He may seek prestige or ego-satisfaction within the group rather than observing this behaviour in others. His heart may be moved by tragedy but he may forget to record its impact upon his fellow-members. In consequence, he may fail to note these important details which may appear to him so commonplace as not to merit any attention.

It is clear that in both, the participant and non-participant types of observation, the problem of observation-control is not solved. To the degree that the investigator becomes a participant his experience becomes unique, peculiarly his own. Thus, any other researcher would not be able to record the same facts. There is thus less standardization of data. In short, his role of observer is handicapped somewhat by his being a participant.

Non-participant observation does answer some of these objections. But a purely non-participant observation is difficult. We have standard set of relationships or role patterns for the 'non-member' who should be ever present but never participating. Both the subject-group and the outsider are likely to feel uncomfortable. And, naturally, for many research situations it is almost impossible for the outsider to be a genuine participant in all ways. The sociologist cannot, for example, become a criminal in order to study a criminal gang. Sometimes, it is possible to take part in a great many activities of the group, just to avoid the awkwardness of complete non-participation while taking the role of an observer for other activities. This strategy was employed by Leplay a century ago in his study of European working class families. In certain studies, the investigators have participated as members of the family taking part in games and dances. They nevertheless made clear that their purpose, above anything else, was to gather facts.

Principal Difficulties in Observations

It is necessary to recognize pertinently the obstacles to impartial observation. The first social scientist to list and discuss these intrinsic difficulties was Herbert Spencer. In his 'Study of Sociology', he devoted four chapters to the subject. Spencer pointed out that many social phenomena, unlike the bulk of natural phenomena, are not directly perceptible, but often have to be established by putting together many details which are naturally dispersed in space and time.

Spencer next commented on the barriers to correct observation and the interference which results from the emotional engagement of the social investigator in the subject of his study. Of particular importance, in this context, is the fact of interrelatedness of the observer to the situation being observed.

We have to consider three main causes of distorted observation. These are: (i) those due to the inadequacies of our sense-organs; (ii) those due to the interdependence of observation and inference; and (iii) those typical to the social sciences, i.e., those due to the impossibility of observing human beings without influencing their actions and being influenced by them. We now turn to a discussion on these points.

(i) Inadequacies of Our Sense Organs: Traditionally we tend to regard our sense organs as reliable, though perhaps not as powerful as we would like them to be. But in fact our sense organs operate in a highly variable, erratic and selective manner. Psychologists have conducted experiments which have shown that what man perceives on a particular occasion depends greatly on his state of mind and body at the time. There is a wealth of evidence to show that it is thoroughly unsafe to rely on the everyday observation.

(ii) Observation and Inference: Observation and inference are inseparable. Anything that impinges on our senses has a meaning for us largely to the extent we relate it to what we already know. Without any frame to start with, new experiences are isolated, unidentifiable, and meaningless. The research worker with no frame of reference sees much, but identifies little. The researcher with too rigid a frame of reference sees only such things as confirm his preconceptions. Thus, we are faced with the very awkward and serious difficulty that our senses are not, even under the most favourable conditions, the means for providing us with 'objective knowledge' about what we set out to observe. There are various possible ways of coming to grips with this difficulty. One way is to ignore it. Even if out observations are not very objective, they are, it may be argued, at least able to prove to our personal satisfaction that what we see is true. There is the danger that non-controlled observation is likely to give us the feeling that we know more than we actually do, about what we have seen. The data are so real and vivid, hence our feelings about them so strong that we sometimes tend to mistake the strength of our emotions for the depth of comprehensions.

(iii) Observer and Observed: We must pay some attention to another critical problem in social science, viz., the face of observation itself modifying the situation being observed, so long as social science research is based on documentary data, there is obviously no reason to fear that distortions will arise from this source. But social science research involves human observers and the interactive human subjects.

(iv) Observer-Caused Effects: The researcher's efforts to study a phenomenon always affects the phenomenon and is most likely to change it. The observer is invariably a part of the same environment as is the phenomenon he is studying. Therefore, the observer like all other aspects of the environment cannot but influence the phenomenon, only,

sometimes the effect may be light that it could be ignored. This is usually the case with the natural sciences except perhaps in chemistry in which the chemist's breath is likely to affect the reaction he is running. The observer effect in medical examination straddles the physical and social sciences; for example, when a doctor takes a patient's blood pressure, fear or excitement may force blood pressure far above the actual level.

The humanness of the observer and his inevitable interaction with the observed are bound to create distorting effects to which we must pay some attention. The critical problem in social sciences is that the existence of observer itself modifies the situation being observed. So long as social science research is based on documentary data, there is obviously no reason to fear that distortions will arise from this source. But social science research involves human observers and the interactive human subjects.

One way of allowing for observer interference when it cannot be prevented is to vary the amounts and kinds of observer participation when all else is held constant; for example, in a factory being observed for the structure of human relations the observers may vary the amount of time they spend with the workers and the degree of friendship and hostility towards the workers during the time they interact with the workers. If such variations on the part of the observers produce no differences then it would be secure to conclude that observer is not an important source of variations. As an added control it could be possible to bring the observer into situation in which nothing else is changed from normal and then measure whether or not his presence alone would cause any differences.

Prof. Wirth once said, "A society is possible in the last analysis because the individuals in it carry around in their heads some sort of picture of that society. If the participants regard the changed situation as an abnormal one which does not fit into their conception of the world, their self consciousness will be aroused, their behaviour will be disturbed and the situation will not adapt itself in a way enabling the investigator to predict a similar adaptation in natural circumstances. The presence of an observer, even merely as one extra person in the interacting situation, will lead to distortion."[5]

REFERENCES

(1) Madge: *op. cit.,* p. 177.

(2) Selltiz, *et al., op. cit.,* Chapter on 'Observation.'

(3) See Chapter on 'Observation' in Selltiz, Jahoda, *et al., op. cit.*

(4) Madge: *op. cit.,* p. 131.

(5) Madge: *op. cit.,* p. 128.

Chapter XI

The Interview Method

Human behaviour, for the initial one or two years of life is mostly non-verbal. It is only later that human beings engage in oral-verbal acts if external circumstances permit them to do so. They may subsequently be able to include written-verbal acts if the social system they live in is adequately developed to a level as to be conducive to this.

The oral-verbal and written-verbal acts have two obvious advantages: (a) they can yield an almost infinite variety of meaningful information, and (b) they can easily be stored. In our culture, verbal acts have been attributed a greater discerning process compared to non-verbal ones.

A tendency often evidenced in literature is to attach moré importance to non-verbal than to verbal acts. The underlying assumption seems to be that the non-verbal acts are more real and basic and the verbal acts epiphenomenal. If there is a discrepancy between what a person does and what he says he does (verbal response), the interpretation is generally that the person lies with his words than with his deeds (non-verbal response).

Let us try to resolve this controversy. We may begin by saying that there is hardly much reason to believe in the complete impossibility of finding a set of verbal responses from which a satisfactory prediction about a future act can be made. If a verbal stimulus elicits a certain verbal response, this may serve at the least, as a basis for the inference of future verbal behaviour. In as much as verbal behaviour occupies a large portion of the total behaviour of humans, this cannot by any means be considered a small achievement.

It is often said that verbal acts are less consequential compared to the non-verbal ones. Non-verbal acts have physical consequences — it is possible to kill with a non-verbal act but not with a verbal one. It may be argued, however, that verbal acts often precede or accompany dramatic non-verbal acts, so that a correspondence may be established between the verbal and non-verbal components of behaviour. It may also be argued that verbal methods (e.g., interviews) may be used to get at what people think or at least what they think but not what they actually express in social situations. But this is a methodological problem relating to constructing the data-collection situation so that valid information may be obtained.

Another problem lies in relation to what is considered the subject-matter, for example, of sociology. It may be contended by critics that verbal methods may be excellent for the study of a person's ideology or convictions but not for the study of communicative acts if these are verbal ones. If sociology is considered a science of interaction amongst people then this argument may be taken very seriously.

It has been said that a person cannot lie with his deeds. To this our reply may be that it all depends on our definition of a 'lie.' If by a 'lie' we mean that there is an inconsistency between what the person knows and inference people may legitimately draw from his overt behaviour, then 'lie' applies equally well to the non-verbal sphere of human behaviour.

This discussion is intended to highlight the fact that the oral-verbal techniques of data collection, despite the criticisms levelled by some against these, are indeed fruitful sources of rich human behavioural data.

The interview technique that we shall discuss in this chapter is one verbal method of securing data. Another verbal method of securing data is the questionnaire, which we shall consider in the next chapter. The main difference between the interview and the questionnaire methods is that the former involves presentation of oral-verbal stimuli and reply in terms of oral-verbal responses (oral stimuli — oral responses), whereas the questionnaire method involves presentation of written-verbal stimuli and return of written-verbal response (written stimuli — written responses). The observational methods, as we have seen in the preceding chapter, are restricted mostly to non-verbal acts (nodding, clapping, manipulating things, smiling etc.), i.e., to understanding this behaviour and describing it as it occurs. The observational methods are understandably not so effective in giving information about persons' perceptions, beliefs, feelings, motivations, anticipations, future plans, past and private behaviours. The interview method is quite effective in giving information about all these aspects. G. W. Allport in his classic statement, sums this up beautifully. He says, "If you want to know how people feel, what they experience and what they remember, what their emotions and motives are like, and the reasons for acting as they do — why not ask them?"[1]

The interview approach simply stated, involves a person designated the interviewer asking questions (mostly) in a face-to-face contact (generally) to the other person or persons, designated the interviewee/s who give answers (mostly) to these questions. It does not mean, as the term 'mostly' in the brackets suggests, that all the time it is interviewer who asks questions. On rare occasions, the interviewee may also ask certain questions and the interviewer responds to these. In any case, it is certain that the interviewer initiates the interaction (interview) and the interviewee is at the receiving end.

In so far as it affords a "portrait of human personality", i.e., information about the social background which governs one's scheme of life, one's inner strivings, tensions, wishes and the changes in one's behavioural relations, the interview has been a widely used method in empirical studies. Thomas and Znaniecki used this method to get at some aspects of their subject, 'the Polish Peasant', concerning the patterns of adjustment of immigrants to new social situations. Some of the most sophisticated interview techniques were used in their study entitled, "The Authoritarian Personality" by Adorno and associates. Stouffer and associates used the interview method extensively in their celebrated study entitled "The American Soldier." Interview may be said to be one of the most commonly used techniques (usually employed with other techniques of data-collection but also on occasions, singly) of data collection in studies of human behaviour. The reassessment of the qualitative interviews has helped the interview method attain tremendous importance in contemporary research in the field of social and behavioural science.

Types of Interview

We shall now discuss the different types of interview. The classification of interviews may be effected on the basis of various criteria, these may be classified according to their functions (such as the diagnostic interviews, often used for clinical purposes or interviews engaged in for treatment, e.g., the psychiatric interviews that serve the purpose of catharsis, also called therapeutic interviews), or interviews may also be classified according to the number of persons participating in the process (e.g., group interview or individual interview). Another basis of classifying interviews is the type of approach employed, e.g., structured or unstructured (sometimes also called directive or non-directive interviews). Yet another typology of interviews derives on the basis of whether these are focused on a specific item/issue or not so. Here we briefly discuss some of the major types of interview.

(1) The Structured Interviews

Such interviews involve the use of a set of pre-determined questions and highly standardized techniques of recording. The reasons for standardization is to ensure that all respondents reply to the same questions; that is, any given question has the same meaning for all the respondents. Structured interviews mostly involve the use of fixed, alternative questions. The alternative questions or close-ended questions are those in which the responses of the subjects are limited to certain fixed, pre-designated alternatives. These alternatives may simply be 'yes' or 'no' or may consist of a series of anticipated replies out of which the respondent picks any one (or more) which is closest to his position. Structured interviews may also involve the use of open-ended questions but the questions and their order are pre-determined. The interviewer is, however, free to repeat the question if the reply is not to the point. Generally, the interviewer has no freedom to waive a question except to get clarification of the subject's responses and these questions must be non-directive or non-suggestive.

(2) Unstructured Interviews

Unstructured interviews, as opposed to the structured ones, are characterized by a far too greater flexibility of approach to questioning the respondents. Compared to the structured interview, the non-structured ones involve relatively much lesser standardization of relevant techniques and operations. Consequently, the investigator is never certain as to what the respondents will give out as information.

Interviewers in this type of interview, do not follow a system or list of pre-determined questions. Respondents are encouraged to relate freely and frankly their concrete experience with little or no directions from the interviewer. The respondents are allowed and freedom to talk on whatever events seem significant to them, to provide their own definitions of the social situation, report their own foci of attention and reveal their attitudes and opinion as they deem it.

The flexibility of the unstructured interview properly utilized helps to bring out the affective and value-laden aspects of the subjects' responses and to determine the personal significance of his attitudes. Such interviews permit a free-flowing account of the personal and social contexts of beliefs and feelings. This type of interview achieves its designated purpose depending on the extent to which the subject's responses are spontaneous rather than forced; specific, concrete and self-revealing.

In a non-structured interview, the interviewer is allowed a much greater freedom to ask, if he feels so, any supplementary questions, or if the situation so demands to omit certain questions, to change the sequence of questions and if need be, to offer explanations and clarifications. The interviewer has much greater freedom to record the responses according to his own frame of judging significance, relevance, and convenience. He is free to include some aspects and exclude others from his record, highlight certain responses and ignore or underplay others. Granted such freedom, the interviewer has both advantages as well as disadvantages.

Such a flexibility frequently results in lack of comparability between one interview and another. Further, analysis of the unstructured responses is much more difficult and time-consuming than that of the structured responses secure during the structured interviews.

The non-structured interviews usually demand deep knowledge and skill on the part of the interviewer. The interviewer is expected to possess not only the general skill, and capacity demanded of any sympathetic listener, but also the specific ability to adopt temporarily the beliefs and attitudes of each of his informants.

The collection of material by such a flexible means is inevitably slow and normally only a small sample can be expected to be covered. Because of the unrestricted range of subjects on which the respondents may desire to discuss, it is very difficult to articulate the recorded responses of different interviews into a single scheme.

We may now point out the major advantages of the non-structured interview. In so far as such interviews facilitate free and uninhibited responses from the respondents, the informant has the facility to be much more open and articulate. His accounts in the hands of a skilled researcher may fertilize into very fruitful insights and hypotheses. In explanatory/formulative studies, such interviews are indeed the cenrtral technique of collecting information. As Johan Galtung says, "The advantage of unstructured response is to be unprecise; that they permit the unexpected response."[2]

Such interviews also have the advantage of leaving a favourable impact on the informant who will have acquired in the process of interview a certain element of skill in self-analysis and thus be in full sympathy with the subject-matter as also with the substance of the interview record.

The above discussion also suggests by way of contrast, the major merits of the structured interviews, these being the comparability of interview records, uniformity which facilitates bringing these different records into some unified conceptual scheme affording dependable basis generalization. Being more economical, structured interviews afford a larger coverage in terms of respondents. Lastly, they demand lesser skills on the part of the interviewer.

We shall now consider some of the major types of unstructured interview and partially structured interview.

(a) Focused Interview : The main objective of this type of interview is to focus attention on the given experience of the respondent and its possible effects. The interviewer knows in advance the aspects of a question he has to cover. The list of aspects is derived from his formulation of the research-problem, from hypothesis based on a psychological or sociological theory, from his knowledge of the situation or the experience in which the respondent has participated. Thus, the interviewer has a definite framework of topics to be covered but he has more or less complete freedom to decide the manner and the sequence in which the questions would be asked. The interviewer has freedom to explore reasons and motives to probe further in directions he thinks would afford clues. In such interviews, although the respondent is free to express completely his own line of thought, the direction of the interview is mainly in the hands of the interviewer. The interviewer wants a definite type of information and as such his task is to confine the respondent to a discussion on such issues with which he seeks conversance.

The focused interviews have been used effectively in the development of hypotheses about the aspects of specific experience that may expectedly lead to change in attitude on the part of those exposed to experience.

Obviously, the more detailed a researcher's knowledge of the situation in which the person being interviewed has participated and the more specific his hypothesis, the more precisely he can outline in advance the questions to be covered in course of the interview.

(b) The Clinical Interview : This type of interview is quite similar to the focused interview, the primary difference between them being that the clinical interview is concerned with broad underlying feelings or motivations or with the course of individuals' life experience, rather than with the effects of the specific experience, as in the focused interview. As in the focused interview, here too, the interviewer knows in advance what aspects method of eliciting information is more or less completely left to his discretion. The most common types of clinical interviews are those conducted during social case work in psychiatric clinics and in prison administration.

(c) The Non-Directive Interview : Although a few books on research techniques use the terms non-directive interview and unstructured interview almost interchangeably or synonymously, we shall prefer to treat these as distinct. In the non-directive interview, the imitiative is completely in the hands of the respondent. The term 'non-directive' received its currency from a type of psychotherapy in which the patient is encouraged to express his feelings without any questions or suggestions from the therapist. In a more limited sense, non-direction is implicit in most interviewing, i.e., although the interviewer is expected to ask questions about the given topics, he is not supposed to bias or direct the respondent to one rather than another response. In non-directive interviewing, however, the interviewer's function is simply to encourage the respondent to talk about the given topic with a bare minimum of direct questioning or guidance. He encourages the respondent to talk fully and freely by being alert to the feelings expressed in the respondent's statement and by warm but non-committal recognition of the subject's feelings. The non-directive interviewer's function is primarily to serve as a catalyst to a comprehensive expression of the subject's feelings and beliefs and of the frame of reference within which his feelings and beliefs take on a personal significance. To achieve this result the interviewer must create a completely permissive atmosphere in which the subject is free to express himself without fear of disapproval, admonition and advice from the interviewer.

Against the backdrop of the above discussion covering some of the major types of interviews, we may say that each one has its own strong points as well as limitations and that each is suited to a particular kind of situation and patently desirable in obtaining specific kinds of data.

Despite the varied manifestations and version of interview methodology, we may point out the major overall advantages and limitations of the method in a general way.

Advantages of the Interview Method

(1) The personal interviews, compared especially to questionnaires usually yield a high percentage of returns.

(2) The interview method can be made to yield an almost perfect sample of the general population because practically everyone can be reached by and can respond to this approach. It will be remembered that the questionnaire approach is severely limited by the fact that only the literate persons can be covered by it. Again, the observational approach is also subject to limitations because many things or facts cannot be observed on the spot.

(3) The information secured through interviews is likely to be more correct compared to that secured through other techniques. The interviewer who is present on the spot can clear up the seemingly inaccurate or irrelevant answers by explaining the questions to the informant. If the informant deliberately falsifies replies, the interviewer is able to effectively check them and use special devices to verify the replies.

(4) The interviewer can collect supplementary information about the informant's personal characteristics and environment which is often of great value in interpreting results. Interview is a much more flexible approach, allowing for posing of new questions or check-questions if such a need arises. Its flexibility makes the interview a superior technique for the exploration of areas where there is little basis for knowing what questions to ask and how to formulate them.

(5) In as much as the interviewer is present on the spot, he can observe the facial expressions and gestures etc., of the informants as also the existing pressures obtaining in the interview-situation. The facility of such observations helps the interviewer to evaluate the meaning of the verbal replies given by informants. For example, hesitation, particular inhibitive reactions etc., may give rise to certain doubts about the reliability of the responses and the interviewer may then ask indirect questions to verify his doubts.

(6) Scoring and test-devices can be used, the interviewer acting as experimenter. At the same time, visual stimuli to which the informant may react can be presented.

(7) The use of interview method ensures greater number of usable returns compared to other methods. Returned visits to complete items on the schedule or to correct mistakes can usually be made without annoying the informant.

(8) The interviewer can usually control which person or persons will answer the questions. This is not possible in the mailed questionnaire approach. If so desired and warranted group discussions may also be held.

(9) A personal interview may take long enough to allow the informant to become oriented to the topic under investigation. Thus, recall of relevant information is facilitated. The informant can be made to devote more time if, as is the case, the interviewer is present on the spot to elicit and record the information. The interviewer's presence is a double headed weapon, the advantageous aspect of it being that face-to-face contact provides enough stimulation to the respondent to probe deeper within himself. As we have suggested, interviewer acts as a catalyst.

(10) The interviewer may catch the informant off his guard and thus secure the most spontaneous reactions than would be the case if mailed questionnaire were used.

(11) The interview method allows for many facilities which aid on the spot adjustments and thus ensure rich response material. For example, the interviewer can carefully sandwich the questions about which the informant is likey to be sensitive. The interviewer can also change the subject by observing informant's reactions or give explanations if the interviewee needs them. In other words, a delicate situation can usually be handled more effectively by personal interview method.

(12) The language of the interview can be adapted to the ability or educational level of the person interviewed. Therefore, it is comparatively easy to avoid misinterpretations or misleading questions.

(13) The interview is a more appropriate technique for revealing information about complex, emotionally-laden subjects or for probing the sentiments underlying an expressed opinion.

Major Limitations of the Interview Method

(1) In terms of cost, energy and time, the interview approach poses a heavy demand. The transportation cost and the time required to cover addresses in a large area as also possibility of non-availability or 'not at home', may make the interview method uneconomical and often inoperable.

(2) The efficacy of interviews depends on a thorough training and skill of interviewers as also on a rigorous supervision over them. Failing this, data recorded may be inaccurate and incomplete.

(3) The human equation may distort the returns. If an interviewer has a certain bias, he may unconsciously devise questions so as to secure confirmation of his views.

(4) The presence of the interviewer on the spot may over stimulate the respondent, sometimes even to the extent that he may give imaginary information just to make it interesting. He may tell things about which he may not himself be very

sure. He may also get emotionally involved with the interviewer and give answers that he anticipates would please the interviewer. It is also possible that the interviewer's presence may inhibit free responses because there is no anonymity. The respondent may hesitate to give correct answers for the fear that it would adversely affect his image. Some fear of this information being used against him may grip him.

(5) In the interview method, the organization required for selecting, training and supervising a field staff is more complex.

(6) It is the usual experience that costs per interview are higher when field investigators are employed. This is especially so when the area to be covered is widely spread out.

(7) The personal interview usually takes more time. Sometimes, the interview lasts for hours on end and the interviewer cannot check the free flow of the respondent's replies for fear that it may disrupt the 'rapport.' Added to this is the time spent for journeys to and fro to the addresses and the possibility of not always being able to meet them.

(8) Effective interview presupposes proper rapport with the respondent and controlling of interview atmosphere in a manner that would facilitate free and frank responses. This is often a very difficult requirement, it needs time, skills and often resources. Secondly, it is not always possible for the interviewer to judge whether the interview atmosphere is how it should ideally be and whether or not 'rapport' has been established.

(9) Interviewing may also introduce systematic errors. For example, if the interviews are conducted at their homes during the day, a majority of informants will be housewives. Now if the information is to be obtained from the male members, most of the field-work will have to be done in the evening or on holidays. If this be the case, only a few hours can be used per week for interviewing.

(10) Many actions human beings carry out are not easily verbalized, but easily observed. Through observation a social process may be followed as it develops. Verbal techniques such as interview may give valuable reports, but post hoc, unless one is dealing with rather unusual respondents capable of acting and being interviewed at the same time.

We shall now discuss some of the prerequisites that ensure successful interviewing. The quality of interviewing depends, firstly on a proper study-design. It should be noted that even the most skilled interviewer will not be able to collect valid and useful data, if the schedule of questions is inadequate or unrelated to the objectives of research. If a well-designed, standardized schedule can elicit the required information, a staff of ordinary men and women, properly selected and trained, can serve well enough.

Within the limits of a study-design, there is some room for the art of interviewing to come into play. Interviewing is an art governed by certain scientific principles. The interviewer's art consists in creating a situation wherein the respondents' answers will be reliable and valid. This ideal requires a permissive situation in which the respondent is encouraged to voice his frank opinion without the fear of his attitudes being revealed to others.

The basic requirement of successful interviewing, understandably, is to create a friendly atmosphere; on of trust and confidence that will put the respondent at ease. Through subsequent stages, the interviewer's art consists in asking questions properly and intelligently, in obtaining a valid and meaningful response and in recording the responses accurately and completely.

Let us consider how the interviewer can create a friendly interview atmosphere. It is the interviewer's approach that really does the trick. The interviewer should introduce himself briefly and explain clearly the purpose of his study. Interviewer's approach should be positive. His aim should be to interview everyone included in the sample. It is possible that a small proportion of respondents will be suspicious or hostile and the large number may require a little encouragement and persuasion.

Many people are flattered to be selected for an interview. The interviewer should answer any legitimate questions and clear any doubt the respondent has. He should also if need be, explain that the respondent should not be afraid of being identified and that interview is not a test and that the interviewer just wants to know how people feel about certain issues and the only way to find out, is to ask them.

The interviewer's manners should be friendly, courteous, conversational and unbiased. He should represent the golden mean — neither too grim, nor too effusive, neither too talkative nor too timid. The main idea should be to put the respondent at ease so that he will talk freely and fully. It helps if the interview starts with the casual conversation about weather, pets or children. An informal conversational interview, above all, is dependent upon a thorough mastery by the interviewer over the actual questions in the schedule. He should be able to ask them conversationally rather than real them stiffly. He should know what questions are coming next so that there will be no awkward disruption of smooth interaction. Fundamentally, the interviewer's job is that of a reporter. He should not act as an adviser, custodian of morality, curio-seeker or debator. He should not show surprise or disapproval of a respondent's answer. He should show an interested disposition toward his respondent's opinion. On his own, he should never divulge his own. The interviewer must keep the direction of interview in his own hand, discouraging irrelevant conversation and trying to keep the respondent on the track.

Next, we turn to consider how the interviewer should ask his questions. The interviewer must be alert to the importance of asking each question exactly as it is worded unless the interview is unstructured. Interviewers should remember that even a slight rewording of a question can so change the stimulus as to elicit answers in a different frame of reference. The interviewer should refrain from giving unwarranted explanation of questions because this also may change the frame of reference or inject bias into the response. If each interviewer were permitted to vary the questions according to his sweet will, the resulting responses recorded by different interviewers may not be comparable. If at all the interviewer has to offer any explanation to the respondents, he should offer only those that he has specifically been authorized to do. Should the respondent fail to understand the question, the interviewer may advisedly repeat it slowly and with proper emphasis.

Questions must be asked in the sequence they appear on the schedule. Varying this order will change the respondent's frame of reference since each question sets up a frame of reference for the following questions. Thus, if the sequences vary from interviewer to interviewer, the responses will not be comparable. The interviewer must make it a point to ask every question, unless directions permit skipping a few. It may seem that the respondent has given his opinion on a subsequent question in answering an earlier question, but he must nevertheless ask the question in order to be sure. A question may appear to be naïve or inapplicable but the interviewer should never omit asking it. Wherever necessary and appropriate, the interviewer should preface the question with certain conversational phrases to maintain continuity and tempo.

We shall now consider another important requirement of successful interviewing. It is often difficult as interviewers have often experienced, to obtain a specific complete response. This is perhaps the most difficult part of his job. Respondents often qualify or hedge their opinions. They often answer, 'do not know' just to avoid thinking about the question, they misinterpret the question, divert the process of interview by launching off an irrelevant discussion or they give self-contradictory answers. In all these cases the interviewer has to probe deeper.

The test of a good interviewer is that he is alert to incomplete or nonspecific answers. Each interviewer must understand fully the overall objective of each question and what it is precisely trying to measure. A pre-test on the interviewers helps to equip them with such understanding. The interviewer should be able to ask himself after every reply the respondent gives whether the question is completely answered. If the respondent's answer is vague or diffuse or incomplete, effective probe questions should be asked.

The interviewer must be careful at every stage, not to suggest a possible reply, that is, the interviewer should not ask leading questions (i.e., put words into the subject's mouth). The "don't know" reply is another problem of the interviewer. Sometimes, this response may be due to a genuine lack of opinion or knowledge, but at other times it may be a cloak wittingly or unwittingly used by the interviewee to hide many attitudes, fear, reluctance, vague opinions, lack of understanding, etc. The interviewer should distinguish between the different types of 'don't-know response' and repeat the questions with suitable assurances.

An important consideration in successful interviewing relates to recording the responses of interviewees. There are two chief means of recording responses during the interview. If the question is a fixed alternative one, the interviewer need only mark or check an appropriate category. But if the question is open-ended, the interviewer is expected to record the reponse, verbatim.

On pre-coded schedules, errors and omissions in recording the replies are a frequent source of interview-error. In the midst of various tasks that the interviewer is supposed to perform in the course of interviews, viz., trying to pin the respondent down to a specific answer, remembering the sequence of questions, observing facial expressions etc., the interviewer may sometimes neglect to indicate the respondent's reply to some item, overlook a particular question or check the wrong category, etc. Even the best interviewer should, therefore, make it a habit to inspect each interview to make sure that it is filled in accurately and completely. If any information is lacking he should go back and ask the respondent for it. He should correct the errors and omissions in the schedules on the spot. If he has recorded verbatim replies only sketchily, he should correct the weakness right there. It is not at all proper to wait until later in the day or until he returns home at night, since by then he may have forgotten quite a few crucial circumstances of the interview. The interviewer should understand that the omission or inaccurate reporting of a single answer can make the entire interview worthless since the schedule is designed as an integral whole.

In reporting responses to open-ended or free answer questions, the interviewer should give complete, verbatim reporting. It may often be difficult to fulfil this requirement, but apart from obvious irrelevancies and repetitions, this should be the goal. It is necessary that the interviewers have some idea of the coding process. This will ensure that they are able to record responses in such a manner that the coders will be able to reconstruct the whole set of responses correctly in a codified form.

The interviewer should ideally quote the respondents exactly. Paraphrasing the replies, summarizing them in one's own words or "polishing up" any slang or cursing etc., not only might distort the respondent's meanings and emphases but also miss the tenor of his replies.

Although it is frequently difficult to record responses verbatim without using shorthand, a few simple techniques can greatly increase the interviewer's speed and honest reproduction. The interviewer can ask the subject to wait until the interviewer has written the last thought but this may slow down the interview and may have certain adverse effects. In order not to slow up the interview, the interviewer should be prepared to write at the same time as the respondent talks. This may prevent him from watching the expressions of the respondent but some adjustments have got to be made. The interviewer may also use common abbreviations. He may also use a telegraphic style of recording. In doing so, the interviewer must not make the recording incomprehensible to the coders.

One final point related to successful interviewing is, how to minimize bias introduced by the interviewer. Known as the interviewer-"bias", it refers to systematic differences from interviewer to interviewer or occasionally systematic errors on the part of the interviewers in the selection of the samples (e.g., in quota sampling where the selection of interviewees is left to the interviewers), in asking questions, eliciting and recording responses.

Much of what we call interviewer-bias, can be more correctly described as interviewer-differences which are inherent in the fact that interviewers are human beings and not machines and thus they do not work identically or infallibly. The fact that respondents too are human beings with differing perceptions, judgements, etc., simply enhances the differences that would occur if different interviewers were dealing with physical rather than human materials. It is too much to expect, therefore, that the interviewers will return complete, comparable and valid reports.

Even assuming an unbiased selection of respondents, bias in the interview-situation may stem from two sources:

(a) Respondent's perception of the interviewer.
(b) Interviewer's perception of the respondent.

'Perception' here points to the manner in which the relation between the interviewer and respondent is influenced and modified by their wishes, expectations and personality structure.

There is a sizable experimental evidence to prove that bias may result under certain conditions in spite of anything the interviewer may do to eliminate it. Respondents have been shown to frequently answer differently when interviewed by people from different social strata or ethnic group or nationality group. For example, the working-class respondents are less likely to talk freely to middle-class interviewers. The magnitude of these effects naturally varies with the way in which the respondents perceive the situation. The biasing effects can often be reduced by altering the respondent's perception of the situation, e.g., by assuring him that his identity will not be revealed but these effects can seldom be completely eliminated.

The interviewers should dress inconspicuously so that their appearance will not adversely sensitize certain categories of respondents. The staff in a large-scale research project should be instructed to interview the respondent privately (unless the whole group is to be interviewed) so that his opinions will not be affected by the presence of some third person and to adopt an informal and conversational attitude in an effort to achieve the best possible 'report.'

It should be noted that not all interview-biassing effects operate through the respondent's perception by an interviewer. Some respondents may be totally immune to the most crucial biasings characteristics of the interviewer. The other dimension, we must consider in this context, is the interviewer's perception of the respondent. This is as important a source of bias as the respondent's perception of the interviewer. No matter how standardized the schedule and how rigidly the interviewer is instructed, he still has much opportunity to exercise freedom of choice during the actual interview. Thus, it is often his perception of the respondent that determines the manner in which he asks questions, the way in which he probes, his classification of responses to pre-coded questions and his recording of verbatim answers.

The interviewers often have strong expectations from respondents and as such, stereotypes are likely to come into play during the interview. On the basis of their past experience, judgements or prior answers received from other respondents, the interviewers may often quite unconsciously assume that they are inferior to him or that they are hostile, deceptive or ignorant, etc. Such expectations will affect their performance. For example, a 'No response' from an educated well-to-do respondent may be probed into on the assumption that an opinion may be lurking somewhere or the interviewer may think that the respondents do not mean what they say. Experiments have shown that the interviewers tend to select from long verbatim answers those parts that most closely conform to their expectations, beliefs or opinions and discard the rest.

An important source of bias arises from the interviewer's perception of the situation. If he sees the results of the study as a possible threat to his interests, he is likely to introduce bias. Such difficulties can be overcome by proper motivation and supervision. The interviewers being human, such biasings factors can never be overcome completely. Of Course, their effects can be reduced by standardizing the interview so that the interviewer has as little free choice as possible. If interviewers are given clear and standard instructions on questioning procedures, on the classification of responses etc., their biases will have lesser chances of operation.

It should not be overlooked, however, that if the interviewer's freedom is restricted, correspondingly, the opportunities for effective use of his insight are restricted too. The more responsibilities the interviewer is given for questioning and evaluating the respondent's opinions, the more likely it is that bias will result. This calls for a very careful selction of some middle course.

In so far as bias, in the sense of different interviewers not returning exactly the same responses from equivalent respondents, can never be totally eliminated, the main responsibility of the director of the research project is to select, train and supervise his staff in such a way that any net result of bias will be at a minimum. He must be aware of the possibilities of bias at various points so that he is in a position to discount their effects in his analysis.

REFERENCES

(1) Cf. Selltiz, *et al., op. cit.,* p. 236.

(2) Galtung, *op. cit.,* p. 120.

Chapter XII

The Questionnaire

As was noted in the previous chapter, the observational methods are less effective in giving out information about personal beliefs, feelings, motivations, expectations or future plans. To be sure, they provide no information about a person's past or his private behaviour since inherently such behaviour is beyond the pale of observation. The questionnaire, the interview and the projective methods are eminently suited to obtaining such information.

In this chapter, we shall be concerned with the questionnaire as an instrument of data-collection. In quite a few books devoted to research methodology, the terms 'Questionnaire' and 'Schedule' are treated as synonyms. Technically, however, it is desirable to differentiate between them. A questionnaire consists of a number of questions printed (or typed) in a definite order on a form (or set of forms). The form/s are usually mailed to the respondents who are expected to read and understand the questions and reply to them in writing in the relevant spaces provided for the questions on the said form/s. Ideally, the respondent has to answer the questions on his own, i.e., totally unaided. A schedule also has a reference to proforma containing a set of questions. The researcher/interviewer puts to respondents the questions from the proforma in the order as these are listed and records the replies. In certain situations, the schedules may be handed over to the respondents and the interviewer may get these filled in his presence, offering necessary explanations with reference to the questions if and when necessary.

The signal advantage of the questionnaire method is that it offers great facility in collecting data from large, diverse and widely-scattered groups of people. The distinctive characteristic of the questionnaire has been aptly summarized by Johan as 'Written-verbal stimulus' and 'Written-verbal response.' It is used in gathering objective, quantitative data as well as for securing information of a qualitative nature. In some studies, the questionnaire is the sole research tool utilized but it is more often used in conjunction with other methods of investigation. In the questionnaire (as also in the interview) technique, great reliance is placed on questions which he is exposed to as also for data on his behaviour. The subjects' reports may not be taken at face value; these may be interpreted on the basis of other available knowledge about them (subjects) or in terms of some psychological principles. Needless to say, the questionnaire (also interview) approach can normally help obtain only materials that the respondent is willing and able to report.

It is well worth noting that persons are not only reluctant to openly report their feelings, plans, fears and so on; they may in point of fact, be unable to do so. We may not be aware of many of our beliefs and hence may not be able to report them. Nevertheless, each one of us has a unique opportunity to observe himself and to that extent one is in a position to and often will communicate this knowledge about himself to others. But such reporting or communication, especially one that diagnoses and explains why one's behaviour was what it was, requires qualities of penetration much beyond the reach of average persons. It is given to only a few to be able to engage in self-diagnosis. The capacity to peep into depths of one's personality is conspicuous by its absence among the people at large. It is precisely this that works to the detriment of the efficacy of the questionnaire method. Despite the limitations of self-report, it is often possible and useful to get people's own accounts of their feelings, attitudes, etc., by means of questionnaires.

Let us now turn to discuss the typical advantages of the questionnaire as compared to other major methods of collecting data for research.

(1) In so far as the questionnaire is usually mailed to the respondents and contains specific, clear-cut directions, the persons charged with the collection of data need not exert themselves on offering additional explanations or instructions. It is obvious that the questionnaire technique does not call for any special skills of training on the part of investigators in the field.

(2) Since the questionnaire approach makes it possible to cover, at the same time, a large number of people spread over a large territory, it is decidedly more economical in terms of money, time and energy. Other methods do not afford such a facility.

(3) The questionnaire, by its very nature, is an impersonal technique. Uniformity from one measurement situation to another is provided by virtue of its standardized working of questions, standardized sequence of questions and fixed or standardized instructions for recording responses. This alleged uniformity, viewed from the psychological angle, is often more illusory than real. A given question in spite of its 'standardized' wording could have different meanings for different persons. Careful trial-testing and helping respondents to understand the questions in the course of administration may, however, go a long way toward ensuring uniformity of questions in the questionnaire and as such, making the replies comparable.

(4) Yet another typical merit of the questionnaire is that it ensures anonymity. The respondents have a greater confidence that will not be identified as holding a particular view or opinion. The subjects feel more free to express views that they think would arouse disapproval or get them into trouble. It has been found that there is often a marked difference between the replies to the questionnaire and those to the interviews. The difference stems from the element of anonymity that is characteristic of the questionnaire approach. Anonymity is not, however, the best method of eliciting replies at all times. Complex issues like familial adjustment which are bound to have strong emotional overtones may not be inquired into by means of the anonymous tool that a questionnaire is. Here a personal understanding and permissive manner on the part of an interviewer may prove effective.

(5) The questionnaire places less pressure on the respondents for immediate response. The subject, given ample time, can consider each point carefully before actually putting his reply in writing. If there is some kind of pressure for time on the subject (as is often the case in interview) he may reply with the first thought that comes to his mind. It should, however, be noted that pressure on the subject for immediate response has a certain advantage in situations where spontaneous responses matter.

The foregoing discussion also hints at some of the disadvantages or limitations of the questionnaire. We shall deal with these at some length.

(1) One of the major limitations of the education questionnaire is that it can be administered only on subjects with a considerable amount of education. Complex questionnaire requiring elaborate written replies can be used indeed on a very small percentage of population. It is seen that even the highly educated persons may have little facility for writing and even granting this, very fey have the motivation and the patience to write as much as they might speak out. Thus, questionnaires are hardly appropriate for a larger section of maintaining interest on the contemporaneous burden of writing and of maintaining interest on the subjects is quite heavy, the number of questions they may be asked as also the fullness of response is severely limited.

(2) In a mailed questionnaire, the proportion of returns is usually low; it may sometimes be as low as 10%. Among the factors that may affect the returns are the sponsoring agency, the attractiveness of the questionnaire, its length, nature of the accompanying appeal, the care of filling out the questionnaire and of mailing it back, inducements for replying and the kind of people to whom questionnaire is sent, etc. Even under the best of circumstances, a considerable proportion may not return the questionnaire.

(3) In a questionnaire, if the respondent misinterprets a question or writes his reply unintelligibly, there is very little that can be done to correct this. In this approach there is no facility for repeating questions, explaining them or seeking clarification of a particular response. In questionnaire approach, the validity of respondents' reports can hardly be appraised. The researcher here is in no position to observe the gestures and expressions of the respondents. He cannot follow-up the inconsistencies or contradictions in the replies.

(4) The usefulness of the questionnaire is restricted to issues on which the respondents have more or less crystallized views that can be simply expressed in words. The rigidity of questionnaires and the inability to explain elaborately in writing one's 'abnormal', anti-social feelings and behaviour coupled with the fact that the subject has to render his response in writing — all go against frank discussion of socially-tabooed issues raised in a questionnaire.

(5) The success of the questionnaire approach depends upon the 'sense of responsibility' among the subjects. A serious attempt at filling out the questionnaire-format presupposes, among other things, the awareness on the part of the subjects of their responsibility to the larger institution of science. Only then may responsible help be forthcoming. Such an awareness, even in countries where education is quite advanced, is difficult to come by.

(6) A significant limitation of the questionnaire is that the researcher/investigator is not in a position to vary the stimuli or social atmosphere impinging upon the subjects according to his designs. Certain other approaches to data collection do allow this facility to a greater or lesser extent; the stimuli or atmosphere as he questions the subjects. Such a flexibility characteristic of the interview approach is conspicuously absent in the questionnaire. This flexibility is indeed a very valuable asset. Johan Galtung has offered a very apt analogy that sums up our discussion. He likens interview to the musical symphony; waves after waves of sound impinging upon the audience. The questionnaire, on the other hand, has been likened to presentation before subjects of stimuli in the manner of a painting, various shades of colour spread over the canvas. In other words, the interview method involves presentation, one after the other, of stimuli on the continuum of time whereas in the questionnaire, these are presented in space.[1]

Typology of Questionnaires

The types of questionnaire vary widely. Questionnaires may be classified in a number of different bases. The classification of questionnaires may be based on the variable of structure. Accordingly, we have :

(a) structured/standardized questionnaire;

(b) unstructured/non-structured questionnaire.

Structured questionnaires are those in which there are definite, concrete and preordained questions with additional questions limited to those necessary to clarify inadequate answers or to elicit more detailed responses. The questions are presented with exactly the same wording, and in the same order to all the respondents. The reason for standardization is to ensure that all the respondents are replying to the same set of questions. The form of the question may be either closed (i.e., categorical) or open (i.e., inviting free response); the important point is that they are stated in advance, not constructed during the questioning. Standardized questionnaires may differ in the amount of structuring of the questions used. They may present fixed alternative answers to questions so the respondent just chooses the appropriate one, or they may leave the respondent free to answer in his own words. Extensive use of structured questionnaire is made, for example, in studies of the cost of living expenditure, and investment practices, etc. The most famous of the structured questionnaires are all those by the Census Bureau for the population and Housing Censuses.

Fixed Alternative Questions are those in which the responses of the subject are limited to the stated alternatives. These alternatives may be simply yes or no. The following is an example of fixed-alternative question: To what social class would you say you belong : (a) middle class, (b) lower class, (c) working class, or (d) upper class?

Open-ended question are designed to permit a free response from the subject rather than one limited to certain stated alternatives. The distinguishing characteristic of open-ended questions is that they merely raise as issue but do not provide or suggest any structure for the responsedent's reply. The respondent is given the opportunity to answer in his own terms and in his own frame of reference. When open-ended questions are used in standardized interviews, the questions and their order are predetermined and the task of the interviewer is to encourage the respondent to talk freely and fully in response to the questions included in the interview schedule and to make a verbatim record of his replies.

Relative Advantages/Disadvantages of Open-ended and Closed Questions

Fixed alternative or closed questions have the advantage of being 'standardizable', simple to administer, quick and relatively inexpensive to analyse. The analysis of responses to open-ended questions is often complex, difficult and expensive. Sometimes the provision of alternative replies helps to make clear the meaning of the question. Respondents are more likely to understand the question when the alternative replies are provided. The function of alternative responses is to clarify the dimensions along which answers are sought. One of the principal values of open-ended question is its use as an exploratory tool before opinion has crystallized or before the research objectives have been clearly defined. The closed question may require the respondent himself to make a judgement about his attitude rather than leaving this to the interviewer or coder.

Most of these advantages of fixed alternative questions have their attendant limitations. One of the major drawbacks of the closed question is that it may force a statement of opinion. Many individuals do not have any clearly-formulated or crystallized opinions on many issues. Closed questions are ill-equipped to reveal these. Although the wording of questions is the same for all respondents, different respondents are likely to make different interpretations, some of which may be quite different from those intended but it is much more likely to go undetected in the former. Closed questions are more efficient where the possible alternative replies are known, limited in number and clear-cut. Thus, they are appropriate in securing factual information (e.g., age, home-ownership, income) and in eliciting opinions on matters on which people hold clear views. Open-ended questions are desirable when the issue is complex. Closed questions have the advantages of focusing the respondent's attention precisely on the dimensions with which the investigator is concerned. But they do not provide information about respondent's own formulation of the issue, the frame of reference in which he perceives it, the factors that are important for him and motivations that underlie his opinions. When these matters are the focus of interest, open-ended questions are justly warranted.

Kinds of Questionnaire Items

The information sought by the questionnaire may be classified under three heads:

(1) Identificatory Information: The following items may be included under this category: Questionnaire case, cross-reference, questionnaire number, name of survey, name of agency sponsoring the survey, name of individual or family interviewed, sex of informant, relationship of informant to family head, address of the case, telephone numbers, interviewer's name or initials, co-operation of the informant ant notes as to the confidential treatment of returns.

(2) Social Background and Factual Data: The following items may be included under this category: Age of head of the family and family members, marital status, education, religion, political preference, union membership, family size and composition, occupation of the head of the family or of the respondent, employment, family income, socio-economic status, etc.

(3) Subject-matter of the Survey: The informant may be asked a direct question on the facts as he understands or remembers them. Certain information can be obtained rather easily by asking straightforward questions. The opinions which

he holds are not so readily ascertained. First, is the so-called "information questions.' When knowledge about the topic is definitely correlated with the opinions held, these information questions are particularly important. The opinions may be elicited only from those who are in a position to hold them.

A second approach is that of "seeking advice." The informant is usually flattered by the fact that his advice is considered important. This approach has been used effectively in a study of factors associated with family size.

Another approach which opinion-pollers use is the "exploratory questions." In questions of this type, the informant is given a sufficient background of information about the survey topic to make sensible judgement.

Designing the Questionnaire/Schedule

Several considerations should be borne in mind while designing a schedule or questionnaire. Careful planning, about the physical design of the questions, careful selection and phrasing of the questions definitely affect the number of returns as also the meaning and accuracy of the findings.

(1) The physical appearance of the questionnaire affects the co-operation the researcher receives. In a mailed questionnaire, an attractive looking questionnaire is a plus point for co-operation. Conversely, an unattractive one may cause the recipient to put it aside.

(2) As pointed out earlier, schedules are usually filled by the investigator whereas the questionnaire generally by the respondent himself. This consideration as to who is to record the responses must go into designing a schedule / questionnaire. If a highly-trained investigator is to do the questioning and enter the replies, the form should be different from the one drawn up for the informant to fill out. The terminology and questions should be adapted to the type of people who will give the information. For example, a questionnaire addressed to experts who are thoroughly conversant with the subject-matter of the survey can be much more technical than one directed to a random sample of the population. In designing questionnaires that are to be filled out by people from different walks of life, the level of education, the biases, and the interest or other characteristics which affect the ability and desire to fill in the form truthfully and correctly should be taken into consideration.

(3) The choice of words is understandably an important consideration. The information must grasp the spirit of the question rather than its precise wording.

(4) In inquiries of certain aspects, it may be important for certain questions to follow certain others so that proper "set" is developed. Special attention must be given to the sequence of the items/questions.

(5) If the number of questions is small, their arrangement on the questionnaire will not require detailed planning. When the number of questions is large, they should be condensed in a very limited space.

(6) The purpose of the questions is another important consideration. It may be to ascertain facts, to test the 'knowledge' of the informant or discover his beliefs or attitudes. If opinions are desired, for example, care must be exercised to see that the questions do not just bring out only the points of fact.

(7) If the questionnaire is to be used for a periodic survey, the questions should be designed with a view to uniformity and comparability of results.

(8) Questions must be designed with the possible difficulties of analysis well in view. Analysis is facilitated to the extent the information is in a form which is readily amenable to classification and tabulation.

Physical Form of the Questionnaire

(1) *Size:* The size of a questionnaire depends to some extent on the scope of the survey and the number of items to be included. The basic question is, what size of the questionnaire is preferable? This can be best answered by considering the advantages and disadvantages of various sizes. If the schedules are small, they can be carried easily in pockers and brought out only after the respondent has answered the call. If the questions can be put on handy cards, sorting, counting, filing, checking, etc. in the office are facilitated. Investigators object to carrying a large folder because their identity may be mistaken. The questionnaire should not be too cumbersome for respondents.

It is best to use only one side of the form, the reverse being left blank for special remarks by the recorder. If both sides are to be filled out, filing and sorting the schedules become difficult.

Mailed-questionnaires should be large enough to provide adequate space for comments if such supplementary material is desired. Charts, diagrams and pictorial material may be introduced in main questionnaires to sustain and recreate interest on the part of the recipient, but such material usually requires considerable space. In order to avoid too large a schedule, a booklet may be used.

(2) *Quality and Colour of Paper:* The schedule is handled a great deal after it reaches the office. Therefore, the paper should be durable. If sorting and counting are to be done by hand, a strong flexible card with a smooth surface is desirable. The less conspicuous the schedule, the less likely the objections to giving information. Ordinary white and light-coloured schedules are preferable from the collection point of view.

When planning mailed questionnaires, it may be desirable to use a colour which will attract the recipient's attention. In certain marketing studies, yellow paper was found to have the highest percentage of returns but dark colours were not effective. When several questionnaires are sent out in a sequence, alternation of colours elicits more returns than a single colour.

(3) *Arrangement of Items on the Questionnaire:* Questions which belong together should be arranged so. When the question is dependent upon the answer to the preceding one, it should be given a subordinate place. Paying due attention to the appearance of the questionnaire will avoid many errors and ensure a higher percentage of usable returns than would be obtained from a poorly-arranged questionnaire.

Choice of Questions[2]

(1) The researcher should include only such questions as have a direct bearing on the problem itself or on the evaluation of the methodology abopted for study.

(2) Questions whose answers can be secured more accurately easily and effectively from other source may be excluded.

(3) The selection of questions should be done with an eye on the subsequent tabulation plan.

(4) In drawing up the schedule or questionnaire, other studies or surveys on comparable material should be kept in mind. As far as feasible, identical items, terms, definitions, and quantitative units of measurement should be employed.

(5) Care should be taken while asking personal questions or those which may embarrass the respondent.

(6) Only such factual questions, to which most of the informants can reasonably be expected to know, should be asked. Frequently, duration, vividness, interest, meaningfulness and setting are some of the important factors that help securing the required information.

(7) Questions that are likely to yield inaccurate responses should be avoided. People often resort to a form of wishful thinking in answering questions on such matters as the level of education they have had, the jobs they have had, the jobs they have held, etc.

(8) Questions which involve too much mental effort on the part of the informant should be avoided, e.g., entailing mathematical calculations.

Wording of Questions

Understandably great care is required in formulating the questions. Reliable and meaningful returns depend to a large on this. Even when factual information is to be secured, certain precautions relating to phrasing of questions are necessary. Even greater care must be exercised when opinions are to be obtained. Since words are likely to affect responses, respondents with limited vocabularies are likely to be suggestive. If questions are beyond the comprehension of the respondent, he may just choose one of the alternative responses without any idea as to the meaning of his response.

Suggestions for Wording Questions

(1) Simple words which are expectedly familiar to all potential informants should be employed. This should be done without making the questions appear too elementary for those of higher mental or educational level. This is often possible and it is here that art of question-framing comes in. A question that contains long, dependent or conditional clauses may confuse the informant.

(2) Formulate the questions so specifically as to yield the exact information that is needed. The more specific the question, the greater the usability of the answer to it for tabulation purposes.

(3) Avoid multiple-meaning questions. Such items that will give rise to confusion should be formulated as two or more questions.

(4) The researcher should not make use of ambiguous questions. Ambiguity may arise if terms are beyond the vocabulary of the respondent. If the phrasing is too complex or in general terms, the informants may start with entirely different assumptions. The best means to this end is to pretest the questions.

(5) All questions which produce biased answers may be regarded as 'leading questions.' Questions worded in such a way as to suggest the answers may be avoided. For example, to the question, "Do you regularly visit the library?" many people will an swer "yes", even though they may not be doing so.

(6) Answers to questions in which prominent personalities are mentioned will be conditioned by the informant's personal feeling towards them. Indiscriminate ban on important names is not, however, desirable.

(7) Danger words, catch-words, stereotypes or words with emotional connotations should be avoided. Names of political parties and political figures may colour the responses, hence such use may be avoided.

(8) Chapin suggests the occasional use of "slant side-questions." For example, when respondents were asked, "Are you married?" most of them replied in the negative but when the question was changed to "Where is your wife?", a much higher percentage was discovered to be married.

(9) Most people like to feel that they are reasonable, intelligent, penerous, understanding and prestigious members of their community. They thus tend to answer questions in terms of what they "ought" to think or feel about a situation. Hence, caution must be exercised in the use of phrases which reflect upon the prestige of the informant.

(10) The question must allow for all possible responses. Thus, provision for such indefinite answers as "don't know", "no choice", "doubtful", other (specify) should be made.

(11) The alternatives in multiple-choice questions must be realistic and not far fetched. They should conform more or less to the way people really think and feel about the issues involved. If the alternatives are phrased in terms of

concrete situations, the questions will be more meaningful. When framing the alternatives, it should be borne in mind that people answer questions in terms of the relative value of the choices presented in the questions and not in terms of absolute universe of preferences.

(12) The amount of writing required on the schedule or questionnaire should be reduced to the minimum. Since most handwriting is poor, there is the danger of misinterpretational errors. Whenever feasible, symbols may be used for replies.

(13) A few questions that will serve as checks on the accuracy and consistency of questions as a whole should be designed. Questions that bring out the same facts but are worded differently and placed in different sections of the questionnaire afford a check on the "internal consistency" of the replies.

(14) Questions inviting responses toward socially accepted norms or values should be avoided. Such questions often fail to indicate a person's real opinion.

(15) Seemingly unreasonable questions should be justified by using an explanation why they are worth asking.

On Questionnaire Construction

The investigator should fist discover the extent to which the desired data are already available in published reports and decide whether all or part of the needed data can be obtained through a formal questionnaire. The entire process of questionnaire-construction can be divided into following aspects:

(i) Information to be sought.
(ii) Type of questionnaire to be used.
(iii) Writing a first draft.
(iv) Re-examining and revising questions.
(v) Pre-testing and editing the questionnaire.
(vi) Specifying procedure for its use.

(i) The formulation of the problem provides the starting point for developing the questionnaire. The investigator must decide what aspects of the problem are to be dealt with in a particular study.

(ii) The appropriate form of questions depends on the mode of administration, the nature of information sought, the sample of people and the kind of analysis and interpretation intended.[3] The investigator must also decide whether to use closed or open-ended questions. The use of follow-up questions or probes is advisable at many points in connection, especially, with free responses. The questionnaire should anticipate where they are required and should provide the appropriate wording. Usually, several alternatives are needed, depending upon the preceding reponses. For example, if the answer is too general and vague, the follw-up question may be "What do you mean?"

(iii) The best sequence of topics should be carefully considered when framing the questions. Some closely-related questions may be asked in order to measure consistency and for checking the reliability of responses. At this stage of questionnaire-framing all available suggestions need to be utilized. Questionnaires previously drafted on similar lines may prove quite helpful.

(iv) Next, the questionnaire should be scrutinized for technical defects, quite apart from biases and blind spots arising due to personal values.

(v) Pre-testing is necessary to find out how the questionnaire works and whether changes are necessary before launching off the full-scale study. The pre-testing of instrument provides a means for solving unforeseen problems in its administration in the field. It may also indicate the need for additional questions or deletion of others. If substantial changes are warranted, a second pre-test may be conducted. Sometimes, a series of revisions and pre-testing is required. After pre-testing, the final edition is done to ensure that every element passes scrutiny of content, form, sequence of questions, spacing and arrangement. Editing is intended to make the questionnaire as clear and as easy to use as possible.

(vi) The questionnaire itself should contain simple, straight-forward directions, indicating, just what the respondent is supposed to do.

Sequence of Questions

It is essential to examine the order in which questions are to be asked. Many a refusal and misunderstanding can be avoided by proper arrangement of questions. Questions should be arranged logically. The question arrangement makes it possible to determine the directions of the response. The opening questions should be such as to arouse human interest. The respondent then is less likely to refuse to co-operate.

The opening questions should be such as are easy to answer. Questions which might embarrass the informant should be placed in the middle or at the end of questionnaire. Questions on economic status, or those that test the knowledge of the respondent and those of an intimate personal nature should be put at the end. Questions seeking personal information should be put at the end. Questions to which the informant may be sensitive should not be put at extreme end because this may leave him with wrong impressions and make it difficult to question him later. Since there is the likelihood of the mail-informant losing interest as he proceeds to fill in the questionnaire, important questions should advisedly be put at beginning.

REFERENCES

(1) Galtung Johan, *op. cit.,* p. 117.
(2) See Penn, S.I.: *The Art of Questions,* Princeton: 1951.
(3) Also see Lazarsfeld, Paul: *The Art of Asking Why,* National Markiting Review, Vol. I., 1935.

Chapter XIII

The Projective Techniques

A projective test involves the presentation of a stimulus situation devised or selected, because it will mean to the subject not what the experimenter has arbitrarily decided it should mean, but rather whatever it must mean to the 'personality' who gives it his personal, private, idiosyncratic meaning and organization. The assumption underlying the projective test is that the individual's organization of the relatively unstructure stimulus situations is indicative of the basic trends in his perception of the world and his response to it.

Projective techniques were first devised by psychologists and psychiatrists concerned with the diagnosis and treatment of patients afflicted by emotional disorders. Such tests attempt to give a comprehensive, picture of the individual's personality structure, his emotional needs or his conflicts and complexes. The use of such tests, however, requires intensive specialized training. In so far as certain tests have often been employed with advantage in the investigation of certain kinds of problems in sociology, social psychology and anthropology, we shall mention only some of the more frequently used tests.

In projective tests, the individual's responses to the stimulus situation (a photograph or a symmetrical but meaningless ink-blot design) are not taken at their face value. The stimuli may arouse in the subjects many different kinds of reactions. There are thus, no 'right' or 'wrong' answers. The emphasis is on his perception or the meaning he gives to it and the way to which he organizes it or manipulates it (perception). The nature of the stimuli and the way in which they are presented do not clearly indicate the purpose of test or the way in which the response is to be interpreted. The individual is not asked to asked to talk about himself directly. The ostensible subject-matter or stimulus may be a photograph, a picture, an ink-blot, etc. However, the responses to these stimuli are interpreted as indicating the individual's own view of the world, his personality structure, his needs, tensions and anxieties, etc.[2]. As stated earlier, the are interpreted in terms of some pre-established psychological conceptualization of what the preson's responses to the stimulus (test situation) mean.

Rorschach test: One of the more frequently used projective techniques is the Rorschach test. This test consists of ten cards having prints of ink-blots. The design is symmetrical but meaningless (see the picture below):

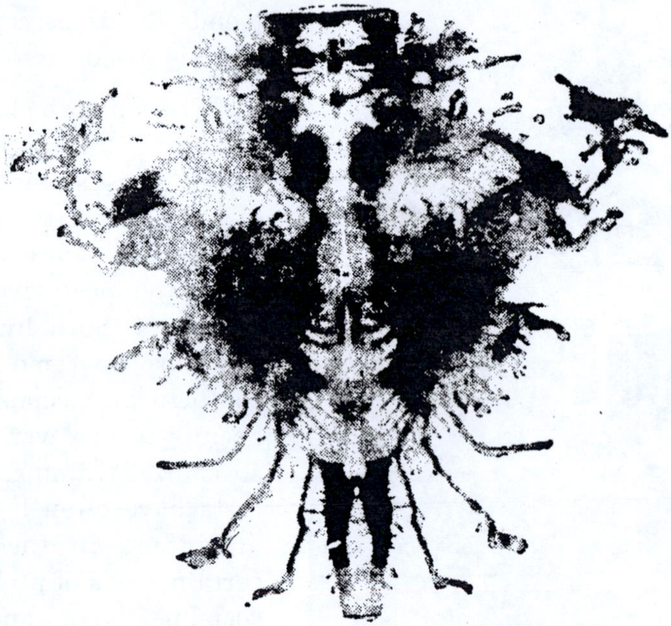

The subject is asked "What might this be?" The subject's responses, e.g.," This could be two women gossiping" or "Reminds me of the human lungs" or "A butterfly",etc., are interpreted on the basis of some pre-established psychological framework .

Obviously, the task of interpreting as to what a particular response means in terms of the subject's personality characteristic, is indeed, a very difficult, tricky and specialized one. Interpretations may not always be the same for different scientists working on the same response. There is also the problem of validity.

Thematic Apperception Test (T.A.T.): This is another often used projective test. The test consists of a series of pictures about which the subject is asked to tell stories.

Some of these pictures deal with the ordinary day-to-day events while others may represent unusual situations. The stories that subject tell constitute the basis for the investigator to draw certain inferences about their personality, tensions, adaptive aspects of behaviors and experessive aspects, etc. such inferences rest on the assumption that what the respondent perceives in the test-material represents in some way, externalization or projection of process within himself.

Tomkins-Horn Picture Arrangement Test: This test has a somewhat more specific focus. It is designed for group-administration. It consists of 25 plates each containing three sketches that may be arranged in various ways to portray a sequence of events. The subject is asked to arrange them in a sequence which he considers to be most reasonable. The responses are interpreted as providing evidence regarding conformity to norms, social orientation of the respondent, optimism-pessimism, etc.

Word-Association Test: The subject is presented with a list of words; after each one, he has to respond with the first word that comes to his mind. For example, if the stimulus-word is "black" the subject may respond immediately by saying "white", or someone may respond by saying "sheep" or "Negro." The content as also the rate of the subject's response may indicate the likely areas of emotional disturbance.

Sentence-completion Test: In this test, the first few words of a possible sentence are given and the subject is asked to complete it. Different subjects may complete the sentence differently. This also affords clues to areas of the subject's emotional disturbance and his attitudinal structure.

Doll Play Test: This test is especially suited for children. The child-subject is given a set of dolls representing adults or children of both sexes or members of different ethnic groups. The subject may be asked to show how these dolls would act in specified circumstances. The children may be allowed to play with the dolls freely. The manner in which they organize the dolls and work out various arrangements would indicate their attitudes or prejudices, etc., towards the class of persons represented by the dolls.

It is important to note that each of these tests, in addition to the specific function ascribable to each, also affords a basis for broader interpretation of the individual's personality. Many of these techniques have been subjected to critical scrutiny. Consequently, standardized methods of administration, scoring and interpretation have come to be established. Nevertheless, questions have been repeatedly raised about their validity, and evidence on this point to date is from conclusive.

Despite this limitation, the projective tests have been used with advantage in studies concerned with relation of individual personality to social and cultural factors. For example, Adorno and colleagues in their study entitled, "The Authoritarian Personality" used T.A.T. pictures as one of the means for assessing the personalities of individuals who scored low on the scale of anti-semitism and ethnocentrism, i.e., those who were less prejudiced. With a view to identifying the relation between culture and personality, anthropologist Du Bois in her study of the people of Alor administered a

Rorschach test to a number of villagers of Alor to see the conrrespondence a Rorschach test to a number of villagers of Alor to see the correspondence between the personality patterns and cultural behaviour.

The projective techniques have also been devised and utilized to investigate the content of an individual's attitudes some social objects. These techniques share some of the characteristics of the projective methods already described. They encourage a free response on the part of the individual; they do not ask him to talk about himself directly or about his own views and feelings. In so far as the purpose of these tests is to tap specific attitudes, the test-materials usually provide a more specific subject-matter than do those used in tests for assessing broad personality patterns. In these tests as in others ,the aim is to prevent the transparency of the test as best as possible. It is well worth noting that transparency of purpose (if masking is not feasible) is not necessarily a serious disadvantage.

Even when the purpose of a projective to the subjects, the projective tests are definitely preferable (if attempts at interpretation do not suffer owing to incompetence) for the following reasons:

(a) The subject may find it easier to express himself if he is not talking about his own feelings and attitudes explicitly)

(b) The subject may be unable to describe his feelings and attitudes as accurately as they may be discerned in the projective tests.

(c) It is possible that sometimes access to certain populations of potential subjects may be withheld if the topic under investigation is made explicit to subjects.

(d) The projective test may produce more extensive information than a questionnaire or even an interview, even if its purpose is not concealed to the subjects.

Quite a few projective techniques for the study of attitudes have also been devised. These very in the extent to which they can camouflage their purpose and requisition a certain measure of skill at recording and analyzing the responses. We shall briefly describe the major techniques used for the study of social attitudes. Abundant caution in their use and interpretation, however, is necessary.

Verbal Techniques

(1) Word Association Test: In this test a number of words are presented to the subject, one by one, and he is asked to indicate the first thought that he associates with each word. The speed of response and its emotional concomitant, as well as its content may constitute valuable indicators of attitude.

(2) Sentence Completion Technique: This is another kind of verbal technique. We have already discussed it earlier. The content of responses (in terms of completing the incomplete sentences) may provide considerable insight into the person's attitudes. This technique has been used for studying attitudes of various kinds. M.Kerr used it, for example, in the study of national stereotypes held by the English. Some of the sentence beginnings employed in this study were as under:

(i) When I think of Russians, I think of....

(ii) If you invite an American to your home, he may....

(3) Story and Argument completion Techniques : In these tests the subject is given just enough of a story or argument to focus his attention on given issue but not enough to indicate how it will eventually turn out. He is then asked to supply a conclusion to the story or the argument. His response, i.e., the way he supplies the ending argument, is assumed to betray his deep-seated biases.

(4) Projective Questions: The subject is asked to respond to a vague question, e.g., who are you/ Such question may take the form of asking about a possible event in the future or about an imaginary event. The subject's response is taken to be indicative of his perceptions, beliefs, attitudes, etc., which would have predisposed him to answer the question the way he had done. Sometimes projectives questions take the form of asking about other people's views, the assumption being that the respondent will find it easy to put cirtical or unpopular views which he cannot openly express, into the mouths of other people.

(5) Description: This involves asking the respondent to describe the kind of person who would behave in a specified way. For example, the subject may be asked to describe the people who freely mix with a member of a specified ethnic group.

Pictorial Techniques

Pictorial techniques, many of them borrowed from well established clinical procedures, have along been popular in the study of social attitudes.

(1) T.A.T.: Proshansky was one of the first to use the T.A.T. type of pictures in the study of social attitudes. Ambiguous pictures of situation involving labour were mixed with the regular T.A.T. pictures. The subjects were asked to describe what they thought the pictures represented. Pictures of T.A.T. have been used in several studies of attitudes toward minority groups. For example, Adorno and associates in their "Authoritarian Personality" presented four pictures especially aimed at uncovering attitudes towards minority groups, alongwith the regular T.A.T. pictures.

Fromme (1941) presented to subjects political cartoons, each with four alternative captions, representing different dimensions of attitudes. The subjects were asked to choose the alternative that in their view, fitted each cartoon best.

(2) The Rosenzweig Test: It uses a cartoon format in which one character is represented as saying something. There is a blank space for another character and the subject is asked what this send character would probably say. J.E. Brown applied a modified version of the Resenzweig test for used in the study of ethnic attitudes.

Play Techniques

The techniques involving manipulation of dolls have been used in investigating the attitudes of young children. Dolls have been used in investigating the attitudes of young children. Dolls clearly representing different ethnic or racial groups, say 'white' and 'coloured' dolls, may be given to the children. They may be asked to play out specific scences such as arranging a birth-day party. The inclusion or exclusion of certain types of dolls as well as the roles assigned to them would provide a score of the child's attitudes toward the racial or ethnic groups. Hartley and Schwartz combined doll-play with pictorial material in studying inter-group attitudes of childrens.

Psychodrama and Sociodrama Techniques

These techniques require that the subject act out a role, either as himself (Psychodrama) or as somebody else (sociodrama) as he would in a real-life situation. For example, a subject may be asked to play the role of a co-worker of some other racial group in some hypothetical situation (e.g., when the boss called him for an explanation). The manner in which he plays the role, the history or backdrop that he creates for the roles, etc., may provide considerable insight into his attitudes. Psychodrama and sociodrama are among the few tools available for systematic investigation of social skills.

It should be noted toward the conclusion of this discussion that although the projective tests have provided a very potent tool for getting at the data of personal and private character, these present formidable difficulties all their own. One of the persistent difficulties in regard to data obtained by these means is that of interpretation. What a particular response of the subjects really means is a question that does not find any unanimity of opinion. In view of this difficulty, one can only say that a much closer investigation of validity is needed. Some of the studies carried out to date have given encouraging evidence of correspondence between the results of an indirect test and those provided by an independent criterion.[3] Other studies have, however, revealed discrepancies. Between different measures. These raise serious questions about what these various tests really succeed in measuring. More attention, therefore, would need to be paid to validation of projective tests before they can make their full contribution to social research.

REFERENCES

(1) See Selltiz, Jahoda, *et al.*, *op. cit.*, chap. Projective Techniques.

(2) See Bell, J.E., *Projective Techniques: A Dynamic Approach to the Study of Personality*, Longmans Green, New York, 1948.

(3) Also see Abt, L. and Bellak: *Projective Psychology*, Knoff, New York, 1950.

Chapter XIV

The Scaling Techniques

We had on an earlier occasion stated that social research necessitates that distinctions of degree rather than of kind be measured. The researcher may want to ascertain, for example, whether Mr. X is more favourably disposed toward an issue than Mr. Y. Although making such distinctions of degree is justly a function of analysis rather than of data collection, the desire to be able to identify such distinction influences the form in which data are collected. This means that the questions asked to the respondents must be such as to give information on which judgements of degree can be based. Mostly the distinctions of degree are incorporated in the measuring instruments themselves.

Broadly, techniques for registering differences in degree are of two types. In the first type, one makes a judgement about some characteristic of an individual and places him directly on a scale defined in terms of that characteristic. A scale is a continuum extending from the highest point (in terms of a characteristic, e.g., favourableness) agreement, etc. and the lowest point, i.e., the lowest degree in terms of the characteristic; there being several intermediate points between these two poles. These scale positions are so related to each other that the second point indicates a higher degree in terms of a given characteristic as compared to the third. In the technique of the (first) type we shall be presently considering how the rater places the individual on a rating scale set up in such a way that various degrees of the characteristic in question (for example, the favourable or unfavourable attitude toward co-education in colleges) are indicated. The person making the judgement as to where to assign a particular response of the individual on the scale, may be the particular individual himself or an observer, an interviewer or a coder, etc.

The second type of technique for registering differences of degree consists of questionnaires constructed in such a way that the score of individual's responses assigns him a place on a scale.

For example, if the researcher is interested in an individual's attitude toward co-education in colleges, the individual respondent is asked to reply to a series of questions relevant to co-education or to indicate his agreement or disagreement with a series of statements. From his replies to these statements or questions, a score is computed; this score is taken as indicating his/her position on a scale representing various degree of favourableness or unfaourableness toward co-education.

The rating scales and attitude scales, both have the object of assigning individuals to positions with different numerical values in order to make possible the distinctions of degree. Let us now consider some of the major types of rating scales in which the rater places the person or object being rated at some point along the continuum, a numerical value being assigned to each point.

Graphic Rating Scales : This perhaps is the most widely used rating scale. In this type, the rater (who may be the subject himself) indicates his rating by simply making a mark (✔) at the appropriate point on a line of statements that run from one extreme of the attribute or characteristic in question to the other extreme. Scale-points with brief descriptions may be indicated along the line, their function being to help the rater in localizing his rating. The following scale may illustrate a graphic rating scale. Let us say the characteristic we wish to ascertain is peoples' views in ragard to participation of workers in the management.

Feels strongly that workers should be allowed full participation (in management)	Generally feels that workers should be given an opportunity	Is ambivalent. Partly favours, partly disfavours worker's participation	Generally feels workers should not be given opportunity of participation	Strongly feels that workers should not be allowed to participate in management

One of the major advantages of these scales is that they are relatively easy to use and provide scope for fine discriminations of degree. A reference must be made to certain precautions to be taken in designing and using them. Statements so extreme that they are not likely to be used should be avoided. Secondly, descriptive statements should be ordered to correspond as closely as possible, to the numerical points on the scale.

Itemized Rating Scales : These are also known as numerical scales. In this type, the rater selects one of a limited number of categories that are ordered in terms of their scale positions. Scales with five or seven categories have generally been employed but some have used even as many as eleven points. Barker, Dembo and Lewin in their study of the effects of frustration on constructiveness of play among young children constructed a seven point scale for rating constructiveness. They drew specific illustrations of points on the scale indicating degree constructiveness. In the above study, "The toys are examined superficially", the fourth point indicating moderate manipulation of the toys, and the seventh point indicating the highest degree of constructiveness was "play showing more than usual originality."

In general, the more clearly defined the categories, the more reliable the ratings are likely to be. Of course, how much specification is needed depends on the fineness of distinctions warranted by the purpose of the study and, the nature of the material, etc.

Comparative Rating Scales : In this category of rating scales, the positions on the scale are expressly defined in terms of a given population, a group or in terms of people with known characteristic. The rater/respondent, for example, may be called upon to indicate whether an individual's problem-solving skill or some other attribute most closely resembles that of Mr. X or Mr. Y or of Mr. Z, etc., all of whom may be known to him (the rater), in the matter of skill or attribute. Or again, a rater may be asked to estimate the ability of an individual to do a certain kind of work in the context of the ability to the total group of persons engaged in the above kind of work and whom the rater has known. The rater then may indicate whether the individual is more capable than 10% of them or 20% of them, etc.

Rank Order Scale : Here the rater is required to rank subjects/persons specifically in relation to one another. He indicates which person rates the highest in items of the characteristic being measured, which person is next highest and so on.

We have said above that in the rating scales, the rater himself may be the subject to be rated. This is called self-rating. Self rating has certain typical advantages. The individual (rater himself) is often in a better position to observe and report his feelings, opinions, etc. than anyone else is. But if the individual is not aware, as is not unusual, of his biases, beliefs or feelings or is aware of such feelings but does not wish to express them for certain reasons (such as fear or image conversation) then self-rating procedure may prove to be of little value. It must be reckoned that an individual's conception of what constitutes a particular position, say extreme position, may be quite different from that of the others making comparable self-rating.

Despite these failings, self-rating has proved useful in measurement of attitudes. With respect to certain attributes or attitudes, e.g., intensity, importance, etc., self-rating has come to be reckoned as the only satisfactory source of information. Clear specifications of the dimensions to be rated and definition of the frame of reference or standard against which ratings are to be made, may reduce the possibilities of distortion in self-ratings.

Let us briefly discuss some of the cautions that one should ideally heed in constructing and using the rating scales.

There is a possibility that if more than one characteristic of a person is to be judged, the rater may carry over a generalized impression of the persons from one rating to the next. Thus, if a rater considers a person to be intelligent and he believes that intelligent persons are better adjusted, he is likely to rate the persons as well-adjusted, as well as 'intelligent.' This is known as the spill-over or 'halo effect' which needs to be guarded against.

Another type of error is the 'generosity error.' Here the tendency of the rater is to overstimate the desirable qualities of subjects whom he likes. Murray and associates have identified 'contrast error' in which the rater has a tendency to see others as the opposite of himself in a trait. Yet another error emanates from the tendency of the raters to avoid making extreme judgements and to assign individuals to the more moderate categories.

Constant errors such as those described above, may be minimized by training raters and by making them aware of the possibility of such biases. Of course, specific types of errors can be arrested by taking specific steps. For example, the generosity error may be reduced by using relatively neutral descriptive terms for the scale positions rather than by using evaluative ones. 'Halo effects', may be reduced by having various ratings of a person made independently.

Potential Sources of Unreliability in Rating

Let us now discuss the sources of unreliability in rating. One frequent source of unreliability among different raters is the fact that different raters do often use different frames of references for describing persons in terms of a question. For example, the rating of a person as 'liberal' derives its meaning from the rater's reference groups. The way to minimize unreliability is to train the raters carefully as also pay due attention to the construction of the rating scale. Clear definitions of the characteristic being measured and of various positions on the scale, as well as a clear specification of the reference group can be of some help in distinguishing between the adjacent positions on the scale.

Number of Scale Points

The decision as to how many scale positions or categories are to be used in the rating scale will depend on the degree of differentiation one would desire in measurement; this in turn would be dictated by the research purpose or hypotheses. The following factors also affect the above decision : (a) the discriminative ability of the raters (their training and experience); (b) the kind of characteristic to be judged (whether these are easily discernible or not); (c) the conditions under which ratings are to be made (whether they are based on voluminous extensive data or limited data).

It would be necessary and advisable to use a less differentiated scale (consisting of a limited number of points or positions) if complex attributes are to be judged and experienced raters are not available.

In many studies, ratings are made during the process of analysis by coders who have studied the data secured from the field. Here the reliability of rating can be substantially improved by having several raters work as a team making independent judgements, comparing their ratings, discussing discrepancies, etc.

The 'simplicity' of rating scales commends their use to many a researcher. But there is no denying the possibility that their simplicity may be deceptive. Often so much time is required to establish adequate reliability that the procedure becomes uneconomical. Yet it is true that despite the attendant difficulties a rating scale may be just about the only instrument available for a given purpose. So is the case at least at the present stage of development in social research techniques. Furthermore, the rating scales have a wide range of application; they can be used in connection with data collected by any method, e.g., observation, interview documents or projective techniques, etc.

Validity of Rating Scale

In regard to the problem of validity of the rating scales which is perhaps the most significant problem arising in the use of such scales investigators in general have assumed that their rating scales are valid when the following conditions obtain :

(a) When the characteristics being measured are relatively "objective", that is, their meaning can be uniformly understood by different raters.

(b) The ratings are actually made under optimal 'desired' conditions, e.g., well constructed scales, trained raters, specified common frames of reference, etc.

Attitude Scales[1]

As was stated in the beginning of the chapter, a second type of technique for registering differences of degree consists of questionnaires constructed in a manner that the score of an individual's response places him on a scale. In this approach, the individual does not directly describe himself in terms of his position (rather than himself) on the dimension in questions; rather he expresses his agreement or disagreement with a number of statements relevant to the issue. On the basis of his responses, he is assigned a score or numerical value. The score a person gets indicates his position on the dimensions. Since this technique has been generally used in the measurement of attitudes, the readers can appreciate the rationale behind entitling this section 'attitude scales.'

It was said that the attitude scales are constituted of various statements or items relevant to an issue (like nationalization of banks, coeducation, inter-caste marriages, etc.). The individual subjects respond in a particular manner to these statements. To these modes of response, particular scores are assigned. Let us consider what criteria are used in selection of statements or items for inclusion in an attitude scale. There are two such criteria.

Criteria for Inclusion of Items in Scale

The statements or items must elicit responses that are psychologically related to the attitude being measured. For example, in a scale measuring attitude toward co-education, the following statement may be said to have a manifest relationship to the attitude being measured : "Girls should have an educational atmosphere uncontaminated by boys." It should be remembered however, that it is often advantageous to have statement that appears on the surface to have no relationship to the attitude in question, since it may prevent the respondent from concealing or distorting his attitude. *Adorno* and associates used many such indirect statements in their study of the authoritarian personality. In the case of such seemingly unrelated statements, care must be taken to see that before they are accepted as relevant measures, their relation to the attitude is clearly demonstrated.

The second criterion requires that the scale differentiates clearly between people who are at different points along the continuum of the attitude being measured. The items or statements need to be such that they discriminate not merely between opposite extremes of attitude (i.e., favourable and unfavourable) but also among individuals who differ slightly (e.g., moderately favourable and neutral). As we shall see, some types of scales provide for the identifications of moderate positions by permitting the expression of various degrees of agreement or disagreement with explicit statements that are clearly favourable or clearly unfavourable to the issue.

Types of Scales

The way in which a scale discriminates among individuals depends on the way in which the scale is fashioned and the method of scoring employed. In some scales, the statements/ items form a gradation of such a nature that the individual agrees with only one or two of these and disagrees with the remaining statement on their side of those agreed to. Such scales in which a person's response fixes his positions, are called the Differential scales. In other type of scales, the individual indicates his agreement or disagreement with each statement and his total score is computed by adding scores assigned to his responses to each of the statement comprising the scale. Such scales may be called Summated scales. Yet another type of scales is set up in such a way that the statements or items form a cumulative series. Principally, an individual whose attitude is at a certain point on the dimension being measured will answer favourably all the items on one side of this point and answer unfavourably all those on the other side of this point. These are called Cumulative scales. Let us discuss each of these types of scales in turn.

Differential Scales : These scales used for the measurement of attitudes are closely associated with the name of *L.L. Thurstone,* hence are often called Thurstone-type scales. Thurstone-type scale consists of a number of statements whose position on the scale has been determined by a ranking operation performed by judges who are persons whose judgements about the relative rank of different statements along a dimension can be relied on. Various method of securing judgemets of scales-position have been, viz., the method of paired comparisons, the method of equal-appearing intervals, etc.

The method of equal-appearing intervals is most commonly used in the construction of this scale. This procedure is as under:

In selecting the statement for the scale and assigning scores to them, the following procedure is used : (a) The researcher gathers a large number of statements (several hundred) conceived as related to the attitude being investigated. (b) A large number of judges (upto 300) working independently, are requested to classify these statements into eleven categories or piles. Each of the judges is requested to place in the first pile the statements which he thinks are most unfavourable to the issue (or, most progressive or most permissive, depending upon the dimension along which the statements are to be placed) in the second pile, those he considers next most unfavourable and proceeding thus, in eleventh pile, the statements he considers most favourable. The sixth position on this continuum is defined as the point at which the attitude is 'neutral.' The first pile (i.e., statements rated as most unfavourable) carries the score of 11 while the statements assigned the last pile carry a value of 1 (each). (c) The scale value of any one statement is computed as the mean or median position to which it is assigned by the group of judges. Statements that have too broad a scatter, that is, whose evaluation by different judges varies very widely, are discarded as ambiguous or irrelevant. (d) A final selection of statements is made, taking evaluated items or statements that spread out evenly along the scale from one extreme position to the other (scale values like 10.3, 9.4, 8.4, 7.5, 6.4, 5.3, 4.5, 3.4, 2.6 and 1.6) may be included in the scale to be administered.

The resulting scale is thus a series of statements, usually about twenty, the position of each statements on the scale having been determined by the judges' classification. The subjects are asked during the administration of the scale questionnaire to check mark the statement or statements with which they agree or to check two or three statements that are closest to their position.

In *MacCrone's* study of attitudes toward 'natives' in South Africa using the *Thurstone-type* scale, the statement which was judged as one with *extremely* unfavourable import for the natives and having the scale value 10.3 was, "I consider that the native is only fit to do the 'dirty' work of the white community." The most favourable statement having a scale value of 0.8 was "I would rather see the white people lose their position in this country than keep it up at the expense of injustice to the native." Between these two opposite extreme statements were a number of statements arranged according to their scale-values (from higher of lower).

Of course, the scale values are not shown on the questionnaire and the statements are usually arranged in a random order. The mean (more preferably the median) of the scale values of the items the individual checks is interpreted as indicating his position on the scale of favourable-unfavourable attitude (or any other dimension) toward a given issue.

The *Thurstone* method of equal-appearing intervals has been widely used. Such scales have been utilized to measure attitudes toward varied inssues such as war, religion, and various ethnic groups. The *Thurstonetype*, scale has also been adopted for the analysis of documentary data such as newspaper editorials.

The *Thurstone* scale is most appropriate and reliable if the scale is measuring just a single attitude and not a complex of attitudes. If the responses of an individual scatter widely over statements having scale values differing widely, his attitude score is not likely to have the same meaning as a score with little scatter. The scattered responses may also be interpreted to mean that the subject has no clear attitude toward the issue or that his attitude is not organized in a manner assumed by the scale.

Several objections have been raised against the Thurstone-type scale. The major ones may be listed as under:

(a) The procedure involved in constructing such a scale is very cumbersome. This involves, as we have seen, a lot of work such as preparing several hundred statements relevant to the issue taking care that different shades of attitudes are represented, getting these statements rated by a large number of judges and then choosing the most reliable statements constituting a smooth continuum, etc.

(b) Another justified criticism of this scale is that, since a subject's score is the mean or median of the scale-values of several statements he checks, there is the likelihood that the same total score obtained by different persons may express different attitudinal patterns. For example, an individual checks two items (statements) have scale-values 8.6 and 7.6 respectively. His score will be $8.6 + 7.6 \div 2 = 8.1$ (the mean of scale-values). Now another individual may check three statements having scale-values $10.4 + 5.5 \div 3 = 8.1$ (approx). Thus, two individuals get rated as being equivalent in regard to their attitude even though the latter's choice of statements and the scatter of his responses is appreciably different from that of the former.

(c) The statements comprising the scale have a reference to varied dimensions of an issue and hence cannot really occupy different positions on a single continuum.

(d) Yet another objection concerns the extent to which the scale values assigned to statements are influenced by the attitude of judges themselves. Although some earlier studies, notably by Hinckley and MacCrone, had come to the conclusion that the attitudes and backgrounds of the judges do not affect the position of various statements on the scale, more recent researches notably by Hovland and Sherif (1952) and by *Kelly* and associates (1955) have come out with findings suggesting that the attitudes and backgrounds and even the intelligence of the judges do affect the scale-values they assign to the statements. Such findings cast serious doubts on the meaning of the scale positions and the distances between them. It should be noted, however, that even these studies found a high agreement in the rank-order in which the different groups of judges arranged statements along the continuum. Thus, according to most writers on research methodology, the Thurstone-type scale despite this weakness may be said to constitute a reasonably satisfactory ordinal scale. In practice, if individuals agreed with only a few contiguous items on the scale, the Thurstone scale would provide highly satisfactory ordinal scales since in this case the score would have a clearer meaning.

Summated Scales : A summated scale like the differential scale just discussed, consists of a series of statements to which the subject is asked to react. The main difference between the two is that unlike the differential scale or favourable statements definitely favourable or unfavourable toward a given issue are used in the scale (the intermediate shades being excluded). The respondent/subject indicates his agreement or disagreement and degree thereof with each item. Each response is given a numerical value corresponding to its favourableness or unfavourablenss. The summation of the scores of individual's responses to all the separate statements gives his total score. This score represents his position on the continuum of favourable-unfavourableness toward an issue.

The type of *summated scale* most frequently used in the study of social attitudes follows the pattern devised by *Likert*. Therefore, it is customarily referred to as the Likert-type scale. In this scale, the subjects are asked to respond to each of the statements in terms of several degrees of agreement or disagreement; for example, (I) strongly approve, (II) approve, (III) undecided, (IV) disapprove, (V) strongly-disapprove. We can see that these five points constitute the scale; at one end of the scale is strong approval, at the other end is strong disapproval and between them lie intermediate points. The subject indicates with reference to each statement where he stands on this scale. Each point on the scale carries a score or a value. Response indicative of the most favourable attitude (strongly approve) is given the highest score of 5 or + 2, while the one conveying most unfavourable attitude (strongly disapprove) is given the least score, i.e., 1 or 2. The following will make it clear:

Statement No. I : Coeducation should be made compulsory				
I	*II*	*III*	*IV*	*V*
Strongly approve 5(or + 2)	Approve 4(or + 1)	Undecided 3(or 0)	Disapprove 2(or – 1)	Strongly disapprove 1(or – 2)

Of course, the score values corresponding the scale positions do not appear on the questionnaire supplied to respondents.

The procedure for constructing a Likert-type scale is as follows:

(a) The investigator assembles a larger number of statements considered relevant to the attitude being investigated, which are either clearly favourable or clearly unfovourable.

(b) The statements are administered to a small sample of subjects, i.e., representation of those on whom the questionnaire is to be finally administered. The subjects indicate their response to each item by checking one of the categories of approval or disapproval on the scale below each statement.

(c) The responses to various items are scored in such a way that a response indicative of the most favourable attitude is given the highest score (or highest positive score). It is important that the responses are scored consistently in terms of the attitudinal direction they indicate. Whether 'approve' or 'disapprove' is a favourable response *vis-a-vis* an issue depends on the content and wording of the statement. For example, with reference to the following statements, its disapproval by a subject will indicate favourable attitude toward the issue.

Statement No. II : Co-education has nothing but evil in store for students.				
I	*II*	*III*	*IV*	*V*
Strongly approve 1 (or-2)	Approve 4 (or-1)	Undecided 3 (or 0)	Disapprove 4 (or + 1)	Strongly disapprove 5 (or + 2)

It may be noted that in the above illustration, the order or scale-values of the positions has been reversed. Comparing it with the scale used for statement No. I, we find that for statement No. I the position I (strong approval) had the scale-value of 5 (or + 2), the same position as used for statement No. II has the scale value of 5 (or + 2). This is quite understandable, because the person who strongly disapproves statement No. II which in terms of content is the opposite of statement No. I, i.e., expresses unfavourable view about co-education.

(d) The next step in the procedure is to compute the total score of the individual by adding his item-scores (i.e., scores received for separate statements).

(e) Finally, the responses are analysed to determine which of the statements discriminate most clearly between the high scores and the low scores on the total scale.

In other words, the investigator exerts to identify the items which have a high discriminatory power. The items with low discriminatory power or those that do not show a substantial correlation with the total score are eliminated to ensure that the questionnaire is internally consistent, that is, every item or statement is related to the same general attitude.

The Likert-type scale has several advantages over the Thurstone scale.

(1) It permits the use of items that are not manifestly related to the attitude being studied. This is so because in the Likert method any item (statement) that is found empirically consistent with the total score can be included. Unlike Thurstone type scale, there is no necessity of agreement among judges that restricts the items (statements) to content which is obviously related to the attitude being studied. As was indicated earlier, it is a great advantage to be able to use items that do not, on the face of it, appear to have a direct relationship to the attitude being studied.

(2) The Likert type scale is generally considered simpler to construct. At least, the procedure of construction is less cumbersome.

(3) It is likely to be more reliable than a Thurstone type scale comprising the same items. The Likert type scale permits the expression of several degrees (usually five) on the continuum of agreement-disagreement, whereas the Thurstone type scale allows for a choice between only two alternative responses, i.e., accptance or rejection.

(4) The range of responses permitted to a statement in the Likert type scale provides more precise information about the individual's opinion on the issue.

It should be noted, however, that the Likert type scale does not provide a basis for saying how much more favourable one is, compared to another, or for measuring the amount of change after some experiment or exposure. Thus, in effect, the Likert scale does not rise to a stature higher than that of an ordinal scale.

One major weakness of the Likert scale is that often, the total score of an individual has little clear meaning in as much as many patterns of response to the various statements may produce the same score. We have already noted this is regard to the Thustone type scale. But this lacuna applies with even greater force to the Likert scales, since they provide a greater number of response possibilities. So in Likert scale as in the Thustone type scale, the meaning of identical total scores of two or more persons may be markedly different. Pragmatically viewed, it may appear that the scores on the Likert type questionnaire often provide a basis for a rough ordering of people on the characteristics being measured.

Cumulative Scales: *Cumulative scales* like the earlier scales are made up of a series of items with which the respondent indicates agreement or disagreement. The distinctive feature of a cumulative scale is that the items therein are ordered or related to one another in such a way that an individual who replies favourably to item No. 3 also automatically replies favourably to item No. 2 and No. 1 and one who replies favourably to item No. 4 also reacts favourably to items Nos. 3, 2, and 1 and so on. Thus, all individuals who react to a given item favourably have higher scores on the total value scale than the individuals who react to that items unfavourably. The individual's score is computed by counting the number of items he answers favourably. This score places him on the scale of favourable-unfavourable attitude provided by the relationship of the items to one another.

One of the earliest scales for measurement of attitudes, the *Bogardus* social distance scale, was intended to be a scale of the cumulative type. The social distance scale which has become a classic technique in the measurement of attitudes toward ethnic or racial groups lists a number of relationships to which members of a given ethnic group might be admitted. The respondent is asked to indicate for specified ethnic or racial groups the relationships to which he would be willing to admit members of each group. This attitude is measured by the closeness of relationship that he is willing to accept or the social distance that he would wish to maintain.

The Borgardus scale is illustrated below:

Relationship I would accept		*Group I English*	*Group II Negro*	*Group III French*	*Group IV Chinese*
(1) To close kinship by marriage	1	1	1	1	1
(2) To my club as personal chums	2	2	2	2	2
(3) To my street as neighbours	3	3	3	3	3
(4) To employment in my occupation	4	4	4	4	4
(5) To citizenship in my country	5	5	5	5	5
(6) As visitors only to my country	6	6	6	6	6
(7) Would exclude from my country	7	7	7	7	7

The respondent is directed to circle or tick off (✔) each of the classifications (relationship categories) to which he would be willing to admit the average member of a particular ethnic, racial or nationality group (neither the best members nor the worst, he has known). The answers are supposed to reflect the respondent's first feeling reactions.

In the above scale, it is reasonable to expect that a respondent who ticks off 3 in relation to French, i.e., indication of his willingness to have them as his neighbours, would ordinarily also tick off 4 and 5, i.e., accepting them as employees in his occupation and accepting them as citizens in his country. But he would not tick off 6 and 7, because these are statements connoting exclusion. If an individual does not tick off 3, then it is reasonable to except that he will not tick off 1 and 2, since these are statements indicating even closer relationships (marriage and friendship) compared to 3 (neighbourhood).

The underlying assumption that these items form a cumulative scale (with reference to America) has, by and large, been borne out. In practice, however, some reversals may occur. For example, one who would object to living in the same neighbourhood with a particular group would not object to having these people in an informal social club (i.e., accepting 2, but rejecting 3).

The reason may be their dirty living habits or domestication of certain pets which are a nuisance to the neighbourhood. Experience has demonstrated, however, that such reversals, while possible in individual cases, do not obtain in regard to an entire group of respondents. It should be noted that reversals can be interpreted by postulating the intrusion of some extraneous factors such as repondent's apprehension that land values may fall if members of a particular group (of low social status) were to live in his neighbourhood. After 1940, there has been a rapid development of techniques for determining whether the statements form or a scale in the ideal sense ideally have. This led to a methodological emphasis on the development of unidimensional scales, that is, scales consisting of statement that do no refer to issues extraneous to the characteristic being measured.

It had been pointed out by a number of investigators that the Thurstone or Likert scales contain statement about various aspects of the characteristic under consideration and thus these statements belong in fact, to two or more different scales. Thus, scales using statements are in fact 'multi-dimensional' scales. For example, in a scale that was designed to measure attitude toward war (a Thurstone-type Scale), the most favourable statement was, "war is glorious" and the most unfavourable statement was "There is no conceivable justification for war" and its mid-point was "I never think about war and it does not interest me." Carter pointed out that these statements could hardly be considered as falling along a straight line, since they refer to different aspects of the phenomenon of war.[2] It is understandable that combining statements referring to different aspects of the phenomenon, e.g., war, makes it impossible to specify exactly what the scale is measuring. In such a scale characterized by multi-dimensionality, there is a very high possibility of the subject's response being scattered along statements which differ widely in their scale-value; this makes it difficult to give any clear meaning to the score based on the average of the scale-values of statements checked by the individual.

A notable attempt to approach this problem has been made by *Guttman*. The technique developed by Guttman, known as 'scale analysis' or the 'Scalogram method' has for its main purpose, to ascertain whether the attitude or characteristic being studied actually involves only a single dimension. In the Guttman procedure, a universe of content (the attitude or characteristic under study) is considered to be unidimensional only if it yields a perfect or almost perfect cumulative scale. That is, it should be possible to arrange all the responses of any number of subjects into a pattern such as the one given below:

The important thing about this pattern is that if it holds good, i.e., the given score on a particular series of items (statements) always has the same meaning. That is, if one knows a subject's score, he can tell, without consulting his questionnaire, exactly which items the subject must have endorsed.

Samuel Stouffer points out the characteristic feature of the *Guttman technique* thus: "...it must be possible to order the items such that, persons who answer a given question favourably all have higher ranks than persons who answer the same question unfavourably. The response to any item provides a definition of the respondent's attitude."[3] This quality of being able to reproduce the responses to each item knowing only total score is called 'reproducibility', which is one of the major tests of whether a set of items constitutes a scale in Guttman's sense. Let us take an illustration for added clarification. Consider the following items, with which the respondents are asked to agree or disagree:

(1) Co-education in the long run helps subsequent marital adjustments. Agree ________ disagree.

(2) Parents should send their sons and daughters to co-educational institutions. Agree ________ disagree.

(3) Co-education should be made compulsory by an Act of law. Agree ________ disagree.

If these items were found to form a perfect cumulative scale, then we would have all individuals with a score of 2 on the scale believe in the first statement that 'co-education helps adjustment among sexes' and believe, of course, in the second statement that 'parents should send their children to co-educational institutions' but not in the third statement that 'co-education should be made compulsory by law.'

In practice, speaking of social research perfect cumulative or unidimensional scales are rarely if ever found. But approximations to them can be developed. Scalogram analysis uses several criteria for deciding whether or not a particular series of statements may be regarded as a unidimensional scale. As we have stated, the most important of these is the reproducibility of the responses. The proportion of the subject's responses which fall into the scale pattern presented above, provides a measure of the extent to which particular responses are reproducible from the total score. Guttman has set 0.9 as the level of minimum reproducibility.

The Guttman techique may rightly be regarded as a method of determining whether a set of statements forms a unidimensional scale. It affords no guidance, however, for selecting statements that are likely to form a unidimensional scale. The scale discrimination technique developed by Edwards and Kilpatrick is a method of selecting a set of items likely to form a unidimensional scale. The procedure suggested is as under:

(a) A large number of statements dealing with the issue concerning the study is collected. Items that are ambiguous, irrelevant, neutral or too extreme are eliminated by inspection.

(b) As in the Thurstone method, a large number of judges are requested to place the remaining statements in eleven piles according to their degree of favourableness–unfavourableness toward the issue. The unreliable items are discarded and each of the remaining items is assigned a scale value (median position).

(c) These statements are then transformed into a Likert type scale by providing for expression of various degrees of agreement disagreement in response to each of the items. This scale is administered to a large group of subjects and their responses are analysed to determine which of the items discriminate most clearly between the high scorers and the low scorers on the total scale. Such items as have the highest discriminatory co-efficients in their scale interval (say, all items having scale value between 7.0 and 7.9 or 6.0 and so on) are selected in twice the number that is actually wanted for use in the final scale. For each scale interval, an equal number of items is selected.

(d) The statements or items in the resulting list are arranged in order in their scale value. The list is sub-divided into two counter-parts of questionnaire. The even numbered statements are assigned to one and the odd numbered ones are assigned to the other questionnaire.

But the unidimensional scales do suffer from certain limitations which we would do well to note.

(1) Unidimensional scales hardly constitute a reliable basis for assessing attitudes of persons towards complex objects or phenomena or for predicting the behavioural responses of individuals towards such objects or phenomena. For instance, 'war' or 'modernity' is a complex concept hence, the unidimensional scales do not quite help us to measure the attitudes of men toward these intricate concepts of war and modernity. It is, of course, possible to construct and use unidimensional scales for the implications of war for economy, health, morality etc., in independent studies. Although these dimensions of war do affect the final shape of persons' attitudes towards war, independent enquiries basing their assessment on unidimensional scales would hardly afford us a total perspective about a person's attitude toward 'war' in all its many-splendoured implications.

Secondly, a scale may be unidimensional for some persons but not so for others. In our discussion on cumulative scales, we had shown how the items on the scale may not constitute a cumulative series for one and all. Differences in educational levels and experience are reflected in a person's subjective evaluation of the scale items and as such a person may indicate his disagreement to item No. 2 but not to item No. 3 on the cumulative scale. Harding and Hogerfe have in their study demonstrated how a single scale did not, in effect, function as a unidimensional scale on the three different categories of workers.

REFERENCES

(1) See, Edwards, A.L.: *Technique of Attitude Scale Construction,* Appleton-Century Craft, New York, 1957.

(2) Selltiz, *et al.: op. cit.,* 373.

(3) *Ibid.,* p. 374.

Chapter XV

Sociometry

In this chapter, we shall be dealing at length with a special technique known as Sociometry which involves collecting and organizing data relating to interpersonal relationship and sentiments.

The sociometric technique is closely identified with the work of *J.L. Moreno*, entitled, *Who Shall Survive?* Sociometry is concerned with charting out the attractions and repulsions among the members of a group, among groups (miniature social systems) or sub-groups or between the subgroup and individuals. Sociometry involves a set of operations that depart fundamentally from the method employed by *Emory Boradgus* for the measurement of social distance.

Helen Jennings,[1] one of the pioneer in the field of sociometric studies, described sociometry as a device for a graphic and straight-forward portrayal of the total configuration of relations among the members of a group at some given point in time. Such a picture affords at a glance, the main lines of communications and the whole kaleidoscope of attractions and repulsions among members of the group. For *Franz,* "Sociometry is a method used for discovery and manipulation of social configuration by measuring the attractions and repulsions among individuals in a group."[2]

The basic technique employed in sociometry is the sociometric test; sociometric techniques have a reference to a cluster of devices, sociometric test included, which consist in having each member in the group with whom he/she would like to or would not like to engage in some activity that is relevant to the life of the group. Depending on the character of the group, the members may be asked to indicate whom (from among the other members of the group) he/she would like to be associated or not like to be associated with, in play, studies, problem-solving, dinner, lending and borrowing, etc.

What type of interactions among members become the focus of the researcher's attention depends, besides his objectives, on the nature and functions of the group. Generally, sociometric studies employ observation, questionnaires and interview schedules. Sometimes, examination of records may also be employed to secure the relevant information. But sociometry should more properly be considered a method of analysis rather than simply a method of data-collection.

The researcher needs to conduct observation of the behaviour of members if he wants to know the actual happenings in the group. During such an observation, the researcher concentrates on how the members behave, how they interact with one another, what the nature of their relationship is, who initiates interaction (orientation role) and who plays the object-role, etc.

Suppose, we conduct an observation aimed at ascertaining the pattern the students of a class in a public school exhibit in respect of exchanging the New Year Greetings. We may find that one student may be taken to be the most popular member of the class as much as he receives maximum number of greetings; a sociometric 'star,' to use the language of sociometry. We may also find that a few students do not receive any greeting cards. In sociometric terminology, these are the 'isolates.' We may further find that there has been among students, incidence of mutual exchange of greeting cards, e.g., A sends to B and B sends to A. This is known as the 'mutual choice.' In the course of our observations, we may come across some cliques, i.e., sub-groups of students, within each of which mutual exchange of greetings has taken place.

The sociometric questionnaires and interviews are employed in securing information from each persons about the other members of the group with whom they would like to or would not like to engage in a particular type of interaction, as also, their thoughts about this interaction. Questions included in the sociometric questionnaire/schedule are directed toward seeking information from each person in the group as to which other members of the group he would like or not like as his playmate, roommate, colleague, etc. Sometimes, the person is asked to name all the persons in the group whom he would like to choose or reject; that is, there is no restriction on the respondent to confine his choice or rejections to the first three or four persons in order of preference. But if the group is numerically large, the individual respondent is usually asked to indicate his choices or rejections to the first few persons in order of perference.

Moreno himself insisted on soliciting unrestricted number of choice or rejections, i.e., he recommends that the respondents should be allowed to indicate the total range of choice or rejections without any limitations. There is, of course, no denying that such a freedom allowed to the individual members of the group would go a long way in affording a sensitive and objective portrait of the interpersonal relations in the group. But, practical considerations often warrant a restriction on the individual respondent to indicate his choice or rejections only upto a certain numerical limit (three or four). As has been said above, if the group subjected to sociometric analysis is a large one, such a restriction largely becomes necessary.

Suppose, we want to administer a sociommetric test in a class of students. We may ask each student of the class to indicate which three (or more) students he would like to invite for a birthday party at his place and what his order of preference would be among those he would like to invite. We may also ask each student to indicate which three (or more) students he would not like to invite to his birthday party and what would be his order in rejection.

If the respondents believe that their choices or rejections would be used as a basis for the actual restructuring of the group or for effecting subsequent arrangements or rearrangements, there is a greater likelihood of their responding to the sociometric questions in all sincerity. At least, this is the usual and reasonable assumption. So in the sociometric studies, the researcher normally prefaces his questioning with the assurance to the respondents that their choices in respect of play, living arrangements and studies, etc., will be taken into active account while effecting modifications in prevailing conditions or in making subsequent arrangements.

Despite the fact the Moreno and associates had employed the sociometric method with extreme care and their insistence was on the use of this method only under certain conditions, the sociometric method has been used quite extensively and quite often without much caution. The popularity of this method may be attributed to the facility and graphic character of the 'sociogram' which may be aptly described as a diagrammatic means of presenting in essential basics the outline of inter-personal relations among the members of a group and the sentiments underlying these relationships. Sociometric data can also be summarized by means of N x N table. Such a tabulation is basic to matrix analyses.

Let us try to understand the N x N tabulation with the help of an example. Suppose we asked each one of the fifteen students who comprise a class, whom (among the other fourteen) they would like to invite for a birthday party. Suppose also, that we asked each student to in order of his/her preference. We can present these data, in a N x N table (since group has fifteen students, the table will be a 15 x 15 table).

The digits 1, 2, 3 shown in the various cells of the table below indicate the preferences. 1 represents the first preference choice. As shown in the table below, A has given first preference to B as an invitee to the birthday party. Similarly, the digits 2 and 3 in the table indicate respectively the second and third preferences. As can be seen in the table, C has given second preference to A and third preference to E. Similarly, D has given first preference to A, second to C and third to E. Thus, on the whole, the sociometric matrix, illustrated above, portrays in a quite intelligible manner the interpersonal relations among the students of a class.

	Chosen														
	A	*B*	*C*	*D*	*E*	*F*	*G*	*H*	*I*	*J*	*K*	*L*	*M*	*N*	*O*
A		1		2		3									
B	1			2	3										
C	2	1		3											
D	1		2		3										
E	2	1	3												
F				1	3			2							
G		3		1	2										
H				2	3		1								
I	1				2		3								
J	2		1				3								
K	2		1											3	
L				2			1		3						
M	3				1							2			
N							1		2	3					
O			1							3			2		
I	3	3	3	2	1	–	3	–	–	–	–	–	–	–	–
II	4	–	1	4	2	–	–	1	–	1	–	1	1	–	–
III	1	1	1	1	4	1	2	–	1	–	2	–	–	1	–
Total	8	4	5	7	7	1	5	1	1	1	2	1	1	1	0

The very same data may be presented in the form of a sociogram.

SOCIOGRAM: SHOWING PATTERNS OF CHOICE AT THE BIRTHDAY PARTY

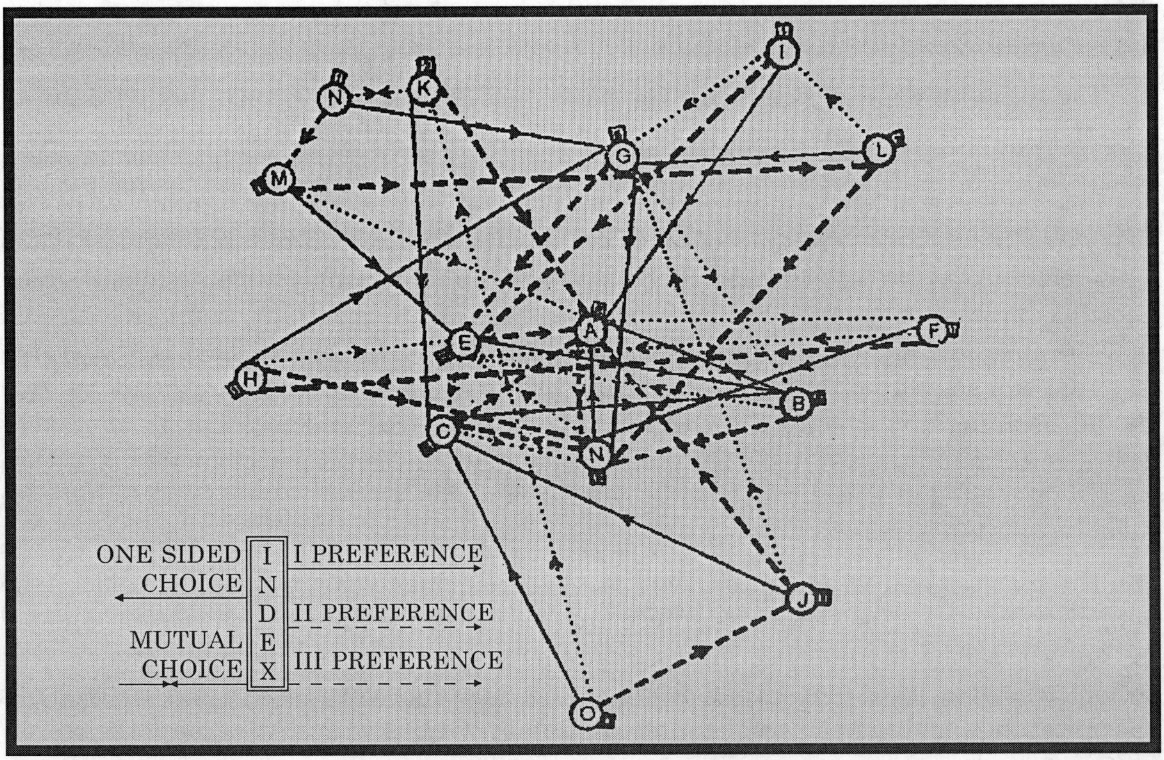

Examining the sociogram presented above, we find that A is the most frequently chosen person. He has secured the highest number of choices, i.e., eight. Out of these, three are first preference choices, four second preference and one third preference. In the language of sociometry we may designate A as the 'star', e.g., he is the most popular student in the group. In terms of the total number of choices, D and E (who have secured 7 choices each, irrespective of preferences) come next. But preference wise, their standing is not comparable to A, since D has only 2 first preferences whereas E has only 1. It is worthy of note that C, G and B have secured respectively a total of 5, 5 and 4 choices but each of them has received 3 first preferences. B has secured first preference choice from A who is the 'star' (as such this first preference choice, qualitatively speaking, amounts to more than any other first preference choice). Such qualitative differences are important aspects of sociometric analysis. In the sociogram, we find that O has not been chosen by a single student and is thus an isolate in sociometric parlance. Some instances of mutual choices also appear in the sociogram, e.g., A has chosen B and B has reciprocated A's sentiment. Similarly, K and N have given third preference choices to each other. The sociogram also presents mutual choices that are qualitatively unequal, e.g., D has indicated his first preference choice for A but A has given a second preference choice to D.

If we had a group considerably larger than the one represented by the sociogram, the corresponding figure might have shown the existence of sub-groups or cliques within the larger group.

The sociogram above, represents the pattern of choices with respect to invitation to a birthday party. We could have also asked the students of the class questions with a view to knowing the pattern of choices/rejections in regard to other criteria. For example, "whom would you choose as your playmate?" or "with whom would you like to share your lunch?" etc., are some of the questions that could be asked. It should be noted with reference to the sociometric questions that the situations or events about which questions are asked must be the ones the members of the group are familiar with and that the questions should appear realistic in the context of the group. That is, the events or situations should not appear very outlandish or far-fetched to the respondents and should meaningfully fit into the cognitive structure of respondents. Lastly, it is very desirable to maintain a fair measure of consistency between the sociometric structure we are interested in and the criteria in respect of which we ask respondents to indicate their acceptance or rejection.

The questionnaires and interviews are the principal instruments involved in the administration of sociometric tests. These are easy to administer and can be reformulated to suit situations of differing kinds. Students engaged in testing the reliability of sociometric data have found that despite a considerable variation in the individual's specific choices and the patterns of inter-personal relations within the group, the scores/ indexes based on the sociometric data are fairly stable.

Sociometric methods have been used with advantage in the studies of leadership, friendship pattern, group structures, social adjustments, minority prejudices, morale, public opinion, etc. In the field of psychiatry too (especially, group therapy) the use of sociometry has proved very fruitful.

Among the pioneering studies of leadership using the sociometric technique, the one conducted by *Helen Jennings* on girl students deserves special mention. *Jennings* calculated the choice-scores for each student on the basis of the choices or rejections received by each of them. This study revealed that there was a close correspondence between the leadership status of the students in the community and the choice-scores received by them in the study. One of the most significant findings of *Jennings'* study has been that leadership does not depend on any definite constellation of traits or personality characteristics; it depends rather on the behavioural contributions made by the person in reference to other members of the group.

Festinger, Schachter and Back have employed the sociometric technique in their study of the effects of residential patterning on friendship patterns. The study brought to light the fact that while factors such as age, interests, socio-economic status, etc, are important in the formation of friendly relations, ecological factors have a significant contribution to make in the initial formation and reinforcement of friendship relations. *Crisswell* employed the sociometric technique in her study of ethnic group prejudices. She has been able to show clearly that racial prejudices among children develop only after a certain age.

Roethlisberger and *Diskson* in their well-known study entitled 'Management and the Worker' have described by means of sociometric diagrams, the interpersonal relationship among workers in the 'Bank wiring room,' an experimental group culled out of the larger complex the 'Hawthorne Electrical Works.' Many a time, it is not feasible to study the interpersonal relations in the context of some specific concrete situation. At such times the individuals are asked to participate in an imaginary play situation or socio-drama with a view to assessing the nature of their attitudes. The socio-drama has diagnostic as well as therapeutic implications for the participants.

Merits: The variables that sociometric measure represent are typically social and as such, deal with the basic data the sociologists in the main, are primarily interested in individuals in interaction within a miniature social system are effectively represented, affording thus, an insight into the social environment as perceived by the subject. Knowledge of the "subjective frame of reference" aids understanding of the situation. Sociologists, social psychologists and, to a lesser extent, social anthropologists and psychiatrists have employed sociometric measures with advantage. *Moreno's* insistence that sociometric finding should be utilized for restructuring the situation under study has led to use of these measures being employed in the fields of education, industry, military, mental health, and broadly, in social engineering.

The interdisciplinary appropriateness of the sociometric devices makes out a strong case for their relevance to a field where there is interest in cross-disciplinary integration. Furthemore, these are devices an independent researcher can use without large-scale resources. Sociometric findings have direct implications for the situation under study. This is an additional merit of these techniques in terms of action-research. Nor is it all; these techniques while generating a high degree of interest and co-operation in the subjects, also provide acceptance indices and operative definition for a number of empirical concepts. Small wonder, the social, behavioural sciences have been impressed by sociometric devices as evidenced from the frequent employment of these techniques in various areas of their scientific concern.

Limitations: Let us now discuss some of the cautions and limitations a research employing sociometric techniques ought to be familiar with. These cautions in some cases relate to (a) the manner of employing these techniques; in others, they relate to (b) shortcoming inherent in the very nature of sociometric techniques.

The sociometric measures provide only one of the multiple means of viewing interpersonal relations. More often than not, additional evidence gathered through other means of providing information about the physical, social, cultural and psychological aspects of the situation is a prerequisite to an interpretative understanding of the phenomena, the sociometric techniques are conventionally applied to. *Moreno* rightly recommends the use of spontaneity tests and interviews to yield clues to the determinats of sociometric responses. For example, a person indicating his choice for a member of his own ethnic group may have done so owing to his personal acquaintance with the member chosen; not so much for reasons of ethnicity.

Suppose, it was seen in the course of a sociometric study of children belonging to different socio-economic classes that the middle class children are generally inclined to choose children of their stratum as playmates. What would this finding mean? If we found that the (chosen and the choosers) middle class children live in the same locality and as such are acquainted with one another, this would mean that residential factor is a significant one in determining inter-personal choices. Children belonging to different socio-economic groups usually live in different localities, hence the possibility of contacts between children of different strata is bound to be less. Consequently, the middle class children are understandably not inclined to choose children of other groups as their playmates. Hence, any conclusion that the act of middle class children in not choosing children of other socio-economic or cultural groups is a reflection of prejudice. It would not be a reflection of reality.

This does not however, mean that the element of prejudice as a historical fact is not involved in patterning the choices of children anywhere. For instance, in fact the segregation of people of different creeds, castes and racial stocks, i.e., their living in separate communities/localities may in part, be attributed to prejudice.

Sociometric techniques constitute an integral part of the efforts of *Moreno* and associates at propounding a mature behavioural theory of inter-personal relations. The sociometric techniques acquire their distinctive character from this theory. But a few researchers may be tempted to misuse these techniques. John Madge[3] has sounded an explicit caution bearing upon this possibility.

The tendency to ignore other kinds of data and to ascribe a special empirical status to sciometric data may retard motivation to introduce measure necessary for a fruitful and wider application of sociometry. *Lindzey and Borgatta* contend that there has been very little in the way of systematic, theoretically derived research aimed at exploring the kinds of conditions and variables related to sociometic response.[4]

The relative lack of systematic and cumulative investigations is rooted in the tendency to rely solely upon the sociometic measures: Thus far, sociometric studies have been confined mostly to educational and institutional groups, while other pertinent groups have not been investigated sociometrically.

Multivariate conception of the nature of inter-personal relation may hopefully lead to research that will be of basic importance to the understanding of group process. Besides, such systematic research would promote greater understanding of the sociometric instruments. Lack of concern for linking of the formulations to empricial data (characteristic of *Moreno*) has had the effect probably of deterring a more cautious and persistent approach to relations between theory and sociometric data. *Leeman* has presented base-line mathematical model to represent sociometric choice which may lead to a more systematic approach to sociometric data.

Again, the sociometric investigators have paid scant attention to the criterion of sociometric questions. The importance of selecting an appropriate criterion for sociometric analyses has been emphasized time and again. Relevant here is the distinction between 'essential' and 'auxiliary' criteria (proposed by *Moreno*), the essential criteria being those that refer to central activity under study. Crisswell has distinguished between 'one-way' and 'two-way' sociometric questions while *Jennings* suggests a distinction between 'Psyche' and 'Socio' group. These distinctions need to be stressed since a failure to select the criterion carefully does affect the quality of data adversely and such data may not lend themselves to analysis of any consequence.

The question of what the choices under various criteria mean, as also, of the kinds of variable that can best be measured through the use of certain criteria, are questions that rightly deserve careful consideration and yet have often been neglected. One of the objections raised in this connection is that the investigator employing sociometry does not often know what a choice means for the subject. This objection refers to the questions of relevance of various criteria for providing data in regard to particular dimensions.

The demand that the investigator should "know" what a response actually means to every subject is not very proper; the important things, however, is the extent to which an order imposed upon subjects on the basis of response can be related to pertinent independent measures.

Despite the phenomenal advances made in the analysis of sociometic data in the last few decades, characteristic flaws still persist, the most serious of these being the "tendency to capitalize illegitimately upon chance-variation" and to treat such variations as socially significant.[5]

'Near sociometric' and 'quasi-sociometric' studies which are ramifications of the 'pure' sociometric studies, have also been conducted quite fruitfully in situations where strict conformity to the requirements of 'pure' sociometric studies is beset with practical problems. Sociometric self-rating, group participation scale, multirelational sociometric survey and 'Guess who techniques' etc. are some of the methodological devices, quite similar to the sociometric tests.

REFERENCES

(1) See Goode and Hatt: *op. cit.,* pp. 249, 50.

(2) Cf Young: *op.cit.,* p. 355.

(3) Madge: *op.cit.,* p. 233.

(4) See Lindzey, Gardner (Ed.) : *Handbook of Social Psychology,* Addison Company, New York, 1953, Chapter 'Sociometric', Vol. II.

(5) *Ibid.*

Chapter XVI

The Case Study Method

The method of exploring and analyzing the life of a social unit/entity, be it a role-incumbent (person), a family, an institution or a community, is customarily known as case study method. The aim of case study method is to locate or identify the factors that account for the behaviour patterns of a given unit, and its relationship with the environment. The case data are always gathered with a view to tracing the natural history of the social unit, and its relationship with the social factors and forces operative and involved in its surrounding milieu. In sum, the social researcher tries, by means of the case study method, to understand the complex of factors that are working within a social unit as an integrated totality. Looked at from another angle, the case study serves the purpose similar to the clue-providing function of expert opinion. It is most appropriate when one is trying to find clues and ideas for further research.

Burgress has highlighted the special potency of the case materials for understanding complex behaviour and situations in specific detail. He refers to these data as a social microscope.

The major credit for introducing case study method to the field of social investigation must go to Fredrick *Leplay*. The English social philosopher, *Herbert Spencer,* was among the first to use case materials in his comparative studies of different cultures. *William*

Healey, resorted to the case study method in his study of juvenile delinquency. *Healey* realized that the problem of juvenile delinquency was too complex to be understood simply on the basis of available statistical data. Hence, he declared himself in favour of the case study method which afforded a deeper and rounded understanding of the phenomenon. Anthropologists and ethnologists interested in the systematic description and study of the primitive as well as modern cultures have liberally utilized the case study method. Cora Dubois, Robert Redfield and Oscar Lewis, to mention some of the prominent names, have liberally employed the case study method. Historians have resorted to this method for portraying some historical character or a particular historical period and describing the developments within a national community. Many a novelist and dramatist has used some semblance of the case study method for presenting a word picture of characters.

The case study method received the necessary impetus and recognition as a systematic field-research technique in sociology with the well-known study, "The Polish Peasant" by Thomas and Znaniecki. In the course of this study, made extensive use of life history documents and made them their chief instrument in reaching out to the actual experiences and attitudes of individuals and groups as well as in securing "a cross-section of the entire process of their social becoming."[1] They scrutinized a large number of personal diaries, letters, autobiographies and other types of case materials with a view to getting at the concrete details of the individual and collective behaviour of persons in a given cultural context. Thomas and Znaniecki aimed at reconstructing a chronologically continuous and complete word-picture of the feelings of individuals subjected to particular experiences, of their ideas about the relations they have with others and the impact of these on them. Thomas and Znaniecki maintain that the case data constitute 'the perfect type of sociological material' in so far as they represent a more enlightening and fundamentally more reliable record of personal experiences, with a wealth of concrete detail, vivid memories, tension situations, and multifarious reactions to social situations which would escape the attention of the most skilled investigators using other techniques.

Thomas and Znaniecki contend that the social science has to resort to the use of data other than the case-history or life history simply because of the practical difficulty in securing, at the moment, a sufficient number of such records encompassing the totality of sociological problems and the enormous amount of work involved in an adequate analysis of all the personal data necessary to fully characterize the life of a social group. In India, quite a few monographs on rural and tribal communities have resorted to the case study method.

Social scientists ultimately aim at some kind of generalization or theory-building. Whether the case data can be regarded as sufficiently typical or representative affording a secure basis for theory-construction is a question that has been plaguing the social scientists for quite some time. The issue has been a subject of controversy among the social researchers. Hence, it is important to thrash out the question whether the materials offered by case history may be considered an adequate basis for generalizing with respect to the category of cases that the particular case under study represents.

Stouffer, Kinsey and *Adorno* among others, have had occasion to study a large number of cases. These social scientists found a remarkable uniformity among independently conducted studies of large groupings in different socio-cultural and temporal contexts. The opinions of Stouffer, Kinsey etc., in regard to the reasonably high generalizability afforded by case data are in tune with those of Thomas and Znaniecki. Anthropologist Franz Boas too, on the basis of his several case studies of the 'primitive' groups, came to the conclusion that human nature anywhere is of one piece.

But, the fact of uniformity among cases does not warrant the conclusion that the cases under study are the typical representatives of the larger category of cases they were drawn from. It is indeed improper to overstress the element of uniformity since the similarity among cases hardly, if ever, extends to all the dimensions there are to life.

While human behaviour may vary according to situations, it is usually possible to identify the 'basic' human nature in the midst of such variations. This is the assumption that underlies collection of case data. All human beings experience certain physiological tension; certain experiences are ubiquitous, e.g., birth, death, sex drive, fatigue, etc. As *DuBois* an anthropologist, rightly points out, that the comparative studies of personalities as determined by variations in culture are possible simply because of certain basic homogeneity or similarity evidenced in mankind. Psychologist *G.W. Allport* contends that some statements about human nature broadly apply to each individual or to each member of a larger group. As such there does not appear to be any reason why a quest for identifying the innate human tendencies cannot capitalize on personal case data.

Various media and techniques have been utilized by researchers in the course of certain excellent case studies, they managed to turn out. *Nels Anderson,* who conducted a case study of the 'Hobos', got to know about their inner lives through the medium of their poetry, folk-songs, ballads and other cultural manifestations. *Anderson* collected their photographs published in journals and newspapers. He also collected from several institutions the statistical and other types of information about life of the *Hobos,* collecting relevant bits of information from such diverse sources, Anderson could offer a systematic account of the inner life of the Hobos and the practical ethics of their organization. *Warner* and associates have, in the course of their case studies entitled. The *Yankee City Series,* made use of various methods and techniques of data collection. Personal interview, observation, questionnaire, statistical records, etc., were the diverse means employed by them. In sum, various researchers have employed a number of different means and techniques to get at data substantiating, supplementing and verifying the information gained through the case study method.

The specific method of case study would depend upon wit, commonsense and imagination of the person doing the case study. The investigator makes up his procedure as he goes along. Saturating oneself in the situations is very important. Some anthropologists believe that case studies of less than several year's duration are likely to be misleadingly superficial. Bronislaw Malinowski, a doyen among anthropologists, gives a vivid argument on this point.

"Living in village with no other business but to follow native life, one sees the customs, ceremonies and traditions over and over again, one has examples of their beliefs as they are actually lived through and full body and blood of actual native life fills out soon the skeleton of abstract constructions. That is the reason why working under such conditions, the ethnographer is enabled to add something essential to the bare outline of tribal constitution, and to supplement it by all the details of behaviour, setting and small incident." [2]

Let us now turn to discuss the criteria for evaluating the adequacy of the case history or life history which is of central import for case study. *John Dollard* has proposed seven criteria for evaluating such adequacy. [3]

These are as follows :

(1) The subject must be viewed as a specimen in a cultural series. That is, the case drawn out from its total context for the purposes of study must be considered a member of the particular cultural group or community. The scrutiny of the life histories of persons must be done with a view to identifying the community values, standards and their shared way of life.

(2) The organic motors of action must be socially relevant. That is, the action of the individual cases must be viewed as a series of reaction to social stimuli or situation. In other words, the social meaning of behaviour must be taken into consideration.

(3) The strategic role of the family group in transmitting the culture must be recognized. That is, in as much as the individual case is a member of a family, the role of the family in shaping his behaviour must never be overlooked.

(4) The specific method of elaboration of organic material onto social behaviour must be clearly shown. That is, case histories that portray in detail how basically a biological organism, the man, gradually blossoms forth into a social person, are especially fruitful.

(5) The continuous, related character of experience from childhood through adulthood must be stressed. In other words, the life history must be a *Gestalt* or configuration depicting the inter-relationships between the person's various experiences. Such a Gestalt affords a comprehensive understanding of a person's life as a continuum.

(6) The 'social situation' must be carefully and continuously specified as a factor. One of the important criteria for the life history is that a person's life must be shown as unfolding itself in the context of and partly owing to, specific social situations.

(7) The life history material itself must be organized according to some conceptual framework, this in turn would facilitate generalizations at a higher level.

The criteria just discussed stress the specific chain of coordinated, related continuous and configurated experiences in a cultural pattern which motivate social and personal behaviour. The criteria laid down by *Dollard* are principally perfect but some of these are hard to materialize and to be translated into practice.

Dollard tried to articulate the diverse events depicted in the life histories of persons in the course of repeated interviews, utilizing psychoanalytical techniques in particular situational contexts. His criteria of life history emanate directly from this experience. While the life histories have their independent importance as research documents, the interviews of their writers can afford, as Dollard observes, rich insights into the nature of the social situations experienced by them.

A person's life is quite complex indeed. There is till date no technique that can bring in some kind of uniformity and consequently, ensure the cumulativeness of case history materials by disentangling the complex totality that is human life. But although case data are not amenable to rigorous analysis, a skilful handling and interpretation of such data may help developing insights into cultural conflicts and problems born out of culture change.

Gordon Allport has suggested the following with a view to broadening our perspective in relation to case data.[4]

(1) If the life history has been written in the first person, it must be as complete and coherent as possible.

(2) Life histories should have been written for knowledgeable persons. That is, if the enquiry is sociological, the writer should write it on the assumption that its readers will be sociologists.

(3) It is advisable to supplement case data by observational, statistical and historical data since these provide standards for assessing the reliability and consistency of the case materials. Besides, such data afford a basis for generalizations.

(4) Efforts should be made to ascertain the reliability of life history data by examining the internal consistency of the material, repeat interviews with the person and personal interviews with the members of the subject's own group who are well acquainted with him.

(5) A judicious combination of techniques of data collection is a prerequisite for securing data that are culturally meaningful and scientifically significant.

(6) Life histories or case histories can be regarded as an adequate basis for generalization to the extent that these are representative or typical of a particular group.

The researcher engaged in the collection of case data cannot afford to ignore the unique or atypical cases. He should take account of them as exceptions. As *Thomas* points out, there is no sharp line of division separating the normal from the abnormal in concrete human life.

Case histories are replete with valuable information of a personal private nature. This information helps the researcher to portray not only the personality of the person and the social situation impinging upon him but also in formulating relevant hypotheses. Though critical of documentary materials generally, Blummer gives the credit due to them by pointing out that the personal documents afford an opportunity for the researcher to develop his spirit of inquiry. The researcher can conduct a more effective analysis of a particular aspect if he has acquired an intimate acquaintance with it by means of personal documents. Blummer does not, at the same time, lose sight of the limitations of the personal documents. He points out that independently, these documents hardly fulfill the criteria of reliability, adequacy and representativeness, but to exclude them from any scientific study of human life will be a blunder in as much as these documents are necessary and significant both for theory building and practice.

Despite the formidable limitations case data suffer from, these are used, not infrequently, by sociologists, psychologists, industrial psychologists, psychiatrists and anthropologists. In so far as the effectiveness of psychiatric diagnoses and treatment depend on the case studies, psychologists have laid heavy stress on a deep-going and comprehensive study of person's lives. Gordon Allport has recommended in strong terms the use of case data.

The knowledge of particulars is truly the beginning of codified knowledge. It is out of our acquaintance of the concrete persons that the desire to know nature and understand its springs is born. The first step is to understand the concrete individuals and all the complexity of their nature. If we are in haste about analyzing and classifying, we shall be running the risk of cutting down the emotional anchorages, organizations and natural identifications characterising the personal life of an individual may not be adequately represented. Hence, the psychologist must understand life as it is being lived.

On this view, the totality of life processes that is reflected in the well-ordered life history documents is invaluable in stimulating insights. The life history documents that afford a basis for comparisons contributing to statistical generalizations and drawing of inferences about the uniformities in human behaviour are indeed of great value. There is no provision of ordered data about personal lives of people that rightly comprise the basis of the psychological science. The final aim of science is to understand, control and make predictions about human life and to the extent this expectation of science is borne out by the personal documents in terms of preparing the ground for psychiatric treatment, the theoretical and practical importance of personal documents should be considered as beyond doubt.

A case may be considered the gateway to and at the same time the final destination of abstract knowledge. It is the interpretations of the peculiar and the concrete that contribute to the continual growth of abstract knowledge.

In 1929, *Read Bain* vigorously attacked the value and validity of case life history materials as significant scientific data. It was Bain's contention that these materials do not provide knowledge of the "impersonal, universal, non-ethical, non-practical, repetitive aspects of phenomena."[5]

The foregoing remarks to Bain point to some of the major deficiencies of the life history data. The "subject", says Bain, "may write what he thinks the investigator wants.... The greater the 'rapport' the (greater the subjectivity).... The subject is more likely to be self-justificatory than factual (characterized by) over and under-statement, convenient forgetting and (fantasy).... Case situations are seldom comparable.... in a pluralistic universe of discourse.... Since the subject tells history in his own words, logical concepts, units of scientific classification, have to be read into it or out of it by the investigator."[6]

Prof. Bain has since his initial objection, changed considerably his stand vis-à-vis the case study research. In his subsequent modified stance. Bain states that most of the dangers (see his remarks above) will be avoided as a matter of routine by those who are well-trained in the modern methods of collecting such materials and in the scientific techniques of assembling, classifying and processing data. The case data according to Bain are useful for diagnosis, therapy and other practical case problems. Case studies and life histories, he says, are an aspect of idiographic research and thus, a necessary prerequisite for any nomothetic (abstract) science.

Bain concedes that, by and large, case study affords fruitful hypotheses as also the data which may be useful in testing them and that without these, generalized social science would be handicapped.

Tremendous improvements in the techniques of case studies have been registered during the past few decades. *Elton Mayo, Alfred Kinsey, Carl Rogers* and *M. Komarovsky* are some of the researchers who have used the new techniques of collection, recording and processing case data.

During the last few decades, case study techniques have shown a steady trend toward formalization, that is, case studies can now be conducted in such a manner that the data are amenable to quantification and statistical treatment. Case study techniques have become indispensable for therapeutic and administrative purposes. The materials collected by research-minded social workers can be very useful of 'pure' or 'basic' research. It should be remembered, however, that the social caseworker's orientation is substantially different from that of a social researcher. The social researcher, is primarily interested in comparable case data and persistently searches for similarities or uniformities that enable him to classify or analyse data to formulate ultimately the law of their occurrences and relationship. He does not regard specific case situations as a sufficient basis for understanding human behaviour; rather he views the cases under study as the possible examples of a line of reasoning by which the researcher might be enabled to develop new concepts or theories or test the existing conceptual schemes.

REFERENCES

(1) Young: *op. cit.*, p. 231.

(2) Simmon J.L.: *op. cit.*, p. 272.

(3) Dollard, J.: *Criteria for the Life History*, Yale University Press, 1935, pp. 8-31.

(4) Cf. Young: *op. cit.*, pp. 261-62.

(5) *Ibid.*, p. 262.

(6) *Ibid.*

Chapter XVII

Sampling : Method and Techniques

In this chapter, we shall be addressing ourselves to an important problem concerning the practical formulation of social research. This problem relates to the estimation of certain characteristics of a 'universe' or 'population' on the basis of a study of the characteristics of a portion (or a sample) of it. The method consisting of the selecting for study, a portion of the 'universe' with a view to drawing conclusions about the 'universe' or 'population' is known as sampling.

Sampling, however, is not typical of sciences only. In a way, we frequently practise in our day-to-day lives some crude versions of sampling. The housewives, for example, press a few pods of boiled rice in the cooking pot to be able to declare that it is ready to be served. Understandably it is not feasible to examine each and every grain in the pot, and more important, doing so is not necessary either. Our day-to-day experience testifies to the fact that, by and large, it is possible to make some kind of a general statement about the 'universe' by observing only a few items or elements, i.e., a sample drawn therefrom. Statistical sampling thus, is only a methodological version of our everyday experience and quite commonly employed procedure. A statistical sample ideally purports to be a miniature model or replica of the collectivity or the 'population' constituted of all the items that the study should principally encompass, that is, the items which potentially hold promise of affording information relevant to the purpose of a given research.

A.L. Bowley, whose pioneering work on sampling statistics in the realm of social sciences won him academic and official recognition in the early twenties of the last century, arrived at certain conclusions about the 'universe' of his study by resorting to the method of sampling. Bowley sampled out for his study, one family for each group of twenty families. His conclusions, based on the sample were found to be to a considerable extent consistent with the subsequent findings of *Charies Booth* and *B.S. Rowntree* who worked on a much more comprehensive canvas. Bowley's work demonstrated very clearly that the sampling technique effecting, as it typically did, considerable economies of time, money and effort, also afforded worthwhile conclusions. The use of sampling in social sciences has steadily increased ever since. During the last few decades, sampling techniques have assumed great importance.

As was stated at the opening of the chapter, a sample is a portion, selected from the 'Population' or 'Universe.' The terms *'Population'* and *'Universe'* have been used here in a very specific sense. 'Population' is not necessarily synonymous with a population of a community or a state. 'Population' in the manner it is used in sampling statistics is constituted of all the individuals, things, events, documents or observations (on a single or many individuals) etc., belonging to a designated category characterising specific attributes which a particular study should principally cover. The 'population' or the 'universe' of a study dealing, for instance, with 'the views of college students of 'X' city about co-education', will consist of all the students studying in various classes in the colleges of the city.

A 'population' contains 'sub-populations.' Thus, the female college students in the city form a 'sub-population' or a stratum of the 'population' consisting of the entire college students of the city. A sub-population or a stratum may be defined by one or more specifications that divide a 'population' into mutually exclusive sections or strata consisting of (a) colleges, and (b) girl students in women's colleges and male students from colleges meant for males only. A single unit or member of the 'population' is referred to as a population element.

It is well to take heed of an important issue raised by *J.L. Simon.*[1] Sample for him is a collection of observations for which one has data with which he/she is going to work. Almost any set of observations for which one has data constitutes a sample.

Every sample principally corresponds to a 'Population' or 'Universe' behind it. But 'Universe' is typically harder to define because it is often an imaginary concept. A universe may be said to be a collection of things or people that one would like to say, his sample was selected from. A universe can be finite or infinite and ill-defined. Infinite universes are harder to understand and it is often difficult to decide which universe is appropriate for a given purpose. For instance, if we are interested in studying a sample of homicides, the issue to decide or settle is which universe the sample comes from. Depending on our objectives, the appropriate universe might be all homicides now living or it might be all homicides who might ever live. The latter concept of homicides is imaginary since some of the items in the universe do not exist. It is infinite too. Those not agreeing with this notion of universe, would be inclined to regard it not as the collection of people/objects that they would say the sample was drawn from, but the collection from which the sample was actually drawn. This view equates the universe to the sampling frame which is an empirical representation of the theoretic universe in which one is interested. The sampling frame is always finite and existential. The former notion of the universe is pragmatic.

A *'census'* refers to a count or a study of all of the elements in the 'population.' As is quite obvious it is generally more economical in time, efforts and money to get the desired information for only some of the elements (sample) than for all of them, i.e., the population. When we select some of elements (sample) with the intention of finding out something about the 'population' from which they are taken, we refer to that sub-group of elements as a 'sample.' Our expectation, in studying the sample, is of course, that what we find out from the sample, will be true of the 'population' as a whole. Actually this may not be the case, since after all, a sample is only a part of the 'population.'

How far would the information or finding we get from the sample, approximate the finding we would get if the totality, i.e., the given 'population', were studied and whether or not our finding based on the study of a sample is likely to differ from the finding that we would get if the given 'population' as a whole was studied, by more than a specific margin, would depend greatly on the way sample is selected.

Of course, we can never have the full assurance that our sample returns reflect the state of the 'population' with respect to the characteristics we are studying, unless we have simultaneously conducted a complete comparable study of the 'population' (in which case the very purpose of and gains accruing from sampling would be nullified). We can, however, devise sampling plans which if properly executed, can guarantee that if we were to repeat a study on a number of different samples, each of the same size, drawn from the given 'population', our findings would not differ from the true findings which we would get if the given 'population' as a whole were studied, by more than a specified value in at least a specified proportion of samples drawn from the population. That is, it is possible to devise a sampling plan about which we can have a good measure of confidence — that the findings based on our sample of a given size drawn from a given 'population' will not differ or deviate from the 'true' finding, i.e., the 'population' — finding by more than a certain value, so that a tolerably reliable picture of the state of affairs in the population can be had from the sample-findings.

In actual practice, however, we do not go on repeating the study, i.e., go on recording responses or measurements for the same set of items on an indefinite number of samples drawn from the given 'population.' But the mathematical knowledge of what would happen in repeated studies on these samples, enables us to infer that with a given sample there is a probability that a certain proportion of estimates based on samples drawn from a population will be close to the population value, i.e., true value (i.e., will not deviate far from this value) and thus give out a reasonably good or dependable estimate of the population value which is the true value.

For a researcher who decides to study a sample with the intention, naturally of arriving at a reliable estimate about the 'population', it is very important that he should be able to say with a substantial measure of confidence that his sample-finding/estimate closely approximates the 'true', i.e., population finding; otherwise studying a sample will have no meaning. As was stressed earlier, a sample is studied with a view to drawing conclusions about the 'population' or 'universe' that the sample is assumed to represent. Thus, the measure of confidence that the researcher would like to place in his sample findings must be 'substantial.' This means that the probability of the sample finding being a reliable indicator of the 'true' finding, i.e., finding that would have been arrived at, if the 'population' in its entirety were investigated, must be quite high.

A sampling plan for a study is devised largely taking into view the level of accuracy and confidence in the findings of the study. Research projects differ in regard to the levels of aspiration for accuracy of and confidence in their findings (based on study of a sample). A sampling plan which warrants the insurance that the chances are great enough that the selected sample is sufficiently representative of the population to justify our running the risk of taking it as a basis for estimating the characteristics (of researcher's concern) in the population, may be called representative sampling plan. Representative sampling plan is one major strategy employed by scientists to decrease the likelihood of misleading findings.

In social sciences, the measure or level of confidence is conventionally fixed at .95 (i.e., 95%). Quite obviously, no purpose will be served by fixing the level of confidence at .5 (50%) since this would simply amount to saying that there are 50% chances that the sample finding will be a very close approximation of the 'true', i.e., population value and again, that there are 50% chances that the sample value will not be a good estimate of the 'true' value. It is, like saying that there is one chance in two that it will rain and also the same chance that it will not rain. Such an equivocal statement does not have any worthwhile import, for it is so pointless. On the contrary, a 95% *level of confidence* with regard to the sample would lend us assurance that one can safely assume that the sample value will most probably afford a good estimate of the 'true' (population) value; since, 95% level of confidence would mean that the researcher has at this probability or confidence level the assurance that there are 95 chances out of 100 that his sample-finding will be a close estimate of the true finding and conversely, the odds are 5 against 100 that his sample-finding will be a bad estimate of the population findings.

There is another way of looking at this, too. Suppose 100 samples, each of the same size as the one actually selected by the researcher were drawn from a 'population', then 95% *level of confidence* or probability would mean that out of these 100 samples, 95 samples will be good estimates of the 'population' while only the remaining 5 samples will be bad or foul estimates of the population.

Thus, the researcher aiming at 95% level of confidence carries a great deal of assurance that the sample selected will give out findings which will represent the state of affairs (in regard to his specific concerns) in the 'population.' The underlying assumption is, of course, that the researcher's sample belongs to the category of the 95% good samples and not to the 5% bad samples. The researcher's sample happening to belong to the category of the 5% bad samples is a possibility which, however rare, cannot be overlooked. More about this a little later in this chapter.

Before we proceed to discuss the types of sampling design and various sampling procedures involved in implementing designs, it may be helpful to understand in a general way the general advantages and limitations of sampling.

(1) Obviously, a sample can afford an estimate of the characteristics of the population in a much shorter time than would be possible otherwise. This time-saving advantage is especially important for studies of our modern dynamic society which is characterized by rapid changes. Unless shortcut methods, e.g., sampling strategies, are devised for measuring social situations, the measurement is out of date before the study on the 'population' is conducted.

(2) Sampling makes the study much less expensive. Fewer people need to be interviewed. A smaller staff is required to collect, process and tabulate the data. Money saved by sampling procedure may be used to dig out more details about the cases under study and to intensify analysis of data. From the administrative point of view, it is often impossible to conduct a study of the total 'population.' The typical difficulties in such a case relate to hiring of a large staff, the task of training and supervising them, etc.

(3) When small samples are used, it becomes possible to give more attention to each return that is received and to check their accuracy. This contributes significantly to the trustworthiness of tabulations and analysis.

It should be remembered, as was suggested earlier, that sampling in some sense is always employed in all studies, since it is clearly impossible to study all the manifestations of phenomena for all times and places. It is well worth noting that even the census is but a sample of the country's population at a given point of time. No sooner it is taken than it is a sample of the past. Hence, quite so often, there is no alternative to sampling.

Sampling, however, is not without its limitations. Here we may point out the major ones.

Sampling demands exercise of great care and caution, otherwise the results obtained may be incorrect or misleading. When the characteristics to be measured occur only rarely in the population, a very large sample is required to yield cases that will give statistically reliable information about it. Often, small samples hamper analysis of data since there are not enough cases for breakdown tables and sub-classifications.

We may do well to note that complicated sampling plans may in the long run require more than a complete 'population' count. This is particularly true if the sample is a large proportion of the total population and/or if complex weighing procedures are used.

Sampling Designs

The basic distinction in the modern sampling theory is between *Probability sampling* and the *Non-probability sampling*. It would help us to understand the above distinction if we can appreciate the nature and meaning of the concept of *probability*.

The idea of probability or chance arises when one is not sure about something, that is, when one does not have enough information and therefore can only guess. Chance implies uncertainty about the future course of events and about their prediction. Thus, chance is, in a sense, the expression of man's ignorance about the shape of things. *Descartes* suggested, "when it is not in our power to determine what is true, we ought to act in accordance with what is most probable."[3]

A way to appreciate the concept of probability is to view the probability of an event occurring as the proportion of times the event has taken place in the past; usually based on a long series of observations. Underlying the while-collar workers' action of buying insurance is the probability that an adult white-collar worker will not die during the period for which he intends to buy an insurance policy at a specific premium. This, however, cannot be held to be a satisfactory definition of the events which have never or only very rarely occurred in the past and hence one is not in a position to reasonably reckon the proportion of times events occurred one way or the other, in the past.

In fact, we do employ the concept of probability all our lives, while taking all decisions we have ever taken and conclusions ever drawn. We decide to visit a public park with our families on a day and at a time when there is a low probability of the park being too crowded. We bet heavily on hand of cards when there is, we feel, a high probability that we have the best combination. A hospital decides not to expand its bed-capacity when administration feels that the probability of many more hospitalization cases arriving is low.

If someone were to ask us what the outcome of a cricket match will be, there is a chance that we will be wrong, no matter what we have to say for an answer. Whenever the situation is such that there is a chance that you could be wrong because of the uncertainty involved, the concept of probability comes as a help. The concept of probability helps us to answer a question like, "what is the likelihood that 'X' will win the election or 'A' team will win the match?" is illustrative of the concept of probability.

If the chances of an event like victory are 1 (one) in 5, the probability is 1/5 = 0.2; or if the chances are 1 in 100 the probability is 0.01. Similarly, if from a population or universe of 100 cards we wish to draw a sample of 10, by a method like lottery which ensures equal chance of selection to every card, we allow each card representing a number, 10 out of 100 chances of being included in the sample (.1 probability). Those items/members represented by cards would have each, by the same token, 90 out of 100 chances (.9 probability) of being excluded from the sample.

The concept of probability is especially useful when one has selected a sample from the population and wants to know the population (e.g., one wants to know the probability or the degree of likelihood that the average value of a population characteristics, say, income, will not differ from the average income value of the sample by more than a certain amount). The concept of probability also helps us to answer another type of important question, i.e., "What is the probability that the sample was taken from a given universe (so represents it) rather than from some other universe, so that one can safely draw conclusions about the population from the sample evidence?"

The estimation of probability with respect to each item or member in the universe facilitates mathematical determination of the sample-size corresponding to our aspirations in regard to the representativeness of sample finding vis-a-vis universe. We shall deal with this exhaustively, a little later.

We now turn to understand the method of estimating probability.[4] We begin with seeing how the ordinary or unconditional type of probability is estimated; for example, how may the probability of drawing an ace from a pack of playing cards (the pack comprising 52 cards) be estimated?

One possible way of estimating the probability of drawing an ace from pack of cards is based on our experience with playing cards. If we have watched card games casually over a long period of time we might roughly say on the basis of our experience that the probability of an ace coming up is about 1 in 10 or 1 in 15 (The actual mathematical probability is 4 to 52.)

Similarly we might make an estimate based on experience as to the probability that two cards of the same denomination (e.g., two aces) will turn up in the same hand of three cards dealt from a card pack. General information and experience are also the source for estimating the probability that a particular team will win the soccer tomorrow or that drought will hit a particular region next year, and so on. In sum, we simply put together all our relevant prior information and experience and put forth a guess.

Another important source of probability estimates is empirical, involving systematic investigation with repeated trials on phenomenon — a frequency series. In the case of estimating the probability of drawing an ace from a pack of cards, the empirical procedure is to shuffle the cards, deal one, record whether or not the card is an ace, replace the card and repeat the steps a lot many times. The proportion of times we observe an ace come up is the probability estimate based on a frequency series. Observation of frequency series might help one to estimate the probability in other contexts.

Yet another source of establishing probability estimates is enumeration, i.e., counting the probabilities. For instance, by examination of a common die we can understand that there are six different possible numbers that can come up when the die is cast. We can then determine that the probability of getting a 1 (one), say, is 1/6 and that of getting a one and a two is 2/6 (1/3) because two of the total six possibilities are a combination of one and two. We can by the same token, determine that when rolling two dice, there are two possibilities of getting two sixes (one from each die) out of thirty-six possibilities (i.e., a probability of 2 out of 36 or 1/18). It should be noted that determination of probabilities by this method, i.e., by counting, is possible if only two conditions are present, viz., firstly, the totality of possibilities is known hence limited, and secondly, the probability of each particular probability is known (the probability of all sides of the die surfacing is equal, i.e., 1/6).

Probability estimates can be established through mathematical calculation, too. If we know by other means that the probability of a spade coming up is 1/4 and the probability of an ace of spade coming up is 1/52 (1/4 x 1/13). If we know that the probability of spade coming is 1/4 and that of diamond 1/4, then we can calculate that the probability of getting a spade or a diamond will be 1/2 (i.e., 1/4 + 1/4). What is important here is not so much the particular calculation procedures but the fact that one can often calculate the desired probability on the basis of already known probabilities. It is possible to estimate probabilities by mathematical calculation only if we know by other means the probabilities of some related events. It is not possible, therefore, to mathematically determine the probability of a tribal boy picking up a couple of words correctly from our dialect. Understandably, some empirical knowledge is necessary to help one estimate this.

The concept of probability is especially useful when one has selected a sample from the 'population' and wants to know the probability of the degree of likeness between the sample and the population (i.e., one wants to know the probability of the degree of likelihood that the average value of a population characteristic, say, income, will not differ from the average (income) value of the sample characteristic by more than a certain amount). The concept of probability also helps us to answer another type of important question, i.e., "what is the probability that the sample was taken from a given universe (so represents it) rather than from some other universe, so that one can safely draw conclusions about the population from the sample-evidence?"

In social science, the most generally used probability statements are of the 'conditional' probability type. A typical conditional probability relates to obtaining of the samples (by chance) if various samples of a given size were taken from a given population say, A. For example, what is the probability of getting a sample of five persons in a row with an income of above Rs. 1,000 p.m., if samples of this size are randomly chosen from the 'population' of persons whose average monthly income is Rs. 1,000? The answer to such a question is given by examination of the frequency series generated by populations like the given population. For example, we write down 'over Rs. 1,000' and 'under Rs. 1,000' respectively on a large number of equal-sized cards and put them into a basket. We then draw five cards by a lottery method several items and see how often the five cards drawn are all over Rs. 1,000. This is the *'Monte Carlo Method'* of estimating probabilities.

Another way of answering such a conditional probability question is by mathematical calculation. For example, if half the cards in the basket have numbers below Rs. 1,000 and half of them, over Rs. 1,000, the probability of getting five cards marked above Rs. 1,000 in a row is 1 in 2^5, i.e., $1/2^5$ (1/32) or 0.321.

The social science researcher has to resort to probability statistics when having posed a scientific question about the nature of the social world he marshalls data that do not lend any clear-cut support to a certain conclusion and, at this stage, he does not want to or cannot collect more data. The pre-requisite to using probability statistics is to translate the scientific question into a statistical one. One must, of course, know in certain terms, what probability he wants to determine, before he is in a position to pose a probability (statistical) version of a scientific question.

For example, if a researcher starts with a question, "Does a particular vitamin arrest chances of boldness?" and administers the vitamin to ten persons and does not do so to other ten persons who are similar to the first group of ten in relevant respects. His sample thus comprises only 20 people and he may not for practical reasons want to have a large sample. If it is seen during the experiment that eight out of ten 'vitamin' people do not show increased baldness while six out of the ten 'non-vitamin' persons show signs of increasing baldness, what is the conclusion? Does the vitamin arrest chances of baldness?

One way to translate the above question into a statistical probability question is to ask, "Do the 'vitamin' persons belong to the same universe as the 'non-vitamin' people?" In other words, the researcher is asking whether the 'vitamin' persons have the same chances of developing baldness as the 'non-vitamin' persons. This boils down simply to asking "Whether the vitamin has bettered the chances of those (against baldness) who took it and has thus removed them from the original universe characterized by its original chances of baldness." The original universe to which the non-vitamin persons must still belong is the 'bench-mark' universe. Subsequently, the researcher may put up a bench-mark hypothesis (null hypothesis) that the vitamin still has the same chance of resisting baldness as the 'non-vitamin' persons. Thus, asking the question "Whether vitamin arrests the chances of baldness" is the same thing as asking whether persons who take 'vitamin' belong to the same universe as the 'non-vitamin' persons or belong to a different universe which now has different chances of developing baldness.

The Probability Sampling Design

The essential characteristic of probability sampling as should be clear from the foregoing discussion on the concept of probability, is that one can specify for each element of the population the probability or the statistical chance of its being included in the sample. In the simplest case, each of the elements has the same or equal probability of being included in the sample, and conversely, of being excluded from the sample. This, however, is not a necessary condition; what is necessary is that for each element there must be some specifiable probability that it will be included in the sample.

Probability sampling is the only approach that makes possible the formulation of determinable representative sampling plans. That is, the investigator, if he used probability sampling, can estimate the size of a sample (or sizes of various components of complex sample) that he will need if he does not want the sample to differ by more than a specified amount from the finding or result that a study of total population would yield. We shall now discuss the major versions of probability sampling.

(i) Simple Random Sample

Simple random sampling is in a sense, the basic theme of all scientific sampling. It is the primary probability sampling design. Indeed, all other methods of scientific sampling are variations of the simple random sampling. An understanding of any of the refined or complex variety of sampling procedure presupposes an understanding of simple random sampling. A simple random sample is selected by a process that not only gives to each element in the population an equal chance of being included in the sample but also makes the selection of every possible combination of cases in the desired sample size, equally likely. Suppose, for example, that one has a population of six children, *viz.*, A, B, C, D, E and F. There will be the following possible combinations of cases, each having two elements from this population, viz., AB, AC, AD, AE, AF, BC, BD, BE, BF, CD, CE, EF, DE, DF, and EF, i.e., in all 15 combinations. If we write each combination on equal sized cards, put the cards in a basket, mix them thoroughly and let a blind-folded person pick one, each of the cards will be afforded the same chance of being selected/included in the sample. The two cases (the pair) written on the card picked up by the blind-folded person thus, will constitute the desired simple random sample. If one wishes to select simple random samples of three cases from the above population of six cases, the possible samples, each of three cases, will be, ABC, ABD, ABE, ABF, ACD, ACE, ACF, ADE, ADF, BCD, BCE, BCF, BDE, BDF, BEF, CDE, CDF, CEF, and DEF, i.e., 20 combinations in all. Each of these combinations will have an equal chance of selection in the sample. Using the same method, one can select a simple random sample of four cases from this population.

In principle, one can use this method for selecting random samples of any size from a population. But in practice, it would become a very cumbersome and in certain cases an impossible task to list out all possible combinations of the desired number of cases. The very same result may be obtained by selecting individual elements, one by one, using the above method (lottery) or by using a book of random numbers.

The book of tables comprising list of random numbers is named after *Tippet* who was first to translate the concept of randomness into a book of random numbers. This book is prepared by a very complicated procedure in such a manner that the numbers do not show any evidence of systematic order, that is, no one can estimate the number following, on the basis of the preceding number and *vice-versa*. Let us discuss the two methods of drawing a simple random sample.

Lottery Method

This method involves the following steps: (a) Each member or item in the 'population' is assigned a unique number. That is, no two members have the same number, (b) Each number is noted on a separate card or a chip. Each chip or card should be similar to all the others with respect to weight, size and shape, etc., (c) The cards or chips are placed in a bowl and mixed thoroughly, (d) A blind-folded person is asked to pick up any chip or card from the bowl. Under these circumstances, the probability of drawing any one card can be expected to be the same as the probability of drawing any other card. Since each card represents a member of the population, the probability of selecting each would be exactly the same. If after selecting a card (chip) it was replaced in the bowl and the contents again thoroughly mixed, each chip would have an equal probability of being selected on the second, fourth, or nth drawing. Such a procedure would ultimately yield a simple random sample.

Selecting Sample with the Help of Random Numbers

We have already said what random numbers are. These numbers help to avoid any bias (unequal chances) to items comprising a population, of being included in the sample in selecting the sample. These random numbers are so prepared that they fulfill the mathematical criterion of complete randomness. Any standard book on statistics contains a few pages of random numbers. These numbers are generally listed in columns on consecutive pages. Following is a portion of a set of random numbers:

42827	70203	78569	60281
41519	84612	30877	37989
39273	91905	33891	31641
48225	65290	85998	11528
56506	27841	56560	28947
29280	51213	96336	79288
73184	26689	05928	65869
52677	23027	51511	87251

The use of the tables of random numbers involves the following steps: (a) Each member of the population is assigned a unique number. For example, one member may have the number 77 and another 83, etc. (b) The table of random numbers is entered at some random point (with a blind mark on any page of the book of tables) and the cases whose numbers come up as one moves from this point down the column are included in the sample until the desired number of cases is obtained. Suppose our population consists of five hundred elements and we wish to draw fifty cases as a sample. Suppose we use the last three digits in each number of five digits (since the universe size is 500, i.e., three-digital). We proceed down the column starting with 42827; but since we have decided to use only three digits (say the last three), we start with 827 (ignoring the first two digits). We now note each number less than 501 (since the population is of 500). The sample would be taken to consist of the elements of the population bearing the numbers corresponding to those chosen. We stop after we have selected 50 (the size decided by us) elements. On the basis of the above section of the table, we shall be choosing 12 numbers corresponding to those chosen. We shall choose 12 cases corresponding to the numbers 237, 225, 280, 184, 203, 190, 213, 027, 336, 281, 288, 251.

Characteristics of Simple Random Sample

We shall start by considering one very important property of the simple random samples; this being, that larger the size of the sample, the more likely it is that its mean (average value) will be close to the 'population' mean, i.e., the true value. Let us illustrate this property by supposing a population comprising six members (children). Let the ages of these children be respectively: A=2 years, B=3 years, C=4 years, D=6 years, E=9 years and F=12 years. Let us draw random samples of one, two, three four and five members each from this population and see how in each case, the sample means (averages) behave with reference to the true 'population' mean (i.e., 2+3+4+6+9+12 = 36/6 = 6). Table following illustrates the behaviour of the sample means as associated with the size of the sample.

Table showing the possible samples of one, two, three, four and five elements (children, from the population of six children of ages *2, 3, 4, 6, 9* and *12* years respectively):

A Samples of 1 case each		*B Samples of 2 case each*		*C Samples of 3 case each*		*D Samples of 4 case each*		*E Samples of 5 case each*	
Sample	*Mean*	*Sample*	*Mean*	*Sample*	*Mean*	*Sample*	*Mean*	*Sample*	*Mean*
2	2	2,3	2.5	2,3,4	3	2,3,4,6	3.8	2,3,4,6,9	4.8
3	3	2,4	3.0	2,3,6	3.7	2,3,4,9	4.2	2,3,4,6,12	5.4*
4	4	3,4	3.5	2,4,6	4.0	2,3,6,9	5.0*	2,3,4,9,12	6.0*
6	6*	2,6	4.0	3,4,6	4.3	2,3,4,12	5.2*	2,3,6,9,12	6.4*
9	9	3,6	4.5	2,3,9	4.7	2,4,6,9	5.2*	2,4,6,9,12	6.6*
12	12	4,6	5.0*	2,4,9	5.0*	3,4,6,9	5.5*	3,4,6,9,12	6.8*
		2,9	5.5*	3,4,9	5.3*	2,3,6,12	5.8*		
		3,9	6.0*	2,3,12	5.7*	2,4,6,12	6.0*		

	4,9	6.5*	2,6,9	5.7*	3,4,6,12	6.2*	
	2,12	7.0*	2,4,12	6.0*	2,3,9,12	6.5*	
	3,12	7.5	3,9,6	6.0*	2,4,9,12	6.8*	
	6,9	7.5	3,4,12	6.3*	3,4,9,12	7.0*	
	4,12	8.0	4,6,9	6.3*	2,6,9,12	7.2	
	6,12	9.0	2,6,12	6.7*	3,6,9,12	7.5	
	9,12	10.5	3,6,12	7.0*	4,6,9,12	7.8	
			4,6,12	7.3			
			2,9,12	7.7			
			3,9,12	8.0			
			4,9,12	8.3			
			6,9,12	9.0			
36/6 = 6	90/15 = 6		120/20 = 6		90/15 = 6		36/6 = 6
17% +	33% +		50% +		67% +		83% +

* Indicates that the sample mean does not differ or deviate by more than one unit from the population mean (which is 6 years).

\+ Indicates percentage of sample means which deviate by not more than one unit from the population mean.

In the given table, all possible random samples of various sizes (i.e., 1, 2, 3, 4 and 5) and their corresponding means are shown. The true (population) mean is 6 years. This mean can of course be calculated by adding up the mean-values of the total combinations of the elements in the population for any given sample size. In the table we see, for example, that for the sample size of three elements there are 20 possible combinations of elements, each combination having an equal chance of being selected as a sample according to the principle of probability. Adding up the mean-values of these possible combinations shown in the table, we get the total score of 120. The mean will be 120 ÷ 20 = 6, which is also, of course, the population mean. This holds good for other columns too.

Let us now examine the table carefully. We shall find that for samples of one element each (column A) there is only one mean-value which does not deviate by more than 1 unit from the true population mean of 6 years. That is, all others, viz., 2, 3, 4, 9 and 12, deviate by more than one unit from the population mean, i.e., 6. As we increase the size of the sample, e.g., in column B, where the sample size is 2, we find a greater proportion of means (averages) that do not deviate from the population mean by more than 1 unit.

The above table shows that for the sample of two, there are 15 possible combinations and hence 15 possible means. Out of these 15 means there are 5 means which do not deviate from the population mean by more than 1 unit. That is, there are 33% of the sample means which are close to the population mean within +1 and –1 units. In column C of the table, we see that there are 20 possible combinations of elements for the sample-size of three elements, each. From out of the 20 possible sample-means, we find that 10, i.e., 50% do not deviate from the population mean by more than 1 unit. For the sample size of four elements, there are 67% of means which are within the range of +1 and –1 unit from the true (population) mean. Lastly, for the sample size of five elements, there are much more, i.e., 83% of such means or estimates. The lesson surfacing out of our observations is quite clear, viz., the larger the sample, the more likely it is that its mean will be close to the population mean.

This is the same thing as saying that the dispersion of estimates (means) decreases as the sample size increases. We can clearly see this in the above table. For the sample size of one (column A) the range of means is the largest, i.e., between 2 and 12 = 10. For the sample size of two the range is between 2.5 and 10.5 = 8. For the sample size of three, four and five, the range of variability of means is respectively 3 to 9 = 6, 3.8 to 7.8 = 4 and 4.8 to 6.8 = 2. It will also be seen from the table that the more a sample mean differs from population-mean the less frequently it is likely to occur.

We can represent this phenomenon relating to simple random sampling clearly with the help of a series of curves showing the relationship between variability of estimates and the size of sample. Let us consider a big population of residents. One can imagine that their ages will range between below 1 year (at the least) and above 80 years (at the most). The normal and reasonable expectation would be that there are lesser cases as one approaches the extremes and that the number of cases goes on increasing progressively and symmetrically as we move away from these extremes. The mean-age of the population is, let us say, 40 years. Such a distribution of residents can be represented by a curve known as the normal or bell-shaped curve (A in the diagram following). Let us now suppose that we take from this population various random samples of different sizes, e.g., 10,100 and 10,000. For any of the sample-size we shall get a very large number of samples from the population. Each of these samples will give us a particular estimate of the population mean. Some of these means will be over-estimates and some under-estimates of the population characteristic (mean or average age). Some means will be very close to it, quite a few rather far. If we plot such sample means for a particular sample-size and join these points we shall in each case, get a normal curve. Different normal curves will thus represent the values of sample-means for samples of different sizes.

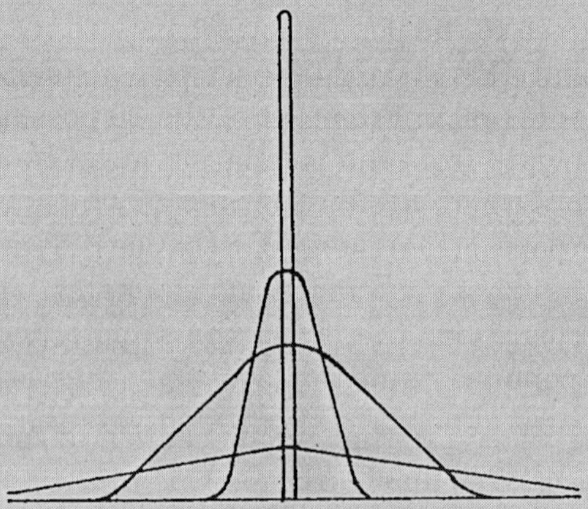

Distribution of Mean-values
For Samples of Different Sizes

A : Normally Distributed Data
B : Estimated Means of Samples of 10
C : Estimated Means of Samples of 100
D : Estimated Means of Samples of 10,000

Fig. 17.1

The above diagram approximates a picture of how the sample-means would behave relative to the size of the sample. The curve A represents the locations of ages of single individuals. The estimated means of samples of 10 individuals, each, from the curve B that shows quite a wide dispersion from true population-mean (40 years). The means of samples of 100 individuals each, form a normal curve C which shows much lesser deviation from the population mean. Finally, the means of the samples of 10,000 from a curve that very nearly approximates the vertical line corresponding to the population mean. The deviation of the values representing curve D from the population mean would be negligible, as is quite evident from the diagram.

It can also be discerned very easily from the above figure that for samples of any given size, the most likely sample-mean is the population-mean. The next most likely are the mean values close to the population mean. Thus, we may conclude that the more a sample mean deviates from the population-mean, the less likely it is to occur. And lastly, we also see what we have already said about the behaviour of the samples, namely, the larger the sample the more likely it is that its mean will be close to the population-mean.

It is this kind of behaviour on the part of the simple random (probability) samples with respect to the mean as well as to proportions and other types of statistics, that makes it possible for us to estimate not only the population-characteristic (e.g., the mean) but also the likelihood that the sample would differ from the true population value by some given amount.

One typical features of the simple random sampling is that when the population is large compared to the sample size (e.g., more than, say, ten times as large), the variabilities of sampling distributions are influenced more by the absolute number of cases in the sample than by the proportion of the population that the sample includes. In other words, the magnitude of the errors likely to arise consequent upon sampling, depends more upon the absolute size of the sample rather than the proportion it bears with the population, that is, on how big or how small a part it is of the population. The larger the size of the random sample, the greater the probability that it will give a reasonably good estimate of the population-characteristic regardless of its proportion compared to the population.

Thus, the estimation of a popular vote at a national poll, within the limits of a tolerable margin of error, would not require a substantially larger sample than the one that would be required for an estimation of population vote in a particular province where poll outcome is in doubt.

To elaborate the point, a sample of 500 (100% sample) will give perfect accuracy if a community had only 500 residents. A sample of 500 will give slightly greater accuracy for a township of 1000 residents than for a city of 10,000 residents. But beyond the point at which the sample is a large portion of the 'universe' there is no appreciable difference in accuracy with the increases in the size of the 'universe.' For any given level of accuracy, identical sample sizes would give same level of accuracy for communities of different population, e.g., ranging from 10,000 to 10 millions. The ratio of the sample-size to the populations of these communities means nothing, although this seems to be important if we proceed by intuition.

Systematic Sampling

This type of sampling is for all practical purposes, an approximation of simple random sampling. It requires that the population can be uniquely identified by its order. For example, the residents of a community may be listed and their names rearranged alphabetically. Each of these names may be given a unique number. Such an index is known as the 'frame' of the population in question. Suppose this frame consists of 1,000 members each with a unique number, i.e., from 1 to 1,000. Let us say, we want to select a sample of 100. We may start by selecting any number between 1 to 10 (both included). Suppose we make a random selection by entering the list and get 7. We then proceed to select members; starting from 7, with a regular interval of 10. The selected to select members; starting from 7, with a regular interval of 10. The selected sample would thus consist of elements bearing Nos. 7, 17, 27, 37, 47, ... 977, 987, 997. These elements together would constitute a systematic sample.

It should be remembered that a systematic sample may be deemed to be a probability sample only if the first case (e.g., 7) has been selected randomly and then every tenth case from the frame was selected thereafter. If the first case is not selected randomly, the resulting sample will not be a probability sample since, in the nature of the case, most of the cases which are not at a distance of ten from the initially chosen number will have a Zero (0) probability of being included in the sample. It should be noted that in the systematic sampling when the first case is drawn randomly, there is, in advance, no limitation on the chances of any given case to be included in the sample. But once the first case is selected, the chances of subsequent cases are decisively affected or altered. In the above example, the cases other than 17, 27, 37, 47... etc., have no chance of being included in the sample. This means that systematic sampling plan does not afford all possible combinations of cases, the same chance of being included in the sample. Thus, the results may be quite deceptive if the cases in the list are arranged in some cyclical order or if the population is not thoroughly mixed with respect to the characteristics under study (say, income or hours of study), i.e., in a way that each of the ten members had an equal chance of getting chosen.

Stratified Random Sampling

In the stratified random sampling, the population is first divided into a number of strata. Such strata may be based on a single criterion (e.g., educational level, yielding a number of strata corresponding to the different levels of educational attainment) or on combination of two or more criteria (e.g., age and sex), yielding strata such as males under 30 years and males over 30 years, females under 30 years and females over 30 years. In stratified random sampling, a simple random sample is taken from each of the strata and such sub-samples are brought together to form the total sample.

In general, stratification of the universe for the purpose of sampling contributes to the efficiency of sampling if it establishes classes, that is, if it can divide the population into classes of members or elements that are internally comparatively homogeneous and relative to one another, heterogeneous, with respect to the characteristics being studied. Let us suppose that age and sex are two potential bases of stratification. Now, should we find that stratification on the basis of sex (male / female) yields two strata which differ markedly from each other in respect of scores on other pertinent characteristics under study while on the other hand, age as a basis of stratification does not yield strata which are substantially different from one another in terms of the scores on the other significant characteristics, then it will be advisable to stratify the population on the basis of sex rather than age. In other words, the criterion of sex will be more effective basis of stratification in this case.

It is quite possible that the process of breaking the population down into strata that are internally homogeneous and relatively heterogeneous in respect of certain relevant characteristics is prohibitively costly. In such a situation, the researcher may choose to select a large simple random sample and make up for the high cost by increasing (through a large-sized simple random sample) the total size of the sample and avoiding hazards attendant upon stratification. It should be clearly understood that stratification has hardly anything to do with making the sample a replica of the population. In fact, the issues involved in the decision whether stratification is to be effected are primarily related to the anticipated homogeneity of the defined strata with respect to the characteristics under study and the comparative costs of different methods of achieving precision. Stratified random sampling like the simple random sampling, involves representative sampling plans.

We now turn to discuss the major forms or stratified sampling. The number of cases selected within each stratum may be proportionate to the strength of the stratum or disproportionate thereto. The number of cases may be the same from stratum to stratum or vary from one stratum to another depending upon the sampling plan. We shall now consider very briefly these two forms, i.e., proportionate and the disproportionate stratified samples.

Proportionate Stratified Sampling

In proportionate sampling, cases are drawn from each stratum in the same proportion as they occur in the universe. Suppose we know that 60% of the 'population' is male and 40% of it is female. Proportionate stratified sampling with reference to this 'population', would involve drawing a sample in a manner that this same division among sexes is reflected, i.e., 60:40, in the sample.

If the systematic sampling procedure is employed in a study, the basis on which the list is made determines whether or not the resulting sample is a proportionate stratified sample. For example, if every 7th name is selected in a regular sequence from a list of alphabetically arranged names, the resulting sample should contain approximately 1/7th of the names beginning with each letter of the alphabet. The resulting sample in this case would be a proportionate stratified alphabetical sample. Of course, if the alphabetical arrangement is completely unrelated and irrelevant to the problem being studied, the sample might be considered a random sample with certain limitations typical of the systematic samples discussed above.

Various reasons may be adduced for sampling the various strata in unequal or dissimilar proportions. Sometimes, it is necessary to increase the proportion sampled from strata having a small number of cases in order to have a guarantee that these strata come to be sampled at all. For example, if one were planning a study of retail sales of clothings in a certain city at a given point of time, a simple random sample of retail cloth stores might not give us an accurate estimate of the total volume of sales, since a small number of establishments with a very large proportion of the total sales, may happen to get excluded from the sample. In this case, one would be wise in stratifying the population of cloth stores in terms of some few cloth stores that have a very large volume of sales will constitute the uppermost stratum. The researcher would do well to include all of them in his sample. That is, he may do well at times to take a 100% sample from this stratum and a much lesser percentage of cases from the other strata representing a large number of shops (with low or moderate volume of turn-over). Such a disproportionate sampling alone will most likely give reliable estimates in respect of the population.

Another reason for taking a larger proportion of cases from one stratum rather than from others is that the researcher may want to subdivide cases within each stratum for further analysis. The sub-strata thus derived may not all contain enough number of cases to sample from and in the same proportion as the other sub-strata, hence would not afford enough cases to serve as an adequate basis for further analysis. This being the case, one may have to sample out higher proportion of cases from the sub-stratum.

In general terms, it may be said that greatest precision and representation can be obtained if samples from the various strata adequately reflect their relative variabilities with respect to characteristics under study rather than present their relative sizes in the 'population.' It is advisable to sample more heavily in strata where the researcher has a reason to believe that the variability about a given characteristic, e.g., attitudes or participation, would be greater. Hence, in a study undertaken for predicting the outcome of the national elections employing the method of stratified sampling, with states as a basis of stratification, a heavier sample should be taken from the areas or regions where the outcome is severely clouded and greatly in doubt.

Disproportionate Stratified Sampling

We have already suggested the characteristics of the disproportionate sampling and also some of the major advantage of this sampling procedure. It is clear that a stratified sample in which the number of elements drawn from various strata is independent of the sizes of these strata may be called a disproportionate stratified sample. This same effect may well be achieved alternatively by drawing from each stratum an equal number of cases, regardless of how strongly or weakly the stratum is represented in the population.

As a corollary of the way it is selected, an advantage of disproportionate stratified sampling relates to the fact that all the strata are equally reliable from the point of view of the size of the sample. An even more important advantage is economy. This type of sample is economical in that, the investigators are spared the troubles of securing an unnecessarily large volume of information from the most prevalent groups in the population.

Such a sample may, however, also betray the combined disadvantages of unequal number of cases, i.e., smallness and non-representativeness. Besides, a disproportionate sample requires deep knowledge of pertinent characteristics of the various strata.

Optimum Allocation Sample

In this sampling procedure, the size of the sample drawn from each stratum is proportionate to both the size and the spread of values within any given stratum. A precise use of this sampling procedure involves the use of certain statistical concepts which have not yet been adequately or convincingly introduced.[5]

We now know something about the stratified random sampling and its different manifestations. Let us now see how the variables or criteria for stratification should be planned. The following considerations ideally enter into the selection of controls for stratification:

(a) The information germane to institution of strata should be up-to-date, accurate, complete, applicable to the population and available to the researcher. Many characteristics of the population cannot be used as controls since no satisfactory statistics about them are available. In a highly dynamic society characterized by great upheavals in the population, the researcher employing the strategy of stratification typically runs the risk of going quite wrong in his estimates about the sizes of the strata he effects in his sample.

(b) The researcher should have reasons to believe that the factors or criteria used for stratification are significant in the light of the problem under study.

(c) Unless the stratum under consideration is large enough and hence the sampler and field workers have no great difficulty locating candidates for it, it should not be used.

(d) When selecting cases for stratification, the researcher should try to choose those that are homogeneous with respect to the characteristics that are significant for the problem under study. As was said earlier, stratification is effective to the extent that the elements within the stratum are like each other and at the same time different relative to the elements in other strata.

Let us now consider the merits and limitations of stratified random sampling in a general way:

(1) In employing the stratified random sampling procedure, the researcher can remain assured that no essential groups or categories will be excluded from the sample. Greater representativeness of the sample is thus assured and the occasional mishaps that occur in simple random sampling are thus avoided.

(2) In the case of more homogeneous populations, greater precision can be achieved with fewer cases.

(3) Compared to the simple random ones, stratified samples are more concentrated geographically, thereby reducing the costs in terms of time, money and energy in interviewing respondents.

(4) The samples that an interviewer chooses may be more representative if his quota is allocated by the impersonal procedure of stratification than if he is to use his own judgement (as in quota sampling).

The main limitation of stratified random sampling is that in order to secure the maximal benefits from it in the course of a study, the researcher needs to know a great deal about the problem of research and its relation to other factors. Such a knowledge is not always forthcoming and quite so often waiting is long.

It should be remembered that the viewpoint of the theory of probability sampling, it is essentially irrelevant whether stratification is introduced during the procedure of sampling or during the analysis of data, except in so far as the former makes it possible to control the size of the sample obtained from each stratum and thus to increase the efficiency of the sampling design. In other words, the procedure of drawing a simple random sample and then dividing it into strata is equivalent in effect to drawing a stratified random sample using as the sampling frame within each stratum, the population of that stratum which is included in the given simple random sample.

Cluster Sampling

Typically, simple random sampling and stratified random sampling entail enormous expenses when dealing with large and spatially or geographically dispersed populations. In the above types of sampling, the elements chosen in the sample may be so widely dispersed that interviewing them may entail heavy expenses, a greater proportion of non-productive time (spent during travelling), a greater likelihood of lack of uniformity among interviewers' questionings, recordings and lastly, a heavy expenditure on supervising the field staff. There are also other practical factors of that sampling. For example, it may be considered less objectionable and hence permissible to administer a questionnaire to three or four departments of a factory or office rather than administering it on a sample drawn from all the departments on a simple or stratified random basis, since this latter procedure may be much more disruptive of the factory routines. It is for some of these reasons that large-scale survey studies seldom make use of simple or stratified random samples; instead, they make use of the method of cluster sampling.

In cluster sampling, the sampler first samples out from the population, certain large groupings, i.e., "cluster." These clusters may be city wards, households, or several geographical or social units. The sampling of clusters from the population is done by simple or stratified random sampling methods. From these selected clusters, the constituent elements are sampled out by recourse to procedures ensuring randomness.

Suppose, for example, that a researcher wants to conduct a sample study on the problems of undergraduate students of colleges in Maharashtra. He may proceed as follows:

(a) First he prepares a list of all the universities in the state and selects a sample of the universities on a 'random' basis.

(b) For each of the universities of the state included in the sample, he makes a list of colleges under its jurisdiction and takes a sample of colleges on a 'random' basis.

(c) For each of the colleges that happen to get included in the sample, he makes a list of all undergraduate students enrolled with it. From out of these students, he selects a sample of the desired size on a 'random' basis (simple or stratified).

In this manner, the researcher gets a probability or random sample of elements, more or less concentrated, geographically. This way he is able to avoid heavy expenditure that would otherwise have been incurred had he resorted to simple or stratified random sampling, and yet he need not sacrifice the principles and benefits of probability sampling.

Characteristically, this sampling procedure moves through a series of stages. Hence it is, in a sense, a 'multi-stage' sampling and sometimes known by this name. This sampling procedure moves progressively from the more inclusive to the less inclusive sampling units the researcher finally arrives at those elements of population that constitute his desired sample.

It should be noted that with cluster sampling, it is no longer true that every combination of the desired number of elements in the population is equally likely to be selected as the sample of the population. Hence, the kind of effects that we saw in our analysis of simple random samples, i.e., the population-value being the most probable sample-value, cannot be seen here. But such effects do materialize in a more complicated way, though, of course, the sampling efficiency is hampered to some extent. It has been found that on a per case basis, the cluster sampling is much less efficient in getting information than comparably effective stratified random sampling.

Relatively speaking, in the cluster sampling, the margin of error is much greater. This handicap, however, is more than balanced by associated economies, which permit the sampling of a sufficiently large number of cases at a smaller total cost. Depending on the specific features of the sampling plan attendant upon the objects of survey, cluster sampling may be more or less efficient than simple random sampling. The economies associated with cluster sampling generally tilt the balance in favour of employing cluster sampling in large-scale surveys, although compared to simple random sampling, more cases are needed for the same level of accuracy.

Multi-phase Sampling

It is sometimes convenient to confine certain questions about specific aspects of the study to a fraction of the sample, while other information is being collected from the whole sample. This procedure is known as 'multi-phase sampling.'

The basic information recorded from the whole sample makes it possible to compare certain characteristics of the sub-sample with that of the whole sample. One additional point that merits mention is that multi-phase sampling facilitates stratification of the sub-sample since the information collected from the first phase sample can sometimes be gathered before the sub-sampling process takes place. It will be remembered that panel studies involve multi-phase sampling.

Non-probability Sampling Design

The distinctive characteristic of non-probability sampling design in contradistinction to the probability sampling design is that sampling procedure adopted in this design does not afford any basis for estimating the probability that each element in the population has an equal chance of being included in the sample. In such a sampling, there is no assurance that every element has some specifiable chance of being included in the sample.

It is clear that for the non-probability type samples there is no way of estimating as to how much confidence may be placed in the sample returns as to their being within a specified margin of error. The major forms of non-probability samples are : (a) Accidental samples, (b) Quota samples, and (c) Purposive or judgement samples.

Let us Discuss these in Turn

(a) Accidental Samples: In accidental sampling, the researcher simply reaches out and picks up the cases that fall to hand, continuing the process till such time as the sample acquires a desired size. The researcher, for example, may take the first 150 persons he meets on any one of the pedestrian paths of a street, who are willing to be interviewed or to provide the kind of information he is seeking. Similarly, a welfare officer, wanting to make certain generalizations about the factory workers may study the workers of a particular department in the factory where he is working. A journalist, wanting to know how the 'people' feel about an issue may choose to interview cases conveniently available from different walks of life, e.g., teachers, workers, taxi-drivers, retail shopkeepers, housewives and others who are presumed to reflect public opinion. In such a sample, there is, of course, no other way of estimating the bias (difference between the average sample value and the true population value) except by doing a parallel study with a probability sample or by undertaking a complete census. If one uses an accidental sample, one can only hope and pray that he is not being too grossly misled by his sample findings which constitute the basis for estimating the state of the 'population.' This does not mean, however, that accidental samples do not have any place in scientific research. This type of sampling, besides being economical and convenient, can also afford a basis for stimulation of insights and working hypotheses. Where too much accuracy is not needed or where pre-occupation is with tentative clues to hypothesis-formulation (as in exploratory studies), the procedure of accidental sampling is quite useful.

(b) Quota Samples: One of the most commonly used methods of sampling in marketing researches and election polls is the method of quota sampling. The basic objective of quota sampling is the selection of a sample that is a replica of the 'population' with respect to which one would wish to generalize. Quota sampling, by and large, affords the insurance that diverse elements in the 'population' will be included in the sample and that these elements will be taken account of in proportions in which they obtain in the population. Suppose, we are sampling from a 'population' of girl-students comprising the total number of girls studying in co-educational institutions and those studying in institutions for girls only. Suppose, there is a sharp difference between the two sub-populations in respect of the characteristics we wish to measure. This being so, the results of the survey would almost certainly give out an extremely misleading picture of the total 'population', if we did not include an adequate proportion of girls studying in the co-educational institutions. The quota sampler anticipating such possible differences between sub-groups will try to ensure the inclusion in his sample of enough number of cases from each stratum to afford a reliable picture of the total 'population.'

Quota Sampling Usually Proceeds in Three Steps

(1) The population is classified in terms of properties known or assumed to be pertinent to the characteristics being studied.

(2) The proportion of the population falling into each class is determined on the basis of the known, assumed or estimated composition of the population in respect of the above.

(3) Lastly, each observer or interviewer is assigned a quota of respondents. The responsibility of selecting the respondents or subjects is theirs. The quotas are so fixed that the total sample observed or interviewed would reflect the proportions among the classes as determined in the previous step (i.e., 2).

Since the observer or interviewer has the final say in the selection of the subjects, the selection of items/cases depends on the judgement of the interviewer/observer.

It often happens in practice, however, that the various components of the sample are not in the same proportion as the corresponding strata in the population. The interviewers might not have followed their instructions correctly and faithfully. Disproportion between the samples and properties of population are more likely to occur, especially, in respect of the less manifest traits which not have been included as a part of the specifications for interviewer's/observer's/quotas. It should be noted that the inadequacy in the sample can be corrected during the analysis by weighing the different strata in terms of their proportions in the population (involving multiplication or division of results by the appropriate corrective figures).

Thus, the critical requirement in quota sampling is not that the various strata in the population be sampled in their correct proportions; it is rather that there should be enough cases from each stratum to make possible an estimate of the population-value and secondly that we know the proportion of each stratum in the total 'population.' If these two conditions are met, the estimates of values for the various strata can be combined to give an estimate of the total population value.

Despite these precautions in the course of selecting the sample and corrections effected during the course of analysis, quota sampling may produce serious errors since it involves, undeniably, an accidental sampling procedure. A part of the sample in any particular class constitutes an accidental sample of the corresponding stratum of the population.

Data for fixing quotas are generally drawn from previous census results and certain contemporary sources. When drastic changes are taking place in society, the estimated quotas may be seriously in error and produce misleading results.

A great deal depends on the interviewer/observer's judgement in sampling. In general, the observer or interviewer may be assumed to fill his quotas in a manner that suits his own convenience. The interviewer is more likely to select people similar to himself in many respects. Thus, the stratum-wise samples may not be representative of the strata in the population. The interviewer/observer is seldom so well-informed compared to the researcher (if the two are different) hence left to choose samples by himself, he is likely to introduce two biases, (a) of classification of subject and (b) non-random selection.

The result of quota sampling may often not be seriously in error but whether or not they are, is extremely difficult to establish. We have no assurance that the quota sample will give reliable results within a certain limit of tolerance. And since random sampling, hence the probability principle, is not involved at any stage, the errors of the method cannot be determined by statistical procedures.

As we have seen earlier, mathematical corrections may be effected if there are disproportions in samples from various strata. But this step depends on our advance knowledge about the true proportions of strata in the 'population.' For certain populations, one does not just know this and here the only control that an investigator can avail of is the sampling process itself.

There is by now enough experience with quota sampling so that its vulnerability to certain types of biases can be controlled.

(c) Purposive or Judgement Samples: The basic assumption behind judgement or purposive sampling is that with the exercise of good judgement and appropriate strategy one can handpick the 'right' cases to be included in the sample and thus develop samples that are satisfactory in relation to one's research needs. A common strategy of purposive sampling is to pick cases that are judged to be typical of the population in which one is interested. The selection of elements proceeds under the assumption that errors of judgement in the selection will tend to counter-balance each other.

In other words, when practical considerations pose serious hazards in the way of adopting, probability sampling, the researcher looks for a subgroup which is typical of the 'population' as a whole (in respect of some characteristic that he is interested in). The sub-group is the 'barometer' of the 'population.' Observations are restricted to this sub-group and conclusions from these observations are generalized to the total 'population.' For example, a researcher interested in the effect of rural electrification on traditional social institutions may choose as his sample a particular village where electrification has been effected, say, about a couple of years back. He makes his observations in this village and believes that what obtains here would also obtain with very little variation in other villages that have also been electrified. There is, however, no demonstrable basis for such a belief, it may ultimately turn out to be ill founded. Judgement or purposive sampling is very precarious, because much stronger assumptions must be made about the population and sampling procedure than are required while employing probability sampling. Secondly, sampling errors and biases cannot be computed for this type of samples since sampling procedure does not involve probability sampling at any stage. Data secured on the basis of judgement or purposive samples, at best, point to certain hypotheses but in general they cannot be used as a basis for the statistical testing of hypotheses. Thus, judgement sampling has great utility in exploratory or formulative studies aiming as they do at obtaining insights that would help posing problems or formulating hypotheses for research.

Combinations of Probability and Non-probability Sampling

If sampling is carried out in a series of stages, it is possible to combine probability and non-probability principles in one sampling design. One or more stages of sampling can be carried out according to the probability principle and the remaining stages according to the non-probability principle.

To take an example, the investigator may begin by selecting clusters using cluster (probability) sampling strategy but, at the final stage, he may select classes of elements as quota samples. Thus, the sampler may select a probability sample of districts in a state; within each of these districts, he may choose a probability sample of development blocks and finally, within each block he may select quota samples controlled for the stages of community development, i.e., I, II, III, etc.

The advantage of such a design is that the major economies of quota sampling occur in obtaining the particular cases for the sample. It is relatively less expensive to select by recourse to the probability principle, areas within which the final stage of sampling will take place. There is some evidence to prove that quota samples taken in selected areas are more successful in controlling certain variables than is the case when the control of these variables depends on the judgements of interviewers or observers. Combining probability and non-probability procedures in certain instances, may involve an opposite strategy. The investigator may take a probability sample of elements within a non-probability sample of areas; the areas are selected as a purposive or juegement sample. The districts (in the above example) may be selected on the ground that these have been particularly successful in reaching the developmental targets (or the reverse) and from each of these, the sampler then selects a probability sample of the developmental blocks. The typical districts selected purposively may be regarded as defining a population. If a probability sampling is completely applicable and hence one can estimate the degree of confidence that may be placed in the assumption that findings of the sample are a good representation of the 'population' returns. The researcher can then generalize the inferences based on this restricted sub-population to the national population, subject to the assumption that the typical districts are still typical of their respective stages. So long as and to the extent that this assumption is valid, the sampling plan described above will produce most dependable results at a minimum cost.

Let us now discuss at some length the special applications of non-probability sampling. It was suggested earlier that the major advantages of non-probability sampling procedures are convenience and economy. Investigators continue to use non-probability sampling methods and justify their use on grounds of practical experience, expediency and facility. They may, of course, in the same breath concede the theoretic superiority of the probability sampling. Many practical samplers, however, argue that in many cases, the superiority of the probability sampling is only 'on paper' or 'notional.' They point out that many a time, the way the probability sampling plans are actually implemented, the theoretical advantages of probability sampling get nearly nullified. There can be many slips in carrying out the probability sampling plan. For instance, some of the cases selected in the sample may refuse to be interviewed or not be available, interviewers may omit some of the questions in the process of interviewing, compromises may be effected by allowing interviewers to substitute other respondents when the originally selected cases are not found at home and so on. The sample actually interviewed, therefore, may not be a probability sample of the universe in the strict sense of the term.

Moreover, there are circumstances in which probability sampling is unnecessary or inappropriate. For example, in exploratory studies, the researcher's goal is to obtain ideas, new insights and experienced critical appraisals just to help him pose a research problem or hypothesis. The researcher conducting such studies does not carry out the studies of samples with the purpose of being able to generalize to the populations that are being sampled. Thus, he selects a purposive sample. The respondents are selected precisely because of their special experience, exposures and competence, the market-researchers are typically content with accidental or purposive samples, which are selected in such a way that the likelihood of difference among the elements in the sample is maximized. They may be looking for ideas to be transmitted, say, to the persons in charge of advertising the products rather than putting across correct estimates of the population distribution.

Sometimes there is no way out but to resort to the non-probability sampling. If one is trying to find out something, for example, about the experiences of people who had to leave, say, Sri Lanka, owing to certain political developments, he has no realistic choice but to rely on informants who happen to be available, here and now. Of course, the researcher's choice here is between data that do not permit a statistical assessment of the margin of error, etc. and no data at all. This does not mean, of course, that one is not concerned with the possibility of error; it is only that he places his reliance on internal consistency of data and its coherence with other information that he might have come to secure.

We must remember that there are many important considerations in research, in addition to the sampling design. It may, therefore, be necessary to balance one consideration against another. Sometimes, wisdom lies in a better and more accurate sampling design being given up in favour of more sensitive method of data collection. It is in this light that we should understand why the use of non-probability sampling may on occasions be justified. Of course, the decision whether it would be better to gather more adequate or in-depth information based on a not very sound sample or less adequate information based on a sounder sample, is by no means an easy one to arrive at. It is in terms of the research-purpose that the researcher may take such a decision.

For example, in a study of factors related to the use of narcotics by boys in juvenile street gangs, Chein and Associates (1957) used a sample of social group-workers who had spent quite sometime winning the confidence of gang boys. This sample was an accidental sample of group-workers and since they could give information about only those gang boys with whom they had worked, the sample of gang members about whom information could be had was also an accidental sample. But considering the facility with which more dependable information about the gang could be had from these group-workers, the researchers preferred an accidental (non-probability) sample to probability sample of gang members (assuming that it was possible to get such probability sample).

Thus, in his scientific wisdom, the researcher has to carefully weigh the gains and liabilities of various research procedures. He may, under certain circumstances, sacrifice the probability principle in his sampling procedure to gain a deeper understanding through more sensitive and dependable instruments of securing information.

The Problem of Sample Size

We shall now consider one of the trickiest problems relating to sampling, viz., the problem of sample size. "What should be the adequate size of the sample in relation to the size of population?" "How big ought to be a sample?" are questions often asked by research students. No decisive answer to this question can be given. This is because the question of size can be answered only when we are sampling elements for the population in such a manner that each element has the same chance of being included in the sample, i.e., when we are adopting the probability design of sampling. As we had said earlier in this chapter, only the probability design makes possible the formulation of representative sampling plans. Hence, makes it possible of the formulation of representative sampling plans. Hence, the question, "how large the sample should be in order to be representative of the population of a designated size?" presupposes the probability sampling procedure. Failing this procedure, representativeness of the sample howsoever large can only be a matter of hope and conjecture.

The general misconceptions in regard to the size of the sample is that the size of the universe from which the sample is drawn determines the number of cases needed to yield an adequate or representative sample of that universe. We shall do well to note right away that the emphasis should be placed not upon the number of cases in the universe but on their number in the sample. We have discussed this at some length earlier while considering the merits of a random sample.

Definition of an Optimum Sample

Let us turn to consider the criteria for obtaining optimum sample for any given study. An optimum sample for a study may be defined as that sample which fulfils the requirements of efficiency, representativeness, reliability and flexibility. That is, the sample should be small enough to forestall unnecessary expense and large enough to help the researcher avoid sample-error beyond the limit to tolerance. It should be large enough to yield statistically representative and significant results in all tabulations of any import but it need not be so large as to result in wastage of funds, retarding the project and achieving needlessly high precision. The sample should yield the desired estimates with the required level of reliability at a minimum cost. It should be remembered that in practice efficient sampling involves making the most of available resources in terms of technique and organization of statistical data and adjusting, as best as possible, to the limitations of time, funds and personnel, originally imposed on the study. In addition, it should be possible in some instances to expand or contract the sample-size to meet unforeseen exigencies arising in the course of the study. In certain situations, reliability and efficiency may be improved by effecting the desired changes in the size of sample.

At the level of practice, these ideals can be approached but rarely realized and so one cannot be expected to choose the correct sample size.

The choice of the size of sample for a given study is affected by several factors, which we now turn to discuss. These factors are interrelated and vary greatly in different studies with respect to their relative importance in determining the sample size.

(1) The Nature of Population (homogeneous-heterogeneous) : The size of the sample in a study will depend upon the degree of homogeneity of the population. The more homogeneous the population, fewer the cases required to yield a reliable sample of it and conversely, the more heterogeneous the population more the cases required to constitute a reliable sample of it.

The size of sample required for a satisfactory study of a heterogeneous population can be cut down by classifying the population into strata. Some of these strata will be more homogeneous and others less so. More homogeneous strata can be represented by smaller samples than the relatively heterogeneous ones. This is so because the more homogeneous a stratum, the better can a random sample of a given size represent it, i.e., more alike will be the cases in the sample hence, less variable their mean.

(2) Complexity of Tabulation : In making a decision about the size of the sample, one must also take into account the number of categories and classes into which the findings are to be grouped and analyzed. The greater the number of categories, the larger would be the total sample needed to yield reliable statistical measures of them. Even though a sample may seem quite adequate for the main tabulation, the number is likely to thin down very quickly when detailed tabulations are prepared. For example, a sample of 1,000 students might seem like an adequate number for a survey designed to ascertain the proportion of students favouring co-education. Let us say that only 25% are in favour (250 students). If the researcher wanted to go further and know the type of students who favoured co-education, he would have to classify these respondents further, on the dimensions like, whether they had a prior experience of the co-educational institution? Which social class they come from? What kind of family background they have? What was the nature of their experience (if any) of the co-educational institution? And so on. Proceeding thus, the researcher may finally find only 10 or 15 cases of a particular type (viz., no prior experience of co-education, middle class, orthodox family background, etc.). Such a sample can afford only a very flimsy basis for arriving at significant and generalizable conclusions about the relationship among variables.

The size of sample chosen should be large enough to give reliable measures of the smallest important categories. When data are broken down into smaller and smaller sub-classes, the number of cases falling into various cells soon becomes so small that statistical measures computed from the cell entries are likely to be unreliable. Thus, intensiveness of tabulation is a factor that has importance for the decision relating to sample-size.

(3) Problems Relating to Collection of Data : Usually, the size of the sample must be kept within the numerical limit of cases which can be secured with given funds and time. The volume of data is affected by length of the questionnaire/schedule, the number of field-workers, the dispersion or concentration of cases in a geographical area, the refusal-rate, the losses of cases, the type of sampling employed and finally, the method of data-collection.

The transportation cost involved in getting from one address to another and in call-backs (second or third call) must be considered when deciding the size of the sample. While planning the sample-size, the researcher must always anticipate that he may fall short in the collection of the number assigned for questioning. People migrate, die, are unable to give information owing to illness, go vacationing or on business, cannot be located, refuse to answer, addresses prove wrong, and so on. It is a good policy to plan to obtain information from every case in the sample if humanly possible. This means that considerably more time will be required than what would be required if only accessible and cooperative cases are obtained. However, it is better to have a smaller sample without bias than a large sample which is likely to be unrepresentative of the universe for reason of bias.

(4) Type of Sampling : Generally, a smaller sample will suffice when stratification is employed. This is because the effect of stratification is to resolve the relatively heterogeneous totality into a number of individually homogeneous sub-samples. More heterogeneous the population, the greater the economy of cases possible through stratification.

In sampling known as double sampling, the researcher combines a large random sample (for the collection of a few basic items of information) with a very small controlled or stratified sample (from which detailed or complicated information is secured). The detailed data from the small stratified sample can be expanded to represent the universe by using the procedure of weighing in proportion of the frequencies found in the large random sample. The requirement here is that the size of the random sample should be large enough to yield reliable weights for the various strata. The stratified sample itself inquires fewer cases compared to simple random sample because the sample in each stratum needs to be representative of that stratum and not of the 'universe.'

One important factor in determining the necessary number of cases is the size of the sampling units. In fact, larger the sampling unit, the greater the number of cases which will be needed for individual tabulation.

The Mathematics of Sample-size

We now turn to ponder over the basic practical question "How to determine the sample-size which will yield the desired degree of precision as stipulated by the researcher for a given study?" The sampling problem is, of course, the same in all studies, i.e., to estimate or predict something about the population on the basis of knowledge of something about the sample.

The researcher must know what kind of statistics on the sample will serve the purpose, e.g., percentages, averages, standard deviation, etc., for such an estimation. This is important because different kinds of statistics are useful depending on the desired degrees of precision in sample returns which in turn are afforded by different sample-sizes. Averages and percentages are the more commonly desired statistics, we shall therefore deal specifically with the question of sample-sizes corresponding to the desired degrees of precision in respect of averages and percentages.

Since the sample drawn by the researcher is only one of the many possible samples of the universe that he might have happened to choose, he needs to know how much reliance he can place on the sample as the representative of the 'universe' about which he wants to know something or with reference to which he wishes to generalize. He needs to know how large the sample should be to give him a satisfactory level of precision. This calculation is possible by recourse to mathematics since in random sampling (probability sampling design) where every item in the universe has a specifiable probability of inclusion in the sample, the precision of prediction or estimate is related to the square root of the number of items in the sample.

Before proceeding with the calculation of the requisite size of the sample for a given study, it is necessary in practice, to secure some preliminary information about the population or universe. If the researcher intends to use the sample to make an estimate of the average measure of particular characteristic in the universe, he needs to have some preliminary estimate to the standard deviation (dispersion) in the distribution of the values of items in the universe with respect to the given characteristic. The researcher who comes to know the range of values (the spread) in respect of a particular characteristic in the universe can get a preliminary estimate of the standard deviation by dividing this range by 6, since the standard deviation of the (finite) universe may for all practical purposes be taken to be around 1/6 of the full range of variation. In other words, the range of dispersion of a distribution may be taken to comprise 6 standard deviation units. The preliminary information about the universe may be had by means of a pilot study, results of past surveys, from reports published by statistical bureaus, reckoning of experts in the field, etc.

As stated earlier, the researcher, before proceeding to calculate the size of the sample, must decide the expected level of precision of the estimates. This expectation is based, in the main, on the purpose of the study. In other words, the researcher must decide (a) how much error in the estimate to be derived from the sample (as compared to the true value, i.e., value of the 'universe') may be tolerated (called margin of error or limit of accuracy) and (b) with how much assurance can it be said that the estimate will fall within this margin of error (called, level of confidence or probability). We have already said something about these concepts earlier. It will be proper, however, to consider these in greater detail, presently.

(a) Margin of Error or Limit of Accuracy: The basic question here is: 'How much is the percentage or average to be secured from the study of the sample likely to vary from the true mean (of the population) and may still to be tolerated?' The researcher might tolerate 5% error or he might require accuracy within a limit of 2%. It all depends on

how accurately or exactly he wants to know certain facts. Let us suppose that the researcher wishes to know in advance which of the two candidates contesting the election is going to win the seat. If the voting is going to be close, the researcher can afford to tolerate only a smaller error if he is to be practically certain. He may, for example, set the permissible error at less than 2%. On the other hand, if the election appears to be one sided, and quite biased in favour of a particular candidate, the researcher may be able to predict the results even with a much larger error in the estimate. If the sample-survey happened to reveal that 60% of votes would go in favour of a candidate, an error as high as 9% might be tolerated. In this case, even if the sample-poll had drawn the most unfortunate sample deviating 9% from the true value, the true value would still be 51%, i.e., 1% above the 50% which is the critical point. Thus, both estimated value of 60% and true value of 51% would be above the critical point (i.e., 50%) and the prediction would be reliable.

(b) Probability or Confidence Level: In addition to limit of accuracy, the researcher must also decide with reference to his study, how much confidence he would like to place in the sample-estimates being as close to the true estimate as to be within the limits of tolerance or accuracy set by him for the study. In certain situations, he may want to be exceedingly sure that his estimates (based on the sample) will be within 51% of the true value whereas in certain other situations, he may be satisfied with a little lesser degree of assurance. In social science research, two degrees of probability or confidence are very well-known and often used. One of these is 0.95 level of probability, i.e., there will be 95 chances out of 100 that the sample estimate will not exceed the limits of tolerance or margin or error, and the second level is the 0.99 level, of probability, i.e., it is likely that in 99 chances out of 100 the sample estimate will not exceed the margin of error aimed at. The level of confidence may even be set at 0.999, that is, the sample estimate would not deviate from the true value (of universe) beyond the limits of tolerance in 999 chances out of 1000. For certain purposes, the researcher may aim low and set the probability level at 0.67 (i.e., 2 out of 3).

The chances that a particular sample drawn for a study will yield an estimate of the universe which is within the margin of error, depend upon the variation among the samples that may be drawn from the universe. If the values secured from the samples tend to deviate considerably from the true value, then the chances of any given sample-value staying within the permissible limits of error are poor.

The standard error is the measure which tells us what the chances of a sample staying within the permissible limits are. It is a measure of variation in sampling estimate which could be expected in random sampling. As we have seen earlier, random samples tend to follow the laws of probability and the sample-estimates tend to cluster around the true value of the universe. These estimates can be represented by a bell-shaped or normal curve. The mid-point of this curve represents the true value (of the universe) and the maximum variation or deviation of a random sample-estimate from this true value is about three times the standard error. The standard error is thus about

1/6th of the entire range of random sampling variation. For all practical purposes, however, the standard error is taken as 1/4th of the range of variation, since the extreme variations occur very rarely. Probability tables show that 95 out of 100 sample estimates can be expected to fall within the limit +2 and –2 standard errors. This means that if we have set our level of confidence or probability at 0.95, our problem will be to draw a random sample with a standard error which is about ½ (half) of our margin of error. For a higher level of probability, we would have to draw a sample with a standard error, that is a still smaller fraction of the margin of error.

It should be noted that the standard error gets smaller (higher precision) as the samples get larger. To double the precision, the sample size must be multiplied by 4, i.e., increased four times; to treble it, the sample-size must be multiplied by 9; to quadruple it, by 16 and so on. This only means that precision increases as the square-root of the number of cases in the sample, a statement we had made earlier. Statisticians have prepared tables which show the probability of sample estimates coming within the various standard error limits. These limits are generally stated as + (plus) and – (minus). Such tables readily show, for instance, that 95% of the random sample estimates fall within the limit of +1.96 and –1.96 standard errors, about 68% of the estimates fall within the limits of +1 and –1 standard error and 99% of the estimates fall within the range of +2.57 and –2.57 standard errors, and so on.

In full consideration of (1) the margin of error and (2) the probability or confidence level, the researcher can proceed with the calculation of a desired sample-size. *Mildred Parten* has given the following formula for calculating the sample size, when the statistic to be estimated is the percentage.[6] This is obviously a transposed variation of a standard error formula.

$$\text{Size of sample} = \frac{\text{P.C.}\,(100 - \text{P.C.})Z^2}{T^2}$$

In the above formula, P.C. means the preliminary estimate of the percentage (from the universe).

Z means the number of standard error units which are found (from the normal probability table) to correspond to the required probability level.

T means the margin of error which may be tolerated (5% or 2%).

Parten has given the following formula for calculating the sample size for predicting or estimating the mean value of the universe in regard to a specified characteristic at a certain level of confidence and aimed at a given margin or error or limit of tolerance.

$$\text{Sample size} = \left(\frac{\delta + Z}{T}\right)^2$$

Where δ stands for the preliminary estimate of standard deviation of the universe.

Z stands for the number of standard error units corresponding to the required probability or confidence level.

T stands for the margin of error that may be tolerated.

Let us take a concrete example and work out the sample-size. Suppose we wish to estimate the average annual income of families inhabiting a certain 'middle class' locality of a city.

Let us say, we have set our margin of error at Rs. 100/-, i.e., we will tolerate the sample estimate within plus or minus 100 from the true mean of the population in respect of income. Suppose we have set the probability or confidence level at 0.95. Suppose also that from a survey conducted a few years back, we estimate the standard deviation in respect of annual income of the population (locality) to be Rs. 500/-. The value of Z, i.e., the standard error units corresponding to the probability of 0.95 is 1.96.

Substituting these values in the formula given above, we have

$$\text{Size of sample} = \left(\frac{500 \times 1.96}{100}\right)^2$$

$$= (9.8)^2$$

$$= 95$$

This means that a random sample of 95 cases (families, which are the sample units) should give us an estimate of the mean of the given 'universe' within the set margin of error and at the desired level of confidence or probability, respectively, of Rs. 100/- and 0.95. If we tighten the margin of error and set it at Rs. 50/-, the number of cases in the sample, i.e., the required size of the sample will be four times as large (i.e., 380) as the size required for the earlier margin of error (Rs. 100/-).

If another locality is characterized by greater homogeneity in respect of income and suppose, thus, that the standard deviation in income terms is only 100, the size of the sample for the above margin of error will be much lower. In other words, the use of the formula illustrates the lesson we had learnt earlier, namely, greater the homogeneity smaller the sample required and greater the accuracy aspired for, larger the sample-size needed.

The repeated use of such terms as the margin of error and level of confidence and other numerical expressions of probabilities and sample sizes, may tend to create the impression that a sample-size calculated by a formula will guarantee a desired precision. It should be remembered, however, that the relations shown in the statistical tables of probability represent normal expectations in an ideal random sampling. But in as much as the actual sampling is rarely ideal, the relations expressed in tables cannot be expected to hold. The general difficulty and rarity of ideal sampling should understandably make one skeptical about results which are exactly according to expectations. This does not, however, mean that the researcher should not use or prefer the exact sample-size computed on the basis of the probability formula. In fact, this is precisely what he should do because it is his best bet. He should not, however, insist on this exact size if practical considerations make it inexpedient.

A substantially different approach to the problem of determining the desired sample-size is the 'stability test.' This consists in collecting data for relatively small sub-samples and keeping a running record of the distribution of the returns. When after a point, the addition of more sub-sample does not change the results significantly, the researcher may assume that the total sample drawn thus far has become adequate, size-wise.

But this procedure may well be regarded as wasteful of time because it amounts in effect to a researcher engaging in a series of separate surveys spread over a considerable period of time. It has been argued that this procedure is uneconomical in that more schedules are collected than are actually needed, since the tapering off to the point of approximate stability cannot be located with any certainty until the curve has maintained its level for a while. But this does not seem to be a serious limitation when compared with the conservative practice of many reputable studies which collect more than the necessary/minimum number of items as a sample.

The main advantage of this type of stability test is that instead of depending upon calculations based on preliminary information, one simply increases the overall sample-size unit it is observed to be sufficient. The empirical check of watching the returns and stopping when they stabilize seem straightforward and convincing.

The chief danger of this procedure lies in the fact that the successive sub-samples collected are not likely to spread over the universe. Results may stabilize even though they do not represent the population. In fact, the less representative the sub-sample, the more likely is the addition of more cases to yield the same result and throw up the appearance of stabilization. Unless sub-sample is a cross-section of the universe, there will not be a supersensitive sample upon which to observe the approaching stabilization. The basic requirement of this procedure is that a growing representative sample must be available for observation. The expenses and the difficulty of collecting successive sub-samples which are spread over the universe are the major reasons why this is not likely to be representative.

The empirical stability test can be very effective, however, when the sub-samples are properly drawn and collected. The method is most appropriate for interview-surveys covering relatively small areas or community such as a town or a city because then, it is not so difficult or expensive to make each sub-sample a random sample of the population.

A more refined form of empirical control compared to stability test is a relatively recent development called Sequential Analysis. The general procedure involved, here, is to keep adding to the sample and at the same time keep testing the sample for significance until the minimum sample is accumulated that will provide the required level of significance.

REFERENCES

(1) Simon, J.L. : *Basic Research Methods in Social Sciences,* Random House, N.Y. 1968, Chapter on Sampling and Protability.

(2) See Cauls, Peter : *The Philosophy of Sciences, of Van Nostrand,* Co N.Y. 1965, p.p. 214-17.

(3) Kline, C.F. : *Mathematics Cultural Approach,* Addison-Wesley, 1962, p. 652.

(4) Simon, J.L. *op. cit.,* chapter : *Sampling and Protability.*

(5) Ackoff, R.L. *op. cit.,* chapter : *Sampling Design.*

(6) Parten, M. Swrveys, *Polls and Samples,* Harpersuternational.

(7) Simon, J.L. *op. cit.,* chapter on *Sampling and Protability,* pp. 312-6.

Chapter XVIII

Analysis of Data and Interpretation

Quite a few preceding chapters were addressed to the varied techniques of data collection employed by social scientists and the methodological rationale underlying them. The question that naturally follows is : "What is to be done with the data that are collected?" In this chapter, we shall deal with this question.

After the data have been collected, the researcher shifts his centre of attention to their analysis. Analysis of data involves a number of closely related operations that are performed with the purpose of summarizing the collected data and organizing these in such a manner that they will yield answers to the research questions (or suggest hypothesis or research questions, if no such questions or hypotheses had initiated the study).[1]

Some writers on research methods effect a clear distinction between analysis of data and the processing of data. Johan Galtung, for example, defines the two phases of research operations as under:[2]

(a) Processing of data refers to concentrating, recasting and dealing with data such that they become as amenable to analysis as possible.

(b) Analysis of data for *Galtung*, may be considered as having a reference to the process of viewing the data in the light of hypothesis or research questions, as also, the prevailing theories and drawing conclusions that will make some contribution in the matter of theory formulation or modification.

Quite a few other writers notably *Selltiz, Jahoda et al.,* do not make such a precise differentiation. For them analysis of data, as a comprehensive process involves processing, *i.e.,* operations designed to facilitate and increase amenability of data for analysis, as also, the operations designed to draw generalization or test hypothesis. We shall largely adhere to this conception of analysis which is indeed much more inclusive.

It should be made clear at this point that the steps typically envisaged in the analysis of data as related to a study will vary depending on the type of the study. If there exists a set of clearly formulated hypothesis to start the study with, then each hypothesis can be seen as a norm prescribing a certain action to be taken vis-a-vis the data. More specific the hypothesis, the more specific the action. In such studies, the analysis is almost completely a mechanical procedure. The task of analysis is reduced to just arranging the appropriate combinations of data and reading them off against the hypothesis to be tested whether they are tenable or liable to be rejected as false. This, however, is a very rare possibility in social science research.

In most studies data are collected more according to hunches or vague clues rather than in reference to specific hypotheses. These data are, therefore, analysed inductively rather than deductively, by means of procedures discovered or arrived at during the process and not by any prescribed set of rules.

The dividing line between analysis of data and interpretation is difficult to draw. In fact, the two processes are symbiotic and merge imperceptibly. If analysis involves organizing data in a particular manner as we have said it does, then, it is mostly the interpretative ideas that govern this task. If the end-product of analysis is the setting up of certain general conclusions then what these conclusions really mean and reflect is the bare minimum that the researcher must feel obliged to know. Interpretation is the way to this knowledge. Thus the task of analysis can hardly be said to be complete without interpretation coming in to illuminate the results.

Since interpretation, as we have explained, is often inextricably interwoven with analysis, it may properly be conceived of as a special aspect of analysis rather than a distinct operation. It may, however, help our understanding if for a moment we treat it as a separate operation, just to be able to appreciate what it involves. We may say that interpretation is an aspect of the research-operation which is geared to exposing our conclusions by linking them to (*i.e.,* viewing them in the light of) other available knowledge or established theories and principles. Thus, interpretation helps one understand what the given research finding really means and what the underlying abstract principle is, of which the research finding is just one concrete manifestation or reflection at the concrete level of empirical observations. Hence, interpretation is the process which unravels the abstract that lies buried in the concrete. It helps us understand the 'why' of the findings. Interpretation makes it possible for us to appreciate why the relations between variables, as expressed in the findings, are what they are. It helps us to understand that the concrete observation or finding is but one instance of the operation of a theory or principle and on this basis to draw inferences about things seemingly quite unrelated to it. We shall return to a more detailed discussion of interpretation later.

It should be remembered that while analysis and interpretation become the foci of a researcher's attention only after the data are in, the entire research process right from its inception is governed and guided by a concern for these two operations. All the preceding steps in the study are taken with these future tasks of analysis and interpretation in view. The concern for analysis and interpretation, enters almost all the earlier phases of all the research exercise.

In any successful study, the anticipated tasks of analysis and interpretation largely determine what goes on before and conversely, the analysis of data in many a study is designed before the data are collected (with the possible exception of exploratory or furmulative studies where the researcher has no idea as to what kind of answers he wants the data to give out since he does not have any specific question for a start).

Although the extent or early concern with both these subsequent operations will vary from study to study (as was suggested with reference to the exploratory studies), it is safe to assert that no scientific enquiry should be planned without anticipating what will be needed to be done when the data are in and without a concern for the possible interpretation of the research findings. Failing this, the investigator may discover a bit too late that he cannot proceed with the analysis because certain relevant data are missing.

Problems of analysis and interpretation also vary from study to study. Typically, they present greater difficulties in exploratory or formulative studies than in experimental investigations.

Let us now discuss at some length each of the processes involved in the broad operation which we have called the analysis of data. Our discussion will include: *(a)* classification or establishment of categories for data, *(b)* application of categories to raw data through coding, *(c)* the tabulation of data, *(d)* statistical analysis of data, and *(e)* inferences about causal relations among variables. We shall deal with these procedures in the above order.

A. Establishment of Categories or Classification of Data

Social science research generally involves a large variety of responses to different kinds of questions asked or stimulti presented to the sample or 'population' of respondents.

These responses may be verbal or non-verbal. Clearly, if a large number of different kinds of responses are to be organized such that they can be used in answering the research questions, or in drawing generalizations, they must be grouped into a limited number of categories or classes. To take a simple example, suppose a questions is put to respondents, "Are you in favour of the objective type examination for college students?" The responses of the respondents may possibly be grouped under four broad categories, as under:

(*a*) "Yes" responses.

(*b*) "No" responses.

(*c*) "Don't know", "Can't say" etc., responses.

(*d*) "Did not reply."

Suppose another question asked to the respondents is, "To which social class would you say you belong?" The responses of the respondents may be grouped into the following categories:

(*a*) Upper class.

(*b*) Middle class.

(*c*) Lower class.

(*d*) "Can't say."

(*e*) Other responses (like, "I don't believe in social classes." "It hardly matters swhere I belong" etc.).

A prerequisite to taking a decision about the categories to be instituted for grouping the data is that the researcher must select some appropriate principle of classification. The research question or hypothesis, if any has been formulated, provides a good logical basis for selecting a classificatory principle. Suppose, the hypothesis in a study is: "Students who have had an experience of studying in co-eduational schools will have more favourable attitude toward the system of co-education." Here, obviously, one of the principles of classification of responses will be whether or not the respondent has had prior experience of co-educational system. Another basis of classifying responses would be the degree of favourableness or unfavourableness expressed toward the co-educational system. Other bases of classification may also be invoked, depending on what further associations are to be scrutinized. The first basis of classification would yield two categories of responses:

(*a*) said, they had a prior experience of co-education;

(*b*) said, they did not have any prior experience of co-education.

These two categories contain within themselves the entire range of responses (assuming, of course, that no respondent refused to answer or did not respond or gave some 'other response.' No responses on the above assumption are beyond the compass of these two categories. These two categories together form what is known as a "category-set."

A 'category-set' must meet the following three requirements:

(1) The set of categories should be derived from a single classificatory principle. This requirement is quite understandable because if more than one principle of classification is employed, a single response may be claimed by more than one category. Thus, the categories will not be independent of each other. For example, if we have three categories constituting the category-set, *e.g.,* male, female, child, deriving obviously, from two classificatory principles, namely, sex and age respectively, then any one case (respondent) may be covered by more than one category in the category-set. For example, a child may also be a male, a female may also be a child and so on. The classificatory principle may, however, be a compound one, *i.e.,* made up of two or more criteria, *i.e.,* male child, female child, etc.

(2) The second requirement is that the category-set should be exhaustive, that is, it should be possible to place every response in one of the categories within the set. 'No response' should be left out for want of an appropriate category in the set that will include it. Whatever be the responses, it must be covered by some category within the set. For example, if the people of the world were to be clasified on the basis of their racial stock, the category-set constituted of three categories, namely, *(a)* Caucasoid, *(b)* Negroid and *(c)* Mongoloid, would clearly not be an exhaustive category-set in accord with the requirement outlined above, since it does not contain a single category in which many of the Indian people (and some others) can find a place.

(3) The last requirement is a corollary of the first one, namely, that the categories within the set should be mutually exclusive; that is, the categories should not overlap. Thus, no response would be claimed by more than one category within the set.

Establishment of categories for data characteristic of social sciences is not always an easy task. The classificatory principle may often be a compound one (as opposed to simple, unitary). The task of drawing out all the mutually exclusive categories which together would exhaust the total universe of responses, on the basis of a compound classificatory principle, is indeed an exacting one, demanding imagination. It is a great help in such cases to reduce the attributes costituting the compound principle of classification to symbols or codes and draw out by means of the technique of *Boolean expansion,* the entire range of possible categories comprising the category-set. Let us take a very simple example. Suppose the researcher considers three attributes, *e.g.,* sex (male of female), age (below 21 years of age or above 21 years of age) and marital status (married or single) as constituents of his single (but compound) principle of classification and reduces these to symbols as under:

Male = S, female = $\overline{S}$

Below 21 years of age = A, Above 21 years of age = $\overline{A}$

Married = M, Single = $\overline{M}$ *

The resulting category-set will be the exhaustive totality consisting of all possible combinations of these three attributes that comprise the compound classificatory principle. The possible combinations, *i.e.,* categories, will be $2^3 = 2 \times 2 \times 2 = 8$ in number.

These are as under:

(1) $S\ A\ M$

(2) $\bar{S}\ A\ M$

(3) $S\ \bar{A}\ M$

(4) $S\ A\ \bar{M}$

(5) $\bar{S}\ \bar{A}\ M$

(6) $\bar{S}\ A\ \bar{M}$

(7) $S\ \bar{A}\ \bar{M}$

(8) $\bar{S}\ \bar{A}\ \bar{M}$

Decoding, *i.e.,* substituting the real connotations for the symbols, we get eight mutually exclusive categories which read as under:

(1) Males below 21 and married.

(2) Females below 21 years and married.

(3) Males above 21 years and married.

(4) Males below 21 years and unmarried.

(5) Females above 21 years and married.

(6) Females below 21 years and unmarried.

(7) Males above 21 years and unmarried.

(8) Females above 21 years and unmarried.

By the same token, if the compound classificatory principle is constituted of four attributes, we shall have $2^4 = 2 \times 2 \times 2 \times 2$, *i.e.,* 16 mutually exclusive categories. It should be clear now how this method of establishing categories, rather than intuition, makes the task of classification much easier and fool-proof.

It is obvious that the establishment of a set of categories is relatively easy if the responses obtained from the respondents during the study are fairly simple and clear-cut and so the categories can be easily defined in an unambiguous way. Although this is the way categories should always be defined, the task is much more difficult with certain types of content. To such hypothetical content, we turn, presently.

Suppose in a study the researcher asked the male students, "How would you say the female students feel about studying in the same college with male students like you?" The answers are likely to range from indications of highly favourable attitudes (imputed

---

For the sake of convenience, we have taken only two sub-classes under marital status, *i.e.,* married and single. We are aware that there are certain other possibilities, viz., widow, widower, divorced, etc.

to female students) to imputations of highly unfavourable attitudes. Suppose, these are some of the answers received from respondents.

(1) 'They like the idea.'

(2) 'I don't think they mind.'

(3) 'They think it lowers them.'

(4) 'I don't come in contact with them, so I wouldn't know.'

(5) 'They hate it.'

(6) 'Some of them like it, some don't.'

(7) 'They want to study here so they can say they are no less than the males.'

(8) 'In a purely ladies' college they would miss much, so they seem to like it here.'

In regard to the above responses it would not be difficult to evolve a simple set of categories based on the classificatory principle of favourable versus unfavourable attitudes imputed to girl students. But we find that both favourable and unfavourable answers convey different shades of meanings.

The male student who says, "They (the girl students) want to study here so they can say they are no less than males" conveys something different from one who says, "They like the idea." Similarly, the male student who says, "They think it lowers them" is again saying something different from the one who says, "They hate it."

Thus, we see that two attributes, *i.e.,* (1) imputation of favourable or unfavourable attitudes to girls, and (2) explicit reference or absence of reference to benefits or harm supporting favourable or unfavourable attitudes are two significant constituents of a compounded principle of classification. The categories in the category-set in accord with the ideal requirements of a category-set discussed earlier, may be put down as under:

(1) Favourable attitude imputed to girl students, explained in terms of benefits they derive from studying in the same college with male students (for example, 7th and 8th answers).

(2) Favourable attitude imputed to girls without explicit reference to benefits gained from studying in the same college with males (*e.g.,* statement No. 1).

(3) Neutral or accommodative attitude imputed to girls (*e.g.,* statement No. 1).

(4) Unfavourable attitude imputed to girls, explained in terms of disadvantages (negative benefits) they derive from studying in the same college with male students.

(5) Unfavourable attitude imputed to girls without explicit reference to disadvantages or losses resulting from co-education (*e.g.,* statement No. 5).

(6) Other answers, can't say, no answer, don't know (*e.g.,* statement No. 4).

The above illustration would give an idea as to how very complex a classification in social science can get. Working with such complex categories requires considerable care and effort at classification. Even when categories have been worked out carefully their use will present greater problems than the use of categories more narrowly and exactly defined. If a male student in the above example says. "they like it alright here, they know why" it is a moot question whether or not this statement implies a benefit. Thus, additional rules would have to be established to deal with such answers.

It must be said even at the cost of some repetition that although in principle, it is possible to use many attributes of responses for formulation of category-sets, in practice, this is often unnecessary, uneconomical and unrewarding since not all of these classficatory principles bear upon the objective of the study.

Let us now turn to consider the problem of selecting a classificatory principle for categorizing unstructured material (*i.e.,* information collected by unstructured tools).

In studies using structured instruments for gathering data relevant to clearly-formulated research questions or hypothesis, the appropriate principle for classification of responses are fairly clearly prescribed by the nature of the questions and the secured responses. In working with unstructured material or data, however, the first problem is to arrive at decisions about which aspects of the material are to be categorized, *i.e.,* what classificatory principles are to be used in establishing categories.

In exploratory studies which definitionally do not start with a well-formulated problem or explicit hypothesis, the decision about the classificatory principles is difficult to arrive at. At the time of data collection, the investigator does not know which aspects may turn out to be most important. He must therefore, collect a large amount of data of unstructured type. In the course of analysis, the researcher is faced with the problem of dealing not only with unstructured materials but also with a big volume of them.

It is advisable when analyzing data of an exploratory study to develop working hypothesis that will yield workable satisfactory classificatory principles. The researcher is required to read carefully through all his material, being all the time alert to the latent clues in data. Such clues are often secured through studying materials on subjects or situations that contrast with the ones he is studying. Such a study helps the investigator to see the important differences between the two situations. Another procedure to get at such clues is to put together one's cases into groups that seem to have a close kinship or appear to belong together and then ask oneself what led him to feel that the cases he placed in a single group are alike. Yet another approach that may stimulate clues for formulation of working hypothesis is to note matters that seem surprising in view either of certain theoretical expectations or common sense and then to search for possible esplanation of the surprising or unanticipated phenomena.

It should, however, be remembered that even with clear-cut hypothesis, the analysis of unstructured material presents special problems. Firstly, there is always the possibility that information on a given point may be missing from some of the documents. There is also the likelihood of a great deal of material not having a direct bearing on the hypothesis. Besides, there is the problem of deciding on the size of units of the material to which the categories are to be applied. For example, if a researcher was using case-records kept by welfare agencies, he must decide which unit (*e.g.,* clients, statements, acts, social workers, sessions with the client or the entire record) is most appropriate in providing answers to his specific research questions.

B. Coding

Coding consists in assigning symbols, usually numerals to each answer which falls in a predetermined class. In other words, coding may be regarded as the classification process necessary for subsequent tabulation. Through coding, the raw data are transformed into symbols that may be tabulated and counted. This transformation is not however automatic, it involves great deal of judgement on the part of the coder. 'Coder' is the official title for a person who is assigned the responsibility to give particular codes to responses after the recorded notes have been brought to the office. It should be remembered, however, that often the judgement as to which response should be assigned a particular code, is made by a person other than the one who goes by the official designation of 'coder.'

Coding may take place at three different points in a study at each of which, different kinds of persons may be responsible for assigning codes to the raw data. In many a study, the respondent himself may be asked to assign codes to his own reaction or situation. This is true for many poll-type and multiple-choice questions. For example, when the respondent is asked to indicate which of the classes (say income groups) he belongs to, *e.g., (a)* below 3000 rupees p.m., *(b)* Rs. 3001/- to Rs. 6000/- p.m., *(c)* Rs. 6001/- to Rs. 9000/- p.m., *(d)* Rs. 9001/- and above, the respondent codes his response simply by ticking off his position among the given alternatives. The second point at which the coding can take place is when in the course of data collection, the interviewer or observer categorizes the subjects' responses. This is what is being done when an interviewer or observer employs a rating scale to describe a person's response or behaviour. The final point at which coding can take place is, of course, when the raw uncategorized data (collected especially throuh unstructured instruments of data-collection) are deposited in the project office and the official coders here exercise their judgement to assign particular codes to particular responses or data.

Let us briefly compare and contrast the pros and cons of coding by the official coders in the office and coding by the interviewers or observers done in the course of data-collection in the field.

The interviewers or observers are in a position to notice the situation as well as the individual's behaviour. Thus, they have more information upon which to base their judgements in regard to the appropriate categorization of responses as compared to the coders working on the basis of written records which may not give a complete idea about the real meaning of the response. Another advantage of coding by data-collectors themselves is that, both time and labour can be saved.

On the contrary, coding in the office by coders has certain signal advantages. Coding of complex data which requires time for reflection should advisedly be done by the office-coders.

On the spot coding judgement made by data-collectors may not be as discerning as judgements made with more time for deliberation. The judgement of data-collectors may be coloured by many factors, *viz.,* respondent's appearances, accents and responses to previous questions, mannerisms, etc. Secondly, there is a danger of the data-collectors lacking in uniformity when coding responses. Thus, comparability of data obtained from a large number of respondent is hampered. Thirdly, the interviewers or observers may develop their own personal frames of reference in respect of the material that they are coding. This would tend to make their categorizations unreliable, after a time. A common frame of references is easier to obtain and maintain in the office-coding operation than in the field.

Let us discuss some of the important problems related to reliability in coding. There are many things that may operate to make the judgement of coders unreliable. Some of the factors may arise from the data to be categorized, some from the nature of the categories that are to be applied and still others may emanate from the coders themselves. We shall now consider briefly some of these factors and the ways they can be guarded against.

Many of the difficulties that occur in coding result from the inadequacies of data. Frequently, the data do not supply enough relevant information for a reliable coding. This could be due to deficient and inadequate data-collection procedures. These difficulties, however, can generally be overcome by careful editing of data. The process which consists in scrutinizing the data to improve their quality for coding known as *editing.*

When the data-collector hands in his material to the project office, the possibility of eliminating many potential coding difficulties still exist. A careful examination of the data as soon as they are collected and if necessary, a systematic questioning of the interviewers or observers helps avert many coding problems.

Not only does editing help to avoid later coding problems, it may also substantially improve the quality of data-collection by pointing out where the interviewers or observers might have misunderstood instructions or might not have recorded data in sufficient detail. In fact, editing should be done in the course of pre-testing the interview or the observation-schedule training the interviewers or observers and in fact throughout the period of data-collection. Editing at the project office goes a long way in removing coding problems. Thus, editing must be done while the interviewers or observers can be easily made available for questioning.

As we have suggested, editing involves a careful scrutiny of the interview or observation schedules. These should be checked for:

(1) *Completeness:* The editors need to see that all items are duly filled in. A blank space next to a question in an interview schedule, for example, may mean either 'no response' or 'Don't know' or refusal to answer or inapplicability of question, or the question having been omitted by oversight, etc.

(2) The editor should examine the interview or observation schedules to find out whether the handwriting or the symbols or codes assigned by interviewer or observer can be easily understood by the coder. It is always advisable to check for *legibility* when the material is handed in and if necessary to get the interviewer or observer to rewrite it. If this is not done, coding may get stuck up at a stage when the interviewers or observers may not easily be recalled for questioning.

(3) Editing also involves examining the schedules for *comprehenstibility*. It often happens that a recorded response is perfectly comprehensible to the interviewer or observer, but not intelligible to the coder because the context of behaviour or response is not known to the coder. Systematic questioning of the data-collectors will clear off confusion and ambiguities and improve considerably the quality of coding.

(4) The data should also be examined or checked to find out whether there are certain inconsistencies in regard to the responses recorded in the schedule. For example, a respondent might have said in response to one of the earlier questions that he had never met people of particular group and yet, in response to a later question he might have said something about visiting certain people of this group in course of his rounds. If such is the case, there is an obvious need to enquire into this inconsistency, and get it clarified through questioning the data-collectors.

(5) It is also necessary to check the degree of uniformity with which the interviewers have followed instructions in collecting and recording data. Coding may be hampered if a response is recorded in units other than those specified in the instructions.

(6) It should be noted that some response may simply appear to be irrelevant for the purpose of the investigation. This is likely to happen if a question is not clearly worked or not intelligently asked. The data should thus be carefully examined with a view to segregating the inappropriate responses from the appropriate ones.

The value of the categorization of data depends naturally on the soundness of cateogries employed. It is necessary that the categories besides being relevant to the purpose of research are also defined from a conceptual point of view. Coding will be unreliable if the categories are not defined clearly in terms of indicators that are applicable to data, here and now. In practice, the categories are defined by means of examples from the data in hand. It is very helpful if illustrations from data show not only what kind of responses typify the category but also help to distinguish the houndary-line between seemingly similar categories.

It is obvious that the quality of coding is affected by the competence of the coders. The training of coders is thus an important step in any study. The training of coders may proceed by the following stages:

Firstly, the various codes are explained to the trainess (coders) and illustrated with examples from the data to be categorized.

Secondly, all the trainee-coders then practice on a sample of the data, problems that arise are discussed by the coders as a group with the supervisor to develop common procedures and definitions.

Thirdly, clues resulting from practice-coding are used to effect revisions in the categories to make them better applicable to the material and to put in writing the procedures and definitions that have evolved during the preliminary coding.

Fourthly, at some point in the practice period when relatively few new problems arise, the coders work on an identical portion of data without consulting one another or the supervisor. The consistency or the reliablity of coding is then computed to determine whether it is feasible to begin coding in right earnest.

Depending on the results of reliability or consistency checks, it may be decided to eliminate the categories that seem too unreliable or to spend more time in training coders or to eliminate coders who are most inconsistent and so on.

Lastly, periodical checks are made to ensure that coders do not become careless with more experience or that they do not develop personal idiosyncratic methods of handling new problems in the material. To ensure uniformity, and decision that is made after coding has begun should be communicated to all coders without delay.

Obviously, the consistency and appropriateness with which a given type of answer is assigned to a given category will have an important bearing on the outcome of analysis. hence, it is important to check the reliability of coding and to increase the agreement among coders as much as possible. It is, of course, difficult to set any given level of reliability as the standard to be attained. Different types of material present different degrees of difficulty in achieving reliability. As a rule, the more structured the material to be coded and hence simpler the categories used, the higher the reliability.

It should be noted that the types of codes used in a study will differ according to whether the data are to be tabulated by machine or by hand. If the data are to be sorted manually, a word-description of the classes is satisfactory. Also abbreviations or letters of alphabates, *e.g.,* 'Y' for Yes, 'N' for No, etc., may be used. Machine tabulation, on the other hand, requires that classes be expressed in numerical symbols, since the machines can only be fed with numerical data. Mechanical tabulation requires the use of punch cards. However, the number of different classes which can be shown on the punch card is limited. In any case, all codes used for machine tabulation can also be used for hand tabulation. If codes are to be put on punch cards of which two sizes are in general use, *i.e.,* 80 column cards and the 54 column cards, it is desirable to use ten on fewer classes/ categories for most items of information or response. The punch card contains 10 numbered spaces and an X and Y in each column making a total of 12 codes that can be used. It is rather complicated procedure to get more than one type of item in a column. For example, nativity and age codes cannot be punched in a single column unless only six age-groupings are used for each.

C. Tabulation

Tabulation is a part of the technical process in the statistical analysis of the data. The essential element in tabulation is the summarization of results in the form of statistical tables. It is only when raw data are divided into groups and counts made of the number of cases falling in these various groups, that it is possible for the researcher to determine what his results mean and to convey his findings to the consumer in a form which can be readily understood. Tabulation naturally depends on establishing categories for raw data, editing and coding of response (punching and running the cards through machines for mechanical tabulation and sorting and tallying for hand tabulation).

Experienced researchers generally develop tabulation plans at about the same time as they draft or construct the data-collection instruments and make sampling plans. The inexperienced researchers seldom concern themselves with tabulation plans until the data have been collected. Of course, it is impossible for the researcher to foresee the entire range of tabulation that will be subsequently desired. He should be familiar enough with his research problem or the subject of investigaiton to be able to draw up tables that will provide answers to the questions which gave rise to the study. The researcher should be able to prepare adequate tabulation plans if he uses the findings from the earlier researches which have elements in common with the one for which the plans are being drawn.

In exploratory studies, a better and safer procedure is to pretest the data-collection instrument on a sample of pupulation of the type that would be covered in the final study. This way, some clues in regard to what kind of tabulation would be meaningful can generally be obtained.

Tabulation, as already suggested, may be done entirely by manual methods; this being known as hand tabulation. Alternatively, it may be done by mechanical methods utilizing automatic and fast power machines for the bulk of data, the process being known as mechanical tabulation. The researcher must decide before he draws detailed tabulation plans for his study, what method of tabulation he would use. This decision will be based on various considerations such as cost, time, personnel, etc. Both hand tabulation as well as mechanical tabulation procedures have their respective merits and limitations. The researcher's alert to these merits and demerits is in a better way to decide which method would be suited to his problem.

We shall briefly review the merits of these two methods of tabulation:

(1) Mechanical tabulation involves much clerical work and specialized operations. Of course, it facilitates speed but the speed may not always be an adequate compensation for extra clerical work.

(2) If the number and types of tables desired are not decided upon before tabulation work is begun, machine-tabulation may be more expedient. But, if hand tabulation is considered to be efficient, the order in which various sorts and counts would be made is determined in advance of tabulation.

(3) A major advantage of machine tabulation is that it facilitates cross-classifications. In large-scale studies where many variables are to be correlated or cross-classified, machine tabulation is reasonably preferable. It is for this reason that mechanical tabulation is used in studies requiring many intercorrelations among variables. But, if the total number of respondents is small, a manual counting of them in accordance with the cross-classificatory principle may be relatively economical.

(4) When there is a great deal of coded information and several punch cards required for each case, hand tabulation may be preferable.

(5) If it is desired to keep the data in a form ready for new tabulation at a relatively short notice punch cards are typically useful. Mechanical tabulation is useful for periodic studies or surveys in which the same type of information is required to be collected at frequent intervals.

(6) The process of sorting and counting is less likely to produce errors if done by machine than if done by hand. Errors, of course, can and do arise in machine tabulation and when they do, they are often very difficult to identify and check. Any errors discovered at coding, editing or field-work stages of the survey may hold up machine-tabulation work. It is often desirable, therefore, to proceed with hand tabulation alongside with the field-work.

(7) Cost of tabulation operations is an important concern of the researcher. Machine tabulation often involves much greater cost since the most of punch cards, charges for punching and verifying, machine charges for sorting and tabulation machines and expenses on hiring specialized services of specific types of machine operators often add up to much more than those involved in hand tabulation.

(8) Another important consideration is time. In mechanical tabulation the work of tabulation as such is done in a very short time, but the preparatory stages as also the training, supervision and possible non-availability of certain types of machines on hire resulting in dislocation of work may all inevitably contribute to wastage of time.

(9) The considerations of convenience can hardly be ignored. If mechanical tabulation demands despatching of raw data to some office far away from the project office, inconveniences involved in packing, transportation, etc., are caused.

(10) Lastly, the amount of commentary material to be recorded and analyzed may also affect the choice of tabulation methods. In some opinion-surveys, the verbatim comments of informants are important. The hand-code card used in hand tabulation alone can provide space for such remarks or comments.

Machines which handle tabulation work are of many kinds. Developments in this field have been extremely rapid during the recent years. Some machines simply sort and count cards, others sort, count and print the results, still others are equipped to perform most complicated statistical operations or calculations. These last-mentioned machines are extremely complex and they must be programmed for a given operation by a specialist in the line.

As was indicated earlier, a table is an exhibit of the numerical data systematically arranged in labelled columns (vertical) and rows (horizontal). A simple or elementary table indicates simple counts of the frequencies with which the various categories in each set occur in the data, for example, the number of people in the sample who have attended high school but not passed, the number of people who have attended college but not graduated and so on. The table given below simply points out the frequencies of visits of fifty respondents to the cinema.

Table 18.1

Showing the Frequency Distribution of a Sample of Respondents based on the Number of Times they Visited the Cinema

Number of visits Per Month	*Number of Respondents*	*Percentage of Respondents*
Never	1	2%
Once	4	8%
Twice	18	36%
Thrice	13	26%
Four Times	7	14%
Five Times	5	10%
Six Times (and more)	2	4%
Total	50	100%

In research, we are often interested in finding out the correlation between two or more variables, *e.g.*, education and income and fertility, simple tables (illustrated above) showing frequency distribution of the respondents in respect of a single characteristic, *e.g.,* education or income or fertility, do not help us see the relationship among two or more variables. The way to see the relationship is by preparing cross-tables or break-down tables. Such tables make possible the grouping of cases that occur jointly in two or more categories, for example, tabulation of the number of cases that are high in education, low in income and have between 2 and 3 children, or the number of cases that are low in education, low in income and have betwen 4 and 5 children and so on. The most elementary form of cross-tabulation the students are familiar with is the college time-table.

Suppose a researcher wants to see the relationship among three variables, *viz.,* occupation, income and fertility. He must employ a scheme of tabulation that will afford all possible combinations of the different categories of these three variables. Cross-tabulation of the data on a hypothetical sample of 100 persons may be presented as under:

Table 18.2

Income Group

Occupation	*below 200*		*201-400*		*401-600*		*601-800*		*801-1000*		*Total*
Fertility	*W.C.*	*B.C.*	*W.C.*	*B.C.*	*W.C.*	*B.C.*	*W.C.*	*B.C.*	*W.C.*	*B.C.*	
No issue	–	–	1	–	3	1	4	1	5	–	15
1 to 2 issues	1	–	4	–	10	3	11	3	6	–	38
3 to 4 issues	5	2	4	3	1	4	1	3	–	2	25
5 to 6 issues	2	8	1	5	–	2	–	–	–	–	18
7 & above	–	3	–	1	–	–	–	–	–	–	4
Total	8	13	10	9	14	10	16	7	11	2	100

In the above table, we have indicated the number of children in rows. This variable of fertility has been divided into five categories, *i.e.,* no issue, 1 to 2 issues, 3 to 4, 5 to 6, 7 and above. So in the margin on the left hand, we have these 5 categories of fertility. We have indicated the income of 100 respondents in columns. The income variable has been sub-divided into five categories, *i.e.,* below Rs. 200, Rs. 201-400, 401-600, 601-800, 801-1000. Thus, we have five columns corresponding to these categories. Again since we have one more variable, *i.e.,* occupation to accommodate, the columns for income have each been sub-divided into two parts corresponding to the two categories in which the occupations have been divided, *i.e.,* white collar occupation and blue-collar occupation. Thus, we have ten vertical columns, corresponding to income and occupation. The number of horizontal rows we have for the categories of the fertility variable is five. Thus, we have ten columns crossed by five rows making up the body of the table. The intersection of the columns and rows has effected 50 (fifty) cells or boxes. Each of these boxes or cells houses a particular number of cases which are different from those in other cells either in respect of income or occupation, in fertility or in any two of these or in all of these. Let us read the table to get some idea as to what it represents.

Out of the total sample of 100 cases, there are 25 who have between 3 and 4 issues. Of these 25, reading from the left-hand side, 5 persons (with between 3 and 4 children) have income below Rs. 200/- and are employed in white-collar occupations. Two persons (with between 3 and 4 children) have income below Rs. 200 and are employed in blue-collar occupations. Let us now take the second row. Of the total respondents, 38 have between 1 and 2 children. 11 (in the 7th cell) who have between 1 and 2 children are from the income group Rs. 601 to Rs. 800 and are employed in white-collar occupation. This exercise should make it very clear that cross-tabulation is an essential step in the discovery of or testing of relationships among the variables contained in the data.

As we have stated, tabulation is a means to present data in a summarizd form in a way that facilitates the required statistical calculations. Data may, however, be presented in other ways, *i.e.,* instead of presenting them in a tabular form, the researcher may present them in the form of diagrams or graphs. Such diagrammatic or graphic representations do have the merit of being intelligible to a less knowledgeable reader. But they suffer from the limitation that they are not so useful as a basis for statistical calculations. We shall return to this point later in this chapter. Let us now proceed to discuss the next operation, *i.e.,* the statistical analysis of data. Tabulation is a prerequisite or a first step in this direction.

D. Statistical Analysis of Data

In research, we are not concerned with each individual respondent. The purpose of research is broader than this. That is, we wish to know much more than simply that a given respondent, for example, has extremely favourable attitude toward disarmament and that another respondent has moderately unfavourable attitudes toward the same issue. But this information is just not enough. Social science researches are generally directed toward providing information about a particular population of respondents mostly via a sample. The sample of the totality might be asked certain questions related to the problem of our study, or be subjected to some form of observation. Let us suppose that we have asked a sample of a thousand college students studying in 'post-graduate' classes a series of questions with a view to securing information about their study habits. Our research would thus be directed toward providing information about the 'population' of 'post-graduate' students of which the thousand cases is a sample.

As a necessary step to characterizing this 'population', we would have to describe or summarize the information about study habits that we have obtained on the sample thereof. Tabulation is just a part of this step. In addition, we must estimate the reliability of generalizations of the 'population' from the obtained data. Statistical methods are useful in fulfilling both these ends.

Statistics, a branch of applied Mathematics, is regarded as mathematics applied to observational data. Conceivably everything dealing with the collection, processing, analysis and interpretation of numerical data belongs to the domain of statistics. However, the term 'statistics' is used in several ways. It denotes a compilation of data such as those found in the labour Gazzette or say, Labour Statistics of the Labour Bureau published annually by the Government of India. The second meaning of the term statistics refers to the statistical principles and methods employed in the collection, processing, analysis and interpretation of any kind of data. In this sense, it is a branch of applied mathematics and helps us to know the complex social phenomena in a better way and lends precision to our ideas.

It is of this field of mathematics which is the subject-matter of this section of the chapter.

Functions of Statistics

Statistics has patently two broad functions. The first of these functions is description and the summarizing of information in a manner so as to make it more usable.

The second function of statistics is induction, which involves either making generalizations about some 'population' on the basis of a sample drawn from this population or formulating general laws on the basis of repeated observations. The two functions of statistical methods can be easily understood by the following example. Suppose it is desired to study the problem of labour unrest in a particular area. The first thing to be done here will be to analyse the various causes of labour unrest and to study the impact of each one of these on the various categories of labour, *viz.,* male workers and female workers or skilled labour and unskilled labour. This kind of analysis will give us an insight into the problem and we may be able to know from such an analysis many important things, *e.g.,* that the involvement of male workers in strikes is much higher than that of the female workers or that the labour unrest in big industries is much higher than in small industries. Such an analysis may lead us to the conclusion regarding the incidence of labour unrest in the country and factors responsible for it. The former example illustrates the process of descriptive sttistics whereas the latter, that of inductive statistics.

The Place of Statistics in Social Research

It is evident that knowledge of basic statistical concepts and techniques is necessary for an intelligent understanding of the generality of life. Out of the welter of single events, social researchers seek general trends; out of the vast and confusing variety of individual chartacters; they continually search for the underlying group characteristics.

There are essentially two reasons why the expertise in statistics and the need to study statistics have grown enormously in the field of social sciences. One reason is that the huge amount of data collected by researchers needs simplification so as to render them capable of being commonly understood without much difficulty. The second and even more important reason is the increasing quantitative approach being currently employed in social science research.

Seemingly statistical considerations enter only at the analysis stage of the research process after the data have been collected, and near to the point in time when the initial plans for analysis are formulated and a sample is to be drawn. But this does not imply that a social researcher can plan and carry out his entire research without any knowledge of statistics and then hand over the data to the statistician for analysis. If a researcher lacked conversance in statistics the results of a costly research project would probably be disappointing if not useless.

Indeed, the problems that will be encountered in analysis and interpretation have to be anticipated at every stage in the research process and in this sense, statistical methods are involved throughout. This implies that statistics is a very useful tool for the social scientist. It is a much more useful tool for exploratory analyses than might possibly be imagined. Most social researches are based on highly tentative theoretical ideas. The variables that need to be controlled in the analysis or even the priorities and sequence of analysis-steps that should be followed are neither precise nor predetermined, researchers are generally awed by the complexity of data analysis no sooner a set of variables is introduced. In these circumstances especially, knowledge of the statistical methods becomes an invaluable tool for the social researcher in disentangling highly complex interrelationships.

Limitations of Statistics

Some of the major limitations of the statistical science and hence the attendant cautions that we need to be alerted about while using statistical techniques in the course of a research exercise are well worth noting.

One of the obvious limitations of statistics is that it is more specifically applicable to problems that are amenable to quantitative expression and treatment. Although qualitative attributes may sometimes be subjected to statistical analysis, these of necessity, have to be translated into quantitative indices by recourse to operational definitions. But then, much would depend on the validity of the operational assumptions. Unfortunately, this is a pit many a researcher falls into, *i.e.,* qualitative data are often operationalised as numerical values without a deeper concern for their validity, in which case, it is rather the poor data that stand to blame and not the statistical science. In as much as many a problem of concern to social scientists is influenced greatly by subjective factors outside the ambit of mathematical treatment, the statistical approach hardly helps in affording us a rounded understanding of the problems.

It is understandable that the statistical laws are applicable to averages of aggregates. These pathetically ignore the individual inricacies of solitary units. Such a neglect may, in certain investigations, lead to merely superficial findings. The social-human sciences typically requisition a keen concern for the unique and the idiosyncratic aspects in society.

Additionally, there is a likelihood that statistics may be misused, so much so that the researcher may be tempted to twist them to suit his fond conclusions or hypotheses.

This also applies equally to the very sensitive tools that the statistical methods afford. They are prone to be misused easily. Thus, great caution needs to be exercised while using them. As we shall have an occasion to see later, the validity of certain statistical methods depends on the nature of data, the levels of measurement, the knowledge of the pertinent aspects of the situations and lastly, the assumptions made vis-a-vis the sample from which the data are secured.

What is most important for us as potential users of statistical methods, therefore, is to bear well in mind that statistics has powerful muscles that can only serve but not direct. Much would depend on the use we want to put it to and whether the situation justifies it. What is given out by statistical computations may not be the final 'truth' since it is basically an approximation of typicality and by nature probabilistic. It is left largely to our interpretative skills to bring out the real message underlying the statistical inferences and propositions.

Proportions, Percentages and Ratios

In order to make the data easily understandable and amenable to analysis and interpretation, the size of the data is considerably reduced and a large number of figures is condensed. However, even after this basic arithmetical operation, data might be fairly voluminous and unwieldy and it may not be easy to draw inferences from them. This difficulty is taken care of by measures like proportions, percentages and ratios.

Proportions

The proportion of cases in any given category is defined as the number in the category divided by the total number of cases. In calculation of proportions, it is presumed that the method of classification has been such that categories are mutually exclusive and the category-set exhaustive. That is, any given individual has been placed in one and only one category.

To illustrate, let us take a nominal scale consisting of four categories with n_1, n_2, n_3, and n_4 cases, respectively. Let the total number of cases be N. Hence, proportion of individuals in the first, second, third and fourth categories are n_1/N, n_2/N, n_3/N, and n_4/N respectively. The following illustration will clarify the point.

Table 18.3

Number of Men and Women in Various Faculties of Subjects

S.No.	*Course*	*Men*	*Women*
1.	Science	75	60
2.	Humanities	160	110
3.	Commerce	82	56
	Total	317	226

The proportion of science students among males is 75/317 or 0.236; the comparable figure for females is 60/226 or 0.265. Other proportions can be computed in a similar fashion and results summarised in tabular form (Table 18.4).

Table 18.4

Proportions of Men and Women in Various Courses

S.No.	*Course*	*Men*	*Women*
1.	Science	0.236	0.265
2.	Humanities	0.505	0.487
3.	Commerce	0.259	0.248
	Total	1.000	1.000

The value of a proportion cannot be greater than unity, i.e., 1. Thus, if we add the proportions of cases in all categories, the result is unity. This is an important property of proportions.

Percentage

The words per cent mean per hundred. Hence, percentage can be obtained from proportions by simply multiplying them by 100. In other words, percentage is the rate per hundred.

The figures in Table 18.4 may just as well be expressed in terms of percentages.

Table 18.5

Proportions and Percentages of Men and Women in Various Courses

S.N.	*Course*	*No.*	*Proportion*	*Percentage*	*No.*	*Proportion*	*Percentage*
1.	Science	75	0.236*	23.6*	60	0.265	26.5
2.	Humanities	160	0.505	50.5	110	0.487	48.7
3.	Commerce	82	0.259	25.9	56	0.248	27.8

$* \ \frac{75}{317} = 0.236 \qquad ** \ \frac{75}{317} \times 100 = 23.66$

Conventionally, percentages are calculated upto the nearest decimal and adjustments are made in the last digits so that totals come to exactly 100.

Ratio

The ratio of any number A to another number B is defined as the numerical quantity obtained by dividing A by B. Suppose that there are 800 male students and 300 female students in M.A. (economics) class. The ratio of male students to female students is 800/300. In calculating ratio the key term is the word 'to.' Whatever quantity precedes this word is placed in the numerator while the quantity following it is treated as the denominator.

In practice, a ratio is either reduced to its simplest form by cancelling common factors or is expressed in terms of a denominator of unity. Thus, the ratio of male students to female studetns in the above example will be written as 8:3 or 2.66 to 1.

Proportion and Percentage

For use of proportions and percentages, the following rules of thumb are important:

(i) Total number of cases should be always reported along with proportions or percentages.

(ii) Percentages must not be computed unless the number of cases on which the percentage is based is in the neighbourhood of 50 or more.

(iii) Percentages may be computed in either direction and careful attention should be given to each table to determine exactly how each percentage has been obtained.

Measures of Central Tendency — Averages

In the preceding section we discussed the various statistical derivatives like ratios, proportions and percentages. These derivatives are not enough to make possible the proper analysis and interpretation of data. It is often essential to represent a set of data by means of a single number which, in a way, is descriptive of the entire set. Obviously, the figure which is used to represent a whole series should neither have the lowest value in the series nor the highest value, it should have a value somewhere between these two limits, possibly in the centre. Such figures are called measures of typicality or central tendency or simple averages.

Before we study these measures, let us learn some of the basic concepts that would be used in calculations.

(1) *Variables:* The concept variable refers to any quantity or characteristic quantities which may possess different numerical values or categories. For instance, time, age, wages and income, etc., are variables.

(2) *Ungrouped Data:* The data collected for the purpose of a statistical inquiry may be simple figures without any form or structure. Data obtained in this way, obviously enough, are in a raw state for they have not gone through any statistical treatment. This shapelessness of data is known as ungrouped data or raw data. Consider the data presented in Table 18.6.

Table 18.6

Roll No.	*Marks*	*Roll No.*	*Marks*	*Roll No.*	*Marks*	*Roll No.*	*Marks*
1	40	11	60	21	43	31	58
2	37	12	38	22	41	32	24
3	61	13	39	23	25	33	71
4	67	14	40	24	42	34	55
5	59	15	51	25	38	35	33
6	70	16	37	26	40	36	65
7	39	17	40	27	50	37	55
8	46	18	72	28	30	38	66
9	68	19	39	29	33	39	40
10	41	20	50	30	54	40	62

Ungrouped data presented in the above manner are not in the form which make them readily amenable to genralization and interpretation. Only a vague impression may be obtained from their perusal.

(3) *Grouped Data:* In order that data are more readily comprehensible, the bulk of data is further reduced by grouping. A first and elementary step in effecting such a grouping of data is by representing the repetitions of a particular mark by tallies instead of corresponding them to the marks obtained.

Table 18.7

Title Tally Sheets showing the Marks obtained by 40 Students

Marks	*Tallies*	*Marks*	*Tallies*	*Marks*	*Tallies*	*Marks*	*Tallies*
24	I	37	II	50	II	63	–
25	I	38	II	51	I	64	–
26	–	39	III	52	–	65	I
27	–	40	V	53	–	66	I
28	–	41	II	54	–	67	I
29	–	42	I	55	II	68	I
30	I	43	I	56	–	69	I
31	–	44	–	57	–	70	I
32	–	45	–	58	I	71	I
33	II	46	I	59	I	72	I
34	–	47	–	60	I	–	–
35	–	48	–	61	I	–	–
36	–	49	–	62	I	–	–

Discrete and Continuous Data: Data may be discrete or continuous. A discrete series is formed from data which are capable of exact measurement. In other words, descrete character of certain kinds of data emanates from the fact that different imaginable values are not possible. A family will have 1, 2, 3, or even 4 children, but it cannot have 3.21 children. Countrarily, one can count the number of workers whose wages are exactly Rs. 350 per week or Rs. 400 per week. This type of data can form a discrete series.

Table 18.8

Frequency Distribution: Discrete Series

S.No.	*No. of children Per Couple*	*No. of Couples*
1.	0	6
2.	1	7
3.	2	11
4.	3	5
5.	4	1
	Total	30

Certain other kinds of data can comprise a continuous series in that all manner of values may be assigned. There are certain items which are not capable of exact measurement like height or weight. We cannot count the number of students whose heights are exactly 160 centimetres. In such cases the data are assigned to groups or class intervals. For instance, we can count the number of students whose heights are between 155 and 165 centimetres. The data of this type are called continuous data (Table 18.9).

Table 18.9

Frequency Distribution: Continuous Series

S.No.	*Height in Centimeters*	*No. of Students*
1.	150–155	12
2.	155–160	15
3.	160–165	18
4.	165–170	17
5.	170–175	15
6.	175–180	14
	Total	91

Each group of 5 consecutive values of heights, namely, 150-155, 155-160, 160-165, etc., is called a class. Since each class subsumes five values, which is the magnitude or width of the class, commonly known as class interval. The first figure of each class is called its lower limit while the last figure of each class is known as the upper limit. Every class interval has a mid-point which is mid-way between the upper and lower limits. Fig. 18.1 illustrates the lower limits, upper limits and mid-points in regard to the classes.

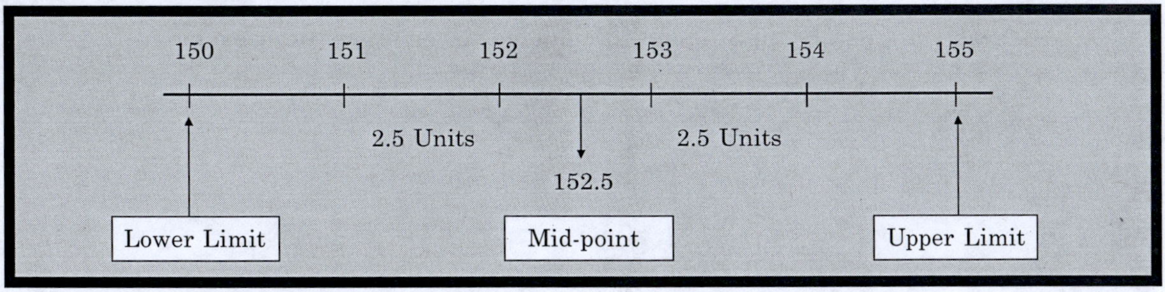

Inclusive and Exclusive Class-Interval: In inclusive class interval, items having values equal to the limits (both lower and upper) of a class are included in the frequency of that class (Table 18.8). On the contrary, when the items equal to the size of either the lower limit or the upper limit are excluded from the frequency reckoning of that class, the class interval is known as exclusive, (Tables 18.9 and 18.10). The data given in Table 18.6 will take the following forms, if classes are inclusive and exclusive, respectively:

Table 18.10

Marks Obtained by 40 Students (Inclusive series)

S.No.	*Marks*	*Frequency*
1.	24–33	5
2.	34–43	16
3.	44–53	4
4.	54–63	8
5.	64–73	7
	Total	40

Table 18.11

Marks Obtained by 40 Students (Exclusive series lower limit excluded)

S.No.	*Marks*	*Frequency*
1.	24–34	5
2.	34–44	16
3.	44–54	5
4.	54–64	7
5.	64–74	7
	Total	40

Table 18.12

Marks Obtained by 40 Students (Exclusive series upper limit excluded)

S.No.	*Marks*	*Frequency*
1.	24–34	5
2.	34–44	16
3.	44–54	4
4.	54–64	8
5.	64–74	7
	Total	40

Central Tendencies

There are three important measures of central tendency or average typically used in social science research, *viz.*, the mean or arithmetic average, the median and the mode.

The Arithmetic Mean

The arithmetic mean is by far the most common among the averages. It is relatively, easy to calculate, simple to understand and widely used in statistical calculations.

The arithmetic mean is defined as the sum of the values of all the items and dividing the total by the number of items. An example will help us learn how to calculate the arithmetic mean. Let us suppose that eight students receive marks: 54, 58, 60, 62, 70, 72, 75 and 77 respectively, in an examination. The mean grade score will be:

$$\text{Mean} = \frac{54 + 58 + 60 + 62 + 70 + 72 + 75 + 77}{8} = 66$$

The procedure in calculating the mean may be expressed in algebraic terms by the following formula :

$$\frac{X_1 + X_2 + X_3 + X_4 + ... + X_N}{N}$$

Where X_1, X_2, X_3, X_4...X_N are the item-values. N represents number of items.

The above formula can be made more compact by assigning to the arithmetic mean the symbol $\overline{X}$ (which is read '*X*' bar) and using the Σ notation. The symbol Σ is capital sigma.

Let ΣX stand for "The sum of the X's"

i.e., $X_1 + X_2 + X_3 + X_4 + ... + X_N$

Then we have:

$$\text{Arithmetic Mean} = \overline{X} = \frac{\Sigma X}{N}$$

Calculating the Mean from the Ungrouped Data

Direct Method: The above formula can be used to calculate arithmetic mean from ungrouped data. The following example would illustrate:

Example: The table given below gives the daily wages received by 15 workers in a certain factory. How do we compute the mean daily wages paid to a worker?

Table 18.13

Daily Wages Paid to Workers

S.No.	*Name of the Worker*	*Daily Wages in (X)*
1.	A	Rs 14
2.	B	Rs 14
3.	C	Rs 15
4.	D	Rs 20
5.	E	Rs 12
6.	F	Rs 16
7.	G	Rs 17
8.	H	Rs 21
9.	I	Rs 14
10.	J	Rs 21
11.	K	Rs 21
12.	L	Rs 22
13.	M	Rs 18
14.	N	Rs 20
15.	O	Rs 13
	N = 15	ΣX = 258

Solution:

If daily wages of worker is represented by $\Sigma X = 258$,

we have $\overline{X} = \dfrac{258}{15} = 17.2$

Mean Daily Wages = 17.2 or Rs. 17.20

Short-cut Method: This short-cut method of computing mean is based on an important property of the arithmetic mean, *i.e.,* the algebraic sum of the deviations of the various item values from their mean is always equal to zero. This also implies that the sum of the deviations of the various values from some arbitrary value other than the arithmetic mean will not be equal to zero.

This property may be well illustrated with the following example:

Table 18.14

S.No.	$\overline{X}$	*Deviation (d) from* $\overline{X} = 0$	*Deviations* (d^1) *from 4 (an arbitrary value)*
1.	6	6.9 = 3	6.4 = 2
2.	7	7.9 = 2	7.4 = 3
3.	9 $\overline{X}$ 45/5 = 9	9.9 = 0	9.4 = 5
4.	11	11.9 = 2	11.4 = 7
5.	12	12.9 = 3	12.4 = 8
N = 5	ΣX = 45	ΣX = 0	Σd' = 25

This phenomenon shall be so for any series of values. Thus, we can assume an arbitrary mean to calculate the deviations of their values from this assumed mean. If the sum of deviations is divided by the number of items and added to the assumed mean, we shall get the actual arithmetic mean.

Symbolically: Arithmetic Mean $\overline{X} = a + \dfrac{\Sigma d'}{N}$

Where $\overline{X}$ is the arithmetic mean,

a is the assumed arithmetic mean.

Σd' is the sum of deviations from the assumed mean.

N is the number of item values.

If we compute mean daily wages paid to workers from the data given in example by this short-cut method it will give us exactly the same answer as we get by the direct method. This is illustrated below:

Table 18.15

S.No.	*Name of the Workers*	*Daily Wages in Rs.*	*Deviation from an Assumed Mean (20) (d')*
1.	A	14	– 6
2.	B	14	– 6
3.	C	15	– 5
4.	D	20	0
5.	E	12	– 8
6.	F	16	– 4
7.	G	17	– 3

8.	H	21	+ 1
9.	I	14	– 6
10.	J	21	+ 1
11.	K	21	+ 1
12.	L	22	+ 2
13.	M	16	– 2
14.	N	20	0
15.	O	13	– 7
N = 15			Σd' = 42

Arithmetic Mean or $\overline{X} = a + \frac{\Sigma d'}{N}$

$$= 20 + \left(\frac{-42}{15}\right)$$

$$= 20 - 2.8$$

$$= 17.2$$

Mean daily wages = Rs. 17.20

Calculation of Arithmetic Mean from Grouped Data

Discrete Series: Direct Method: In discrete series the values of the variables are multiplied by their respective frequencies and the sum of the product so obtained is divided by the sum of the frequencies. The resulting quotient is the arithmetic mean of the series.

Symbolically:

$$\overline{X} = \frac{X_1f_1 + X_2f_2 + X_3f_3 + X_4f_4 + \ldots X_Nf_N}{f_1 + f_2 + f_3 + f_4 + \ldots + f_N}$$

$$= \frac{\Sigma Xf}{\Sigma f} \text{ or } \frac{\Sigma Xf}{N} \; (where\ \Sigma f = N)$$

where $X_1, X_2, X_3, X_4 \ldots X_N$ are the values.

and $f_1, f_2, f_3, f_4 \ldots f_N$ their respective frequencies.

Example 2: The following table shows gains in weight of 65 children during a specified period. Calculate mean weight gained by children.

Table 18.16

Gain in Kg. (X)	*No. of Children (f)*	*Xf*
1.	3	3
2.	4	8
3.	6	18
4.	9	36
5.	12	60
6.	11	66
7.	9	63
8.	7	56
9.	4	36
	N = 65	$\Sigma Xf = 346$

Computation

$$\overline{X} = \frac{\Sigma Xf}{N} = \frac{346}{65} = 5.32$$

Mean weight gained = 5.32 Kg. (approx.).

Short-cut Method: In this method the deviation of each item value from the assumed mean is found out and is mulplied by its corresponding frequency. The algebraic sum of the product is divided by the total frequency (*N*) and added to the assumed mean.

Symbolically $\overline{X} = a + \dfrac{\Sigma f.dx}{N}$

Where '*a*' stands for the assumed mean; $\Sigma f.dx$ for the sum of deviations from the assumed mean; and N for the total number of frequencies.

Calculation of arithmetic mean $\Sigma f.dx$ from the data given in example 2.

Table 18.17

Gain in Kg. (X)	*Name of Children (f)*	*Division from Assumed Mean (5) dx*	*f.dx*
1.	3	– 4	– 12
2.	4	– 3	– 12
3.	6	– 2	– 12
4.	9	– 1	– 9
5.	12	0	0
6.	11	+ 1	+ 11
7.	9	+ 2	+ 18
8.	7	+ 3	+ 21
9.	4	+ 4	+ 16
	N = 65		$\Sigma f.dx = 21$

$$\overline{X} = a + \frac{\Sigma f.dx}{N} = 5 + \frac{21}{65} = 5 + 0.32 = 5.32 \text{ (Approximately).}$$

Mean weight = 5.32 Kg. (Approximately).

Calculation

Continuous Series: Direct Method: In calculating arithmetic mean of a continuous series, we take the mid-value of each class as representative of that class (since it is presumed that the frequencies of that class are concern on mid-point) multiply the various mid-values by their corresponding frequencies and sum of the products is divided by sum of the frequencies. The following example will illustrate the method:

Table 18.18

Distribution of Workers by average Monthly Wages

S.No.	*Monthly Wages (in Rs.)*	*No. of Workers*
1.	110–130	15
2.	130–150	30
3.	150–170	60
4.	170–190	95
5.	190–210	82
6.	210–230	75
7.	230–250	23
		Total (N) 380

Solution: Direct Method

Table 18.19

Monthly Wages in Rs.	*Mid-values (m)*	*No. of Workers (f)*	*m x f*
110–130	120*	15	1800
130–150	140	30	4200
150–170	160	60	9600
170–190	180	95	17100
190–210	200	82	16400
210–230	220	75	16500
230–250	240	23	5520
	N = 380	Σmf = 71120	

Calculation

$$* \text{Mid} - \text{value} = \frac{\text{Lower limit} + \text{Upper limit}}{2} = \frac{110 + 130}{2} = \frac{240}{2} = 120$$

$$\overline{X} = \frac{\Sigma mf}{\Sigma f} = \frac{\Sigma mf}{N}$$

$$= \frac{71120}{380} = 187.16$$

Arithmetic Mean = Rs. 187.16 (Approximately).

Solution: Short-cut Method

Table 18.20

Monthly Wages in Rs.	*Mid-values*	*No. of Workers*	*Deviation from Assumed Mean 180 (dx)*	*Step Deviation (d)*	*Total Deviation (fd)*
110–130	120	15	– 60	– 3	– 45
130–150	140	30	– 40	– 2	– 60
150–170	160	60	– 20	– 1	– 60
170–190	180	95	0	0	0
190–210	200	82	+ 20	+ 1	+ 82
210–230	220	75	+ 40	+ 2	+ 150
230–250	240	23	+ 60	+ 3	+ 69
		N = 380			$\Sigma fd' = 136$

$$\text{Arithmetic Mean } (\overline{X}) = a + \frac{\Sigma fd}{N} \times 1$$

Where '*a*' stands for assumed mean $\Sigma fd'$ for sum of total deviations, '*N*' for total number of frequencies and '*I*' for class interval. Now substituting the values in the formula from the table.

$$= 180 + \frac{136}{380} \times 20$$

$$= 180 + 7.16$$

$$= 187.16$$

Arithmetic Mean = Rs. 187.16 (Approximately).

It is necessary to note that while determining the class interval when the class interval is exclusive (say 15-20, 20-25, 25-30) the method of finding class interval *(i)* will be as follows:

Class interval *(i)* Upper limit and lower limit = 20 – 15 = 5.

If, however, the class-interval is inclusive say (15-19, 20-24, 25-29) the apparent limits are not real limits and hence before finding the class-interval, real limits would need to be determined. In determining the class interval of inclusive series it is assumed that figures have been rounded to the nearest unit given. For example, if the classes are written as 10-14, and 15-19, the lower and upper limits would be considered as 9.5-14.5 and 14.5-19.5, respectively.

Steps in the Short-cut Method

Table 18.21

Procedure for Computing the Arithmetic Mean

Steps	*Procedure*	*Application to Table 18.20*
1.	Assume as the mean or average preferably, the mid-value of a class which is the centre of the distribution or near the centre of the distribution.	The mid-value of the class 170-190 which is at the centre of the distribution, is 180 Assumed mean 180.
2.	Calculate the deviations of the mid-values from the assumed mean.	See table 18.9, Column 4 120 – 180 = 60 180 – 180 = 0 140 – 180 = 40 200 – 180 = 20 200 – 180 = 20 160 – 180 = 20 220 – 180 = 40 240 – 180 = 60
3.	Divide the deviations by a common factor or width of the class interval. These deviations are known as step deviations (d).	$\frac{-60}{20} = -3$, $\frac{-40}{20} = -2$ $\frac{-20}{20} = -1$, $\frac{0}{20} = 0$ $\frac{-20}{20} = 1$, $\frac{40}{20} = 2$ $\frac{60}{20} = 3$
4.	Multiply the step deviations with the respective frequencies of the various classes and find out the sum of the products.	15 × (–3) = – 45, 75 × 2 = 150 30 × (–2) = – 60, 23 × 3 = 69 60 × (–1) = – 60, Σdf = 136 95 × 0 = 0 82 × 1 = 82
5.	Divide the sum of the products by frequencies (N) and multiply the results by magnitude of the class interval (i).	$\frac{\Sigma fd}{N} = \frac{136}{380} = 0.358$ $= \frac{\Sigma fd}{N} \times \text{i} = 0.358 \times 20$ = 7.16 (Approximately)
6.	Add this figure to the assumed mean and the result would be the arithmetic mean of the series.	$= a + \frac{\Sigma fd}{N} \times \text{i}$ = 180 + 7.16 = 187.16 (Approximately)

The procedure for computing arithmetic mean may be schematically expressed as follows:

$$\text{Arithmetic Mean} = (\text{Assumed mean}) + \left[\frac{\text{Sum of the products of the step deviations and the respective frequencies of the various classes}}{\text{Sum of the frequencies}}\right] \times \left[\text{Width of the class interval}\right]$$

The Median

The median is another simple measure of central tendency. We sometimes want to ascertain the position of the middle item, when data have been arranged, or we want to divide a group of students into quartiles by locating the individuals who have exactly 25 per cent of the class below them, or exactly 75 per cent below them etc. These measures are known as positional averages. We define the median as the size of the middle item when the items are arrayed in ascending or descending order of magnitude. This means that median divides the series in such a manner that there are as many items above (or larger than the middle one) as there are below (or smaller than) it.

Location of Median in a Series of Ungrouped Data

To locate the median in ungrouped data-set, first the data are arrayed in ascending or descending order. If the number of items is odd the middle item of the array is the median. If N is even, the median is the average of the two middle items. Symbolically, the median is:

Median (X) = The $\left(\frac{N+1}{2}\right)$ th item in the series arrayed in order of magnitude.

Example: The following table gives the daily wages received by 15 workers in a certain factory. Compute the median wages of the data-set.

Table 18.22

Daily Wages Paid to Workers (N = 15)

S.No.	*Daily Wages in Rs.*
1.	14
2.	14
3.	15
4.	20
5.	12
6.	16
7.	17

8.	21
9.	14
10.	21
11.	21
12.	22
13.	18
14.	20
15.	13

Table 18.23

Items Arranged in Ascending Order of Magnitude (N = 15)

S.No.	*Size of Item*	*S.No.*	*Size of Item*	*S.No.*	*Size of Item*
1.	12	6.	15	11.	20
2.	13	7.	16	12.	21
3.	14	8.	17	13.	21
4.	14	9.	18	14.	21
5.	14	10.	20	15.	22

Solution:

Median (X) = Size of the $\left(\frac{N+1}{2}\right)$ th item in the data-set arrayed in order

$$= \frac{N+1}{2} = \frac{15+1}{2} = \frac{16}{2} = 8$$

Size of 8th item = 17

Median wage of the series = Rs. 17.00.

If the number of items in the series is even, the median is taken as the arithmetic mean of the middle items. If one item is removed from the above example, the median would be:

X = the size of $\left(\frac{14+1}{2}\right)$ th item in the data-set.

= the size of 7.5th item.

Since the median is the 7.5th item in the arrayed series, we need to average 7th and 8th items. The seventh item in Table 18.23 is 16, and the eighth is 17.

Median (X) = the size of 7.5 item $= \frac{16+17}{2} = 16.5$

The median wages of 14 workers is Rs. 16.50

Location of Median in Discrete Series: In a discrete series the frequencies are cumulated and then the value of the middle item is located. The following example will illustrate the steps:

Table 18.24

S.No.	*No. of Children*
1.	3
2.	4
3.	6
4.	9
5.	12
6.	11
7.	9
8.	7
9.	4
	(N = 65)

Table 18.25

Items Arrayed in Order of Magnitude

	Gain in Kgs.	*No. of Children (f)*	*Cumulative Frequency (CF)*
	1.	3	3
	2.	4	7
	3.	6	13
	4.	9	22
Median Class →	5.	12	34
	6.	11	45
	7.	9	54
	8.	7	61
	9.	4	65
		(N = 65)	

Solution:

X = Gain in weight of $\frac{N}{2}$ th item.

= Gain in weight of $\frac{65}{2}$ th item.

= Gain in weight of 32.5 th item.

Median (X) = 5 Kg.

(It is clear from the above Table that the value of items 23rd to 34th is 5. Thus, the value of 32.5th item is also 5).

Determination of Median in a Continuous Series

In a continuous series we do not know every observation. Instead, we have record of the frequencies with which the observations appear in each of the class intervals as in the following Table. Nevertheless, we can compute the median by determining which class interval contains the median.

Table 18.26

Monthly Wages of Workers (N = 380)

	Monthly Wages in Rs.	*No. of Workers (f)*	*Cumulative Frequency (CP)*
	110–130	15	15
	130–150	30	45
	150–170	60	105
Median Class →	170–190	95	200
	190–210	82	282
	210–230	75	357
	230–250	23	380
		$(N = 380)$	

In regard to data given in Table 18.26 the median value is the value on either side of which $\frac{N}{2}$ or $\frac{380}{2}$ or 190 items lie. Now, the problem is to find the class interval containing the 190th item. The cumulative frequency for the first three classes is only 105. But when we move to the fourth class interval 95 items are added to 105 for total of 200. Therefore, the 190th item must be located in this fourth class interval (the interval from Rs. 170 and Rs. 190).

The median class (Rs. 170 – Rs. 190) for the series contains 95 items. For the purpose of determining the point, which has 190 items on each side, we assume that these 95 items are evenly spaced over the entire class interval 170-190. Therefore, we can interpolate and find the value for 190th item. First, we determine that the 190th item is the 95th item in the median class.

? 190 – 105 = 85

Then we can calculate the width of the 95 equal steps from Rs. 170 to Rs. 190 as follows:

$$\frac{190-170}{95} = 0.21053 \text{ (Approximately)}$$

The value of 85th item is 0.21053 × 85 = 17.89. If this value (17.89) is added to the lower limit of the median class, we get 170 + 17.89 = 187.89. This will be the median of the series.

This can be put in the form of a formula.

$$X = L + \frac{\frac{N}{2} - C}{f} \times i$$

Where X = Median

L = Lower limit of the class in which median lies

N = Total number of items

C = Cumulative frequency of the class prior to the median class

f = Frequency of the median class

i = Class interval of the median class

Calculation of Median by Formula

Table 18.27

Monthly Wages of Workers

	Monthly Wages in Rs.	*No. of Workers (f)*	*Cumulative Frequency (CP)*
	110–130	15	15
	130–150	30	45
	150–170	60	105 = C
Median Class →	L = 170–190	95 = f	200
	190–210	82	282
	210–230	75	357
	230–250	23	380
		(N = 380)	

$$X = L + \frac{\frac{N}{2} - C}{f} \times i$$

$$= 170 + \frac{\frac{380}{2} - 105}{95} \times (190 - 170)$$

$$= 170 + \frac{190 - 105}{95} \times (190 - 170)$$

$$= 170 + \frac{85}{95} \times (190 - 170)$$

$= 187.89$ (Approximately).

Median wages = Rs. 187.89 (approx.).

Procedure for Computing Median

Steps	*Procedure*	*Application to Table 18.27*
1.	Obtain cumulative frequency distribution.	0 + 15 = 15, 15 + 30 = 45, 45 + 60 = 105, 105 + 95 = 200, 200 + 82 = 282, 282 + 75 = 357, 357 + 23 = 380 (See col. 3)
2.	Divide N by 2, $\left(\frac{N}{2}\right)$	$\frac{380}{2} = 190$
3.	Locate the interval containing the middle or $\frac{N}{2}$ item. (This is known as median class interval).	The 190th item falls in the class interval 170 – 190.
4.	Find the number of cases below the limit of the interval located in step 3.	Number of cases below 190 is 190 – 105 = 85
5.	Divide the number obtained in step 4 by the number of cases (f) in median class (170 – 190).	$\frac{85}{95} = 0.8497$
6.	Find the width (class interval f) of the median class.	190 – 170 = 20
7.	Compute the median as follows: Lower limit of the median class plus the product of the ratio in step 5 and the width of the median class (step 6)	Median = 170 + (0.8947 × 20) = 170 × 17.89 = 287.89 (apporox.)

The procedure for computing median may be schematically expressed as under:

$$\text{Median} = \begin{bmatrix} \text{Lower limit} \\ \text{of the median} \\ \text{class} \end{bmatrix} + \begin{bmatrix} \dfrac{\dfrac{N}{2} - \begin{matrix} \text{Cumulative frequency} \\ \text{of the class prior to} \\ \text{the median class} \end{matrix}}{\begin{matrix} \text{Frequency of the} \\ \text{median class} \end{matrix}} \end{bmatrix} \times \begin{bmatrix} \text{Width} \\ \text{of the} \\ \text{median} \\ \text{class} \end{bmatrix}$$

The Mode

Another measure which is sometimes used to describe the central tendency of a set of data is the mode. It is defined as the value that is repeated most often in the data-set. In the following series of values: 71, 73, 74, 75, 78, 80 and 82, the mode is 75, because 75 occurs more often than any other value (three times). In grouped data the mode is located in the class where the frequency is the greatest. The mode is more useful when there are a larger number of cases and when data have been grouped. In practice, it is found that a set of grouped data often have more than one mode. Frequency distributions which have one mode are referred to as unimodal. Those with two modes and three modes are described as bimodal and trimodal (more commonly multimodal) distributions.

Calculation of Mode in Discrete Series

In a discrete series the value against which the frequency is the largest would be the modal value. If we look at table 18.25 we will find that 12 is the largest frequency. Thus, 5 being the value against which the frequency is the largest, is the mode of this series. If however, there are more than one value round which figures concentrate it becomes difficult to determine the value of mode. In such cases attempts are made to find out the point of maximum concentration with the help of grouping method. The procedure is as follows:

(i) First the frequencies are added in 'two's, in two ways: (a) by adding frequencies of item numbers 1 and 2; 3 and 4; and 5 and 6; and so on, and *(b)* by adding frequencies of item numbers 2 and 3, and 5, 6 and 7 and so on.

(ii) Then the frequencies are added in 'three's: This can be done in three ways: *(a)* by adding frequencies of item numbers 1, 2 and 3, 4 and 5 and 6 and 7, 8 and 9 and so on, *(b)* by adding frequencies of item numbers 2 and 3 and 4, 5, 6 and 7, 8, 9 and 10; and so on, and *(c)* by adding frequencies corresponding to item numbers 3, 4 and 5, 6, 7 and 8, 9, 10 and 11 and so on.

If necessary, grouping of frequencies can be done in 'four's and 'five's also. After grouping, the size of items maximum frequencies are circled. The item value contains corresponding the maximum frequency, the largest number of times is the mode of the series. This is shown is tables 18.28 and 18.29.

Table 18.28

Gain in Weight for 65 Children During a Specified Period

Gain in Kg.	*No. of Children (1)*	*(2)*	*(3)*	*(4)*	*(5)*	*(6)*
1.	2	6				
2.	4			12		
3.	6		10			
4.	9	15			19	
5.	(12)		(21)			27
6.	(12)	(24)		(33)	(33)	
7.	9	16	(21)			
8.	7			20		(28)
9.	4		11			
	N = 65					

To find out the point of maximum concentration, the data may be arranged in the form of table as follows:

Table 18.29

Analysis Table

Column No.	*Value of Item Containing Maximum Frequency*								
	1kg.	*2kgs.*	*3kgs.*	*4kgs.*	*5kgs.*	*6kgs.*	*7kgs.*	*8kgs.*	*9kgs.*
1.					1	1			
2.					1	1			
3.				1	1	1	1		
4.				1	1	1			
5.					1	1	1		
6.						1	1	1	
No. of time a value occurss				2	5	6	3	1	

Since, value 6 kgs. occurs the largest number of times it is the modal value. Thus, the mode of the series is 6 kg.

Determination of Mode in a Continuous Series

In the case of continuous series, the determination of mode involves two steps. First, the class of maximum concentration is located by the process of grouping. After this, the value of mode is interpolated by the use of the following formula:

$$X = L + \frac{f_1 - f_0}{2f_1 - f_0 - f_2} \times i$$

Here, x stands for the mode, L is the lower limit of the modal class, f_0 stands for the frequencies of the preceding class, f_1 for the frequencies of the modal class, f_2 for the frequencies of the succeeding class and i stands for the class interval or the modal class.

Illustration: Determine mode of the following distribution:

Table 18.30

Monthly Family Income (in Rs.)

	Monthly Income	*Number of Families*
	100-200	5
	200-300	6 = f_0
Median Class →	300-400	15 = f_1
	400-500	10 = f_2
	500-600	5
	600-700	4
	700-800	3
	800-900	2
	Total	$N = 50$

Table 18.31

Location of Modal Class by Grouping

Monthly Income	*f(1)*	*(2)*	*(3)*	*(4)*	*(5)*	*(6)*
100–200	5	11				
200–300	6		(21)	(26)		
300–400	(15)	25			(31)	
400–500	10		15			30
500–600	5	9		19		
600–700	4		7		12	
700–800	3					9
800–900	2	5				

Table 18.32

Analysis Table

Column	*Class Containing Maximum Frequency*							
	100-200	*200-300*	*300-400*	*400-500*	*500-600*	*600-700*	*700-800*	*800-900*
(1)			1					
(2)			1	1				
(3)		1	1					
(4)	1	1	1					
(5)		1	1	1				
(6)			1	1	1			
No. of times a class occurs	1	3	5	3	1			

Therefore, 300-400 group is the modal group. Using the formula of interpolation, *viz.*:

$X = l_1 + \dfrac{f_1 - f_0}{2f_1 - f_0 - f_2} \times i,$ we get the modal value.

Steps	*Procedure*	*Application to Table 18.32*
1.	Find modal class as follows.	*(i)* 5 + 6 = 11, 15 + 10 = 25, 5 + 4 = 9, 3 + 2 = 5, *(ii)* 15 + 6 = 21, 10 + 5 = 15, 4 + 3 = 7.
(a)	Add frequencies in 'two's *(i)* 1 and 2, 3 and 4, 5 and 6, 7 and 8 and write in column (2), *(ii)* 2 and 3, 4 and 5, 6 and 7 and write in column (3).	
(b)	Add frequencies in 'three's *(i)* 1, 2 and 3, 4, 5 and 6, and write in column (4), *(ii)* 2, 3 and 4, 5, 6, and 7, and write in column (4), *(iii)* 3, 4 and 5, 6, 7 and 8, and write in column (6).	*(i)* 5 + 6 + 15 = 26, 10 + 5 + 4 = 19, *(ii)* 6 + 15 + 10 = 31, 5 + 4 + 3 = 12, *(iii)* 15 + 10 + 5 = 30, 4 + 3 + 2 = 9.
2.	Arrange the data as shown in analysis table and find out the class in which maximum frequencies occur largest number of times.	Thus, 300-400 is the modal class.
3.	Find the lower limit of the modal class.	$L_1 = 300$
4.	Find the frequencies of the preceding class.	$F_0 = 6$
5.	Find the class interval of modal class.	$F_1 = 15$
6.	Find the class interval of modal class.	i = 100
7.	Compute the mode by interpolation.	$X = 300 + \dfrac{15-6}{2 \times 15.6 - 10} \times 100$ $= 300 + \dfrac{9}{14} \times 100 = 300 + 64.29$ Thus mode = 364.29 (approx).

The three measures of central tendency discussed at length above not only make different assumptions about the nature of the data but provide also somewhat different kinds of information. The arithmetic mean may be thought of as the point on the scale around which the cases balance, that is, one case at once extreme of the distribution may be counter-balanced by one or more cases at the other extreme of the distribution. If cases are not symmertically distributed around this point, the arithmetic mean may lead one to draw inferences about the group which could be grossly unrealistic, *i.e.,* it may give out a distorted picture of the group in respect of given characteristics. This does not, however, mean that the knowledge of the mean (say, of the mean income of a group) is a pointless information. Whether or not the knowledge of the mean is useful will depend on what one proposes to do with it.

The median also implies a concept of balance, but since it takes account only of the ordinal positions of scores rather than their absolute values, a preson with a very high income may be counter-balanced by a pauper. But in the case of the arithmetic mean it takes a very large number of cases of low income to counter-balance one case of a person who has a very high income.

The use of the mode as a measure of central tendency does away with the idea of a point of balance, since, it is possible to have more than one mode in a distribution. For example, we may find two equally large groups of students, one studying between 1 and 2 hours and another studying between 3 and 4 hours. In this distribution, there will thus be two modes, *i.e.,* the distribution is bimodal. These may also be multi-modal distributions. In case there are, it is perhaps misleading to speak of central tendency. It is also possible for a distribution of scores to have no mode at all, *i.e.,* every score may be occurring about as frequently as every other. In this case too, it is misleading to speak of central tendency, a term suggesting that the cases tend to cluster around some point more or less in the middle of the distribution. In such instance, the arithmetic mean and the median might be useful in bringing out salient aspects of the distributions which they are trying to depict.

In social research, one may also wish to know certain other aspects of how individuals or cases in the sample or 'population' with respect to the variable being measured (*e.g.,* hours of study 'intelligence quotient, etc.') are distributed. One may want to know, for instance, whether the number of students who study for 2.5 hours on an average is about the same as the number that studies for 4.5 hours on an average or whether relatively more students go to cinema three times a month, while few do not go at all and relatively fewer still go to the cinema six or more times a month. If one plotted the figures on a graph indicating the frequency of movie-going on the horizontal axis and the number of people corresponding to each frequency on the vertical axis what would be the shape of the resulting graph. Let us illustrate this on the basis of the above data (few students at the ends, *i.e.,* those not going to films at all and those visiting films four or more times per year and a large number of students visiting films about twenty times a month.)

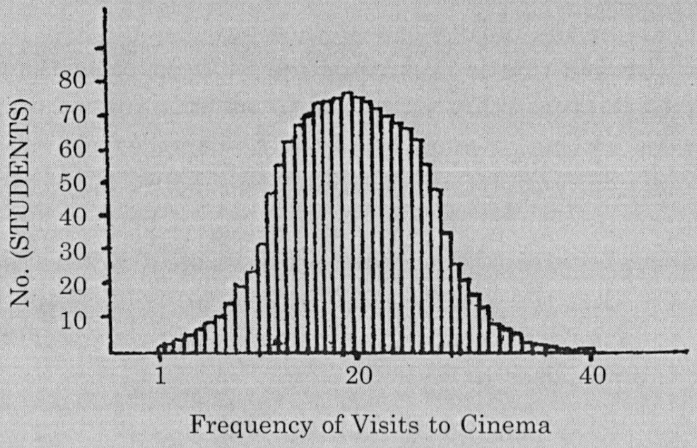

Fig. 18.1

The shape of the above distribution is like a bell (known technically as bell-shaped or 'normal' distribution or symmetrical distribution).

With different kinds of the data characterized by a piling of cases on one side rather than on the other, the curve would be asymmetrical. The figure given below represents a distribution that is asymmetrical.

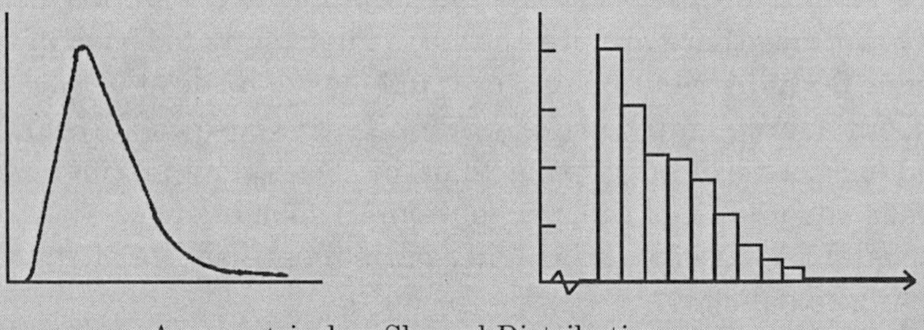

Asymmetrical or Skewed Distribution

Fig. 18.2

With yet another kind of data characterized by pilling up of cases at two (or more) points along the scale with relatively few cases in between, we would get a bi-modal (or multi-modal) distribution. The following figure illustrates a bi-modal distribution.

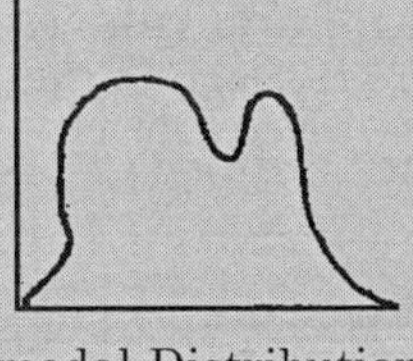

Bimodal Distribution

Fig. 18.3

It should be noted that knowing the shape of the distribution curve is fundamental to the use of efficient statistical methods, since the more efficient methods make specific assumptions about the nature of the distribution curve. It is customary to assume that the distribution curve for any variable is normal but in reality, this may not be so. If it is not, one may see whether other known distribution curves fit the data or whether one can transform the raw data by mathematical manipulation to a known distribution curve. Any standard book of statistics would help clarification on this point.

Measures of Dispersion

In social research, we often wish to know the extent of homogeneity and heterogeneity among respondents with respect to a given characteristic. Any set of social data has values which may characterise heterogeneity. The set of social data is typically characterized by the heteogeneity of values. In fact, the extent to which they are heterogeneous or vary among themselves, is of basic importance in statistics. Measures of central tendency describe one important characteristic of a set of data typically but they do not tell us anything about this other basic characteristic. Consequently, we need ways of measuring heterogeneity — the extent to which data are dispered. The measures which provide this description are called measures of dispersion or variability. The following three distributions shown in Fig. 18.4 will illustrate the importance of measuring the dispersion of statistical data.

Distribution of Mean Values for Samples of Different Sizes

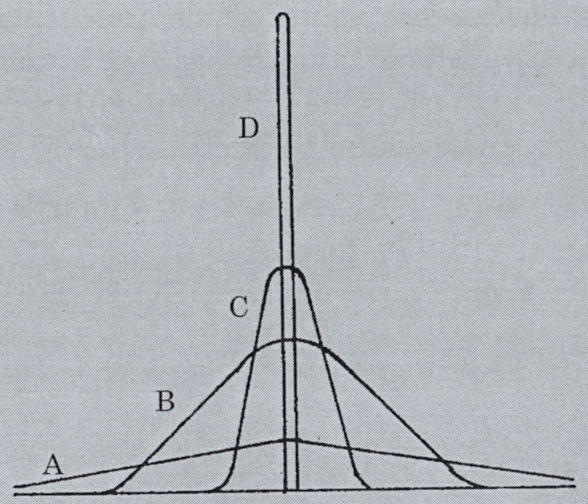

Distribution of Mean Values
for Samples of Different Sizes

Fig. 18.4 Three Curves with the Same Mean but Different Dispersions

It can be seen that the arithmetic mean of all the three curves in the above figure is the same, but the distribution of values as depicted by curve A shows less variability (dispersion) than that depicted by curve B, while curve B has less variability as compared to that shown by curve C. If we consider only the measure of central tendency of distributions, we will miss an important difference among the three curves. To get a better understanding of the pattern of the data, we must also get the measure of its dispersion or variability, we now turn to consider various measures of dispersion.

Range: The range is defined as the difference between the highest and lowest values: Mathematically,

$$R \text{ (Range)} = M_n - M_L$$

where M_n and M_L stand for the highest and the lowest value. Thus, for the data set: 10, 22, 20, 14 and 14 the range would be the difference between 22 and 10, *i.e.*, 12. In case of grouped data, we take the range as the difference between the midpoints of the extreme classes. Thus, if the midpoint of the lowest interval is 150 and that of the highest is 850, the range will be 700.

The only advantage of range, which measure of dispersion is seldom used, is that it can be easily calculated and readily understood. Despite t his advantage, it is generally not a very useful measure of dispersion; its main drawback being that it does not tell us anything about the dispersion of values which are intermediate between the two extremes.

Semi-Inter-Quartile Range or Quartile Deviation

Another measure of dispersion is the semi-inter-quartile range, commonly known as Quartile Deviation. Quartiles are the points which divide the array or series of values into four equal parts each of which contains 25 per cent of the items in the distribution. The quartiles are then the highest values in each of these four parts. Inter-quartile range is the difference between the values of first and third quartiles.

Thus, where Q_1 and Q_3 stand for first and third quartiles, the semi-inter-quartile range or quartile deviation is given by formula

$$= \frac{Q_3 - Q_1}{2}$$

Calculation of Quartile Deviation

Table 18.33

Monthly Family Income (in Rs.)

Monthly Income (in Rs.)	*Number of Families*
100–200	5
200–300	6
300–400	15

400–500	10
500–600	5
600–700	4
700–800	3
800–900	2
Total	N = 50

Solution:

Table 18.34

	Sn. No. (1)	*Monthly Income (in Rs.)* (2)	*Number of Families (f)* (3)	*Cumulative Frequency (CF)* (4)
	1.	100–200	5	5
	2.	200–300	6	11 = c
Q_1 →	3.	300–400	15 = f	26
	4.	400–500	10	36 = c
Q_3 →	5.	500–600	5 = f	41
	6.	600–700	4	45
	7.	700–800	3	48
	8.	800–900	2	50
			N = 50	

Steps	*Procedure*	*Application to Table 18.34*
1.	Find out cumulative frequency *(CF)* and write in column (40).	5 + 0 = 5, 5 + 6 = 11, 11 + 15 = 26, 26 + 10 = 36, 36 + 5 = 41, 41 + 5 = 46, 45 + 3 = 48, 48 + 2 = 50
2.	Find $Q_1 \left(= \frac{N}{4}\right)$	$\frac{50}{4} = 12.5$
3.	Find the interval which contains the Q_1.	Counting to 12.5 items from top (column 4) brings us to the interval with limits 300 to 400.
4.	Find the number of items (*C*) below the lower limit of the interval located in step 3.	Number of items below 300 is 11 = (*C*)
5.	Find the frequency (*f*) in the interval which contains the Q_1.	$f = 15$

6.	Compute the Q_1 as follows:	$Q_1 = l_1 + \frac{N/4 - C}{f}$ (f) $= 300 + \frac{125 - 11}{15} \times 100$ $= 300 + \frac{1.5}{15} \times 100$ $= 300 + (0.1 \times 100)$ $= 300 + 10 = 310$
7.	Find $Q_3 \frac{(3N)}{4}$	$= \frac{3 \times 50}{4} = 37.5.$
8.	Find the interval which contains Q_3.	Counting to 37.5 items from top (column 4) brings us to the interval with limits 500 to 600.
9.	Find the number of item (*C*) below the lower limit of the interval located in step 8.	$C = 36$
10.	Find the frequency (*f*) in the interval which contains the Q_3.	$F = 5$
11.	Compute the Q_3 as follows:	$Q_3 = l_1 + \frac{3N/4 - C}{f}$ (f) $= 500 + \frac{37.5 - 36}{5} \times 100$ $= 500 + \frac{1.5}{15} \times 100$ $= 500 + (0.3 \times 100)$ $= 500 + 30 = 530$
12.	Compute the inter-quartile range.	$= \frac{Q_3 - Q_1}{2}$ $= \frac{530 - 310}{2} = 220$ $QD = \frac{220}{2}$
13.	Compute semi-inter-quartile range or quartile deviation (*QD*).	$= 110$

Quartile deviation is an absolute measure of dispersion. If quartile deviation is to be used for comparing the dispersions of series it is necessary to convert the absolute measure to a coefficient of quartile deviation.

$$\text{Symbolically, coefficient of } QD = \frac{\frac{Q_3 - Q_1}{2}}{\frac{Q_2 + Q_1}{1}} = \frac{Q_3 - Q_1}{Q_3 + Q_1}$$

Applying this to the above illustration we get:

$$QD = \frac{Q_3 - Q_1}{Q_3 + Q_1} = \frac{530 - 310}{530 + 310} = \frac{220}{840} = 0.26 \text{ (Approx.).}$$

Mean Deviation

Range and quartile deviation suffer from serious drawbacks, *i.e.,* they are calculated by taking into consideration only two values of a series. Thus, these two measures of dispersion are not based on all observations of the series. As a result, the composition of the series is entirely ignored. To avoid this defect, dispersion may be calculated taking into consideration all the observations of the series in relation to a central value. The method of calculating dispersion is called the method of averaging deviations (mean deviation). As the name clearly suggests, it is the arithmetic average of the deviations of various items from a measure of central tendency.

As we well know, the sum of deviations from a central value would always be zero. This suggests that in order to obtain a mean deviation (about the mean or any one of the central values), we must somehow or the other get rid of any negative signs. This is done by ignoring signs and taking the absolute value of the differences.

In our hypothetical example, the mean of the number 12, 14, 15, 16 and 18 is 15. This implies that difference of 15 from each of these numbers, ignoring the signs all along and then adding the results, we will get the total deviation. Dividing it by 5, we get:

$$\lambda\bar{x} \text{ (Mean deviation from mean) } = \frac{|d|}{N} = \frac{3+1+0+1+3}{5} = \frac{8}{5}$$

$$= 1.6 \text{ (where } |d| \text{ stands for sum of absolute deviations).}$$

We may therefore say that on an average the scores differ from the mean by 1.6.

Calculation of Mean Deviation in Ungrouped Data (Individual Observations)

Table 18.35

Marks Obtained by Students

Roll Nos.	*Marks obtained (x)*
1.	31
2.	35
3.	38
4.	41
5.	49
6.	54
7.	59
8.	66
9.	68
N = 9	Σx = 441

$$\overline{X} = \frac{\Sigma x}{N} = \frac{441}{9} = 49$$

Table 18.36 (Solution)

Roll Nos.	*Marks Obtained (X)*	*|d| = (X-Mean (49))*
1.	31	18
2.	35	14
3.	38	11
4.	41	8
5.	49 (Mean)	0
6.	54	5
7.	59	10
8.	66	17
9.	68	19
N = 9		Σ|*d*| = 102

$$\lambda\overline{X} = \frac{\Sigma|d|}{N} = \frac{102}{9} = 11.33 \text{ (Approximately).}$$

Calculation of Mean Deviation in Discrete Series

Table 18.37

Gain in Weight for 65 Children During a Specified Period

	Gain in Kgs.	*No. of Children*
	1	3
	2	4
	3	6
	4	9
Median Group →	5	12
	6	11
	7	9
	8	7
	9	4
		$N = 65$

(Solution)

Table 18.38

	Gain in Kgs.	*Number of Children (f)*	*Cumulative Frequency*	*Deviation from Median |d|*	*f|d|*
	1.	3	3	4	12
	2.	4	7	3	12
	3.	6	13	2	12
	4.	9	22	1	9
Median =	5.	12	34	0	0
	6.	11	45	1	11
	7.	9	54	2	18
	8.	7	61	3	21
	9.	4	65	4	16
		N = 65			$\Sigma f\,|d| = 111$

$$\hat{X} \text{ (Median)} = \text{Size of } \frac{N}{2}\text{th item} = \text{Size of } \frac{65}{2}\text{th item}$$

$$= \text{Size of 32.5th item} = 5$$

$$\lambda(X) \text{ (Mean deviation from median)} = \frac{\Sigma f\,|d|}{N} = \frac{111}{65} = 1.71 \text{ (Approx.)}.$$

Calculation of Mean Deviation in Continuous Series

Table 18.39

Monthly Family Income (In Rs.)

Monthly Incomes	*Number of Families*
100–200	5
200–300	5
300–400	15
400–500	10
500–600	5
600–700	4
700–800	3
800–900	3
	N = 50

Table 18.40

Monthly Family Income (In Rs.)

	Monthly Incomes	*Mid Value*	*No. of Families (f)*	*Cumulative Frequency*	*Deviation from Median 400 (d)*	$f\|d\|$
	100–200	150	5	5	250	1250
	200–300	250	5	10= *C*	150	750
Median →	300–400	350	15 = f	25	50	75
Group	400–500	450	10	35	50	500
	500–600	550	5	40	150	750
	600–700	650	4	44	250	1000
	700–800	750	3	47	350	1050
	800–900	850	3	50	450	1350
			N = 50			7400

Steps	*Procedure*	*Application to Table 18.40*
1.	Calculate the median of the distribution.	$\overline{X} = L + \dfrac{\frac{N}{2} - C}{f} \times 1$ $= 300 + \dfrac{\frac{50}{2} - 10}{15} \times 100$ $= 300 + \dfrac{25 - 10}{15} \times 100$ $= 300 + \dfrac{15}{15} \times 100$ $= 300 + (1 \times 100)$ $= 300 + 100 = 400$
2.	Find mid-points of each class.	$\dfrac{100 + 200}{2} = \dfrac{300}{2} = 150$
3.	Find absolute deviations $\|d\|$ of each of the mid-points from median 400.	$\|150 - 400\| = \|- 250.\| = 250$
4.	Find total absolute deviation by multiplying the frequency of each class by the deviation of its mid-points from the median ($f\|d\|$).	$5 \times 250 = 1250$
5.	Find the sum of products of frequency and deviations ($f\|d\|$).	$f\|d\| = 7400$
6.	Compute Mean Deviation	$\lambda(\overline{X}) = \dfrac{f\|d\|}{N} = \dfrac{7400}{50} = 148$

Coefficient of Mean Deviation

To compare the mean deviation of series the coefficient of mean deviation or relative mean deviation is calculated. This is obtained by dividing the mean deviation by that measure of central tendency from which deviations were calculated. Thus,

$$\text{Coefficient of Mean Deviation} = \frac{\lambda}{X}$$

Applying this formula to the previous example, we have,

$$\text{Coefficient of Mean Deviaiton} = \frac{148}{400} = 0.37$$

Standard Deviation

The most useful and frequently used measure of dispersion is the standard deviation or root-mean square deviation about the mean. The standard deviation is defined as the square root of the arithmetic mean of the square of the deviations about the mean. Symbolically,

$$\sigma = \sqrt{\frac{\Sigma d^2}{N}}$$

where σ (Greek letter Sigma) stands for the standard deviation, $\Sigma\, d^2$ for the sum of the square of the deviations measured from mean and N for the number of items.

Calculation of Standard Deviation in Series of Individual Observations

Table 18.41

Marks Obtained by Students

Roll No.	*Marks Obtained*
1	31
2	35
3	38
4	41
5	49
6	54
7	59
8	66
9	68

Solution: Direct Method

Table 18.42

Roll No.	*Marks obtained* X	*(Deviation from mean 49)* $(X - X = d)$	d^2
1	31	– 18	324
2	35	– 14	196
3	38	– 11	121

4	41	– 8	64
5	49	0	0
6	54	+ 5	25
7	59	+ 10	100
8	66	+ 17	289
9	68	+ 19	361
			$\Sigma d^2 = 480$

$$\sigma = \sqrt{\frac{\Sigma d^2}{N}} = \sqrt{\frac{1480}{9}}$$

$$= \sqrt{164.444} = 12.82 \text{ (approx.)}$$

Short-cut Method

Table 18.43

Roll No.	*Marks Obtained*	*Deviation from assumed average 41 (d)*	d^2
1	31	– 10	100
2	35	– 6	36
3	38	– 3	9
4	41	0	0
5	49	8	64
6	54	13	169
7	59	18	324
8	66	25	625
9	68	27	729
$N = 29$		$\Sigma d = 72$	$\Sigma d^2 = 2056$

$$\sigma = \sqrt{\frac{\Sigma d^2}{N} - \left(\frac{\Sigma d}{N}\right)^2}$$

$$= \sqrt{\frac{2056}{9} - \left(\frac{72}{9}\right)^2}$$

$= \sqrt{228.44 - 64}$

$= \sqrt{164.44}$

$= 12.82$ (approx.)

Calculation of Standard Deviation in Discrete Series

In a discrete series the deviations from an assumed mean are first computed and multiplied by the respective frequencies of items. The deviations are squared and multiplied by the respective frequencies of the items. These products are totalled and divided by the total of the frequencies. The standard deviation is calculated by the following formula:

$$\sigma = \sqrt{\frac{\Sigma d^2}{N} - \left(\frac{\Sigma d}{N}\right)^2}$$

The following illustration would explain the formula:

Table 18.44

Gain in Weight for 65 Children During a Specified Period

Gain in kg.	*No. of Children*
1	3
2	4
3	6
4	9
5	12
6	11
7	9
8	7
9	4
	$N = 65$

Table 18.45

Gain in kg.	No. of Children (f)	Deviations from the assumed average (5) d	Total Deviations (f x d)	Deviations squared (d)	fd^2
1	3	– 4	– 12	16	48
2	4	– 3	– 12	9	36
3	6	– 2	– 12	4	24
4	9	– 1	– 9	1	9
5	12	0	0	0	0
6	11	+ 1	11	1	11
7	9	+ 2	18	4	36
8	7	+ 3	21	9	63
9	4	+ 4	16	16	64
	$N = 65$		$\Sigma fd = 21$	$\Sigma fd^2 = 291$	

$$= \sqrt{\frac{\Sigma fd^2}{N} - \left(\frac{\Sigma fd}{N}\right)^2}$$

$$= \sqrt{\frac{291}{65} - \left(\frac{21}{65}\right)^2}$$

$$= \sqrt{4.4769 - 0.1044}$$

$$= \sqrt{4.3725}$$

= 2.09 (approx.)

Calculation of Standard Deviation in a Continuous Series

In a continuous series the class intervals are represented by their mid-points. However, usually the class-intervals are of equal size and thus, the deviations from the assumed average is expressed in class interval units. Alternatively, step deviations are arrived at by dividing the deviations by the magnitude of the class interval. Thus, the formula for computing standard deviation is written as under:

$$\sigma = \sqrt{\frac{\Sigma fd^2}{N} - \left(\frac{\Sigma fd}{N}\right)^2} \times i$$

where i stands for the common factor or the magnitude of the class-interval. The following example would illustrate this formula:

Table 18.46

Monthly Family Income (In Rs.)

S. No.	*Monthly Income*	*Number of Families*
1.	100–200	5
2.	200–300	6
3.	300–400	15
4.	400–500	10
5.	500–600	5
6.	600–700	4
7.	700–800	3
8.	800–900	2
		$N = 50$

Solution :

Table 18.47

S. No.	*Monthly Income (In Rs.)*	*Mid values (m)*	*No. of families (f)*	*Step Deviations from assumed average 450 (d)*	*fd*	d^2	fd^2
1.	100–200	150	5	– 3	– 15	9	45
2.	200–300	250	6	– 2	– 12	4	24
3.	300–400	350	15	– 1	– 15	1	15
4.	400–500	450	10	0	0	0	0
5.	500–600	550	5	+ 1	5	1	5
6.	600–700	650	4	+ 2	8	4	16
7.	700–800	750	3	+ 3	9	9	27
8.	800–900	850	2	+ 4	8	16	32
			N = 50		$\Sigma fd = -12$		$\Sigma fd^2 = 164$

Steps	*Procedure*	*Application to Table 18.47*
1.	Find the mid-points of the various class.	$\frac{100 + 200}{2} = \frac{300}{2} = 150....$
2.	Assume a mid-point as average.	450 = assumed average.
3.	Take the difference of each mid-point from the assumed average (450) and divide them by the magnitude of the class interval to get step deviations (d).	(1) 150 – 450 = – 300 – 300/100 = – 3, ... (2) 250 – 450 = – 200 – 200/100 = – 2, ... (– 3) (5) = – 15 (– 2) (6) = – 12

4.	The deviations are multiplied by the frequency of each class (*fd*).	$\Sigma fd = -12$ (– 3) (– 3) = 9 9 x 5 = 45, ...
5.	Find the aggregate of products of step 4 (*fd*).	$\Sigma fd^2 = 164$
6.	Square the deviations (d^2).	$\sigma = \sqrt{\frac{\Sigma fd^2}{N} - \frac{(\Sigma fd)^2}{N}} \times i$
7.	Squared deviations are multiplied by the respective frequencies (fd^2).	$= \sqrt{\frac{164}{50} - \left(\frac{-12}{50}\right)^2} \times 100$
8.	Find the aggregate of products of step 7 (Σfd^2).	$= \sqrt{3.28 - 0.0576 \times 100}$
9.	Compute standard deviation with the help of the formula.	$= \sqrt{3.2224 \times 100}$ $= 1.795 \times 100$ = 179.51 (approx.)

Coefficient of Variation

The standard deviation represents measure of absolute dispersion. It is also necessary to measure the relative dispersion of two or more distributions. When the standard deviation is related to its mean, it measures relative dispersion.

Karl Pearson has worked out a simple measure of relative dispersion which is generally known as the coefficient of variation.

$$C.V. \text{ or } V = \frac{\sigma}{\overline{x}} (100)$$

The coefficient of variation for the problem in Table 18.47 is:

$$C.V. = \frac{179.51}{426} \times 100 \left[\overline{x} = 426\right]$$

$$= 0.42138 \times 100$$

$$= 42.138 \text{ per cent (approx.)}$$

Correlation

We have discussed so far various statistical methods concerned with the description and analysis of a single variable. In social research, we often wish to know the relation among different variables in the data. One may wish to know, for instance, whether the number of hours students devote for studies is somehow related to their parents' income, to age, etc. In other words, one may be interested in ascertaining whether a change in one variable is associated with or paralleled by variations in another variable, *i.e.,* whether the higher income of parents is associated with high expectations of children in respect of salaries from jobs they will subsequently take up or contrariwise; whether the lower income of parents is correlated with lower expectation of children in regard to salaries from jobs that they aspire to take up.

The most frequently used measure of estimating association among variables is the coefficient of correlation (r).

The correlation coefficient (r) to be discussed presently was introduced by Karl Pearson and is often referred to as product-moment correlation. Coefficient of correlation is calculated to identify the extent or degree of correlation between two variables. It does not mean that their relationship is functional or constant. In other words, correlations in two sets of data need not always be the result of mutual interdependence. Changes in one set of data may be the cause of changes in other set (of data) and there may be a cause and effect relationship between these two sets. But it is equally possible that the changes in the two sets of data are the effects of some third factor which affects both these sets of data. As such, the knowledge about correlation in social sciences, particularly has an extremely limited field of application.

Positive and Negative Correlation

When one variable increases (or decreases) and the other variable changes in the same direction, the relation of the two series is positive; but if the changes in the two variables are in opposite directions, the correlation between the two series is negative. The coefficient of correlation (r) ranges in value from positive one (+ 1.0) down through zero (0.0) to negative one or unity (– 1.0).

Karl Pearson's Coefficient of Correlation (Individual Observations)

To compute the degree or extent of correlation and direction of correlation, Karl Pcarson's method is the most satisfactory.

Symbolically, its formulation is as under:-

$$\mathrm{r} = \frac{\Sigma dx\, dy - N\left(\frac{\Sigma dx}{N}\right)\left(\frac{\Sigma dy}{N}\right)}{N\sqrt{\left(\frac{\Sigma dx^2}{N}\right)-\left(\frac{\Sigma dx}{N}\right)^2}\sqrt{\left(\frac{\Sigma dy^2}{N}\right)-\left(\frac{\Sigma dy}{N}\right)^2}}$$

where dx is the deviation of various items of the first variable from an assumed average and dy, the corresponding deviations of the second variable from the assumed average and N connotes the number of pairs of items.

The application of the formula is explained with reference to the following hypothetical data.

Table 18.48

Marks Obtained by 10 Students in the Theory of Social Research and the Research Project

S. No.	*Marks Obtained in Social Research*	*Marks Obtained in Research Project*
1	40	42
2	26	29
3	70	66
4	32	24
5	52	58
6	30	28
7	48	46
8	48	50
9	42	44
10	62	66

Table 18.49

S. No.	*Marks in Social Research (X)*	*Deviations from ass. ave. 48 (dx)*	dx^2	*Marks in Research Project (Y)*	*Deviations from ass. ave 46 (dy)*	dy^2	*dx.dy*
1	40	− 8	64	42	− 4	16	+ 32
2	26	− 22	484	29	− 17	289	+ 374
3	70	+ 22	484	66	+ 20	400	+ 440
4	32	− 16	256	24	− 22	484	+ 352
5	52	+ 4	16	58	+ 12	144	+ 48
6	30	− 18	324	28	− 18	324	+ 324
7	48	0	0	46	0	0	0
8	48	0	0	50	+ 4	16	0
9	42	− 6	36	44	− 2	4	+ 12
10	62	+ 14	196	66	+ 20	400	+ 280
N = 10	$\overline{x} = 45$	$\Sigma dx = -30$	$\Sigma dx^2 = 1860$	$\overline{Y} = 45.3$	$\Sigma dy = .7$	$\Sigma dy^2 = 2077$	$\Sigma dx.dy = 1862$

Steps	*Procedure*	*Application to Table 18.49*
1.	Assume average of variables X and Y. (Preferably in the neighbourhood of $\overline{X}$).	ass. ave (X) = 48 ass. ave (Y) = 46
2.	Find deviations of item values of X and Y from assumed averages (dx) and (dy)	(X) 40 – 48 = – 8 .... (Y) 42 – 46 = – 4 ....
3.	Square up the deviations (dx^2, and dy^2)	(–8) (–8) = 64 .... = ... (–4) (–4) = 16
4.	Find the products of deviations ($dx.dy$)	(–8) (–4) = 32 .... = ... = ...
5.	Find the aggregates of and dx, dy, dx^2, dy^2 and $dx.dy$.	S dx = –30 Σdy = –7 Σdx^2 = 1860 Σdy^2 = 2077 $\Sigma dy.dy$ = 1862
6.	Compute co-efficient of correlation by the formula	$r = \dfrac{\Sigma dxdy - N\left(\frac{\Sigma dx}{N}\right)\left(\frac{\Sigma dy}{N}\right)}{N\sqrt{\frac{\Sigma dx^2}{N}-\left(\frac{\Sigma dx}{N}\right)^2}\sqrt{\frac{\Sigma dy^2}{N}-\left(\frac{\Sigma dy}{N}\right)^2}}$ $= \dfrac{1862 - 10\left(\frac{-30}{10}\right)\left(\frac{-7}{10}\right)}{10\sqrt{\frac{1860}{10}-\left(\frac{-30}{10}\right)^2}\sqrt{\frac{2077}{10}-\left(\frac{-7}{10}\right)^2}}$ $= \dfrac{1862 - 10(-3)(-0.7)}{10\sqrt{186-9}\sqrt{207.7-0.49}}$ $= \dfrac{1862 - 10\,(2.1)}{10\sqrt{177}\sqrt{207.21}}$ $= \dfrac{1862 - 21}{10 \times 13.30 \times 14.39}$ $= \dfrac{1841}{1914.507}$ = 0.962 (Approx.)

Calculation of Co-efficient of Correlation in a Continuous Series

In case of a continuous series, the data are classified in a two-way frequency table. Computation of coefficient of correlation in respect of grouped data is based on the presumption that every item which falls within a given class interval is assumed to fall exactly at the mid-value of that class.

As an illustration, we shall compute the coefficient or of correlation with regard to following data:

Table 18.50 (a)

Age of Husbands/Wives

Age of Husbands	*Age of wives*					*Total*
	15–25	*25–35*	*35–45*	*45–55*	*55–65*	
20–30	13	1	–	–	–	14
30–40	1	12	2	–	–	15
40–50	–	1	8	1	–	10
50–60	–	–	2	4	2	8
60–70	–	–	–	1	2	3
Total	14	14	12	6	4	50

The formula for the calculation of coefficient of correlation in this case will take the following form:

$$r = \frac{\Sigma dxdy - N\left(\frac{\Sigma dx}{N}\right)\left(\frac{\Sigma dy}{N}\right)}{N\sqrt{\left(\frac{\Sigma dx^2}{N}\right)-\left(\frac{\Sigma dx}{N}\right)^2}\sqrt{\left(\frac{\Sigma dy^2}{N}\right)-\left(\frac{\Sigma dy}{N}\right)^2}}$$

The only change in the above formula in comparison to the earlier one is the introduction of f which stands for frequency.

Applying the formula to the Table 18.50 we get:

$$r = \frac{86 - 50\left(\frac{-28}{50}\right)\left(\frac{-29}{50}\right)}{50\sqrt{\frac{92}{50}-\left(\frac{-28}{50}\right)^2}\sqrt{\frac{91}{50}-\left(\frac{-29}{50}\right)^2}} = \frac{86 - 50\,(-0.56)\,(-0.58)}{50\sqrt{1.84-(0.3)}\sqrt{1.82-0.3364}}$$

$$= \frac{86 - 50 \times 0.3248}{50\sqrt{1.5264}\sqrt{1.4836}} = \frac{86 - 16.24}{50 \times 1.235 \times 1.218}$$

$$= \frac{69.76}{75.211} = 0.9275 \text{ (approx.)}$$

Table 18.50 (b)

				Age of Wives								
				Age Gr 15–25	*25–35*	*35–45*	*45–55*	*55–65*				
				Mid points 20	30	40	50	60				
Age of Husbands				– 20	– 10	0	+ 10	+ 20	*Total*	f.dy	fdy^2	f.dx.dy
		dy	dx	– 2	– 1	0	+ 10	+ 2	f			
Age Gr.	*Mid points*			52_{13}	2_1	0			14	–28	56	54
20–30	*25*	– 20	– 2									
30–40	*35*	– 10	– 1	2_1	12_{12}	0_2			15	– 15	15	14
40–50	*45*	0	0	0	0_1	0_8	0_1		10	0	0	0
50–60	*55*	+ 10	+ 1			0_2	4_4	4_2	8	8	8	8
60–70	*65*	+ 20	+ 2				2_1	8_2	3	6	12	10
			Total	14	14	12	6	4	N = 50	– 29	91	86
			f.dx	– 28	– 14	0	6	8	– 28			
			$f.dx^2$	56	14	0	6	16	+ 92			
			f.dx.dy	54	14	0	6	12	+ 86			

$f.dx = -28,\ f.dx^2 = +92,\ f.dy^2 = .29,\ f.dy^2 = 91,\ f.dx.dy = 86$

Rank Difference Method of Correlation

Where the direct measurement of the phenomenon under study is not possible, for example, of characteristics like efficiency, honesty, intelligence, etc., rank-difference method is applied for finding out the extent of correlation. The formula for computing rank correlation is:

$$R = 1 - \frac{6\Sigma D^2}{N(N^2 - 1)}$$

where R denotes coefficient of rank correlation between paired ranks, D denotes the differences between the paired ranks and N stands for the number of pairs. We shall, with the help of the following example, illustrate the application of the above formula:

Table 18.51

Ranking of Workers According to their Efficiency by two Different Judges

Name of Worker	*Ranking by Judge A*	*Ranking by Judge B*
A	3	4
B	9	7
C	6	6
D	5	8
E	1	1
F	2	3
G	4	2
H	7	5
I	8	10
J	10	9

Table 18.52

Name of worker	*Ranking by Judge A (R_1)*	*Ranking by Judge A (R_2)*	$Dm = (R_1 - R_2)$	D^2
A	3	4	– 1	1
B	9	7	+ 2	4
C	6	6	0	0
D	5	8	– 3	9
E	1	1	0	0
F	2	3	– 1	1
G	4	2	+ 2	4
H	7	5	+ 2	4
I	8	10	– 2	4
J	10	9	+ 1	1
	N = 10		$\Sigma D^2 = 28$	

$$R = 1 - \frac{6\Sigma D^2}{N(N^2-1)}$$

$$= 1 - \frac{6 \times 28}{10 \times (10^2 - 1)}$$

$$= 1 - \frac{168}{10 \times (100 - 1)}$$

$$= 1 - \frac{168}{10 \times 99}$$

$$= 1 - \frac{168}{990}$$

$$= 1 - 0.1696969$$

$$= 0.83 \text{ (approx.)}$$

Calculation of the Coefficient of Correlation by Rank Difference Method

(When there are two or more items having the same value)

If there are more than one item with the same value, a common rank is given to such items. This rank is the average of the ranks which these items would have got, had there been a slight difference in their values.

Suppose the marks obtained by five students are 70, 66, 66, 65, 63, respectively. If these marks are arranged in descending order the figure 70 would receive the first rank, 66 the second rank, 65 the third and 63, the fourth rank. Since, the two students in the example have an equal score their rank is 2. Now they will be given the average rank of those ranks which these students would have secured had they differed slightly from each other. On this assumption, the rank of both the items would be $\frac{2+3}{2}$, *i.e.*, 2.5 and the rank of the next item (65) would be 4.

Thus, the coefficient of rank correlation would need a correction because the above formula $\left[R = 1 - \frac{6\Sigma D^2}{N(N^2-1)}\right]$ is based on the assumtion that the ranks of various items are different.

Where there is more than one item with the same value, a correction factor, $\frac{1}{12}(t^3 - t)$ is added to the value of Σd^2, where t stands for number of items whose ranks are common. This correction factor is added as many times as the number of items with common ranks occur. This is explained in the following example:

Example: Calculate the coefficient of rank correlation from the following data:

Table 18.53

Roll No.	*Marks obtained in Research and Statistics X*	*Rank R_1*	*Marks obtained in Dissertation Y*	*Rank Differences of d^2, R_2 Ranks (d) $R_1 - R_2 = d$*		
1	50	9	60	6	3	9
2	60	5	65	4	1	1
3	60	5	66	3	2	4
4	60	5	70	1.5	3.5	12.25
5	75	1	58	7	− 6	36
6	55	7	48	10	− 3	9
7	68	2.5	62	5	− 25	6.25
8	68	2.5	70	1.5	1	1
9	48	10	52	9	1	1
10	52	8	56	8	0	0
$N = 10$						$\Sigma d^2 = 79.50$

In the above data-set of the X series the number 60 occurs three times. The rank of all three items is 5 which is the average of 4, 5 and 6, the ranks which these items would have secured had they differed slightly from one another. Other numbers 68 in X series and 70 in Y series, have occurred two times. Their ranks are respectively 2.5 and 1.5.

Thus:

$t_1 = 3$, for 60 correction factor would be $\frac{1}{12}(3^2 - 3)$

$t_2 = 2$, for 68 correction factor would be $\frac{1}{12}(2^2 - 2)$

$t_3 = 2$, for 70 correction factor would be $\frac{1}{12}(2^3 - 2)$

The modified formula for coefficient of rank correlation would thus be:

$$R = 1 - \frac{\left[6\Sigma d^2) + \frac{1}{12}(t_1^3 - t_1) + \ldots + \frac{1}{12}(t_n^3 - t_n)\right]}{N(N^2 - 1)}$$

where n stands for the number of items repeated. In regard to the above example the formula will be:

$$R = 1 - \frac{6\left[(\Sigma d^2) + \frac{1}{12}(t^3 - t) + \frac{1}{12}(t^3 - t) + \frac{1}{12}(t^3 - t)\right]}{N(N^2 - 1)}$$

$$= 1 - \frac{6\left[(79.5) + \frac{1}{12}(3^3 - 3) + \frac{1}{12}(2^3 - 2) + \frac{1}{12}(2^3 - 2)\right]}{10(10^2 - 1)}$$

$$= 1 - \frac{6\left[79.5 + \frac{1}{12}(24) + \frac{1}{12}(6) + \frac{1}{12}(6)\right]}{10 \times 99}$$

$$= 1 - \frac{6\left[79.5 + 2 + \frac{1}{2} + \frac{1}{2}\right]}{990}$$

$$= 1 - \frac{6\,(82.5)}{990}$$

$$= 1 - \frac{6 \times 82.5}{990}$$

$$= 1 - \frac{459}{990}$$

$$= 1 - 0.5$$

$$= 0.5$$

A caution relating to the meaning and implication of a coefficient of correlation is quite warranted. The coefficient of correlation, by itself a very useful estimate of relationship, should not be taken as an absolute proof of association among relevant variables in as much as its interpretation depends in a large measure on the size of the sample selected for the study, as also, on the nature of the data collected. A seemingly high coefficient of correlation, say, of 0.80 ($\pm$) may really be quite misleading if the standard error indicative of sample fluctuation is relatively large, or to take a contrary example, a seemingly low coefficient of say 0.45 ($\pm$) may suggest that the relationship among the variables may well be ignored but on the plane of reality, this indication may again be erroneous, since the coefficient of correlation for certain variables may typically be so low that the above correlation coefficient, *i.e.,* 0.45 in comparison would need to be considered relatively quite high for the class of data in question.

However, statistical convention decrees that the coefficient of correlation ranging from 1 to 0.7 ($\pm$) be taken as an indication of 'high' or significant correlation, that ranging from 0.7 to 0.4 ($\pm$) as substantial, that between 0.4 and 0.2 ($\pm$) as low and that below 0.2 ($\pm$) as negligible.

It also needs to be stressed that a high correlation among two variables does not in itself constitute a proof that they are casually related. A significant correlation between variables — for example, between income and size of family or the size of an educational institution and the performance of the students — hardly affords any indication of a casual relationship obtaining amongst them. Suppose we were to find that higher income is inversely correlated with the number of issues (children), *i.e.,* higher the income of parents the lesser their number of issues (the coefficient of correlation is, say, 0.8 which is statistically quite high), we shall be wrong and unjustified in saying that higher income is the cause of lower fertility. It was pointed out earlier that an inference of causality is warranted only if three kinds of proof, concomitant variation, time order and elimination of any other variable as the determining condition of the hypothesised effect, can be secured. In the instant case, following inferences may possibly be drawn in full consideration of the pronounced correlation evident among the variables of income and number of children: *(a)* one might be causing the other, *(b)* both the variables might be the effects of some other cause or causes, and *(c)* the association may be a mere chance occurrence. Causal inferences can obviously be very surely established in an experimental situation. We have considered this when dealing with experimental designs. In social sciences, it is very difficult to set up experiments, so must of the studies are non-experimental ones. Analytical procedures have, however, been devised to draw inferences about causal relationship in non-experimental studies. We shall consider these proceedures later in this chapter.

The social researcher is quite so often interested in estimating the degree of association between attributes, *i.e.,* between variables that are defined qualitatively; for example, he may want to ascertain the degree of association between the sexual attribute and political preference or between nativity and attitude toward a certain social issue. Basically, the problem of association is one of correlation but the association between attributes may not easily become amenable to mathematical treatment as in case of the quantitative measures of variables. A measure of such association among attributes is the coefficient of relative predictability (RP) which is, in fact, a qualitative correlation coefficient.

Certain other measures of association between attributes have been devised by the statisticians. The major estimates of association are based on Chi-square test which is applied to null hypothesis pronouncing association between attributes. The Chi-square test is perhaps the most commonly used test in studies dealing with social-behavioural data. Hence, a fuller exposition of the test is presented in the following pages.

Chi-Square Test

The χ^2 (Greek letter χ^2 Pronounced as Ki-square) test is a method of evaluating whether or not frequencies which have been empirically observed differ significantly from those which would be expected under a certain set of theoretical assumptions. For example, suppose political preference and place of residence or nativity have been cross-classified and the data summarised in the following 2 × 3 contingency table.

Table 18.54

Relationship between Political Preference and Place of Residence

Place of Residence	*Political Preference*			*Total*
	Congress	*Janata*	*Lok Dal*	
Urban	38	20	12	70
Rural	10	26	6	42
Total	48	46	18	112

It is seen in the table that the proportions of urban people are 38/48 = 0.79, 20/46 = 0.34, and 12/18 = 0.67 (rounded to two decimals) for the three political parties in the country. We would then want to know whether or not these differences are statistically significant.

To this end, we can propose a null hypothesis which assumes that there are no differences among the three political parties in respect of nativity. This means that the proportions of urban and rural people should be expected to be the same for each of the three political parties. On the basis of the assumption that the null hypothesis is correct, we can compute a set of frequencies that would be expected given these marginal totals. In other words, we can compute the number of persons showing preference for the Congress party whom we would expect on the basis of the above assumption to be urbanites and compare this figure with the one actually observed.

If the null hypothesis is true, we may compute a common proportion as:

$$\frac{38+20+12}{48+46+18} = \frac{70}{112} = 0.625$$

With this estimated proportion, we would expect 48 × (0.625) = 30 persons affiliated to Congress, 46 × (0.625) = 28.75 persons affiliated to Janata Party and 18 × (0.625) = 11.25 persons affiliated to Lok Dal from out of the 70 urbanites. Subtracting these figures from the respective observed figures from the respective sizes of the three samples, we find 48 – 30 = 18 affiliated to Congress, 46 – 28.75 = 17.25 affiliated to Janata and 18 – 11.25 = 6.25 persons affiliated to Lok Dal from 42 persons from the rural areas.

These results are shown in the following table, where expected frequencies are shown in parenthesis.

Table 18.55

Place of Residence	*Political Preference*			*Total*
	Congress	*Janata*	*Lok Dal*	
Urban	38	20	12	70
	(30)	(28.75)	(11.25)	
Rural	10	26	6	42
	(18)	(17.25)	(6.75)	
Total	48	46	18	112

To test the tenability of the null hypothesis we compare the expected and observed frequencies. The comparison is based on the following χ^2 statistic.

$$\chi^2 = \Sigma \frac{(O-E)^2}{E}$$

where O stands for observed frequencies and E for the expected frequencies.

Table 18.56

Computation of χ^2

O	E	$O–E$	$(O–E)^2$	$\frac{(O-E)^2}{E}$
38	30.00	8.00	64.0000	2.1333
10	18.00	8.00	64.0000	3.5555
20	28.75	8.75	76.5625	2.6630
26	17.25	8.75	76.5625	4.4384
12	11.25	9.75	0.5625	0.0500
6	6.75	0.75	0.5625	0.0833
112	112.00			12.9237
				$\chi^2 = 12.9327$

Before going into further details of the test, we shall introduce the reader to certain terms used in connection with the administration of this test.

Degrees of Freedom

The number of degrees of freedom means the number of independent constraints imposed on us in a contingency table. The following example will illustrate the concept:

Table 18.57

	Affected A	*Not affected* a	*Total*
Inoculated B	AB 14 (20)	aB 26	40
Not inoculated B	AB 16	aB 4	20
Total	30	30	60

Let us suppose that the two attributes *A* and *B* are independent in which case, the expected frequency or the cell *AB* would be $\frac{40 \times 30}{60} = 20$. Once this is identified, the frequencies of remaining three cells get automatically fixed. Thus, for cell, aB the expected frequency must be 40 – 20 = 20, similarly, for the cell *AB* it must be 30 – 20 = 10 and for aB it must be 10. This means that for 2 × 2 table we have just one choice of our own, while we have no freedom in the remaining three cells. Thus, the degrees of freedom *(df)* can be calculated by the formula:

$$df = (c - 1)(r - 1)$$

where *df* stands for the degrees of freedom, *c* for the number of columns and *r* for the number of rows.

Thus, in 2 × 3 table (Table 18.54)

$$df = (3 - 1)(2 - 1) = 2 \times 1 = 2$$

Level of Significance

As stated earlier, the chi-square test is used to examine whether the difference between observed and expected frequencies is due to the sampling fluctuations and as such insignificant or contrarily, whether the difference is due to some other reason and as such significant.

Before drawing the inference that the difference is significant researchers set up a hypothesis, often referred as a null hypothesis (symbolized as H_o) as constrasted with the research hypothesis (H_1) that is set up as an alternative to H_o. Usually, although not always, the null hypothesis states that there is no difference between several groups or no relationship between variables, whereas a research hypothesis may predict either a positive or negative relationship.[3] In other words, null hypothesis assumes that there is absence of non-sampling errors and the difference is due to chance alone. Then the probability of the occurrence of such a difference is determined. The probability indicates the extent of reliance that we can place on the inference drawn. The table values of chi-square are available at various probability levels. These levels are called levels of significance. We can find out from the table the values of chi-square at certain levels of significance. Usually (in social sciences problem), the value of chi-square at 0.05 or .01 levels of significance from the given degrees of freedom is seen from the table and is compared with observed value of chi-square. If the observed value or χ^2 is more than the table value at 0.05, it means that the difference is significant.

Degree of Freedom

To use the chi-square test, the next step is to calculate the degrees of freedom:

Suppose we have a 2 × 2 contingency table like the one in Fig. 1.

	Column 1	Column 2	
Row 1	✓	X	r_1^1
Row 2	X	X	r_1^2
	c_t^1	c_t^2	

Row totals

Column totals

Fig. 1

We know the row and the column totals r_t^1, and r_t^2 and c_t^1 and c_t^2. The number of degrees of freedom can be defined as the number of cell-values that we can freely specify. In Fig. 1, once we specify the one value of Row 1 (denoted by check in the figure) the second value in that row and the values of second row (denoted by *X*) are already determined; we are not free to specify these because we know the row totals and column totals. This shows that in a 2 × 2 contingency table we are free to specify one value only.

Procedure

Table 18.58

Place of Residence and Political Preference

Place of Residence	*Political Preference*			*Total*
	Congress	*Janata*	*Lok Dal*	
	(a)	(c)	(c)	
Urban	38	20	12	70
	(b)	(d)	(f)	
Rural	10	26	6	42
Total	48	46	18	112

Computation for Chi-square

Table 18.59

Cell	*Observed frequencies (O)*	*Expected frequencies (E)*	*O – E*	*(O – E)²*	*(O – E)²/E*
(a)	38	30.00	8.00	64.0000	2.133333
(b)	10	18.00	– 8.00	64.0000	3.555555
(c)	20	28.75	– 8.75	76.5625	2.663043
(d)	26	17.25	8.57	76.5625	4.438405
(e)	12	11.25	0.75	0.5625	0.050000
(f)	6	6.75	0.75	0.5625	0.083333
	$N = 112$	112.00			12.923669

Steps	*Procedure*	*Application to Table 18.58*
1.	Set up a Hypothesis (H_o).	No differences among rural and urban people with respect to political preference. OR There is no association between place of residence and political preference.
2.	Compute expected frequencies (E) by the formula where C_t stands for column total, R stands for row total and N for total number for frequencies.	Cell (a): Observed frequencies (O) = 38 Expected frequencies $(E) = \frac{70 \times 48}{112} = 30$ Cell (b): $O = 10$ $E = \frac{42 \times 48}{112} = 18$ Cell (c): $O = 20$, $E = \frac{70 \times 46}{112} = 28.75$ Cell (d): $O = 26$, $E = \frac{42 \times 46}{112} = 17.25$ Cell (e): $O = 12$, $E = \frac{70 \times 18}{112} = 11.25$ Cell (f): $O = 6$, $E = \frac{42 \times 18}{112} = 6.75$

3.	Compute $(O - E)$.	$38 - 30 = 8$, $10 - 18 = -8$, $20 - 28.75 = -8.75$, $26 - 17.25 = 8.75$, $12 - 11.25 = 0.75$, $6 - 6.75 = -0.75$
4.	Compute $(O - E)^2$	$8^2 = 64$, $(-8)^2 = 64$, $(-8.75)^2 = 76.5625$, $(8.75)^2 = 76.5625$, $(-0.75)^2 = 0.5625$.
5.	Divide $(O - E)^2$ by E: $\frac{(O-E)^2}{E}$	$\frac{64}{30} = 2.13333$, $\frac{64}{18} = 3.55555$, $\frac{76.5625}{28.75} = 2.663043$, $\frac{76.5625}{17.25} = 5.438405$, $\frac{0.5625}{6.75} = 0.0833333$.
6.	Compute $\chi^2 = \frac{\Sigma(O-E)^2}{E}$	$\chi^2 = 12.923669$
7.	Level of significance.	0.05
8.	Compute degree of freedom (*df*).	$df = (r - 1)(c - 1)$ where *df* stands for the degree of freedom, r for number of rows and c for number of columns. $= (2 - 1)(3 - 1)$ $= 1 \times 2$ $= 2$.
9.	Find the value of Chi-square from R.A. Fisher Table values of chi-square at 0.05 level of significance for 2 degrees of freedom.	χ^2 (table value) (Level of significance 0.05 = 5.99 and degree of freedom 2).
10.	Inference.	Since calculated value of χ^2 (= 12.923669) is more than the table value of χ^2 (5.99) at 0.05 level of significance for 2 degree of freedom and hence the null hypothesis (H_0 = N_0 differences among rural and urban people with respect to political preference) is rejected. We, therefore, conclude that there is association between place of residence (rural or urban) and political preference.

Chi-square as a Test of Goodness of Fit

In the previous section we used the chi-square as a test of independence; that is whether to accept or reject a null hypothesis. The χ^2 tests can also be used to decide whether there is a significant difference between an observed frequency distribution and a theoretical frequency distribution. In this manner we can determine how good the fit is of the observed and expected frequencies. That is, the fit would be considered good if there is no significant divergence between the observed and expected data when the curve of the observed frequencies is super-imposed on the curve of expected frequencies.

We must remember, however, that even if proportions in the cells remain unchanged the chi-square value varies directly with the total number of cases *(N)*. If we double the number of cases, the chi-square value gets doubled; if we triple the number of cases we also triple chi-square and so on. The implications of this fact can be illustrated by an example given below:

Table 18.60

Marital Status and Performance in Examination

Marital Status	*Performance in Examination*		*Total*
	Successful	*Not Successful*	
Married	45	30	75
Unmarried	125	50	175
Total	170	80	250

In the present example, the chi-square value is 3.15. On this basis we would naturally infer that the relationship is not a significant one. Now, suppose data had been collected on 500 cases with the following results:

Table 18.61

Marital Status and Performance in Examination

Marital Status	*Performance in Examination*		*Total*
	Successful	*Not Successful*	
Married	90	60	150
Unmarried	250	100	350
Total	340	160	500

Chi-square value as computed from the figures, is now 6.30, which is double the value arrived at in the previous example. The value 6.30 is statistically significant. Had we expressed the results in terms of percentages there would not have been a difference in interpretation. The above examples illustrate a very important point, *viz.*, that chi-square is directly proportional to *N*. Hence, we would need a measure which is not affected merely by a change in the number of cases. The measure phi (ϕ) affords this facility, *i.e.*, the property we desire in our measure. This measure is simply a ratio between the chi-square value and the numerical total of the cases studied.

The measure phi (ϕ) is defined as:

$$\phi = \sqrt{\frac{\chi^2}{n}}$$

that is, the square root of chi-square divided by the number of cases.

Thus, by applying this formula to the two above cited examples we get, in the first case:

$$\phi = \sqrt{\frac{3.15}{250}} = 0.1122497;$$

and, in the second case:

$$\phi = \sqrt{\frac{6.30}{500}} = 0.1122497.$$

Thus, the measure ϕ unlike the chi-square, gives the same result when the proportions in the comparable cells are identical.

G. Udny Yule has proposed yet another coefficient of association usually designated as "*Q*" (more commonly known as Yule's *Q*) which measures association in ? × 2 table. The coefficient of association *(Q)* is obtained by computing the ratio between the difference and the sum of the cross products of the diagonal cells, if cells of the 2 × 2 table are designated as in the following table:

Marital Status	*Performance in Examination*		*Total*
	Successful	*Not Successful*	
Married	a	b	a + b
Unmarried	c	d	c + d
Total	a + c	b + d	

$$Q = \frac{ac - bc}{ad + bc}$$

where *a, b, c,* and *d* refer to the cell-frequencies.

The coefficient of association *Q* varies between minus one and plus one (± 1) as *bc* is less than or greater than *ad*. *Q* attains its limits of ± 1 whenever any one of the cells is zero, *i.e.,* the association is complete (the correlation is perfect). *Q* is zero when the variables are independent (that is, when there is no association), *i.e.,* when $ad = bc$ *and* $Q = 0$.

Application of the above formula is illustrated in the following example:

Let us compute Yule's Coefficient of Association between marital status and performance in examination on the basis of the data presented in the following table:

Table 18.62

Marital Status and Performance in Examination

Marital Status	*Performance in Examination*		*Total*
	Successful	*Not Successful*	
Married	90 (a)	60 (b)	150
Unmarried	250 (c)	200 (d)	350
Total	340	260	500

Substituting the above values in the Yule's formula:

$$Q = \frac{ad - bc}{ad + bc}$$

$$= \frac{(90 \times 100) - (60 \times 250)}{(90 \times 100) + (60 \times 250)}$$

$$= \frac{9000 - 15000}{9000 + 15000}$$

$$= \frac{-6000}{24000}$$

$$= -.25$$

Thus, there is a slight negative association between marital status and performance in examination.

We may look at the problem from another point of view also.

The percentage of married students who failed is $= \frac{60 \times 100}{150} = 40.$

The percentage of unmarried students who failed is,

$$= \frac{100 \times 100}{350} = 28.57 \text{ (Approx.)}$$

Thus, 40 per cent of the married students and nearly 29 per cent of the unmarried students failed in the examination. Hence the poor performance of students may be attributed to marital status.

Causal inferences can be very securely established in an experimental situations. We have considered this issue when dealing with experimental designs. In social sciences, it is very difficult to set up an experiment, so most of the studies are non-experimental ones. Analytical procedures have, however, been devised to draw inferences about causal relationships in non-experimental studies. We shall consider these procedures a little later in this chapter.

In as much as most social researches involve a study of the samples drawn from the 'population' and seek to draw generalizations to this 'population', it is necessary, in the interest of science, to know the extent to which generalizations thus drawn are justified.

Suppose, in a study on samples of male and female students our results show significant differences between the two samples in terms of the number of hours they devote to studies. We may ask whether the differences that are observed reflect the true differences between the male and female students or whether the two 'populations' of students are in fact alike in terms of the hours they devote to studies but the samples drawn from these 'populations' for the study might have differed to this extent by 'chance.' A number of statistical procedures have been designed to enable us to answer such a question in terms of the statements of probability.

When we are comparing samples or studying the difference between experimental and control groups, we normally wish to test some hypothesis about the nature of the true difference between the 'populations' supposed to be represented by the samples under study. In social sciences, we are usually concerned with relatively crude hypothesis (for example, the female students devote more time to their studies than the male students do). We are not usually in a position to consider more specific or exact hypothesis (*e.g.,* which specify in exact terms the difference between the two 'populations'). Suppose, our data show that the sample of female students devotes on an average four hours to studies whereas the sample of male students, only two hours. Clearly, the findings of our samples are in tune with the hypothesis, *i.e.,* female students devote more time to their studies than their male counterparts. But we must constantly bear in mind the possibility that the findings based on our samples may not be exactly the same as the findings we might have obtained had we studied two 'populations' in *toto* (for a detailed discussion see the chapter on sampling). Now, we want to estimate whether we would still have observed more time spent on studies among the female students, had we studied the total 'population'. Such an estimate is possible if we test the 'null hypothesis.'

As was indicated in the chapter devoted to hypothesis, the 'null hypothesis' states that the 'populations' do not differ in terms of characteristics under study. In this case, a 'null hypothesis' would state that in the larger 'population' of students as a whole, sub-groups of the female and male students do not differ in respect of the time they devote to their studies. Various statistical techniques called the tests of significance, some of which were discussed above, have been devised which help us estimate the likelihood that our two samples might have differed to the extent they do, by chance, even if there is actually no difference between the two corresponding 'populations' of male and female students in respect of time devoted to studies. Among the various methods of testing significance, the decision as to which method will be appropriate for a particular study depends on the nature of the measurements used and distribution of the characteristics (*e.g.*, hours of study, number of children, salary-expectations etc.). Most of these tests of significance assume that the measurements constitute interval scale and that the distribution of the characteristic approximates a normal curve. In social research, these assumptions seldom correspond to reality. Recent statistical developments have, however, come out with some kind of a solution to this, in the form of non-parametric tests that do not rest on these assumptions.

We should try to understand at this point the reason why the 'null hypothesis' should be tested when our actual interest is in testing a hypothesis (alternative hypothesis, as it is called) which states that there is a difference between the two 'populations' represented by the samples. The reason is easy to appreciate. Since we do not know the true picture in the 'population' the best we can do is to make inferences about it on the basis of our sample-finding. If we are comparing two samples, there are, of course, two possibilities: (1) either, the populations represented by the sample are alike or (2) they are different. Our samples from two 'populations' are different in respect of some attributes; hours devoted to studies in our example. Clearly, this could happen if the two 'populations' which the samples represent do in fact differ in respect of the said attribute. This, however, does not constitute a definitive evidence that these 'populations' differ, since there is always the possibility that the samples do not exactly correspond to the 'populations' they purport to represent.

We must therefore allow room for the possibility that the element of chance which is involved in the selection of a sample may have given us samples which differ from each other although the two 'populations' from which they are drawn do not in fact differ. The question we may want to ask, therefore, is: "Could we have possibly got samples differing from each other to the extent they do, even if the 'populations' from which they are drawn did not differ?" This precisely is the question which a 'null hypothesis' answers. The 'null hypothesis' helps us to estimate what the chances are that the two samples differing to this extent would have been drawn from two 'populations' that are in fact alike: 5 in 100? 1 in 100? or whatever. If the statistical test of significance suggests that it is improbable that two samples differing to this extent could have been drawn from 'populations' that are in fact similar, we may conclude that the two 'populations' probably differ from each other.

A point to bear in mind here is that all statistical tests of significance and thus all generalizations from the samples to the populations rest on the assumption that the samples are not selected in a manner that bias could have entered into the process of drawing the samples. In other words, the assumption is that the sample we have selected has been drawn in such a manner that all cases or items in the 'population' had an equal or specifiable chance of being included in the sample. If this assumption is not justified, the tests of significance become meaningless and inapplicable. In other words, the tests of significance apply only when the probability principle had been employed in selecting the sample.

To return to our illustration, suppose, our findings show no difference between the two samples: which means that both male and female students in our sample are found to devote equal time to their studies. Can we then say that the two 'populations' of male and female students are similar in terms of this attribute? Of course, we cannot say this with any certainty since there is a possibility that the samples may be alike when the populations actually differ.

But to go back to the case where the two samples differ, we can affirm that the two populations they represent probably differ if we can reject the 'null hypothesis'; that is, if we can show that the difference between the two samples is unlikely to appear if the above 'populations' did not differ. But again, there is some chance that we may be wrong in rejecting the 'null hypothesis' since it is in the nature of probability that even highly improbable events may sometimes take place.

There is another side to it, too. Just as we may be wrong in rejecting the 'null hypothsis,' it is also likely that we may be wrong in accepting the 'null hypothesis.' That is, even if our statistical test of significance indicates that sample differences might easily have arisen by chance even though the 'populations' are similar, it may nevertheless be true that the 'populations' do in fact differ.

In other words, we are always faced with the risk of making any one of the two types of error: (1) We may reject the 'null hypothesis' when in fact it is true, (2) We may accept the 'null hypothesis' when in fact it is false.

The first type of error, we may call the Type I error. This consists in inferring that the two 'populations' differ when in fact they are alike.

The second type of error may be called the Type II error. This consists in inferring that the two 'populations' are alike when in fact they differ.

The risk of making the Type I error is determined by the level of significance we are prepared to accept in our statistical testing, *e.g.,* 0.05, 0.01, 0.001, etc. (that is, 5 in 100, 1 in 100 and 1 in 1000). Thus, if we decide, for instance, that the populations truly differ whenever a test of significance shows that the difference between the two samples would be expected to occur by chance not more than 5 times in 100. This means that if the two 'populations' represented by the sample were in fact similar (in terms of a certain attribute), then we are accepting 5 chances in 100 that we will be wrong in rejecting the 'null hypothesis.' We may, of course, minimize the risk of making Type I error by making our criterion for rejecting the null hypothesis, more strict and tight. We may, for example, decide the level of significance at 0.01, *i.e.,* we would reject the 'null hypothsis' only if the test shows that the difference in the two 'samples' might have appeared by chance only once in a hundred. In essence, what we are saying is that we will reject the 'null hypothesis' if the test shows that out of a hundred samples of a designated size selected from the respective 'populations' by employing the probability principle, only one sample will show difference in terms of the attributes to the extent this is seen in the two samples under study. The criterion for rejecting the 'null hypothesis' can be made even more strict by further elevating the level of significance. But the difficulty here is, that the errors of Type I and Type II happen to be so related to each other that the more we protect ourselves against making a Type I error, the more vulnerable we are to make a Type II error.

Having determined the extent of risk of type I error we are willing to run, the only way of reducing the possibility of Type II error is to take larger samples and use statistical tests that make the maximum use of available relevant information. The situation with respect to the Type II error can be illustrated in a very precise way by means of an "opening characteristic curve." The behaviour of this curve depends on how large the sample is. The larger the sample, the less probable it is that we will accept a hypothesis which suggests a state of affairs that is extremely far off from the state of reality.

In so far as the relationship between the Type I and Type II errors is inverse, it is necessary to strike a reasonable balance between the two types of risk. In social sciences, it has almost become an established practice or convention to reject the 'null hypothesis' when the test indicates that the difference between the samples would not occur by chance more than 5 times out of 100. But the conventions are useful when there is no other reasonable guide. The decision as to how the balance between the two kinds of error should be struck must be made by the researcher. In some instances, it is more important to be certain of rejecting a hypothesis when it is false than fail to accept it when it is true. In other cases the reverse may be true. For example, in certain countries, it is considered more important to reject a hypothesis of guilt when it is false than to fail to accept this hypothesis when it is true, *i.e.,* a person is considered not guilty so long as there is a reasonable doubt about his guilt. In certain other countries, a person charged with a crime is considered guilty until such a time as he has demonstrated his lack of guilt.

In much research, of course, there is no clear basis for deciding whether a Type I or Type II error would be more costly and so the investigator makes use of the conventional level in determining statistical significance. But, there may be some studies in which one type of error would clearly be more costly and harmful than the other. Suppose, in an organization it has been suggested that a new method of division of labour would be more effictive and suppose also that this method would require a lot of expense. If an experiment constituted of two groups of personnel — one operating as experimental group and the other, as control group — is set up to test whether the new method is really beneficial for the organizational goals and if it is anticipated that the new method would entail a lot of expenses, the organization would not wish to adopt it unless there was considerable assurance of its superiority. In other words, it would be expensive to make a Type l error, *i.e.,* conclude that the new method is better when it is not so in fact.

If the new method entailed expenses which were about the same as the old method, then type II error would be undesirable and more damaging since it may lead to failure on the part of the management to adopt the new method when it is in fact superior and as such has long-range benefits in store for the organization.

As we have seen, any generalizations from the sample to the 'population' is simply a statement of statistical probability. Let us say, we have decided to work with a 0.05 level of significance. This means that we shall reject the 'null hypothesis' only if the sample-difference of the magnitude that we have observed can be expected to occur by chance not more than 5 times in 100. Of course, we will accept the 'null hypothesis' if such a difference can be expected to occur by chance more than 5 times out of 100. Now the question is: Does our finding represent one of those 5 times when such a difference might have appeared by chance? This question cannot be definitively answered on the basis of an isolated finding. It may, however, be possible for us to say something about this when we examine the patterns within our findings.

Suppose we are interested in testing the effects of a film on attitudes toward a particular governmental programme, say family planning. We have, let us say, taken full care to keep the desired conditions for experimentation at the maximum. Now suppose that we use as one measure of attitudes toward the programme, only one item, *viz.,* the attitude toward spacing children and find that those who saw the film are more favourably inclined toward this issue than those who did not see the film. Now suppose, the statistical test shows that the difference would not have appeared by chance due to random sampling fluctuations more than once in twenty. Logically, it also means that it might have appeared by chance once in twenty (or 5 times in 100). As we have pointed out, we have no definite way of knowing whether our sample is one among the five in 100. Now, what best can we do?

Let us say, we have asked 40 different questions to respondents, which are reasonable indicators of the attitude toward the family welfare governmental programme. If we are using a confidence level of 5% and if we asked 100 questions we might expect to find statistically significant differences attributable to chance on 5 of them. Thus, out of our 40 questions on various items, we may expect to find statistically significant differences on 2 of them. But, suppose we actually find that on 25 out of 40 questions on those who saw the film had more favourable attitudes compared to those who did not see the film. We may, this being the case, feel much safer in concluding that there is a true difference in attitudes (even though the statistical test indicates that the difference might have arisen by chance on each question 5 times in 100).

Now let us suppose that out of the 40 questions, responses to only one, *i.e.,* about the spacing of children, showed a statistically significant difference between the two groups (those exposed to film and those not). This difference might as well have occurred by chance. On the other hand, it may be that the content of the film actually did influence opinions on this point but not on any other (such as that relating to sterility operations). But unless our hypothesis has specifically predicted in advance that the film would be more likely to affect the attitudes toward spacing of children than the attitudes toward any of the other 39 questions, we are not justified in making this interpretation. Such an interpretation, *i.e.,* one invoked to explain the findings after they surface, is known as the 'post-factum' interpretation, because this involves explanations provided to justify the findings whatever they are. It depends upon the ingenuity of the researcher, as to what explanation he can invent to justify this findings. He can, therefore, justify even the opposite findings.

Merton has very lucidly pointed out that the post-factum interpretations are designed to "explain" observations.[5] The method of post-factum explanation is completely flexible. If the researcher finds that the unemployed tend to read fewer books than they did previously, this may be "explained" by the hypothsis that anxiety resulting from unemployment affects concentration and so reading becomes difficult. If, however, it is observed that the unemployed read more books than previously (when in employment), a new post-factum explanation can be invoked; the explanation being that the unemployed have more leisure and, therefore, they read more books. The critical test on an obtained relationship (among variables) is not the post-factum rationales and explanation for it; it is rather the ability to predict it or to predict other relationships on the basis of it. Thus, our previously unpredicted finding of a difference in attitudes toward spacing of children, even though statistically significant, cannot be considered as established by the study we have carried out.

Since, statistical statements are statements of probability, we can never totally rely on the statistical evidence alone for deciding whether or not we will accept a hypothesis as true. Confidence in the interpretation of a research result requires not only statistical confidence in the reliability of the finding (*i.e.,* that the differences are not likely to have occurred by chance) but in addition, some evidence about the validity of presuppositions of the research. This evidence is necessarily indirect. It comes from the congruence of the given research findings with other knowledge which has withstood the test of time and hence about which, there is considerable assurance. Even in the most rigorously controlled investigation, the establishment of confidence in the interpretation of one's results or in the imputation of causal relationships requires replication of research and the relating of the findings to those of other studies.

It is necessary to note that even when statistical tests and the findings of a number of studies suggest that there is indeed a consistent difference between two groups or consistent relationship between two variables, this still does not constitute the evidence of the reason for the relationship. If we want to draw causal inferences (*e.g., X* produces *Y*), we must meet assumptions over and above those required for establishing the existence of a relationship. (we have already considered this in our treatment of the logic of inferring the causal relationships.)

It is also worthy of note that a result is not socially or psychologically significant just because it is statistically significant. Many statistically significant differences may be trivial in practical social parlance. For example, an average difference of less than one I.Q. point between the urban and rural people may be significant statistically, but not so in the practical day-to-day life. Contrariwise, there are cases where a small but reliable difference has great practical significance. In a large-scale survey, for example, a difference of half or one per cent may represent hundreds of thousands of people and awareness of the difference may be important for significant policy decisions. Therefore, the researcher besides being concerned with the statistical significance of his findings must also be concerned with their social and psychological meanings.

Inferring Causal Relationships: The ideal design of a study that seeks to establish cause and effect was set forth in the chapter on the design of research. Owing to obvious difficulties, such rigid experimental designs can rarely be worked out in social scientific investigations. Most of the inquiries in social sciences are non-experimental in character. In such studies, there are certain empirical obstacles in the way of determining whether or not a relation between variables is causal. It has been repeatedly mentioned that one of the most difficult tasks in the analysis of social behaviourl data is the establishment of cause and effect relationships. A problematic situation owes its origin and the process of becoming, not just to one factor but to a complex of a variety of factors and sequences. The process of disentangling these elements poses a major challenge to the sociological imagination and puts to test the skill of researchers. It is dangerous to follow a 'one-track' explanation which leads to the cause. It is imperative to look for a whole battery of causal factors which generally play a significant role in bringing about complex social situations. As Karl Pearson aptly observes, "no phenomenon or stage in sequence has only one cause; all antecedent stages are successive causes; when we scientifically states causes, we are really describing the successive stages of a routine of experience."[6] Yule and Kendall have recognized the fact that statistics "must accept for analysis, data subject to the influence of a host of causes and must try to discover from the data themselves which causes are the important ones and how much of the observed effect is due to the operation of each."[7] Paul Lazarsfeld has traced the phases involved in the technique he calls 'discerning.'[8] He advocates its use in determining causal relations between variables. Lazarsfeld lays down this procedure:

(a) Verifying an alleged occurrence as under : In order to verify this occurrence, it is necessary to ascertain if the person has actually experienced the alleged situations. If so, how does the occurrence manifest itself and under what conditions, in his immediate life? What reasons are advanced for the belief that there is a specific interconnection between two variables, *e.g.*, loss of employment and loss of authority? How correct is the person's reasoning in this particular instance?

(b) Attempting to discover whether the alleged condition is consistent with objective facts of the past life of this person.

(c) Testing all possible explanations for the observed condition.

(d) Ruling out those explanations which are not in accord with the pattern of happenings.

It is quite understandable that most difficulties or obstacles to establishing causal relationships afflict non-experimental studies most sharply. In non-experimental studies where the interest is in establishing causal relationships among two variables, the investigator must find substitutes for safeguards that are patently built into the experimental studies. Many of these safeguards enter at the time of planning data-collection, in the form of providing for the gathering of information about a number of variables that might well be the alternative conditions for producing the hypothesized effect. By introducing such additional variables into the analysis, the researcher approximates some of the controls that are inherent in experiments. Nevertheless, the drawing of inferences of causality does always remain somewhat hazardous in non-experimental studies.

We shall now discuss some of the problems and the strategies to overcome them, relating to drawing inferences about causality in non-experimental studies.[9]

If a non-experimental study points to a relationship or association between two variables, say *X* and *Y*, and if the research interest is in causal relationships rather than in the simple fact of association among variables, the analysis has taken only its first step. The researcher must further consider (besides association between *X* and *Y*) whether *Y* (effect) might have occurred before *X* (the hypothesised cause), in which case *Y* cannot be the effect of *X*. In addition to this consideration, the researcher must ponder over the issue whether factors other than *X* (the hypothesised cause) may have produced *Y* (the hypothesised effect). This is generally taken care of by introducing additional variables into the analysis and examining how the relation between *X* and *Y* is affected by these further variables.

If the relationship between *X* and *Y* persists even when other presumably effective and possibly alternative variables are introduced, the hypothesis that *X* is the cause of *Y* remains tenable. For example, if the relation between eating a particular seasonal fruit *(X)* and cold *(Y)* does not change even when other variables such as age, temperature, state of digestion, etc., are introduced into the analysis, we may accept the hypothesis that *X* leads to *Y* as tenable.

But it is possible in no small number of cases that the introduction of other additional variables may change the relationship between *X* and *Y*. It may reduce to totally eliminate the relationship between *X* and *Y* or it may enhance the relationship in one group and reduce it in another. If the relationship between *X* (eating of seasonal fruit) and *Y* (cold) is enhanced in a sub-group characterized by *Z* (bad state of digestion) and reduced in sub-group not characterized by *Z* (normal state of digestion), we may conclude that *Z* is the contingent condition for the relationship between *X* and *Y*. This means, in other words, that we have been able to specify condition *(Z)* under which the ralation between *X* and *Y* holds. Now if introduction of *Z* in the analysis reduces or totally eliminates the relationship between *X* and *Y*, we shall be safe in concluding either that X is not a producer of *Y*, that is, the relation between *X* and *Y* is 'spurious' or that we have traced the process by which *X* leads to *Y* (*i.e.*, through *Z*).

Let us turn to consider the situation in which we can legitimately conclude that the relation between *X* and *Y* is spurious.

An apparent relationship between two variables *X* and *Y* is said to be spurious if their concomitant variation stems not from a connection between them but from the fact that each of them (*X* and *Y*) is related to some third variable (*Z*) or a combination of variables that does not serve as a link in the process by which *X* leads to *Y*. The situation characterizing spurious relationship may be diagrammed as under:

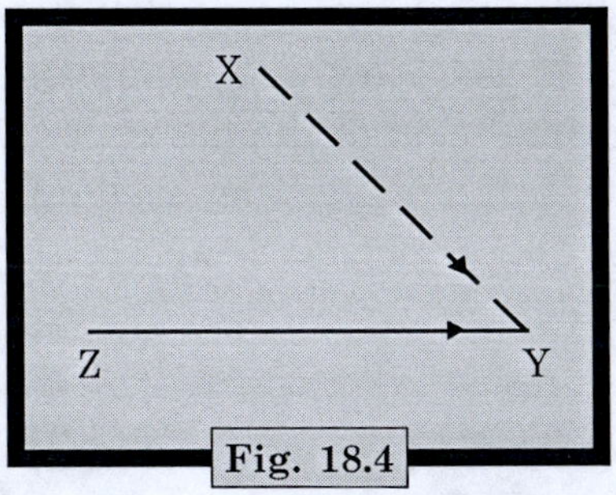

Fig. 18.4

The objective here is to determine the cause of *Y*, the dependent variable (let us say, the monetary expectation by college graduates). The relationship (broken line) between *X* the independent variable (let us say, the grades obtained by students) and the monetary expectation of graduates *(Y)* has been observed in the course of the analysis of data. Another variable *(Z)* is introduced to see how the relation between *X* and *Y* behaves with the entry of this third factor. *Z* is the third factor (let us say, the income-level of the parents of students). We find that the introduction of this factor reduces the relationship between *X* and *Y*. That is, it is found that the relation between higher grade in the examination and higher monetary expectations does not hold itself up, but is considerably reduced when we introduce the third variable, i.e., the level of parents' income. Such an introduction of *Z* brings to light the fact that not *X* but *Z* may probably be a determining factor of *Y*. So the relationship between *X* and *Y* (shown in the diagram by a dotted line) is a spurious one, whereas the relation between *Z* and *Y* is a real one. Let us illustrate this with the help of hypothetical data.

Suppose, in the course of the analysis of data in a study, it was seen that there is a significant correlation between the grades or divisions (I, II, III) that students secured in the examination and the salary they expect for a job that they might be appointed to. It was seen, for instance, that generally the first divisioners among students expected a higher remuneration compared to the second divisioners and the second divisioners expected more compared to the third divisioners. The following table illustrates the hypothetical state of affairs:

Table A (hypothetical data)

Y \ X	I class students	II class students	III class students	Total
Higher monetary expectation	96 (60% approx.)	80	44	220
Moderate monetary expectation	48	240 (66%)	112	400
Lower monetary expectation	16	40	324 (67.5%)	380
Total	160	360	480	1000

It is clearly seen from the table that there is a basis for hypothesising that the grades of the students determine their expectations about salaries. Now, let us suppose that the researcher somehow hits upon the idea that the income-level of the parents *(X)* could be one of the important variables determining or influencing the students' expectations about salaries *(Y)*. Thus, *Z* is introduced into the analysis. Suppose, the following table represents the relationship among the variables:

Table B (hypothetical data)

Y \ X + Z	I class			II class			III class			Total
	H	*M*	*L*	*H*	*M*	*L*	*H*	*M*	*L*	
Higher monetary expectation	*92*	*4*	–	*76*	*4*	–	*44*	–	–	*220*
Moderate monetary expectation	–	*44*	*4*	*4*	*228*	*8*	*12*	*100*	–	*400*
Lower monetary expectation	–	–	*16*	–	*4*	*36*	*4*	*20*	*300*	*380*
Total	*92*	*48*	*20*	*80*	*236*	*44*	*60*	*120*	*300*	*1000*

Note: H.M.L in the horizontal row, dividing each category of the students' grades, stand respectively for high parental level of income, moderate parental level of income and low parental level of income.

The above table clearly shows that the relation between *X* and *Y* has become less significant compared to the relation between *Z* and *Y*. To get a clearer picture, let us see the following table (a version of Table B omitting the categories of *X*) showing the relationship between *Z* and, *i.e.,* parental income level and students' monetary expectations:

Table C (hypothetical data)

Y \ Z	*High level of parental income*	*Moderate level of parental income*	*Low level of parental income*	*Total*
Higher monetary expectation	212 (91.5%)	8		220
Moderate monetary expectation	16	372 (92%)	12	400
Low monetary expectation	4	24	352 (97%)	380
Total	232	404	364	1000

We can very clearly see from the table that, irrespective of their grades, the students' monetary expectations are very strongly affected by the parental levels of income *(Z)*. We see that an overwhelming number of students (*i.e.,* 91.5%) having high monetary expectations are from the high parental income group, 92% having moderate monetary expectations are from moderate parental income group and lastly, 97% having low monetary expectations are from the low parental income group. Comparing this picture with the picture represented by Table A, we may say that the relation between *X* and *Y* is spurious, that is, the grade of the students did not primarily determine the level of the monetary expectations of the students. It is noted in Table A that students getting a higher grade show a significant tendency toward higher monetary expectations whereas the lower grade students have a very marked concentration in the lower monetary expectation bracket. But when we introduce the third variable of parental income, the emerging picture becomes clear enough to warrant the conclusion that the real factor responsible differential levels of monetary expectations is the level of parental income. In Table C, we see a very strong and formidable concentration of cases of students corresponding to the three undermentioned combinations, *viz.,* of higher monetary expectations and higher parental income, of moderate monetary expectations and moderate parental income and of lower monetary expectations and lower parental income, *i.e.,* 5%, 92.1% and 1% respectively.

Tracing the Process Involved and a Relationship Among Variables: As was stated earlier, if a third factor *Z* reduces or eliminates the relationship between the independent variable *X* and the dependent variable *Y*, we may conclude either that the relationship between *X* and *Y* is spurious, or that we have been able to trace the process by which *X* leads to *Y*. We shall now consider the circumstances that would warrant the conclusion that the process of relationship between *X* and *Y* has been traced through a third factor *Z*.

Suppose, in a study the investigators found that smaller communities had a higher average intimacy score, the intimacy score being a measure of the intimacy of association between members of a community arrived at by using an intimacy scale. Suppose, they also found that the middle-sized communities had a lesser intimacy score compared to the small-sized communities and big-sized communities had the least average intimacy score. Such a finding suggests that the size of the community determines the intimacy of association among members of the community.

In other words, the observations warrant the conclusion that the members living in a small-sized community have a greater intimacy of association, whereas the big-sized communities are characterized by a lesser intimacy of association among the members.

The following table presents the hypothetical data:

In the second column of the table, samples corresponding to each of the communities have been shown.

Table A

Size of the Community	*Frequency*	*Average Intimacy Score*
Small-sized community	231	2.40
Middle-sized community	417	2.15
Big-sized community	396	1.65

In the second column of the table, samples corresponding to each of the communities have been shown. In column 3, the average intimacy scores corresponding to types of communities calculated on the basis of the responses given to certain items on a scale relating to the day-to-day associations among members have been shown. It is seen from the table that the average intimacy scores vary inversely with the size of the community, *i.e.,* smaller the size, the greater the intimacy score and conversely, larger the size, the lower the intimacy score.

Now suppose, the investigators got the idea that the three types of communities would differ in terms of opportunities they offer for interaction among members, in as much as the living arrangements, residential patterning, commonly-shared utilities etc., would promote such association. Thus, the investigators would introduce the third factor into analysis of the interaction-potential, *i.e.,* the extent to which the circumstances persons live in are likely to provide opportunities for interaction among themselves. In order to check the hypothesis that it was largely through differences in residential patterning, living arrangements, commonly shared amenities etc., that the three types of communities produced differences in interaction among members of a community, the investigators would consider the size of community and interaction-potential jointly in relation to the average intimacy score. The infraction-potential is thus the third varizble *Z* introduced into the analysis. The interaction-potential is classified, let us say, into *(a)* low interaction-potential *(b)* medium interaction potential, and *(c)* high interaction-potential. The following table represents the hypothetical data:

Table B

Z & Y / X	No.	L Intimacy Score	No.	M Intimacy Score	No.	H Intimacy Score
Small-sized community	21	1.40	60	2.45	150	2.55
Moderate-sized community	114	1.45	120	1.90	183	2.75
Big-sized community	192	1.20 (approx.)	102	1.80 (approx.)	102	2.60 (apporx.)
Total	327	1.30	282	1.98	435	2.64

Reading across the rows in the table, we see that the interaction-potential is strongly related to the intimacy score of the community members, whatever the size of the community. That is, whether we consider the row for small-sized communities, for the middle-sized communities, or for the big-sized communities, there is in each case an increase in the average intimacy score with an increase in interaction-potential. Moreover, reading the entries across the rows, it becomes clear that the size of the community and the interaction-potential bear a significant correlation. For examle, approximately two-thirds of respondents in a small-sized community are living under conditions of high interaction-potential; we also find that a much smaller proportion of the moderate-sized community residents are living under high interaction-potential conditions and a very small proportion of the big-sized community residents under high interaction-potential conditions. Now, we read the intimacy scores down the columns only to find that the relationship between the type of community and intimacy of association has been considerably reduced. In fact, for people living under high interaction-potential conditions, no definite relationship between the size of the community and the intimacy score obtains.

From this set of relationships, the investigators may conclude that the inverse relationship between the size of the community and the intimacy score does hold good, but that one of the major ways in which a particular type of community encourages intimacy among its members is by offering opportunities that increase the rate of interaction amongst them. In other words, the small-sized communities are characterized by a higher average intimacy score because their small size provides a setting for many opportunities for high degree of interaction among members. Big-sized communities, on the other hand, are characterized by a relatively lower intimacy score. But the lower intimacy score is attributable not to the size of the community *per se* but to the fact that a big-sized community cannot offer opportunities for higher interaction among members as the small-sized communities do.

Hence, the investigators rather than concluding that the relationship between the size of the community and the average intimacy score among members is spurious, might conclude that they have been able to trace the process by which *X* (*i.e.,* the type of community) influences *Y* (the intimacy score).

We have so far considered two examples. The former warranted the conclusion that the relation between the variables *X* and *Y* was spurious and the latter the conclusion that the process from X to Y may be traced through Z (*X* to *Z* to *Y*). In both cases, the introduction of a third variable Z reduced or eliminated the relationship between them (*X* and *Y*). One difference may, however, be noted. In the first example, the variable *Z* (*i.e.,* income level of parents) was clearly prior in time to the other two variables (grade of students in the examination and monetary expecations of students). In the second example, the third variable Z (interaction-potential afforded by the communities) did not occur before the assumed causal variable (size of community). It was concurrent with it and might be thought of as starting after it.

The time-sequence of the variables, thus, is an important consideration in deciding whether an apparent causal relationship is spurious. That is, if the third variable Z, which removes or eliminates the relationship between the originally related variables *X* and *Y,* we conclude ususally that the apparent causal relationship between variables X and Y is spurious. But if the third variable Z is known or assumed to have occurred at the same times as *X* or after *X*, it may be in order to conclude that the process by which *X* leads to *Y* has been traced.

We have already seen how in the non-experimental studies, there is always a possibility of interpreting spurious relationship as causal. Thus, to have certain measure of confidence in causal relationship inferred from studies that are non-experimental in character, it is necessary to subejct them to the critical test of eliminating the other possibly relevant variables. For this reason, it is important to collect in the course of study, data on such possibly influential variables other than those with which the hypothesis of the study are centrally concerned.

It was stated earlier that the introduction of a third variable into the analysis may have the effect of intensifying the relationship within one sub-group and of reducing the same in another sub-group. If such be the case, we say that we have spsecified a condition (Z) under which the relationship between *X* and *Y* holds.

Let us now illustrate the process of specification. Suppose, in a community study, we happen to identify a relationship betwee income and educational level. This is shown in the table given below:

Table A (Hypothetical data)

Income / Education	Number	*Perecntage earning less than Rs. 5,000/- Per year*	*Percentage earning more than Rs. 5, 000/- per year*
Graduates	500	32	68
Non-graduates	500	82	18
Total	1000	57	43

We see in the table that the relationship between education and income is a fairly marked one. Higher the education, generally, higher the percentage of cases earning a yearly income of Rs. 5,000/- and above. However, we may decide that the relationship requires further specification. That is, we may wish to know more about the conditions under which this relationship obtains. Suppose, the thought strikes us that the fact of the respondents living in urban-industrial community might positively affect the advantages of education for remunerative employment and hence its reflection in income. On this assumption, we introduce the third factor Z, *i.e.,* those respondents who live in the urban industrial community and those who live in the rural non-industrial community, into the analysis and see how it affects the initial relationship between *X* and *Y* (*i.e.,* education and income). Suppose we get a picture as shown in the following table:

Table B

Respondents living in urban-industrial community (Z)	*Number*	*Perecntage earning less than Rs. 5,000/-*	*Percentage earning more than Rs. 5,000/-*
Graduates	250	20*	80*
Non-graduates	250	80	20
Total	500	50	50
Respondents living in rural-non-industrial community (Z)	*Number*	*Percentage earning less than Rs. 5,000/-*	*Percentage earning more than Rs. 5,000/-*
Graduates	250	80*	20*
Non-graduates	250	90	10
Total	500	85	15

* Approximate

We can see clearly that the Table B reflects a very different relationship between income and education for the people living in the rural-non-industrial community as compared to the one for those living in the urban-industrial community. We see that for those living in the industrial cities, the relationship between education and income is somewhat higher than the original relationship. But, for those living in the rural non-industrial communities the relationship in the above table is considerably lower than the initial relationship. Thus, the introduction of the third factor and the break-down of the original relationship on the basis of the third factor *(Z)* has helped to specify a condition under which the relationship between *X* and *Y* is more pronounced as also the condition under which the relation is less pronounced.

Similarly suppose, we find in the course of a study that people who belong to the higher income category have generally lesser number of children compared to those in the lower income category. Suppose, we feel (on the basis of a theoretic orientation) that the factor of city-dwelling could be important in affecting the relationship. Introducing this factor, suppose, we find that the original relationship between level of income and number of children becomes more pronounced in the city and that it becomes less pronounced among the rural people, than we have identified a condition *Z* (*i.e.,* city-dwelling) under which the relation becomes decisively enhanced or pronounced.

Interpreting the Findings of a Study: Thus far, we have concerned ourselves mainly with the procedures that together comprise, what we call customarily, the analysis of data. The researcher's task, however, is incomplete if he stops by presenting his findings in the form of empirical generalizations which he is able to arrive at through the analysis of data. A researcher who, for example, winds up his research exercise just by stating that "the unmarried people have a higher incidence of suicide as compared to the married people" is hardly fulfilling his overall obligation to science, though the empirical generalization he has set forth does have some value by itself. The researcher in the larger interest of science must also seek to show that his observation points to certain underlaying relations and processes which are initially hidden to the eye. In other words, the researcher must show that his observation has a meaning, much broader and deeper, than the one it appears to have on the surface level. To return to our example of suicide, the researcher should be able to show that his observation that "the unmarried people are characterized by suicide" reflects, in fact, the deeper relationship between social cohesion and rate of suicide (Durkheim's theory). Once the researcher is able to expose the relations and processes that underlie his concrete findings he can establish abstract relationships between his findings and various others.

In essence then, the researcher's work goes well beyond the collection and analysis of data. His task extends to interpreting the findings of his study. It is through *interpretation* that the researcher can understand the real significance of his findings, *i.e.,* he can appreciate why the findings are what they are.

As was stated earlier, interpretation is the search for broader and more abstract meanings of the research findings. This search involves viewing the research findings in the light of other established knowledge, a theory or a principle. This search has two major aspects.

The first aspect involves the effort to establish continuity in research through linking the results of a given study with those of another. It is through interpretation that the researcher can unravel or comprehend the abstract principle beneath the concrete empirical observations. This abstract common denominator having been discerned, the researcher can easily proceed to link his findings up with those of other studies conducted in diverse settings, diverse in matters of detail but reflecting the same abstract principle at the level of findings. Needless to say that the researcher can on the basis of the recognition of the abstract theoretic principle underlying his finding, make various predictions about the concrete world of events quite unrelated seemingly to the area of his findings. Thus, fresh inquiries may be triggered off to test predictions and understandably, such studies would have a relationship with the researcher's initial study.

In a somewhat different sense, interpretation is necessarily involved in the transition from exploratory to experimental research. The interpretation of the findings of the former category of researches often leads to hypotheses for the latter. Since, an exploratory study does not have a hypothesis to start with, the findings or conclusions of such a study have to be interpreted on a 'post-factum' interpretation is often a hazardous game fraught with dangerous implications. Such an interpretation involves a search for a godfather in the nature of some theory or principle that would adopt (*i.e.,* explain) the findings of the study. This quest often turns out to be an exercise on the part of the researcher to justify his findings by locating some suitable theory to fit his findings. As a result quite so often contradictory conclusions may find their 'godfathers' in diverse theories. This aspect of post-factum interpretation, comprising attempts at rationalizing the research findings, should be clearly borne in mind when proceeding with it. On occasions there is, however, no other alternative to it.

Secondly, interpretation leads to the establishment of explanatory concepts. As has been pointed out, interpretation of findings involves efforts to explain why the observations or findings are, what they are. In accomplishing this task, theory assumes central importance. It is a sensitizer and a guide to the underlying factors and processes (explanatory bases) beneath the findings. Underneath the researcher's observations in the course of a study, lies a set of factors and processes which might explain his observations of the empirical world. Theoretical interpretation uncovers these factors. The researcher's task is to explain the relations he has observed in the course of his study, by exposing the underlying processes which afford him a deeper understanding of these relations and point to the role of certain basic factors operating in the problem area of his study.

Thus, interpretation serves a twofold purpose. First, it gives an understanding of the general factors that seem to explain what has been observed in the course of a study and secondly, it provides a theoretical conception which can serve in turn as a guide for further research. It is in this manner that science comes to cumulatively disengage more successfully the basic processes which shape the portion of the empirical world with which a researcher is concerned.

As was stated earlier, interpretation is so inextricably intertwined with analysis that it should more properly be conceived of as a special aspect of analysis rather than a separate or distinct operation. In closing, we are tempted to quote Prof. C. Wright Mills who has stated the very essence of what all is involved in the analysis (involving interpretation) of data. Says Mills, "So you will discover and describe, setting up types for the ordering what you have found out, focussing and organizing experience by distinguishing items by name. This search for order will cause you to seek patterns and trends and find relations that may be typical and causal. You will search in short, for the meaning of what you have come upon or what may be interpreted as a visible token of something that seems involved in whatever you are trying to understand; you will pare it down to essentials; then carefully and systematically you will relate these to one another in order to form a sort of working model....

"But always among all details, you will be searching for indicators that might point to the main drift, to the underlying forms and tendencies of the range of society in its particular period of time."[10]

After a piece of research is terminated, the statement that raises an array of new questions and problems may be made. Some of the new questions constitute the groundwork for new research undertakings and formulation of new theories which will either modify or replace old ones. This is indeed, what research means. It serves to open new and more wider avenues of intellectual adventure and simulates the quest for more knowledge as well as greater wisdom in its use.

REFERENCES

(1) Analysis as involved in Explanatory Studies.
(2) Galtung, *op. cit.,* p. 108. For the sake of convenience, we have taken only two sub-classes under marital status, *i.e.,* Married and Single. We are aware that there are certain other possibilities, *viz.,* widows, widowers, divorced, etc.
(3) H. B. Blalock, *Social Statistics* (Tokyo, 1972, p. 157).
(4) See Ackoff, *op. cit.,* pp. 163-173.
(5) Merton, *op. cit.,* p. 148.
(6) Pearson, T., *op. cit.,* p. 130.
(7) Yule and Kendall, *An Introduction to the Theory of Statistics,* 1950, p. xv. (14th ed).
(8) Young, *op. cit.,* p. 487.
(9) For a detailed discussion, see Selltiz, *et al., op. cit.*
(10) Mills, C. Wright, *Sociological Imagination,* Oxford University Press, 1959, London, p. 223.

Chapter XIX

The Research Report

The research task is barely completed until the report on it is written. The most brilliant findings that a study may have happened to come upon are of little scientific import unless they are communicated to others.

This phase of the research process calls for a set of skills of a somewhat different order as compared to those required by the earlier stages of research. Much of the thrill of research discovery may have worn off by the time the researcher shifts his attention from analysis of data to the preparation of the research report. Nevertheless, the communication of findings, so that they enter the general store of knowledge, is an important part of the researcher's responsibilities and this should receive the same attention as the earlier stages do.

Perhaps the most important point to be kept in mind while writing a research report is its intended function. The purpose of a report is communication with an audience and not with oneself. Although this statement may appear redundant, it is seen that many social research reports give evidence of a struggle for clarification of the author's thoughts and are not designed to communicate ideas meaningfully to an audience about the problems that it would find of interest.[1]

The prerequisite to communicability is that one must be clear about the persons for whom the given report is intended. It is understandable that a report directed to fellow social scientists will be different in certain respects from a report whose purpose is to inform the general public. Whatever the audience, two general considerations must weigh heavily in the minds of the researchers engaged in reporting their researches.

(1) What does this audience (or consumer) want or need to know about the study?

(2) How can this information be best presented?

In this chapter we shall address ourselves to the question of how to present a research report for an audience. The suggestions in this regard shall be directed primarily at the preparation of a detailed report, such as a thesis or a monograph. We may begin with the question of what a research report should contain.

The audience for whom the report is intended, needs to know enough about the study to be able to place it in its general scientific context, and thus, to judge the adequacy of its methods and arrive at an evaluation of how seriously the findings may be taken or to what extent these should be depended upon as guides to future scientific activity and social action. The report should advisedly allude to the following aspects in order that necessary information is afforded to the readers:

(1) An introduction informing the problems the researcher was investigating and the rationale or justification for selecting the problem for investigation.

(2) A discussion of methods/procedures employed by the researcher for sampling out respondents, collection of data and data analysis.

(3) An elaborate presentation on what the findings of the investigation have been, followed by a discussion devoted to what the findings mean or signify at the level of theory and practice and what these findings point to as worthwhile problem-areas for future investigations.

(4) Abstract comprising a brief summary of the introduction and an interpretation section.

(5) An alphabetical list of books and articles cited in the various sections of the report, customarily subsumed under the larger rubric of 'References.'

(6) Appendix (desiredly) comprising copy of the questionnaire schedule used, scales or stimuli employed (as in controlled observation), tables of data which are not so important in relation to the study as to find a place in the body of the report.

We may visualize two possibilities about the final shape of a research report. The first possibility is that the report will closely bring out what the researcher had in mind when he planned the given study. The second possibility is that the form of the report will be prompted by the researcher's active concern for making it the most meaningful document in the context of the findings that have surfaced.

A good research report is understandably the latter since it makes the most sense in relation to the findings a given study, has thrown up. It needs to be appreciated that a study is not irreversibly destined at the time, the problem of research is formulated.

Quite a few times, during the progress of the study, a more adequate statement of the problem itself may come to be developed, new hypotheses may emerge or unforeseen relationship may meet the eye. Hence, the original manner of problem formulation while providing the basic point of reference for the report can always afford some room and margin to accommodate subsequent developments or insights.

The conventional view of the research process held by most persons is that the researcher starts with a formal theory from which he derives some hypotheses, analyses the data collected to see whether or not these hypotheses are confirmed and lays down this sequence of steps in his research report. If research were to proceed in accordance with this neat plan, research reports might well be documented beforehand and the section on results of study could be prepared in a skeletal form awaiting appropriate figures and facts to occupy their designated places. Research barely ever proceeds according to this plan and hence the researcher must be thinking of the report in full view of his data.

There is much more to data analysis than merely checking to see whether the research hypotheses are confirmed and testified to by the data. It also involves, perhaps more importantly, exploring the data to see if some interesting results not originally anticipated show up. For instance, unexpected differences in attitudes toward an issue may be discernible when the data plainly show, for example, that nativity of respondents has an unmistakably strong positive association with the character of the attitudes. It should be remembered that some results may be more informative than mere confirmation or rejection of hypotheses. Some reporters may like to mention these findings tentatively in the report with a view to bringing out their potential use while others are for more intensive research.

But quite a few reporters may feel called upon to focus their reports around these new findings or discoveries, sometimes even ignoring their original hypotheses. Of course, if the study was specifically planned to test certain hypotheses from a formal theory or if these hypotheses were in the nature of propositions arousing wide general interest for certain areas, then the confirmation or rejection of these hypotheses would remain the central focus of the report. It should also be noted that few people would be concerned about knowing whether hypotheses of the researcher were disconfirmed; confirmed hypotheses, understandably, would sustain their interest. A report should not advisedly become a personal history of the researcher's failure to prove the correctness of his speculative notions. The basic purpose of the research report is to inform the concerned audience what the investigator has to learn as a result of his research exercise about matters relating to social reality.

If the research results suggest some instructive and enlightening frame for the presentation of the study, it would be very desirable to adopt the framework in which findings offering new insights into the social-human realm become the center-piece of present action. Report-writing is not a mechanical process; it is largely a matter of good judgement. The judgement typically dawns upon a researcher when he thoroughly understands his data and appreciates what is so outstanding about them.

We now turn to discuss the content of a research report. Each of the sections of the report will be discussed in the order suggested above, at some length.

(i) Introduction: The research report should ordinarily start with a statement of the problem selected for investigation. The reporter should introduce the background and nature of the problem under investigation. Although quite a few times the study might be posing a simple empirical question about human behaviour or might be directed toward a practical problem or some policy-issue, the researcher must place the question or the issue into a larger, theoretical or practical context. This helps the readers to appreciate why the problem is of a general significance and theoretic import.

If the enquiry was planned with a view to making some contribution to certain aspects of social theory, the reporter should summarise the theory or conceptual scheme within which the reporter/researcher is working. Regardless of the nature of the study, it is important that an intelligent but, may be, a non-professional person would be able to understand the nature of problem and appreciate its larger relevance. The report should not contain a lot of jargon except when there is no feasible alternative to it, certain constraints warranting its use. The reader is not always prepared to intelligibly appreciate the problem of research, he is often not conversant with the relevant theoretic structure. Hence, it is important that the general reader is gradually led up to the formal theoretic statement of the problem. Intelligible examples are necessary for illustrating theoretic ideas and the technical terms.

It is extremely desirable that a summary of the current state of knowledge in the area of investigation is presented, once the problem of the study is explained.

The summary should comprise allusions to the previous researches conducted in the problem-area, and pertinent theories relating to the phenomena (if any). A researcher must have familiarized himself with the previous work in the field before designing the study. Most of the literature search should have been done by the time the researcher is ready to write the report. If the researcher was required to recast his study in a somewhat different framework than his initial problem would warrant, he would need to give references he had not previously consulted. That is, he will be obliged to go back to the literature which in the light of the above shift has become relevant. Review of previous work should comprise only the pertinent findings and insights relating to the issue the researcher is dealing with. If such a review article already exists, the researcher will do well to simply address his readers to the review article and present only the bare highlights in the report. Books and articles need to be cited with the author's last name and year of publication.

Towards the end of the section on introduction, it is desirable that the researcher introduces his own study in a brief overview. This affords a smooth transition into the method section which follows the introductory section.

(ii) Method (Design of Study): The readers of the report do like to know in detail how the research was carried out and what its basic design was like. Suppose the research involved experimentation, the readers would like to know the nature of experimental manipulation; the method and points at which measurements were taken and so on. The readers also need to know, in case of the descriptive and exploratory studies, how the data were collected, the nature of questions asked, the strategies adopted by interviewers during the collection of data, the training they had and the recording procedure adopted for recording of responses. The readers also need to know how the observations or replies to questions were translated into measures of the variables with which the enquiry was concerned, in the main, *e.g.,* what questions were asked to estimate the degree of 'commitment' or alienation.

In regard to the sample covered by the study with a view to arriving at general conclusions about the population which the sample supposedly represents, the readers are expected to be told about the general character of the subjects, the number of them covered by the sample, mode of selection etc. Information on these points is crucial for understanding the probable limits of generalizability of the findings, *i.e.,* whether there is any justifiable basis for extending the sample findings to the population. This information can betray the biases of the researcher in selecting the subjects for the study. Thus, the claim of the researcher as to generalizability of findings to population at large could be evaluated. Although meaningful studies based on a small number of cases barely representing a specifiable population are possible, nevertheless, the number of characteristics of the respondent on which the findings are based must be plainly reported so that readers are enabled to arrive at their own verdict regarding the applicability of the given findings to other groups similarly placed in the social structure.

If the researcher has conducted a complex experiment, the report should include some description of the study as it was seen from the viewpoint of the subjects. This would involve a description oif the subjects, the experimental setting, and the variables assessed. The sequence of events in a chronological order also needs to be presented to the reader, who, in a sense, is carried through the experience as though he was a subject.

Even if the reporter customarily reproduces the complete questionnaire/schedule or testing scales in the appendix to the report, a summary of stimulus items, a sample of questionnaire items and scale-items should be included in this section of the report. All this goes a long way toward giving the reader a feel of what it would have been like to be a subject. This has an important bearing on the interpretation of study results, and understandably, the reader is placed thereby in a position to judge the worth of the study results. In quite a few studies the subject/participants are called upon to co-operate actively in the research enterprise. The report should advisedly make a mention of how the participants in the research were compensated for their time and effort and if there was deception practiced on them in the course of the study. Such unethical practices like deception or misinformation about the procedure cannot unfortunately be dispensed with in certain studies. The readers need to be told how these human participants were told about these practices afterwards, the amount of freedom afforded to subjects in the matter of withdrawing their participation, subjection to threats, concealed observations of them, strategies for protecting their anonymity etc., should also be faithfully reported.

(iii) Results of the Study: In simple studies the results are often discussed as they are presented. The section is closed generally with statement that informs the conclusions reached as also the qualifications imposed upon them by the conceptual and practical difficulties faced by the researcher in executing the study-design in a manner he would ideally have desired.

But if the researcher wishes to present different kinds of results before he is able to integrate them or draw any inferences based on them or if he wants to discuss certain matters in the final discussion then the discussion section is better presented separately. Of course, even here there cannot be a pure results section without an attendant discussion. Before the researcher can present his main results there are, in the main, two preliminary things that must concern him. Firstly, he needs to present proof that his study has ensured the conditions for testing the hypotheses and/or for answering the research questions. For example, if the study required of the researcher that he produce two groups radically differing from each other in the character of their emotions, the report must demonstrate that the ratings on the two groups were conclusively different and it was not that the difference occasioned as a matter of chance. In case the investigation required observers to record behaviour of the judges entrusted with rating the responses, the report should present quantitative proof of reliability of the recordings or ratings.

The result section should usually begin with a discussion on the safeguards and strategies adopted by the researcher to negate bias and unreliability in the course of the study. It is quite possible that some of these matters would have already found a place in the meth od section. It is equally likely that in some studies discussion on these matters is rightly postponed to the final discussion section, where researcher tries to adduce alternative explanations of the study results. What should be included at the beginning of the results section so that the readers are satisfied that the stage was successfully set for testing the research hypotheses, is a decision which would be governed by an understanding of the overall state of study results. No hard and fast rules lead to this decision.

Secondly, the method of data-analysis is a matter to be dealt with at the beginning of the results section. The researcher needs to describe the procedure adopted by him in converting his observations into data that may be readily analysed and the procedure adopted for coding and articulation of different observer's ratings. The readers must be told next, about the statistical analysis itself. If this analysis was unconventional or unorthodox and warranted certain statistical assumptions, a detailed discussion giving out the rationale for it, is called for.

This could be the place in the report to afford the readers an overview of the results section, if it is fairly complicated.

The general rule of reporting research findings is to commence with the central findings and then move on to the more peripheral ones. This rule is also applicable to the sub-sections and it is advisable that the basic findings are stated first, followed by elaborations of them, as needed. If the beginning is made with the most central results, the progress in reporting should follow the line suggested below.[2]

(1) The researcher should remind the readers in a conceptual mould, about the question he is asking. For example, is democratic classroom atmosphere more conducive to learning by students as compared to the authoritarian atmosphere?

(2) Secondly, the reporter should remind the readers of the actual operations performed or the actual behaviour measured (which was assumed to be the empirical referent of learning or democratic atmosphere, in our example).

(3) The answer to the question which surfaced as a result of the study should be made known to the readers immediately and unequivocally.

(4) Relevant supporting numbers or figures, substantiating the study result should be given out. For example, $x^2 = 11.2$, df = 2. This should be followed by an elaboration of the overall conclusions. Limitations imposed upon these conclusions by certain factors which might have operated to produce results that may not be expected in a larger class of such situations should be honestly spelt out.

(5) It is necessary that every finding involving a comparison, e.g., between democratic and authoritarian classroom atmospheres, between certain groups or relationship between variables should be accompanied by its statistical level of significance. Failing this, the readers would have no basis of knowing whether or not the findings may be attributed to the chance factor. The inferential statistics though important, do no constitute the core of the narrative and should be subordinated to the substantive results. The real purpose of descriptive statistics or indices should be to present to the readers the behaviour of people as vividly as possible. Effective reporting aims at giving to the readers a 'feel' of the observed behaviour.

(6) Ordinarily, in a detailed research report intended for a knowledgeable readership, every finding considered sufficiently important as to merit some emphasis should be accompanied by a table or graph or figure showing the relevant data. Thus, the reader is in a position to grasp the findings by reading the narration or by looking at the tables or figures, embodying result of interest.

As the writing on the section on results progresses, the reporter should continually keep summarizing and updating the readers' fund of information lest they should be required to look back time and again, to keep in touch with the major points of the researcher's thesis. Towards the end of this section, is demonstrated the statistical reliability of the results. It is often useful to illustrate how particular individuals covered by the study behaved. Besides the illustrative function, this adds richness to the study-findings.

(iv) Discussion : Especially for the more complex studies having more abstract and extensive implications, discussion constitutes a separate section. The section on discussion forms a coherent narration with the introductory section of the report. Concerns of central importance to the researcher in view of his problem and hence embodied in the introduction section should appear again in the discussion for the discussion proceeds from the specific matters about the study through the more abiding and general concerns to the most inclusive generalization the researcher wishes to make.

The discussion should begin with a clear statement of what the researcher has learnt, in the main, from the study. It is very appropriate at this point to place on record the support and non-support of the hypotheses initially posed in the introductory chapter. Each of the new statements made in the discussion section should contribute something fresh to the reader's understanding of the problem. The inferences that may be drawn from the findings should be clearly presented. These may often be at a high level of abstraction. If this be the case, the conceptual or theoretic linkages would need to be explicated.

Let us take an example. If the investigator has found better performance in terms of learning on the part of students, in classroom situations characterized by a 'democratic' atmosphere (democratic atmosphere in the classroom may be said to be characterized tentatively by the freedom allowed to students in respect of choosing the problems for discussion, electing the discussion leader, counter questioning the teacher, etc.), the investigator may conclude that in other situations where such freedom is allowed to participants, *i.e.,* of choosing their problems for discussion or electing their own discussion leader, etc., similar effects will be seen. However, the researcher may wish to carry his inference to a higher level of abstraction, especially if there is some partially developed theory to which it may be possible to link his finding or if there have been other studies in which the specific phenomena are different but these can be understood in terms of the same abstract principle. For example, the investigator may find that the teachers in general feel dissatisfied or unhappy despite the improvement in their salary scales because the 'others' in comparable jobs whose salary scales too were subjected to an upward revision appear to them to have benefitted more by this scale revision. The investigator may treat this state of affairs (characterized by dissatisfaction among teachers despite improvement in salary scales) as an instance of the more abstract concept of 'relative' deprivation. On the basis of this abstract concept, the researcher may be able to link up the finding of his study to those of some other study which reported that in a community hit by a natural disaster some people who had themselves suffered loss of property and bereavement went out to help certain other families because the loss and bereavement suffered by these families as viewed by those who went out to help, was much greater compared to their own. This phenomenon though different from the earlier one in concrete content, can be understood in terms of the same abstract principle which explains the dissatisfaction among teachers despite the increased objective gain. The people who had incurred loss and bereavement in the second example compared their losses to those of the 'significant others' in the community and found that their own losses were much less or that they were much better compared to the 'others', and hence developed sympathy for these 'others' although objectively viewed, they themselves needed to be sympathized with.

The questions that still lie unanswered may also be alluded to. It is quite in order at this point to compare the results of the study with those reported by other investigators. The possible short-comings of the study should be honestly brought out. The readers must be told about the conditions that might have limited the extent of legitimate generalization. Here, the readers should be reminded of the characteristics of the sample studied as also about the possibility that it might differ from the 'population' or 'universe' to which the researcher might want to generalize. The specific characteristics of the method employed by the researcher which might have influenced the results or some factors that might have led to atypical results merit mention. The researcher should not, however, try to invest long involved long involved theories to explain away every 'bump' in the data.

On the contrary, if the study results suggest the beginnings of a new theory which injects amazing clarity into the data and affords a very meaningful view of the problem-area, it would be advisable to rewrite the entire report beginning with the new theory. The aim of scientific reporting is to provide the most informative, instructive and compelling framework for the study right from the first sentence.

(v) Summary or Abstract : In a way, the title of research report itself serve as part of the summary or abstract. Ideally, it conveys the content of the study as accurately and clearly as possible. A potential reader can on this basis decide whether or not to go ahead to read it. Those titles that mention both the dependent and independent variables are obviously the most informative ones.

(vi) References : The section on references comprises a list of all books and articles cited in the text of the research report. These books and articles are arranged alphabetically according to the author's last name, a format that corresponds to the way in which they are cited in a book. The reference should clearly indicate the name of the author, the title of the book or article, the journal in which it appears, the publisher, place of publication and the year of publication.

(vii) Appendix : The appendix to a report consists of copies of materials used in the study, like questionnaire, attitude scale, stimulus materials, drawings of apparatuses, etc. This is expected to help a person who would like to replicate the study. A second appendix might contain tables of data which are too extensive and seemingly too

marginal to be included in the body of the report. This is in the nature of a good turn done to the potential researchers, for this enables them to explore the researcher's data in fine detail and to answer certain questions about the results that might not have occurred to the researcher.

The Style of the Report : We now turn to consider certain basic aspects relating to the study of a research report.[3] The obvious criteria for good reporting are accuracy and clarity. Making the report interesting and writing with flair and 'style' is a subsidiary virtue. Accuracy and clarity must be the principle goals.

It greatly helps to work from an outline. The standardized format detailed above will, of course, go a long way towards organizing the report but a researcher will more probably produce a more coherent report without wasting much time and energy in frequent rewriting if he first organized his main findings. The researcher would do well to check the logic of the sequence of presentation and carefully examine it for any omission of consequence. It is often helpful to start penning the results section first. It is also useful to maintain a constant correspondence between the introduction section and the one devoted to final discussion, to maintain a smooth conceptual narration. It is important that even a non-professional should be able to comprehend on reading the report what the researcher did and for what reason, despite his non-conversance with statistic, complex manipulative study designs or the substantive area of the research problem. Hence, reporting should involve minimum of jargon and use of non-intelligible examples of concepts.

Advisedly, the reporter should read and re-read his own writing taking the role of an intelligent but non-professional reader. He should at each point, feel called upon to ask himself whether he has himself understood the concept he is trying to employ in his report, whether it is unambiguous and so forth. It is a difficult feat to take the role of a non-professional, naive reader, yet it is an overriding requirement in report writing. It may be very helpful to have someone else (friends and reviewers, especially those unfamiliar with the subject-matter area) read the draft and comment upon it. If they find something unclear, their observation needs to be respected. As unclarity detectors, the readers are generally never wrong. The chances of producing a good draft in first writing are small indeed. Good reporting requires a great measures of compulsiveness in attention to details. Since the purpose of a report is to convey information rather than to achieve a literary goal, the reporter can avoid wastage of time by writing the first draft as quickly as possible. Once they are there on paper, he can go back and rewrite the sentences and paragraphs. Rewriting often implies restructuring involves a thorough recasting of the report, even going back to do more data-analysis in support of an argument the researcher is presenting.

A few decades ago, it was conventional to employ third person passive voice in a scientific reporting. This happily, is no longer the norm and the report-writer is free to use the first person and resort to the active voice. The research-reporter may refer to himself as I or we (if there are two or more). It should be noted here, that constant use of 'I' or 'We' may distract the reader from the subject matter. Hence, it is advisable to employ the 'first person' sparingly. Frequent solicitations directed at the 'readers' are also undesirable.

Is the use of past tense more desirable as compared to the use of the present tense? The answer to the question can only be that both have their pride of place in reporting. The past tense should be used while reporting the previous findings tabled by others and while reporting how the re-searcher conducted his study (e.g., the groups were measured before the introduction of the experimental variable) and the specific past behaviours of the respondents covered by the study. The present tense is better used for results that are before the reader and for conclusions of a generic nature (like, thus the parental incomes determine the aspirations of children about incomes from jobs).

It is evident that language can perpetuate stereo-typical notions, hence the reporter is expected to avoid writing in a fashion that reinforces questionable attitudes and assumptions about different communities of people as also the sex roles. Many a time, the use of masculine norms and pronouns are used to refer to both sexes. Such usage like the generic term 'man' intending to connote both men and women is misleading. Researches show that readers visualize and think of male persons when such forms are used. Sadly, language has not caught up with this new awareness. Alternatives too are not totally satisfactory. In most contexts, the simplest alternative is to use the plural like persons or individuals. The reporter must be accurate in his use of pronouns when he is describing his own research or those of others. Readers need to be informed about the sex of the interviewers, observers, experimenters and participants. It is improper to omit or conceal their sex-identity.

Knowledge of sex is quite often crucial. Certain words or terms have a gender-slant, for example; 'manning the project' or 'husbanding resources.' Such terms are better avoided. It should be noted that the use of certain adjectives betrays a bias when their use denotes not different behaviours on the part of men and women but the customary social biases current in evaluating. Some verbs also carry latent bias and inadvertently reveal a stereo-type. It is important that the reporter meticulously avoids sex-role stereo-typing when selecting examples about the sex of home-makers, nurses, doctors, school teachers and so on. The report should not inflict injuries upon the sensible modern view that women's vital needs are similar to men's.

REFERENCES

(1) See Good, C. V.: *On Effective Report Writing*, Phi Delta Kappa, 1941.

(2) See Felsch, R. F. and A. H. Lass: *The Way to Write*, McGraw-Hill, New York, 1955.

(3) Also see Seltiz, C. L. S. Wrightsman, S. W. Cook: *Research Methods in Social Relations*, Holt, Rhinehart and Winston, 1976.

Chapter XX

Research and Theory

Throughout the book, we have been harping on the note that theorizing is an integral part of empirical research just as empirical research has meaning only by reference to a theory or proposition from which it is generated. The scientist is constantly engaged at researching the accepted conclusions of his field; the theoretic propositions he uses. He does this researching by probing for facts of the empirical world that falsify one or more predictions or deductions generated by his accepted conclusions or theoretical models. It is also obvious that during this stage researching involves modification of the existing theoretical schemes or constructions of new theoretical models that are expected to take the place of those no longer able to make sense of or explain the existing state of things.

It is a near convention to view the relationship between theory and research from the vantage point of the former. This leads to asking, "What does research do for theory in the way of testing its utility or correspondence with reality?" If we turn it around, we may ask, "What is there about a theory that has some import for the working researcher?"

These two questions meet at some point of the scientific enterprise but their answers are determined by the direction from which the meeting point is approached. Coming from theory to research, attention is focused on truth, the nature of reality, processes of knowing, and the logic of meaningful statements. Starting from research and moving towards theory, attention turns to such issues as measurement in all its phases, translation of hypotheses into operational terms, reliability of empirical indicators and so on.

There is in evidence an unfortunate tendency in quite a few methodological writings dealing with connections between theory and empirical research to depict these as travellers that move toward each other from their respective starting points but fail ever to meet head on at any point of their journeys.

The rift between empiricists (empirical data gatherers who intend to generalize on empirical data) and theorists, is very old indeed. The great encyclopaedic minds of thinkers like Comte, Spencer and Marx developed grand conceptual schemes on social organization and change. At this time there was already some theorizing which was devoid of empirical reference. Around 1938 the cry voiced through the Journal of Empirical Society of London went up that in the business of Social Science, principles are valid for application only in as much as they are legitimate inductions from facts accurately observed and methodologically classified. The conflict between theorists and researchers, to use Weber's words, the interpretive specialists and the subject-matter specialists, has filtered down to the present day. It is true that theory in social sciences has developed to a great extent independently of systematically pursued research and on the other hand, empirical research has seldom concerned itself with theoretic interest. The result is a deep hiatus. Alongside of this is the erroneous assumption that theory-building and researching are two mutually exclusive domains and that theorists and researchers have to belong to only one of these two schools. In consequence, empiricists have rarely attempted to contribute to theory and are often anti-theoretical; for them theory is mere speculation — sterile dialectic or mysticism. On the other hand, the theorists have equally sadly shown scant regard for empirical work.

Let us appreciate the historical and intellectual backdrop behind the apparent conflict between theory and empiricism.[1]

Firstly, social sciences had their roots in social philosophy. Early masters of social thought were speculative philosophers having a characteristic disdain for any empirical base required for spinning out theoretical schemes.

Secondly, empiricism's emphasis on measurement, quantification and their equation with scientific value has been one major cause of conflict between empirical researchers and theorists since the theorists opined that in human interaction everything cannot be counted and everything that is counted does not count (matter).

Thirdly, empiricists are disillusioned by a plethora of theoretic orientations which appear as social theory since some propositions derived from them are so vague and general that they cannot be systematically tested.

Fourthly, theorists have been disenchanted by a telling discontinuity of empirical research, abundance of facts and decreased empirical generalization.

Principally, however, the scientific activity consists in producing a smashing collision on the highway connecting theory and empirical research. The purpose of such a collision is to generate a genuinely useful insight just as atom smashing produces new knowledge rather than a heap of debris. It is worthy of note that the establishment of Science is marked by a constant oscillation, back and forth, between the empirical and the systematic, i.e., theoretical (or rational).

We have, on earlier occasion, pointed to the limitations inherent in the results of a single research study as also to the need for accumulating systematic knowledge founded on a broader theoretical base. Without such cumulative knowledge steadily flowing from the continuities of empirical research, the insights of social science will necessarily remain limited to the specific settings and problems in which the investigations have actually been conducted. Such a cumulative body of knowledge can be developed, provided empirical studies are theory-oriented and reciprocally, if theory is empirically confirmable.

Meaning of Theory: Scientific theory is a term which comes from the Greek word 'theorein' meaning to look at. A fair translation of scientific theory would be a knowledgeable outlook. There is a sense, of course, in which every one has a world outlook, and thus the meanest of man has his own theory; and to think at all is to theorize. Theory in ordinary speech does not mean this (more usually it means what is called a working hypothesis). Science provides the only systematic and corrigible world outlook not requiring any special suppositions beyond those readily made by ordinary men of affairs. It thus makes possible agreement and collaboration among people who in other respects, would be in severe disagreement.

Theory is a much abused term. It is, therefore, important to distinguish the modern scientific usage of the word 'theory' from other possible meanings it might have come to acquire. In common parlance, theory is identified with speculation. What is 'theoretical' is thought to be unrealistic, visionary or impracticable. *Merton* points out that among sociologists the term 'sociological theory' has had at least six different meanings. In the early days of a science, theories were often the result of arm-chair speculation and had meagre support in empirical data. Theory and observation (empirical facts) became more and more connected as science developed. The social sciences in their present state of development do not always show a close link between research and theory and some current social theories do contain speculative elements, that leap off beyond the evidence of available data. By and large, the intention of a theory in modern science is to summarize existing knowledge, to provide an explanation for observed events and relationships and to predict the occurrence of as yet unobserved events and relationships, on the basis of the explanatory principles embodied in the conceptual scheme. Simply viewed, theory could be understood as a conceptual scheme designed to explain observed regularities or relationships between two or more variables. Writes *Karl Popper* in his *Logic of Scientific Discovery*, "Theories are nets cast to catch what we call 'the world,' to rationalize, to explain and also to master it. We endeavour to make the mesh finer and finer."[2] *Parsons* observes, "The theoretical system (in the present sense) is the body of logically interdependent generalized concepts of empirical reference."[3]

Whereas a theory in the earlier times was considered a final and irrefutable explanation of some class of things or realm of phenomena, in modern science it is always held with some measure of tentativeness, no matter how great the accumulation of findings consistent with it. It is considered as the most probable or most efficient way of accounting for those findings in the light of extant body of knowledge, but is always open to revision. On the whole, it may be said that modern science is modest in regard to its claims in as much as it is fully aware that its findings are all provisional. It does not find itself in a position to make final pronouncements having seen that the river of knowledge has too often turned back on itself. Science has changed not only the face of earth and the life of its people, it has also changed its own face and identity. Today, the scientific mode of thinking plays a more important role than knowledge and erudition, as of old. It has resulted in a method which leads to new knowledge and making a line of thought.

Johan *Galtung* conceives of theory as a set of hypotheses structured by the relation of implication or deducibility.

Formally put, "A theory T is a structure (H, I) where H is a set of hypotheses and I is a relation in H called implication or deducibility, so that H is weakly connected by I."[4]

R. B. Braithwaite's exposition of 'theory' can barely be equalled. For him, "a theory consists of a set of hypotheses which form a deductive system, that is, which is arranged in such a way that from some of the hypotheses as premises all the other hypotheses logically follow. The propositions in a deductive system may be considered as being arranged in an order of levels, the hypotheses at the highest level being those which occur only as premises in the system, those at the lower level being those which occur as conclusions or deductions from higher level hypotheses and which serve as premises for deduction to lower level hypotheses."[5]

Parsons would view the theoretical system as one which ideally tends to become logically closed, to reach such a state of logical integration that every logical implication of any combination of propositions in the system is explicitly stated in some other proposition in the same system.

However, it is well worth remembering that not all theories have a determinate logical structure as Braithwaite's exposition would lead us to 'believe.' Theories may have strong or weak structures. A strong theory structure (tight-knit theory) may be represented as under:

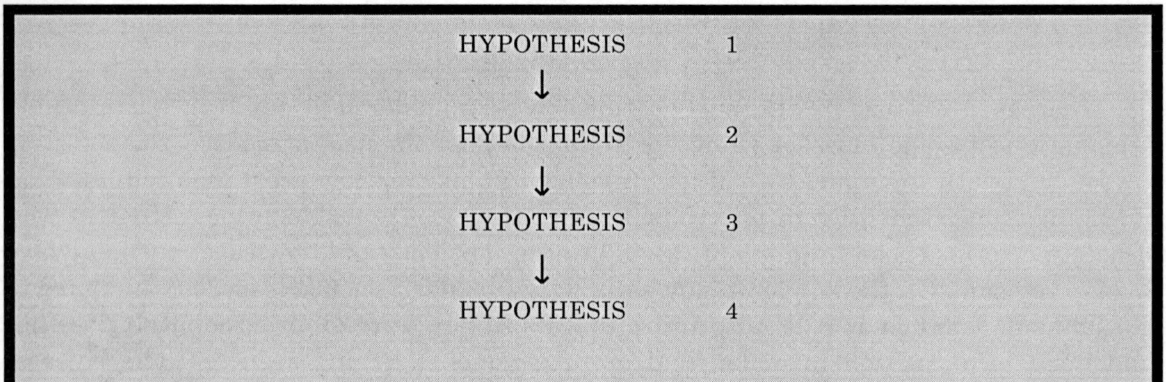

Tight-Knit Theory

Fig. 20.1

From the above representation, it is clear that the lower level Hypotheses which are deductions from the higher level hypotheses are all on the same implication path and that the chain of implication is a neat and unintersected one.

In contradiction, a weakly structured (loose-knit) theory may be depicted as under:

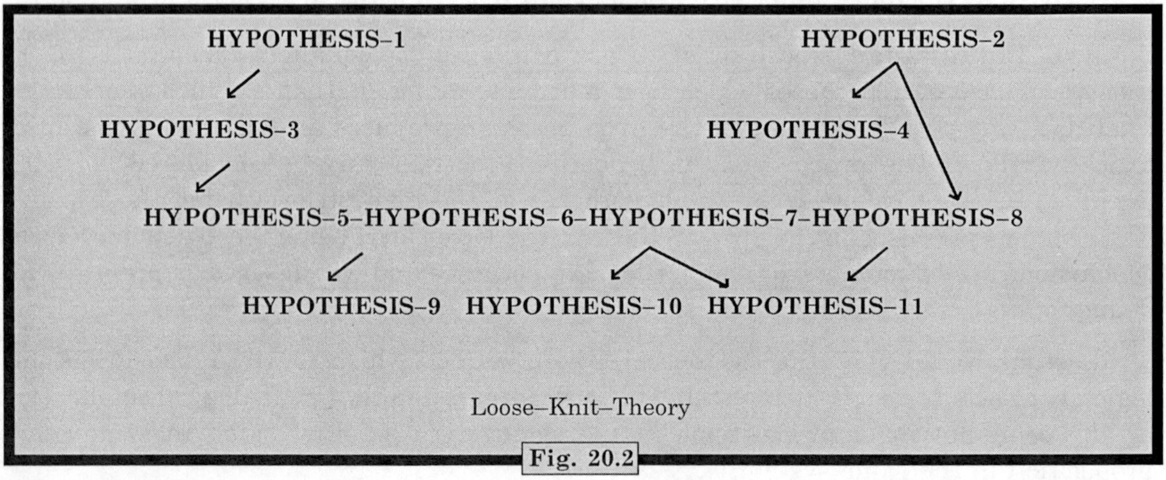

Loose–Knit–Theory

Fig. 20.2

It is obvious that the loose-knit structure unlike the one for tight knit theories (Fig. 20.2) is characterized by the intersection of the implication chains on which the hypotheses are located.

Thus, it would seem as Abel puts it, "All theories fall in two extremes of a simple explanatory principle and a deductive system with an abstract relational structure formed by the theoretical postulates."[6]

Hempel has likened a scientific theory to a network in which terms and concepts are represented by knots and the definitions and. hypotheses by threads connecting the knots.

Says Hempel, "The whole system floats, as it were, above the plane of observation and is anchored to it by the rules of interpretation. These might be viewed as strings which are not the part of the network but link certain points of the latter, with specific places on the plane of observation. By virtue of these interpretative connections, the network can function as a scientific theory. From certain observational data, we may ascend, via an interpretative string, to some point in the theoretical network, and from there proceed, via definitions and hypotheses, to other points, from which other interpretative strings permit descent to the plane of observation,"[7] (See Fig. 20.3).

A theory explains empirical observations, since if anything, it is a mental construction that seeks to model the empirical system. Let us try to understand with the help of an interesting illustration, the nature of theoretical explanation.

In the third century A.D., it was observed that any natural catastrophe, be it an earthquake, flood, drought, famine or pestilence, was followed by persecution of the Christians by the Romans.

In the present century around the thirties (1930-40), it was observed that a fall in the per acre value of cotton in certain southern states of the USA, was followed by incidences of lynching of Negroes by the whites. The underlying similarity in the two

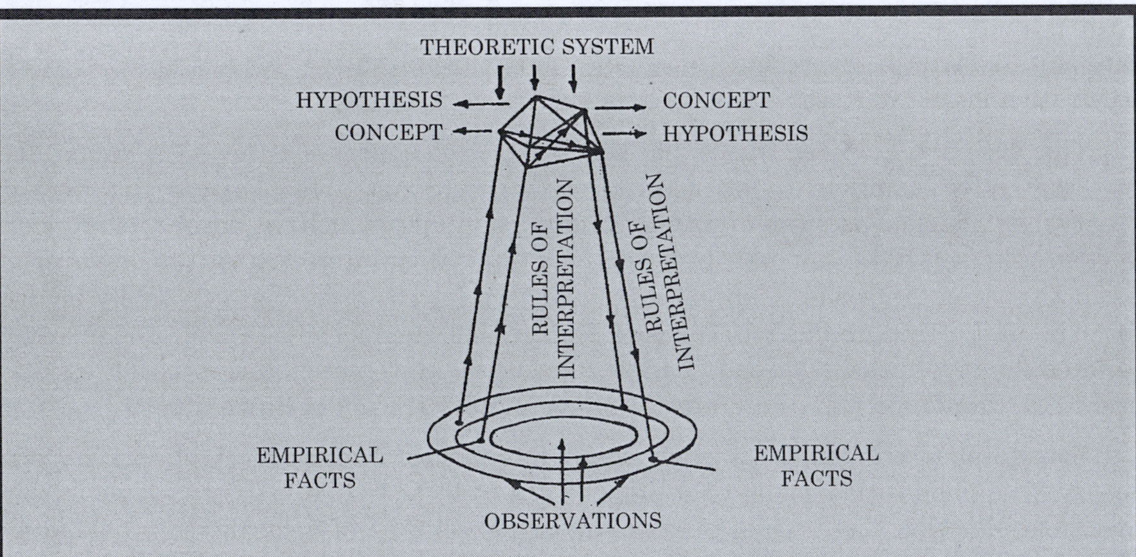

Fig. 20.3 Hempel's Portrayal of Theory.

observations, viz., that catastrophe leads to persecution, is all the more striking because these incidents relate to periods far apart in time as also to different peoples and events. How can we go about explaining this sequence of events?

These two observations of a similar nature can be explained by means of a theory which involves the concepts: frustration, aggression, inhibition and displacement. This theory by Dollard and associates, known as the 'Frustration aggression theory,' is constituted of interlocking hypotheses involving the above-mentioned concepts. The theory in essence states that when a person is frustrated and is inhibited from expressing his aggression directly toward the perceived source of frustration (because the source is powerful and capable of inflicting injuries, e.g., God or Government) he or she will displace his or her aggression toward weaker things (incapable of retaliating to the aggressive acts). Thus, according to this theory both the aggression by Romans against Christians after the occurrence of natural catastrophes or by fall in income of whites, results in aggression but the futility or fear of being directly aggressive against the God or society or Government inhibits the direct expression of aggression against the real sources of frustration and results in its being 'displaced' on to groups which are underprivileged and thus incapable of retaliating.

Hence, with the help of the above theory, an explanation can be offered not only for these two different observations but also of many other events such as the aggressive action of an officer against his subordinates following frustration by his superior officer or the aggressive action of child against a younger sibling or a doll, following frustration caused by its parent's actions. This way, a theoretical perspective brings out in a number of different phenomena the operation of some underlying general principle.

It must, of course, be noted that the 'frustration aggression theory' in its present form is inadequate. It does not account for the variety of relevant phenomena and cannot satisfactorily overcome some objections (Freud shows, for instance, that the frustration may lead to some highly constructive activity too).

This does not, however, mean that the 'frustration aggression theory' is wrong. It is just that it is insufficient, not specific enough and not able to cover the relevant observable phenomena. The limiting conditions under which it applies (the *ceteris paribus* clause) have not yet been defined and this interferes seriously with its predictive value. In social sciences, there are very few theories that can safely be used for explanation and prediction. To speak in terms of Hempel's metaphor, one discovers isolated knots with loose threads hanging, awaiting systematic efforts to tighten them and to tie them together; and quite often, even knots are not yet available.

Something needs to be said here what has hitherto been left implicit. The term theory as applied to the realm of social sciences is in fact used mostly to refer to some logical explanation about social phenomena or a class thereof, logically constructed and systematically organised, that underscores the relationship between two well-defined variables. It is much more than a social law supported by evidence. As a systematic relation between facts, it cannot simply be derived from empirical observations and generalizations by means of rigorous induction. It represents a symbolic construction, theory building is a matter of creative achievement.

As a conceptual scheme reaches out beyond itself, it transcends the observable realm of empirical reality into a higher level of abstraction by means of symbolic construction.

In other words, theoretic statements can in most cases arise by a genetic path between sense-data and theoretical perspectives; out of sense datum statements. But by the time theoretical statements are reached, there is much more than could even be represented in terms of sense-data. A certain open texture is required in scientific theory which can be marred by an insistence on translatability criteria. Theory, if it is to be of any use, is bound to move ahead of the observations which support it in the first place. Thus, theory is not something which can be summed up in terms of observations, measurements or the positive content of our empirical knowledge. Hence, the question that must principally be asked of any statement seeking entitlement as scientific theory is whether it can demonstrate the other phenomena, i.e., not merely the ones on which it rests in the first place. In this sense it stands for the symbolic dimension of experience as opposed to the apprehension of brute fact.

From the very nature of social science theories emanates the limitation characterising these theories, viz., that they often represent speculative exercises and it may not be possible to establish their correspondence with well-defined propositions or laws that can be empirically tested. This state of maturity is a distant goal for most social sciences. The development of these sciences has been marked by a large number of conflicting theoretical perspectives. Social scientists have not yet been able to develop a single inductive procedure or a mathematical model that could test their theories and validate them as applicable to all groups and societies. These theories lie between empirical law and speculative argument. Even a simple hypothesis may be regarded a minor theory and a speculative idea may come to be called theory if it generates at least one fruitful hypothesis, logically.

The theories of social sciences in the light of what has been said above can be verified only in a preliminary way, i.e., not in the strict statistical sense or not by fitting the syndrome of facts having a bearing on the class of phenomena being theorized. Social science theory can aspire for validation mostly by symbolic correspondence.

In the social-behavioural sciences, a quest for true theory could be a futile intellectual exercise. Every theory holds some pieces to the picture puzzle of the social world. A comprehensive picture of social phenomena may be expected to emerge through the integration of a variety of social theories. If it is assumed that nothing exists except the world, then theory is part of the world; a part which stands in some way for the whole; and a comprehensive theory in dealing with the world will have to deal also with itself as a part of this world, just as the map of a country drawn somewhere in that country would have to contain a very much reduced replica of itself. A particular social theory may be likened to a map which showed only roads, or one which showed only railways. Scientific theories are selective; any one science is dealing with only a fraction of what there is to be observed. For that matter, all the sciences taken together will still give a very incomplete account of the world we know, just as the superimposition of all the specialized maps — the road map, the railway map, the demographic map, etc., would still leave indefinitely many concrete facts about the country unexpressed.

It is well-worth reminding ourselves here that no theory is absolutely true since there is no absolute truth in the first place and no theory is a final formulation because ripples of new knowledge are splashing in all the time. These modify or even repudiate the existing theory.

It will serve us well to note that theories which stand repudiated today had their days of glory. For example, at the present time *Comte's* theory of unilineal evolution has been used by experts on modernization to describe progress and evolution in total societies.

Here we need to sound a caution about the possible fallacy of misplaced concreteness which comprises placing of theoretical entities in the same world as the observable ones. Indeed, if they are there at all, they are there by definition, invisibly, which is certainly odd in a world whose claim to existence lies in it being observed. But the invention of theoretical entities is necessary for the progress of science and there is nothing wrong with them as long as they are not thought of as belonging to the observable world. All sorts of possible worlds with all sorts of imaginary constituents, behaving in all sorts of ways may be constructed by science and nobody would have any objection until the scientist tries to force conclusions derived from his hypothetical world upon actions to be carried out in the observable world. In essence, then, the provision of a working replica of the real world is the goal of theory and yet the claim that it is a replica of the real world is always rather presumptions.

The foregoing discussion would suggest that research and theory as co-travellers must proceed toward continuous increments of knowledge. Each has an important contribution to make to the other. A scientist may take one or the other as his starting point, but he must consider at some point of his exercise the bearing of his work on the interrelation between theory and research. That is, if he concentrates on empirical research alone, he must at some point later, examine its relevance to social theory if its potential contribution is to be realized. On the other hand, if his major interest is in the development of theory, he must take into account ways of testing and expanding his theory by empirical research if it is to turn out to be more than just an interesting speculation.

The Role of Theory for Research

The existing body of knowledge inspires the scientist to formulate varied theories and to foretell what new observations would be revealed according to these theories. It should be the purpose of theory to suggest observations by which it may be itself disproved or falsified. Hence, in case observations disagree with the theory, the theory may be considered wrong, but if these agree with the forecasts or expectations based on the theory then it is the task of theory to suggest fresh observations so that it can be researched, revisited and tested again and again. In other words, there is no room for propositions in science which do not really pay their way empirically. Tying down the abstract logical system (theory) to empirical facts is an on going process of science leading to consolidation of existing knowledge and addition of newer dimensions to it.

(1) Theory provides significant guidelines and trails for the conduct of research by pointing to areas that are most likely to be fruitful, that is, areas in which meaningful relationships among variables are likely to be found. If the variables come to be selected such that no relationships between them obtain, the research will be sterile no matter how meticulous the subsequent observations and inferences. A theoretic system narrows down the range of facts to be studied. Theory provides the researcher with a definite view point — a direction — which goes a long way toward helping him enquire into relationships between certain variables selected from among an almost infinite array of variables.[7] As *Oppenheimer* puts it, "in order for us to understand anything we have to fail to perceive a great deal that is there. Knowledge is purchased at the expense of what might have been seen and learned and was not...it is a condition of knowledge that somehow or the other we pick the clues which give us insight into what we have to find out about the world."[8] As a storehouse of meaningful hypotheses a fruitful theory suggests potential problems for study and thus ignites new investigative studies. In fact, a theory can be judged productive (to the extent it can spark off a number of questions. A productive theory suggests potential problems, fruitful hypotheses and provides new perspectives. *Einstein* and *Infeld* observe, "It is never possible to introduce only observable quantities in a theory. It is the theory which decides what can be observed."[9] Only thus can the task of science be reduced to manageability.

Besides suggesting fruitful approaches to phenomena in the general area with which it is concerned, theory also provides leads for research in a different way, viz., by suggesting other kinds of phenomena that may perhaps be understood or explained in the same general terms. Take the example of Cohen's theory of 'delinquent sub-culture'.[10] The Central idea of Cohen's theory is that the delinquent sub-culture evolved by the working class juveniles is a response of these juveniles to deal with the problem of individual adjustment attendant upon the difficulty in meeting the criteria of status as prescribed by the middle-class standards which have to be reckoned with. The delinquent sub-culture provides alternative criteria of status which these children can meet and thus, helps them deal with the problem of individual adjustment.

Cohen's theoretical formulation constitutes a generic approach to the understanding of how and why any sub-culture arises. Thus, such different sub-cultures as those emerging among different professional groups or social classes or small communities may be understood in the same terms. Research on such groups would concentrate on discovering the common problems of adjustment faced by the members and the ways in which the particular patterns of these sub-cultures help members to deal with them. In as much as a theory summarizes known facts and predicts facts which have not yet been observed, it also points to areas which have not yet been explored, in other words, what gaps typically obtain in our knowledge.

Needless to say, such gaps would not be visible if our facts were not systematized and organized. It is thus that theory suggests where our knowledge is deficient. A researcher's acquaintance with the existing theories helps him to select research problems that are likely to prove productive and worthwhile and to avoid enquiries into problems that may prove sterile, yielding no insights. As we have already stated in an earlier chapter, formulation of worthwhile questions is an important step and a precondition to the extension of knowledge. Alerting oneself to the gaps in theory and fact increases the likelihood of formulating significant questions for research.

(2) Another contribution of theory for research is in terms of increasing the meaningfulness of the findings of a particular study by helping us to perceive them as special cases of the operation of a set of more general or abstract statements of relationships rather than as isolated bits of empirical information. A theory typically enhances the meaningfulness of research, since seemingly unrelated findings of isolated studies assume new meaning and significance when they are put into proper theoretical perspective. Let us take the example of observation by Durkheim that Catholics have a lower suicide rate as compared to the Protestants. As an isolated empirical uniformity, the finding would not add greatly to our understanding of suicidal behaviour unless it conceptualized, that is, conceived of as an illustration of a linkage amongst abstractions of a higher order (e.g., Catholicism-Social Cohesion unrelieved anxieties-suicide rate). This done, we are easily able to understand that what was initially taken as an isolated empirical finding of a relationship between religious affiliation and suicidal behaviour is in fact a reflection of a much more general relationship between groups with certain conceptualized attributes (social cohesion) and behaviour of their members. This way, the scope of the original empirical finding gets considerably extended and several seemingly disparate findings can be seen to be the contextual manifestations of the general principle. Similarly, to take another example, the seemingly isolated finding that wives complain of heavy expenditure when the husband's relatives are in the house-guests may be understood on a higher plane of abstraction, to be an instance of the factor of emotional proximity or distance influencing perception. The scope of the findings thus enlarged, other apparently disparate findings may be seen to be interrelated by means of a theoretic thread (*e.g.,* the distorting effect of lack of confidence or morale on perception may be derived from the same theoretical orientation). As a mental shorthand, theory summarises relationships amongst variables in a conceptual framework.

It is through establishng the theoretical pertinence of an empirical finding or uniformity, that we can provide for the cumulation both of theory and research findings. To illustrate, the empirical uniformities about differentials in the suicide rate lend added confirmation to the set of propositions (theory) from which they and other uniformities have been derived. This may be underlined as a major function of theory.

(3) The linkage of the specific empirical findings to a more general concept has another major advantage. It affords a more secure ground for prediction than do these empirical findings by themselves. The theory by providing a rationale behind the

empirical findings introduces a ground for prediction which is more secure than mere extrapolation from previously observed trends. Thus, if studies indicated a decrease in social cohesion among a community of tribals, the theory-oriented researcher would feel secure to predict increased rates of suicide in this group. On the contrary, the a theoretic empiricist would have no alternative but to predict on the basis of extrapolation.

The prediction may be concerned with estimating whether a relationship between two variables, X and Y, which has been observed in the past, will continue in future, or it may be concerned with estimating whether changes in certain conditions will lead to changes in observed relationship (among the variables). To revert to our earlier illustration of delinquency, while Cohen points out that there need not be a direct link between understanding the 'cause' of a phenomenon and finding a 'cure,' his theory nevertheless seems to suggest that a measure intended to reduce gang delinquency is likely to be successful to the extent that it either changes the standards by which working class students are judged in school and (in the community, generally) or helps them to meet and prove equal to those standards.

(4) Whereas an empirical finding as a proposition referring to certain concrete contextual manifestation of a phenomenon does not afford a basis for drawing diverse inferences about what will follow, its reformulation or revamping in theoretic terms affords a secure basis for arriving at the inferences about the varied positive consequences in areas quite remote from the central area to which the given finding relates. For example, the empirical uniformity that Catholics have a lower suicide rate relative to Protestants does not by itself suggest diverse consequences in fields of conduct apparently far removed from that of suicidal behaviour. But once this uniformity is theoretically reformulated, obsessive behaviour and other maladaptive actions may be seen to be related to inadequacies of group-cohesion. (Thus, the lower the degree of social cohesion, higher the rate of mental illness). The imaginative conversion of empirical uniformities into theoretic statements thus increases the fruitfulness of research through successive exploration of its implications (or any empirical uniformity). Theory thus mediates between specific empirical generalization or uniformities and broad theoretical orientations anchored in the intellectual tradition.

(5) In affording broader meanings to empirical findings the theory also attests to their truth. A hypothesis is as much confirmed by fitting it into a theory as by fitting it into facts, because it then enjoys the support provided by evidence for all the other hypotheses of the given theory.

(6) Theory helps us to identify gaps in our knowledge and seek to bridge them up with intuitive, impressionistic or extensional generalizations.

As Karl Jespers said, "It is only when using methodologically classified sciences that we know what we know and what we do not know."[11] This way, theory constitutes a crucially important guide to designing of fruitful research.

Contributions of Research to Theory

The relation between theory and research is not a one way relationship and since the two interact, it will be useful to examine the other direction of the relationship, *i.e.*, the role of empirical research in the development of social theory.

One major function of empirical research is to test or verify hypotheses deduced from existing theories and so to test these. From a well-formulated theory, deductions are made about what will happen in the various situations under specified conditions. These deductions provide hypotheses for empirical research. If a given hypothesis is confirmed by studies designed to test it, such researches may be said to have made a contribution in terms of verifying the entire theoretical structure from which the deduction was made. If, on the other hand, a hypothesis is not confirmed by research, the theory generating the hypothesis must be re-examined to consider whether it should be discarded as invalid or whether a small modification in it would make it consistent with the research findings. Of course, further studies are required to test whether. deductions from modified theory will be supported by empirical observations, *i.e.*, metaphorically, pay their way empirically.

Merton has rightly pointed out that looking at research basically as a structure designed to lest a theoretical model fails to bring home to us much of what actually occurs in fruitful research. Such an image of research exaggerates the creative role of theory in generating hypotheses for the research to test, while it tends to minimize the constructive role of empirical observations for theory.

In fact, "empirical research goes far beyond the passive role of verifying and testing theory. It does much more than just confirm or refute hypotheses. Research plays an active role; it performs... major functions which help variously to shape the development of theory."[12] Cumulative research may be expected through successive approximations to sift out a battery of explanatory variables and establish their interdependence. This is by no means a new species of empiricism nor a new espousal of prerogatives of research against those of theory. It is simply an insistence that theoretic construction alone cannot provide scientifically legitimate grounds for admission of elements into the system (of knowledge). Let us now turn to consider the functions of research for theory.

(l) *Research initiates Theory:* Scientific research sometimes leads to findings that may press for a new formulation as a theory; a new entrant to the existing theoretical corpus of the discipline. It is important to remember, however, that creating a new theory, to use Einstein's metaphor,[13] is not like destroying an old barn and erecting a sky scraper in its place. "It is rather like climbing mountains, gaining new and wider views, discovering unexpected connections between our starting point and its rich environment. But the point from which we started out still exists and can be seen, although it appears smaller and forms a tiny part of our broad view gained by the mastery of the obstacles on our way up."[14]

In the regular course of doing research, especially in the domain of behavioural sciences, there occur accidents in data collection. These accidents involve observations not initially planned in the design of the study. Such unanticipated consequences of research spark off new hypotheses whose confirmation may result in a new theory. Merton terms it the serendipity component of research after the manner of Horace Walpole who coined the term in 1754. The serendipity component refers to the accidental stumbling upon some unanticipated,[15] anomalous[16] and strategic fact. The history of science is replete with instances of how a striking fact accidentally stumbled upon, led to important new theories of great import. Accidental finding that penicillin checks bacterial growth or that many errors in reading and speaking (slips of tongue) are not accidental but have deep and systemic causes, maybe cited as just two among the many examples.

Merton has cited an interesting instance of 'serendipity' in sociological research. Craftown was a suburban housing community of about 700 families of largely working-class status. It was observed in the course of a study that a large proportion of residents were affiliated to and participated frequently in civic, political and other voluntary organizations than had been the case in their previous locale of residence. The surprising fact was that community participation among parents of infants and young children had also increased. The parents when asked how they managed this in spite of having to look after their young children, generally stated that this was possible because there were so many teenage baby-sitters available in the Craftown community. Enquiries, however, revealed that the ratio of teenagers capable of baby-sitting to young children and the infants was far too less in Craftown as compared to that in the communities from where these parents had moved into Craftown.

These researchers were surprised and asked: Were the parents deliberately lying and if so, why? Could there be any vested interests behind their telling such a lie? Various other theories provided possible answers to the above phenomenon but the real clue was inadvertently provided by further interviews with the Craftown residents. The real thing was that although numerically speaking, there were less adolescents in Craftown than in the previous localities, there were more of them whom the parents knew intimately and who therefore existed 'socially' for these parents seeking aid in child supervision. Thus, it was not the absolute number of adolescents that was important, it was rather the number that had a social existence for these parents that really mattered. Put in a more abstract form, this meant that perception (of parents) was a function of (in the adolescents) and this confidence in turn was related to social cohesion (in Craftown). This proposition can be related to the larger body of theory dealing with social perception. Similarly, the concept of relative deprivation (discussed elsewhere in the book) was introduced in an attempt to make sense of surprising and strategic observations made in American Soldier Studies conducted by Stouffer and associates.[17]

In sum, empirical findings emanating from research may suggest new hypotheses and relationships, as well as point to hitherto unknown uniformities, thus leading to formation of new theories and sometimes the elaboration of existing ones.

The attempts to formulate or establish systematic theoretical connections between empirical generalizations in regard to a theoretical social science, for example, in the history of social thought, have been made in various ways. In some cases, they have arisen from direct confrontation with puzzling social phenomena which provoke search for some kind of explanation. The phenomenon may be one which has not hitherto attracted much attention (until its significance was unearthed by the imaginative power of a creative thinker) or it maybe something genuinely new and distinctive in social life. Marx's attempt to explain French revolution and rise of socialist movements belong to this later category. In other cases, it is the dissatisfaction with generalizations or explanatory schemes of earlier thinkers which may have given rise to new theories; for example, Weber took to revision of Marxist theory of the origin of capitalism or Durkheim proposed a new sociological explanation of suicide in contradiction to the diverse explanations which were in currency towards end of the 19th century.

(2) *Research Helps Recasting of Theory:* It is also through the repeated observations of hitherto neglected facts that empirical research helps improve the theoretical model. When an existing theory commonly applied to a subject-matter does not adequately take into account the deviant cases or the non-conforming results, i.e., the ones that are not in accord with predictions suggested by the hypotheses derived from theory, research presses for its reformulation. It is from the evidence contained in the deviant cases that the insights germinate. On the basis of these the existing theory is improved by reformulating it to generate predictions that will encompass all the data, including those initially considered deviant.

The history of social sciences offers many examples where the theoretical model was reformulated to encompass a series of fresh empirical observations. Malinowski in the course of his observation of the Trobrianders found that when these islanders fished by the reliable method of poisoning, an abundant catch was assured and also there was no danger or uncertainty, they did not practise magic. But, on the other hand, in the open sea-fishing which did not promise any certain yield and typically entailed grave danger, the ritual of magic was practised invariably. Stemming from these observation his theory was that magical belief arises to bridge the uncertainties, to fortify confidence, to reduce anxieties and to open up avenues of escape from the seeming impasse. These observations suggested to Malinowski, the incorporation of new dimension into earlier theories of magic, i.e., the relation of magic to the dangerous and the uncontrollable. These new facts were not totally inconsistent with previous theories; it was only that the earlier theories had not taken them adequately into account. In effect, the new facts helped Malinowski develop an enlarged and improved theory.

Another very famous example may be cited. ln the 'Hawthorne electrical studies,' the investigators started with the theory that physical conditions affect work output.

'The investigators were interested in understanding the effects of specific changes in order to identify the optimal conditions. At first, the observers found that improvement in physical conditions did increase the output. But to their surprise, they subsequently found that changes in the direction of poorer physical conditions were also accompanied by increased output. This led to a re-examination of the initial theory. The result was the unearthing of certain important variables that the existing theory had ignored. The fact was that the workers in the experimental group were being made to take in an experiment and were interested in its outcome. As a result, their relationship with their supervisor changed. Their being set as a small group led to a certain cohesiveness among them. These social and attitudinal factors were so important that they obscured the effects of changes in physical conditions. It was not that the physical conditions did not affect the output, but this effect was over-shadowed by the effects of the social and attitudinal factors. The result of this research was a significant broadening of the theory to the effect that output is influenced by factors within the work situation, social as well as physical.

In sum, the results of scientific research very often force a change in the theoretic view of problems which may extend beyond the restricted domain of science itself. Theoretic generalizations must be founded on research results. Once formed and widely accepted, however, they very often influence the development of scientific thought by indicating one of the possible lines of procedure. Einstein and Infeld remark, "Successful revolt against the accepted views results in unexpected and completely different developments becoming a source of new philosophical aspects."[17]

(3) *Research Refocuses Theory:* Empirical research may also refocus theory by shifting the interest of researchers to new areas. Empirical research affects the more general trends in the development of theory. This occurs chiefly through the invention of research procedures which tend to shift the foci of theoretic interest toward those new areas of knowledge that were not hitherto amenable to scientific scrutiny.

We have already seen that a scientific theory summarizes what man can apprehend through his senses or infer from these sensory cues. Research technology is the means by which man as a scientist extends the domain over which sensory cues are perceptible. Refinement in microscopy, for example, improved the resolution of objects with the advance from optical to electron microscopes and thereby extended the perceived sensory cues for the researcher approximately a thousand times. In behavioural sciences, projective tests permit probing of the psychic life of persons in ways not previously attained by depth-interviews and other kindred techniques. Similarly, the development of scaling techniques for attitude measurement now permits the observer to comprehend objectively the patterns of association in expressed attitudes. All forms of correlational and associational analysis provide means for the observer to manipulate observations which in many instances was not possible in experimental situations directly. Research technology is not bound by any fixed limits of possible/refinement. When we reach the point of finest discrimination of human perception, we develop mechanical, electronic apparatuses that are capable of translating their refined cues into those gross enough to fall within the range of human perception.

Constructive imagination increases man's comprehension of his observable world. If the process of thinking involves combining bits of information, then combinations and permutations of such bits provide an unlimited number of possible models that can be the products of man's mind. Each new advance in research technology provides accretions of information-bits. Each model of man's world likewise adds to the sum-total of information. Consequently, the opportunity to construct new theories or models of the world as man sees it, is virtually inexhaustible.

The empirical world would, thus, seem to exchange the predictive power, precision, validity and verifiability of theories. Through the discovery and successive refinements of tools and techniques of methodology more and more theories are enabled to develop higher order propositions possessing greater predictive power.

(4) *Research Helps in Clarifying Theory:* Empirical research develops and refines concepts current in the discipline. Concepts are the essential building blocks of a theory. Operationalization, construction of indices and formalization of research findings enhance the clarity of theoretic concepts and variables.

Clarification of concepts embodied by theory, commonly considered a province peculiar to the theorist, is a frequent result of empirical research. Research sensitive to its own needs cannot easily escape this pressure for conceptual clarification. This is so because a basic requirement of research is that the concepts, the variables or what are often called the units of theory should be defined with sufficient clarity to enable the research to proceed. Research cannot proceed on the basis of concepts phrased in too vague or general terms. For research purposes some concrete empirical indicators of the concepts must be found.

Clarification of concepts ordinarily enters into empirical research by way of establishing indices of the variables under consideration. In non-research speculations and discourses, it is possible to talk loosely about such concepts as 'intelligence' 'morale' or 'social cohesion' without any clear conception of what is entailed by these terms; but these must be clarified if the researcher is to go about his task of systematically observing instances of high or low morale, or high or low intelligence or greater or lesser degree of factionalism or modernization etc. Without devising indices which are observable, fairly precise and meticulously clear, the researcher is bound to be blocked in his venture at the very outset. The movement of thought which was named 'operationalism' is only an instance of the researcher demanding that concepts to be defined clearly enough for the research to proceed with its ordained task.

Emile Durkheim, despite the fact that his terminology and indices now appear to be crude and debatable, did perceive the need for devising indices for his concepts. What often appears in research, as a tendency towards quantification can thus be understood as a special case of inquirers attempting to clarify concepts sufficiently to permit the conduct of empirical inquiry. The development of valid and observable indices is a prerequisite to the use of concepts in any research exercise.

A conception basic to sociology is the 'conflicting social roles.' The conception remains vague and of little value for research until such time as questions such as the following are answered, viz., on what grounds does one predict the behaviour of persons subject to conflicting roles?, or 'when there is conflict, which role takes precedence, or under which conditions does one or another role prove powerful?' More recently, empirical research has pressed for clarification of the key concepts involved in this problem. Indices of conflicting group pressures have been devised and the resultant behaviour in specified situations observed. Thus, a beginning has been made in this direction and effects of cross-pressures on behaviour have been studied. Lazarsfeld, Berelson and McPhee's study entitled 'Voting' (1954) reflects this advance.

It is the experience of researchers that actual testing of any existing theory is likely to redefine it. Often enough, the concepts that have been accepted as simple and obvious turn out to be vague and elusive when we attempt to fit them into facts. Such redefinitions or clarifications may in turn lead to the discovery of new hypotheses. So long as theories use general terms and make rough predictions, it is difficult to disprove them. When we look at certain facts we realize that we would have to sharpen our theories considerably to disprove or prove them.

In sum, the goal of science is to model the sensory world of man for the purposes he defines. These may outcome his need for pragmatic knowledge or simply for comprehension of reality or to grapple with an intellectual challenge. This stance makes of science a never-ending process of data-gathering and of reprocessing old data, of theory-building in areas of curiosity where theories do not already exist and of reconstructing old theories that no longer encompass in their frames, the data they purport to model.

Towards the end of this discussion we would like to answer the question which happens to be posed quite often, viz., whether empirical research first or theory — what is the sequence? To this, our answer would be that every verified empirical proposition presents theory with an explanatory obligation and every theory must face the facts of its own implication in that it must now imply a proposition that has been found to be wrong and false. Theory may inspire research in that it implies one or more propositions concerning which there is no existing evidence, thus calling for 'tying down the abstract logical structure to concrete empirical contents.' Verified relationships may suggest new theories or modifications of old ones. The significance of empirical research lies, thus, not in the facts taken by themselves but in the theoretical implications that may be read into them.

The interaction between theory and empirical research is a matter of striking a judicious balance between quality and quantity. The hollowness of speculative theory without substantive data and the blindness of the raw empiricism without substantive theory have been repeatedly talked about in methodological writings. Empiricists have sought to measure anything and everything and theorists have shunned empiricism as mere fact gathering. In the meanwhile the model-builders have sought to formalize every theory in mathematical terms. This three-pronged attack has done much harm to our perceptiveness and imagination. The only possible solution seems to be that theory and research interact increasingly with each other in a way that they can mutually enhance usefulness of measurement and formalization. It would have to be accepted that no matter how precise the measurement, a quality measured still remains a quality. Quantification is a great asset since it ensures greater reliability and precision in measuring the qualities which are theoretically significant. The indispensable working partner of quantification procedures is obviously the theory that determines what is to be measured.

Hyman advocates the 'following with a view to strengthening the mutually rewarding relationship between theory and research.[18]

1. Greater emphasis be laid on theories of middle range rather than on grand theories. The task of codifying all knowledge relevant to a general theory in social sciences seems incompatible with the temperament of general theorists and is also perhaps beyond their reach at the present time. The middle range concepts are specific and concrete enough for the researcher to appreciate their applicability to his specific problem and sense their translation into operations.
2. What is warranted is a shift from theory to theorizing, for, theorizing implies something in process and activity of one's mind.
3. An eye for the serendipity component needs to be cultivated. From codification of the middle range theories the researcher may come to learn that there are particular anomalous or paradoxical findings he may follow up. He can, thus, become aware of them and be alert to their occurrence. From his methodological training the researcher can develop skills required to search bodies of data which are likely to yield anomalous findings.

It is gratifying to note that the controversy between theorists and the empiricists is cooling off. A growing awareness has dawned upon the scientists, of the need for more intimate interplay between theory and empirical research.

Theory and research may, for purposes of analysis, be conceived of as distinct operations but as necessary complementary components of scientific endeavour, they cannot but be together. Neither is complete without the other.

REFERENCES

(1) See Abraham, M. Francis, *Modern Sociological Theory*, Oxford University Press, Delhi 1982, pp. 21-22.

(2) Cf. Dubin, R., *Theory Building*, Free Press, NY, 1969, p. 5.

(3) Abraham, *op. cit.*, p. 5.

(4) Galtung J., *Theory and Methods Of Social Research,* Allen and Unwin, London, 1967, p. 271.

(5) Cf. Selltiz, *et al., op. cit.*, p. 480.

(6) See, Abraham, *op. cit.*, p. 7.

(7) Selltiz *et al., op cit.*, p. 485.

(8) See, Caws P., *Philosophy of Science,* V Nostrand, 1965, p. 276.

(9) Einstein and Infeld, *op. cit.*, p. 33.

(10) See, Selltiz *et al., op. cit.*, pp. 480-487.

(11) Cf. Caws, P., *op. cit.*, p. 157.

(12) Merton, R., *op. cit.*, p. 157.

(13) *Ibid.*, p. 157.

(14) Einstein and Infeld, *op. cit.*, p. 158.

(15) Unanticipated datum refers to an unexpected observation which bears upon theories not in question when the research was begun.

(16) An observation is anomalous, surprising because (*a*) it seems inconsistent with the prevailing theory or (*b*) with other established facts. This inconsistency provokes curiosity; it stimulates the investigator to make sense of the observation. The researcher explores further. He makes fresh observations, draws inferences. If his hunch based upon anomalous datum proves justified, the surprising datum leads ultimately to a new theory (or an extended theory) strategic datum has a reference to such an observation that permits of implications which bear upon generalized theory. No datum, by itself is strategic. The strategic character of a datum depends on the extent to which the researcher possesses theoretic sensitivity. It is this sensitivity which transforms a seemingly trivial observation into a strategic fact.

(17) Einstein and Infeld, *op. cit.*, p. 55.

(18) See, Abraham, *op. cit.*, p. 37.

Chapter XXI

Social Research and Values

In the preceding chapters, the reader was exposed to a broad spectrum of research techniques; some quite powerful and brilliant. ln this chapter we feel called upon to address ourselves to the following questions: 'Do we know what we are doing with the impressive array of techniques available to the modem social science'? 'Are we using these instruments in a manner that manifest the true objective of science?' These are questions that scholars at different times have never felt tired of posing to the community of scientists. Although questions of this type for a time in the post, did not qualify as meriting any serious attention, the contemporary atmosphere in the fraternity of social scientists warrants that answering them can no longer be postponed.

Carefully viewed, the above questions bring to the fore a prevailing doubt shared possibly by quite a few practitioners of social science about the currently held objectives of science. This implies that the question: what ought to be the true objectives of science, is one that does not have one and the only acceptable answer. That is, alternative answer are possible and the rival groups engaged in the debate on the true objective of science subscribe to diverse or even opposite alternatives. This debate seems to have branched off into main directions, viz., methodological orientation and scientific obligation. These are, verily, aspects that would seem to directly descend from the basic issue on the agenda, viz., the true objectives of science.

Who is to decide? Are the scientists to decide what the objectives of science are and ought to be or should the community at large which supports the institution and thus expects from certain reciprocal returns to decide? To some, the answer may be 'yes' for the former question and 'no' for the latter; for some other the answers may be in the reverse order. For the remaining, the answer may be both, that is, the community of scientists with its set of intellectual values and the community at large with its own set of cultural values and premia, should together settle for or define the true objectives of science and thus, the obligations that a scientist feels he owes to himself would represent a working compromise between the rival thrusts of the scientific values on one hand, and the social values, on the other. Whatever the answers we arrive at, the use of a scale of values is inevitable. How else can we get our answers to questions of this kind? Whatever we may call our basis of judgement: belief, conviction, commitment, ethics, ethos, good sense ... we have come to our answer by opting for a set of values. The answer one has come to, will define for him the objective of his scientific exercise. What one believes to be the true objective of science will, understandably, lead him to question whether the methodological orientation current in the discipline will help him carry out his scientific endeavour fruitfully, in the sense that his product would have a value as defined by the initial objective. Furthermore, the objective once settled from him, the scientists will expectedly be confronted with the task of defining or conceptualizing his obligation or responsibility as a scientist. How should he as a scientist relate himself to the society? What would be his job vis-a-vis the large community? In essence, he will need to opt for a course of action which would involve or would not involve a modicum of preoccupation with certain kinds of values in the course of scientific inquiry or its reporting.

As hinted earlier, stemming from the basic issue of true objectives of science, the prevailing methodological orientation of social sciences generally and sociology and psychology in particular, has in recent decades come in for much criticism. The critique is directed against the glorification of the hypothetico-deductive method—the method typifying the structure of inquiry in physics, as a mode for the development of a system of reliable knowledge in the social science. The critics vehemently object to the wholesale adoption of the hypothetico-deductive model by the social or behavioural sciences. A furious debate about the propriety of the prevailing methodological orientation has thus ensued.

The hypothetico-deductive paradigm as we had an occasion to note in some of the earlier chapters, involves the formulation of a theoretic explanation from a connected set of statements, some of which (premises) logically imply others (theorems). The truth of these theorems of logically deduced expectations (hypotheses) is open to verification by facts secured in the course of empirical investigation. This critics have expressed serious doubts about the value and fruitfulness of the hypothetico-deductive method in social sciences. While admitting that the model represents a valid and productive method of inquiry, the critics point out how this well-thumbed method has failed to deliver the promised goods in the realms of the social and behavioural sciences, if its achievements by way of contributing a body of generally accepted knowledge or empirical laws were to be taken as the measure of its efficiency. Joynson for example, has argued that from a pragmatic point of view the social science have achieved very little, precisely because of the way they interpreted the hypothetico-deductive system. The system has been taken to mean that science can validly study only the objective phenomena which can reliably quantified. Such an interpretation sadly leaves out many internal conditions which are indeed, the important aspects of our personal and social life. Love, ambition and jealousy etc., which are intangible though very real components of our existence, have thus suffered a neglect in as much as these are not directly measurable and hence cannot, on this view, be incorporatated into a scientific explanation. The acceptance of this doctrine, according to critics, inevitably means the choice of topic will be restricted to just those that are amendable to investigation; the prerequisite of amenability being their overt or even obvious character. This also means, the critic stress, that the topics selected in accordance with this criterion will be of a trivial nature in that the findings of investigations centered on such topic will have neither much theoretical nor practical significance. A very relevant anecdote of a drunkard seeks to brings home the point. A drunkard was searching under a street lamp for his keys which he knew he had dropped some distance away. Asked why he did not look for it where he had dropped it, the drunkard retorted, 'because the light is better here."[1] The story has a moral lesson which, so the critique runs, has not been appreciated by the behavioural social science which customarily run after the obvious and measurable and in effect much of the effort "not only in the logic of behavioural science but also in behavioural science itself is vitiated by the principle of the drunkard's search."[2] The behavioural sciences according to the critics, suffer from what Feigl terms a 'phobia about unobservables.' It is the empiricist view of autnomous, objective facts as science's crucial elements that has, in the opinion of the critic, brought the behavioural social sciences to such a sad pass. They cannot make worthwhile contributions to knowledge simply because of their presupposition that only the observable and the objective facts are the ones worth investigating.

It is simple and yet a rarely appreciated point that the scientist is casting a theoretic net with a certain sized mesh into the sea of facts and that his catch is to a large extent the function of that mesh. It would be unwise of the scientist to proclaim that there are no facts in the universe smaller than the mesh size. Feyerabend forcefully argues that there are facts beyond the theoretic net. "There exist also facts which cannot be unearthed except with the help of alternatives to the theory to be tested, and which become unavailable as soon as such alternatives are excluded"[3] Polanyi, Feyerabend, Kuhn and others have espoused the view that premises about the nature of things, the acceptable methodology and data, and the things yet to be discovered constitute integral strands of theoretic net. And thus, in their view, the empiricist characterization of the fishing net of scientists is quite different from the one actually cast in the sea of nature by the practitioners of science. The empiricist theoretic net creates a strong possibility that it will ensure the catch (of empirical evidence) in its favour. These thinkers feel that in actual practice the nets cast by the scientists allow for a lot of flexibility so the scientists can open-headedly contend with and allow room for the possible alternatives. The more accurate portrayal of an active scientist would be a picture of him pursuing his positions in the face of and despite contradictory facts and even the very adverse judgments of his many colleagues. Einstein advised, "if you want to find out anything from the theoretical physicists about the methods they use, don't listen to their words, fix your attention on their deeds."[4]

The critics also contend in reference to a very pertinent question, "would fundamental advances occur in science if the empirical ideal were not met?" that they certainly would occur. They argue that the history of science strongly testifies to the fact that precisely when science has made its greatest advances, when scientific revolutions have occurred, the empiricist ideal has been met least (Feyerabend 1963). They point out categorically that persistence in the face of contradictory facts and the disapproval of those committed to the prevailing paradigm, the intuitive apprehension of a reality as yet undiscovered, the altering of fundamental presupposition or premises by creative act, are all crucial elements in the progress of a science. The classical conception had little or no room for these elements. Ghiselin has tried to present what may be termed the essence of the creative act. He tries to arrive at a statement about creativity on the basis of his analysis of certain typical statements made by great men of science and arts about their own creative processes and spurts. He says, "creation begins typically with a vague even a confused excitement, some sort of a yearning, hunch or other preverbal intimation of approaching or potential resolution .... lt is alike for thinker and artist, the offering of adventure, but adventure, nameless and featureless, which shall be defined by something not even in the periphery of consciousness, but rather implicit in the whole spread of subjective activity."[5] Ghiselin elucidates the prevailing opposition between the innovative individual scientist and the scientific community at large which is given to a model worship.'[6]

Gouldner notes that with method alone we all too easily sink into ritualism, "... it sacrifices the venturesome but chancy insight for the security of controllable routine, penetrating novelty of the shallow familiarity, the broader for the narrow circumstances."[7]

The critics argue that methodology is in the ultimate analysis only a means and its current worship within the social discipline brings to one's mind Robert Merton's ritualist who in effect, sacrifices the ends or goals, having become so involved with the means that clinging to them becomes for him the prized goal. The model worshippers in the social sciences suffering as they typically do from 'methodological inhibition' approximate in their behaviour the ritualistic adaptation which consists in "abandoning (the) goals and clinging all the more closely to the safe routine and the institution norms."[8] It is obvious that the current emphasis on formal verification via quantification would imply that one can hardly know anything by any other means. By this criterion the major insightful works of Weber, Toennies, Simmel, Cooley, Mead and Veblen would not qualify as scientific works. And yet, but for the unwitting violation of the requirement of modern scientism, these thinkers, often referred in certain quarters as 'arm-chair theorists' might perhaps not have been able to formulate certain imaginative concepts like the looking-glass self, the role-taking, conspicuous consumption, etc. Nisbet expressing himself on the implications of contemporary method-worship has only strong words to use in its condemnation. He says "It is hard to think of better way (than the current methodological fetishism) to apotheosize the routine and insignificant."

Under the circumstances, one would legitimately ask whether the ideals of objectivity, hard data, rigid empiricism serve to stiffle original thoughts and potential creativity of scientists. The critics feel that while true creativity cannot be a 'trained' product, serious efforts must be made by the community of scientists to at least provide for such conditions as would permit its initial expression and once revealed, give it full rein.

Adherence of social scientists to the hypothetico-deductive principles implies an absolute reliance on the statistical testing of the null hypothesis. The critics opine that one of the unfortunate expressions of this is that virtually no studies are published where the results do not achieve statistical significance. "Happiness is rejecting a null hypothesis"— so goes a saying current in psychology. So much is made of the null hypothesis that its rejection or otherwise will make or mar a study. Rosenthal's work[9] has shown that there are various subtle and sometimes poorly understood devices whereby the researcher ensures that his hypothesis will be confirmed.

It has been further pointed out by the critics that so often the statistical test which is in fact a relatively simplistic stage in the development of an explanation, has become confused with the explanation itself. Thus, a statistically significant difference or association does not imply necessarily a meaningful understanding of the functional and living relationships between the variables. It has been pointed out that with a sample several hundred strong, it is statistically extremely unlikely that there will exist an absolute zero correlation between any two variables and yet the psychological and sociological significance of a statistically significant coefficient may be a negligible.

We now turn to discuss the other aspect, viz., the scientific obligation, which, as pointed out earlier, has become the subject of a raging controversy especially during the last few decades with scholars like: Lynd, Znaniecki, Redfield, Sorokin, Bierstedt, Gouldner, Nisbet, Mills, Stein, Vidich and Horowitz, to mention just some of the more outstanding, vehemently questioning the ethically neutral or value-free of the social sciences; particularly sociology. Theirs has been, for quite some time in the recent past, a minority voice and the desire within the social and behavioural disciplines to project a scientific image, i.e., to appear quantitatively precise has been so strong all these decades as to over-power and stiffle whatever questions were raised against the value-free stance of these disciplines. These questions were dismissed as inconsequential or scoffed at as acts of sociological heresay.

The controversy over scientific obligation, understandably revolves around the appropriate position of personal values in any scientific research; more so, in social science research. What posture should a social behavioural scientist espouse vis-a-vis the values or ethics? Should they separate their own value-systems from their scientific exercises or should they offer their reasoned judements or suggestions about what should be done in the best interests of the society? (the suggestions being largely based on facts revealed during the scientific investigation). Does the scientific obligation call upon the scientist not commit a value-judgement at any cost or does it lead him to feel committed to offering judgements of value about situations of his scientific concern? Ought the scientific approach be an amoral one or should it involve concern with social values, morality and ethics? These are questions that illustrate the voices from the rival quarters in the debate going on for decades now. The central focus of debate, if its essence is to be laid bare, is whether social science could be value-free and how to maximize the independence of social science from values and ideologies. The social sciences inevitably pose a special problem of this order since they are, by definition, the observations of one set of human beings by another and also in as much as the values are important inputs in all human activity. There is agreement even among the warring sides that the problem referred to above, directly relates to and casts doubts on the scientific status of the social sciences.

Writers like Rudner on one side, have contended that social sciences can be objective in the sense of ensuring independence from values and ideologies. While on the other side, scholars like Mannheim believe that all social thinking is bound to be affected by the cultural milieu of the thinker.

Since the early sixties, the debate seems to have shifted from the discussion of the degree to which social science could be value-free to whether or not its being value-free was desirable. A group of thinkers alluded above, have been forcefully advocating the undesirability of the doctrine of value-free social science and questioning in no uncertain terms, the alleged gains of the value-free social science as practised by the adherents of the 'dogma.' The cry has gone up in the air: Down with the value-free doctrine (in social sciences).

Gray (1968) in a paper entitled 'Value-free Sociology: A Doctrine of Hypocrisy and Irresponsibility'[10] which conveys the main thrust of his contention, has presented a powerful case against a value-free sociology. Gray argues that contributions which sociologists themselves have long regarded as among the most significant ones have not lacked judgements of human value; the power of these works rest, in part on the fact that, value-judgments were made. Even in the work of Max Weber who effected the distinction between statements of fact and statements of value, one comes across his final evaluation of the 'iron cage' of materialism (fostered, in turn, by the rise of bureaucratically organized capitalism) in words quite heavily loaded with values. Gray feels that without the final judgement, the power of Weber's classic work, *The Protestant Ethic and the Spirit of Capitalism,* would have been significantly curtailed. Similarly, Durkheim's classic work, *Suicide,* did not shy away from the value-question. Durkheim discussed at some length the means by which the evil (suicide) could be overcome. Thus, the two great sociologists whom the discipline still regards as among its founding fathers did not just play the role of a disinterested, amoral observer; rather they understood the necessity of being pertinent, i.e., of being concerned with the welfare of mankind. Thus, they felt committed to offering their most reasoned judgments on the theoretic issues of their concern. Gray proceeds to adduce evidences of value-judgments in many a sociological work of several acknowledged masters in the discipline; Comte's advocacy of a sociocracy, Toennies' bias for Gemeinsehaft as opposed to Gesellschaft, Cooley's fascination for primary groups, Veblen's condemnation of conspicuous leisure; all testify to value-commitments on their part. And yet the works of these masters have been considered as particularly significant by sociologists generally. Surely not because an implicit or explicit value position was avoided. Nobody would really advocate that the works of Durkheim, Weber, Cooley, Veblen etc., should be altered to conform to the doctrine of a value-free social science. Insistence on value-neutrality concerning the contributions of these masters, would tantamount to emasculation.

Alvin Gouldner in attempting to explode the myth of a value-free sociology[11] views the value-free doctrine as something sociologists have developed vested interests in. It is somehow useful to those who believe in it. It is according to Gouldner, especially useful to those men who live off sociology rather than for it and who think of sociology as "a way of getting ahead in the world by providing them with neutral techniques that may be sold in the open market to any buyer."[12]

Gray argues that the value-free posture advocated by persons like George Lundberg might be viewed as a cloak ensuring the survival and 'success' of the social scientist's career. The statement by Lundberg[13] that "the services of real (i.e., value-free) social scientists would be as indispensable to Fascists or to Communists and Democrats, just as are the services of physicists and physicians," seems to him to be a message to the followers of the value-free doctrine to stick to it in their own self-interest. For, only that way will they prove useful to any social system, whatever its ideological ilk. Gray urges us to note that the behaviour of the German scientists who conducted fatal 'medical' experiments under the Nazi regime would fall quite logically within the limits of the value-free model. Would one approve of their conduct?

The value-free doctrine of contemporary sociology, for Gray, seems to be hypocritical in that it has fallen short of delivery especially in the most significant works. For him, the doctrine is inappropriate and irresponsible in that it has led people who know most about the nature of social life to think that offering most reasoned judgments about social life was none of their responsibility. 'To whom does the obligation fall? If the social scientist sees in his data an impending racial crisis, is he in any way less of a scientist or compromised if he recommends, to the authorities to take certain measures for the good of the residents concerned? The answer to the question would obviously be 'no'. To be responsible has always been a virtue and yet a value-free, a moral social science doctrine has attempted to convince us otherwise. Lynd asked his value-free sociological colleagues long ago, 'Are we really to be encouraged to continue lecturing on navigation while the ship is going down?'

The value-free dogma, its critics feel, is encouraging just this trend among the practitioners of social science, viz., of refraining from offering well-grounded judgments for the fear that these would lead them to step into a forbidden territory of values and faith; a gorge of alligators, as the value-neutral doctrine conceives of it. It is for this very reason, the critics assert, that as opposed to the writings of Weber and Durkheim, the modern value-free sociology has very little to deliver. Gerth and Landau observe, "By and large, the sociologists of today have shut the world crisis out of their vision focussing their intellectual energy on the crisis of the family while the Chinese revolution involving (many millions)... perhaps the greatest mass movement of mankind is totally neglected."[14] This, the critics feel is the result of their commitment to the value of being value-free.

But then, a question may be asked: 'Who is to sit on judgement over whether the study of Chinese revolution is more important as compared to one focussed on family crises or divorce?' The answer to the question may be discerned in what Robert Lynd has to say about judgments. Says Lynd, "... the outstanding characteristics of a well-trained scientist is his ability to distinguish 'significant' from 'insignificant' problems and data. Good scientific training sensitizes one to important problems ... Research without an actively selective point of view becomes a ditty bag of an idiot filled with bits of pebbles, straws, feathers and other random hoardings."[15] Thus, the answer to the question: 'Who is to judge? is obvious; problems such as racial strife, effects of automation, the viability of the great society, the danger of nuclear annihilation certainly qualify as being among the questions which virtually all intelligent and informed citizens would view as being of consequence. Of Marx, Durkheim, Weber and Mosca, Barrington Moore has the following to say: "....all of them saw as their scientific problem those which the course of history had put on the agenda as the significant ones of their epoch."[16] 'Why the case at the present time should be so different?' ask the critics of value-free social science. Not that social science should be solely social problem or issue-oriented, rather, it should be relevant, as Marx, Weber, Durkheim were; they assert. We surely should not, they argue, avoid issues of real import or consequence just because they require value-judgement or because they are not amenable to the methodological equipment we happen to have at our disposal. To allow the methodological techniques to dicate our human concerns, i.e., the problems were would consider worth inquiring into, would be, according to them the height of intellectual folly. Understandably, it is the issue that is primary. To permit techniques to determine our issue is bound to put us (as it has already) on a methodologically reliable highway which leads, however, into barren · intellectual territory"[17] Ross and Van Den Haag remind their sociological colleagues that to discuss only what is scientifically testable is to ignore much that is vital and to lay undue stress on the trivial.[18]

Gray proceeds to point out that a refusal to make value-judgements amounts, in effect, to tacitly accepting the going value system. The value-free social scientists, according to the critic, are not only no longer truly intellectual, they have assumed a new role as employees, consultants or technicians serving the present establishment which is not at all shy on the matter of values. Consequently, the contemporary sociologists are probably more prosperous but they are, to use Weber's phrase 'specialists without spirit.' Thus, Gray would recommend the legitimacy and, indeed the indispensibility of value-judgement for the sociological discipline; for only thus, can sociology be brought back on the track recommended for it, implicitly or explicitly, by Weber, Durkheim and other significant scholars.

Gouldner suggests that social scientists, because of their competence in the area, are the most suitable people to recommend a certain course of action based, of course, on certain value-judgements, he opines that an attempt to be value-free may in fact, be a attempt to escape from the responsibility that knowledge brings. The doctrine of value-free social science, according to him, resolves these conflicts by making it seem that those who refrain from social criticism are acting solely on behalf of a higher professional good rather than their private interests. (But) in refraining from social criticism both the timorous and the venal may now claim the protection of a high professional principle, and, in so doing, can continue to hold themselves in decent regard. "Persuade all that no one must bell the cat, then none of the mice need feel like a rat."[19]

M. Brewster Smith in his *Social Psychology and Human Values* (1969) asked whether we were willing to apply the prescriptions of cultural relativism (which is an obvious manifestation of value-free social science) to a study of the excesses of Nazi Germany. This would mean that the judgement underlying the excesses must be evaluated in terms of the value position of the society in question. Smith stresses that such an attempt must be regarded as 'legitimation of evil.' There is evil, and it is a moral obligation of social scientists to identify and denounce it, he concludes.

Under the guise of science, the value-free doctrine seems to Gray, to have encouraged to posture of irrelevance and irresponsibility among the social sciences. Consequently the discipline which claims to know the most about social life (Sociology) refuses to investigate significant issues and to deliver its best judgements concerning them for the fear of violating the taboo on value-judgements. The following remarks are pertinent. He says, "To date the value-free doctrine has led us to conclude that this posture of irrelevance and irresponsibility is appropriate. Only when this conclusion is reversed can the sociological discipline hope to rejuvenate on any substantial basis, the intellectual vitality earlier possessed and which only a violation of the value-free doctrine in modern sociology has managed to keep alive. And only then will a worthy and important discipline replace a large amount of well-varified irrelevance with a body of relevant knowledge."[20]

How should a relevant social science proceed, is a question that immediately comes to the mind in the light of the above discussion. A very basic answer to this question according to the critics of value-free social science would be that 'the erroneous and self-congratulatory scientists allegiance to the value-free doctrine must be foregone.' And, one cannot do better than reckon with their advice in the matter.

Human judgement which involves values cannot be done without and as such is inevitable in the selection of a problem for research. We must admit it, and admit actively. With this clear admission of our inescapability from involvement with values, the researcher should proceed to select problems worthy of investigation. The relevance of the problem (its solution) for mankind should be the basic criterion for determining the worthwhileness of the problem.

Having selected a significant problem thus, the researcher should proceed at to investigate it analytically, with as scholoraly and objective a regard for the facts as is humanly possible. The available methodological procedures should be employed as effectively as possible. Finally, having completed the investigation, the researcher should consider it his bounden duty as a representative of the discipline to provide when and where appropriate, his most reasoned judgements concerning the issue. There is, of course, no need to assume that such judgements will 'be beyond question or infallible. They should, rather be taken precisely in the vein in which they are offered... judgements "by the scholar intimately acquainted with the subject offered for the possible enlightenment and betterment of mankind."

The above prescription which, by and large, represents the sentiments of social scientists who are opposed to the value-free posture of their disciplines, to say the least, merits serious consideration. Theirs, as of now, is no more a minority voice.

REFERENCES

(1) See Kaplan, Abraham, *op. cit.,* p. 227.
(2) *Ibid.,* p. 235.
(3) Cochrane, *op. cit.,* p. 152.
(4) *Ibid.,* p. 153.
(5) cf. Kessel. F.S.: *The Philosophy of Science as Practised.* (art) in Cochrane, *op. cit.*
(6) Gouldner, A. W., *Enter Plato;* Routledge and Kegan Paul, London, 1967. p. 338.
(7) Merton, R.. *op. cit.,* p. 204.
(8) Nisbet, R. ct. Cochrane: op. cit., p. 353.
(9) See Rosenthal, R.: *Experimenter Effects in Behavioural Research,* New York, Appleton, Century, Crofts, 1966.
(10) See, (art) *Sociological Quarterly,* 1968, 9, pp. 176-185.
(11) Gouldner, A. W.: *Anti-minotaur: The Myth of Value-Free Sociology,* Social Problems, 1962, 9, p. 199 (418).
(12) *Ibid.,* p. 206.
(13) Lundberg, G.: *Can Science Save Us?* Longmans Green and Co., New York, 1961, p. 56.
(14) Cochrane: *op. cit.,* p. 351.
(15) Lynd R.: *Knowledge for What?* Grove Press Inc., New York, 1964, p. 183.
(16) Cochrane, R.: *op. cit.,* p. 352.
(17) *Fabric of Society,* Harcourt, Bra and Co., New York, 1962.
(18) Ross, R. and Van Den Haag, (art) 1 Cochrane, *op. cit.*
(19) See Gouldner, A. W., *op. cit.*
(20) Gray D. J. (art): *Value-Free Sociology: Hypocrisy and Irresponsibility* in Cochrane, *op. cit.,* p.355.

Index